The
UNIX˙
Programming
Environment

Brian W. Kernighan

Rob Pike

Bell Laboratories
Murray Hill, New Jersey

PRENTICE-HALL, INC.
Englewood Cliffs, New Jersey 07632

* UNIX is a Trademark of Bell Laboratories

Library of Congress Catalog Card Number 83-62851

Prentice-Hall Software Series
Brian W. Kernighan, Advisor

Editorial/production supervision: *Ros Herion*
Cover design: *Photo Plus Art, Celine Brandes*
Manufacturing buyer: *Gordon Osbourne*

This book was typeset in Times Roman and Courier by the authors, using a Mergenthaler Linotron 202 phototypesetter driven by a VAX-11/750 running the 8th Edition of the UNIX operating system.

UNIX is a trademark of Bell Laboratories. DEC, PDP and VAX are trademarks of Digital Equipment Corporation.

10 9 8 7 6 5 4

ISBN 0-13-937699-2
ISBN 0-13-937681-X {PBK}

PRENTICE-HALL INTERNATIONAL, INC., *London*
PRENTICE-HALL OF AUSTRALIA PTY. LIMITED, *Sydney*
EDITORA PRENTICE-HALL DO BRASIL, LTDA., *Rio de Janeiro*
PRENTICE-HALL CANADA INC., *Toronto*
PRENTICE-HALL OF INDIA PRIVATE LIMITED, *New Delhi*
PRENTICE-HALL OF JAPAN, INC., *Tokyo*
PRENTICE-HALL OF SOUTHEAST ASIA PTE. LTD., *Singapore*
WHITEHALL BOOKS LIMITED, *Wellington, New Zealand*

CONTENTS

Preface   vii

1. UNIX for Beginners   1
  1.1 Getting started   2
  1.2 Day-to-day use: files and common commands   11
  1.3 More about files: directories   21
  1.4 The shell   26
  1.5 The rest of the UNIX system   38

2. The File System   41
  2.1 The basics of files   41
  2.2 What's in a file?   46
  2.3 Directories and filenames   48
  2.4 Permissions   52
  2.5 Inodes   57
  2.6 The directory hierarchy   63
  2.7 Devices   65

3. Using the Shell   71
  3.1 Command line structure   71
  3.2 Metacharacters   74
  3.3 Creating new commands   80
  3.4 Command arguments and parameters   82
  3.5 Program output as arguments   86
  3.6 Shell variables   88
  3.7 More on I/O redirection   92
  3.8 Looping in shell programs   94
  3.9 `bundle`: putting it all together   97
  3.10 Why a programmable shell?   99

4. Filters   101
  4.1 The `grep` family   102
  4.2 Other filters   106

iii

4.3 The stream editor sed   108
4.4 The awk pattern scanning and processing language   114
4.5 Good files and good filters   130

5.   Shell Programming   **133**
5.1 Customizing the cal command   133
5.2 Which command is which?   138
5.3 while and until loops: watching for things   144
5.4 Traps: catching interrupts   150
5.5 Replacing a file: overwrite   152
5.6 zap: killing processes by name   156
5.7 The pick command: blanks vs. arguments   159
5.8 The news command: community service messages   162
5.9 get and put: tracking file changes   165
5.10 A look back   169

6.   Programming with Standard I/O   **171**
6.1 Standard input and output: vis   172
6.2 Program arguments: vis version 2   174
6.3 File access: vis version 3   176
6.4 A screen-at-a-time printer: p   180
6.5 An example: pick   186
6.6 On bugs and debugging   187
6.7 An example: zap   190
6.8 An interactive file comparison program: idiff   192
6.9 Accessing the environment   199

7.   UNIX System Calls   **201**
7.1 Low-level I/O   201
7.2 File system: directories   208
7.3 File system: inodes   214
7.4 Processes   220
7.5 Signals and interrupts   225

8.   Program Development   **233**
8.1 Stage 1: A four-function calculator   234
8.2 Stage 2: Variables and error recovery   242
8.3 Stage 3: Arbitrary variable names; built-in functions   245
8.4 Stage 4: Compilation into a machine   258
8.5 Stage 5: Control flow and relational operators   266
8.6 Stage 6: Functions and procedures; input/output   273
8.7 Performance evaluation   284
8.8 A look back   286

9. Document Preparation   **289**
    9.1 The `ms` macro package   290
    9.2 The `troff` level   297
    9.3 The `tbl` and `eqn` preprocessors   301
    9.4 The manual page   308
    9.5 Other document preparation tools   313

10. Epilog   **315**

Appendix 1: Editor Summary   **319**
Appendix 2: `hoc` Manual   **329**
Appendix 3: `hoc` Listing   **335**

Index   **349**

PREFACE

"The number of UNIX installations has grown to 10, with more expected."

(The *UNIX Programmer's Manual*, 2nd Edition, June, 1972.)

The UNIX† operating system started on a cast-off DEC PDP-7 at Bell Laboratories in 1969. Ken Thompson, with ideas and support from Rudd Canaday, Doug McIlroy, Joe Ossanna, and Dennis Ritchie, wrote a small general-purpose time-sharing system comfortable enough to attract enthusiastic users and eventually enough credibility for the purchase of a larger machine — a PDP-11/20. One of the early users was Ritchie, who helped move the system to the PDP-11 in 1970. Ritchie also designed and wrote a compiler for the C programming language. In 1973, Ritchie and Thompson rewrote the UNIX kernel in C, breaking from the tradition that system software is written in assembly language. With that rewrite, the system became essentially what it is today.

Around 1974 it was licensed to universities "for educational purposes" and a few years later became available for commercial use. During this time, UNIX systems prospered at Bell Labs, finding their way into laboratories, software development projects, word processing centers, and operations support systems in telephone companies. Since then, it has spread world-wide, with tens of thousands of systems installed, from microcomputers to the largest mainframes.

What makes the UNIX system so successful? We can discern several reasons. First, because it is written in C, it is portable — UNIX systems run on a range of computers from microprocessors to the largest mainframes; this is a strong commercial advantage. Second, the source code is available and written in a high-level language, which makes the system easy to adapt to particular requirements. Finally, and most important, it is a *good* operating system,

---

† UNIX is a trademark of Bell Laboratories. "UNIX" is *not* an acronym, but a weak pun on MULTICS, the operating system that Thompson and Ritchie worked on before UNIX.

especially for programmers. The UNIX programming environment is unusually rich and productive.

Even though the UNIX system introduces a number of innovative programs and techniques, no single program or idea makes it work well. Instead, what makes it effective is an approach to programming, a philosophy of using the computer. Although that philosophy can't be written down in a single sentence, at its heart is the idea that the power of a system comes more from the relationships among programs than from the programs themselves. Many UNIX programs do quite trivial tasks in isolation, but, combined with other programs, become general and useful tools.

Our goal in this book is to communicate the UNIX programming philosophy. Because the philosophy is based on the relationships between programs, we must devote most of the space to discussions about the individual tools, but throughout run the themes of combining programs and of using programs to build programs. To use the UNIX system and its components well, you must understand not only how to use the programs, but also how they fit into the environment.

As the UNIX system has spread, the fraction of its users who are skilled in its application has decreased. Time and again, we have seen experienced users, ourselves included, find only clumsy solutions to a problem, or write programs to do jobs that existing tools handle easily. Of course, the elegant solutions are not easy to see without some experience and understanding. We hope that by reading this book you will develop the understanding to make your use of the system — whether you are a new or seasoned user — effective and enjoyable. We want you to use the UNIX system well.

We are aiming at individual programmers, in the hope that, by making their work more productive, we can in turn make the work of groups more productive. Although our main target is programmers, the first four or five chapters do not require programming experience to be understood, so they should be helpful to other users as well.

Wherever possible we have tried to make our points with real examples rather than artificial ones. Although some programs began as examples for the book, they have since become part of our own set of everyday programs. All examples have been tested directly from the text, which is in machine-readable form.

The book is organized as follows. Chapter 1 is an introduction to the most basic use of the system. It covers logging in, mail, the file system, commonly-used commands, and the rudiments of the command interpreter. Experienced users can skip this chapter.

Chapter 2 is a discussion of the UNIX file system. The file system is central to the operation and use of the system, so you must understand it to use the system well. This chapter describes files and directories, permissions and file modes, and inodes. It concludes with a tour of the file system hierarchy and an explanation of device files.

The command interpreter, or *shell*, is a fundamental tool, not only for running programs, but also for writing them. Chapter 3 describes how to use the shell for your own purposes: creating new commands, command arguments, shell variables, elementary control flow, and input-output redirection.

Chapter 4 is about *filters*: programs that perform some simple transformation on data as it flows through them. The first section deals with the `grep` pattern-searching command and its relatives; the next discusses a few of the more common filters such as `sort`; and the rest of the chapter is devoted to two general-purpose data transforming programs called `sed` and `awk`. `sed` is a stream editor, a program for making editing changes on a stream of data as it flows by. `awk` is a programming language for simple information retrieval and report generation tasks. It's often possible to avoid conventional programming entirely by using these programs, sometimes in cooperation with the shell.

Chapter 5 discusses how to use the shell for writing programs that will stand up to use by other people. Topics include more advanced control flow and variables, traps and interrupt handling. The examples in this chapter make considerable use of `sed` and `awk` as well as the shell.

Eventually one reaches the limits of what can be done with the shell and other programs that already exist. Chapter 6 talks about writing new programs using the standard I/O library. The programs are written in C, which the reader is assumed to know, or at least be learning concurrently. We try to show sensible strategies for designing and organizing new programs, how to build them in manageable stages, and how to make use of tools that already exist.

Chapter 7 deals with the system calls, the foundation under all the other layers of software. The topics include input-output, file creation, error processing, directories, inodes, processes, and signals.

Chapter 8 talks about program development tools: `yacc`, a parser-generator; `make`, which controls the process of compiling a big program; and `lex`, which generates lexical analyzers. The exposition is based on the development of a large program, a C-like programmable calculator.

Chapter 9 discusses the document preparation tools, illustrating them with a user-level description and a manual page for the calculator of Chapter 8. It can be read independently of the other chapters.

Appendix 1 summarizes the standard editor `ed`. Although many readers will prefer some other editor for daily use, `ed` is universally available, efficient and effective. Its regular expressions are the heart of other programs like `grep` and `sed`, and for that reason alone it is worth learning.

Appendix 2 contains the reference manual for the calculator language of Chapter 8.

Appendix 3 is a listing of the final version of the calculator program, presenting the code all in one place for convenient reading.

Some practical matters. First, the UNIX system has become very popular, and there are a number of versions in wide use. For example, the 7th Edition comes from the original source of the UNIX system, the Computing Science Research Center at Bell Labs. System III and System V are the official Bell Labs-supported versions. The University of California at Berkeley distributes systems derived from the 7th Edition, usually known as UCB 4.xBSD. In addition, there are numerous variants, particularly on small computers, that are derived from the 7th Edition.

We have tried to cope with this diversity by sticking closely to those aspects that are likely to be the same everywhere. Although the lessons that we want to teach are independent of any particular version, for specific details we have chosen to present things as they were in the 7th Edition, since it forms the basis of most of the UNIX systems in widespread use. We have also run the examples on Bell Labs' System V and on Berkeley 4.1BSD; only trivial changes were required, and only in a few examples. Regardless of the version your machine runs, the differences you find should be minor.

Second, although there is a lot of material in this book, it is not a reference manual. We feel it is more important to teach an approach and a style of use than just details. The *UNIX Programmer's Manual* is the standard source of information. You will need it to resolve points that we did not cover, or to determine how your system differs from ours.

Third, we believe that the best way to learn something is by doing it. This book should be read at a terminal, so that you can experiment, verify or contradict what we say, explore the limits and the variations. Read a bit, try it out, then come back and read some more.

We believe that the UNIX system, though certainly not perfect, is a marvelous computing environment. We hope that reading this book will help you to reach that conclusion too.

We are grateful to many people for constructive comments and criticisms, and for their help in improving our code. In particular, Jon Bentley, John Linderman, Doug McIlroy, and Peter Weinberger read multiple drafts with great care. We are indebted to Al Aho, Ed Bradford, Bob Flandrena, Dave Hanson, Ron Hardin, Marion Harris, Gerard Holzmann, Steve Johnson, Nico Lomuto, Bob Martin, Larry Rosler, Chris Van Wyk, and Jim Weythman for their comments on the first draft. We also thank Mike Bianchi, Elizabeth Bimmler, Joe Carfagno, Don Carter, Tom De Marco, Tom Duff, David Gay, Steve Mahaney, Ron Pinter, Dennis Ritchie, Ed Sitar, Ken Thompson, Mike Tilson, Paul Tukey, and Larry Wehr for valuable suggestions.

Brian Kernighan

Rob Pike

CHAPTER 1: **UNIX FOR BEGINNERS**

What is "UNIX"? In the narrowest sense, it is a time-sharing operating system *kernel*: a program that controls the resources of a computer and allocates them among its users. It lets users run their programs; it controls the peripheral devices (discs, terminals, printers, and the like) connected to the machine; and it provides a file system that manages the long-term storage of information such as programs, data, and documents.

In a broader sense, "UNIX" is often taken to include not only the kernel, but also essential programs like compilers, editors, command languages, programs for copying and printing files, and so on.

Still more broadly, "UNIX" may even include programs developed by you or other users to be run on your system, such as tools for document preparation, routines for statistical analysis, and graphics packages.

Which of these uses of the name "UNIX" is correct depends on which level of the system you are considering. When we use "UNIX" in the rest of this book, context should indicate which meaning is implied.

The UNIX system sometimes looks more difficult than it is — it's hard for a newcomer to know how to make the best use of the facilities available. But fortunately it's not hard to get started — knowledge of only a few programs should get you off the ground. This chapter is meant to help you to start using the system as quickly as possible. It's an overview, not a manual; we'll cover most of the material again in more detail in later chapters. We'll talk about these major areas:

- basics — logging in and out, simple commands, correcting typing mistakes, mail, inter-terminal communication.
- day-to-day use — files and the file system, printing files, directories, commonly-used commands.
- the command interpreter or *shell* — filename shorthands, redirecting input and output, pipes, setting erase and kill characters, and defining your own search path for commands.

If you've used a UNIX system before, most of this chapter should be familiar; you might want to skip straight to Chapter 2.

1

You will need a copy of the *UNIX Programmer's Manual*, even as you read this chapter; it's often easier for us to tell you to read about something in the manual than to repeat its contents here. This book is not supposed to replace it, but to show you how to make best use of the commands described in it. Furthermore, there may be differences between what we say here and what is true on your system. The manual has a permuted index at the beginning that's indispensable for finding the right programs to apply to a problem; learn to use it.

Finally, a word of advice: don't be afraid to experiment. If you are a beginner, there are very few accidental things you can do to hurt yourself or other users. So learn how things work by trying them. This is a long chapter, and the best way to read it is a few pages at a time, trying things out as you go.

1.1 Getting started

Some prerequisites about terminals and typing

To avoid explaining everything about using computers, we must assume you have some familiarity with computer terminals and how to use them. If any of the following statements are mystifying, you should ask a local expert for help.

The UNIX system is *full duplex*: the characters you type on the keyboard are sent to the system, which sends them back to the terminal to be printed on the screen. Normally, this *echo* process copies the characters directly to the screen, so you can see what you are typing, but sometimes, such as when you are typing a secret password, the echo is turned off so the characters do not appear on the screen.

Most of the keyboard characters are ordinary printing characters with no special significance, but a few tell the computer how to interpret your typing. By far the most important of these is the RETURN key. The RETURN key signifies the end of a line of input; the system echoes it by moving the terminal's cursor to the beginning of the next line on the screen. RETURN must be pressed before the system will interpret the characters you have typed.

RETURN is an example of a *control character* — an invisible character that controls some aspect of input and output on the terminal. On any reasonable terminal, RETURN has a key of its own, but most control characters do not. Instead, they must be typed by holding down the CONTROL key, sometimes called CTL or CNTL or CTRL, then pressing another key, usually a letter. For example, RETURN may be typed by pressing the RETURN key or, equivalently, holding down the CONTROL key and typing an 'm'. RETURN might therefore be called a control-m, which we will write as *ctl*-m. Other control characters include *ctl*-d, which tells a program that there is no more input; *ctl*-g, which rings the bell on the terminal; *ctl*-h, often called backspace, which can be used to correct typing mistakes; and *ctl*-i, often called tab, which advances the cursor to the next tab stop, much as on a regular typewriter. Tab stops on UNIX systems are eight spaces apart. Both the backspace and tab characters have their own keys on most terminals.

Two other keys have special meaning: DELETE, sometimes called RUBOUT or some abbreviation, and BREAK, sometimes called INTERRUPT. On most UNIX systems, the DELETE key stops a program immediately, without waiting for it to finish. On some systems, *ctl*-c provides this service. And on some systems, depending on how the terminals are connected, BREAK is a synonym for DELETE or *ctl*-c.

A Session with UNIX

Let's begin with an annotated dialog between you and your UNIX system. Throughout the examples in this book, what you type is printed in *slanted letters*, computer responses are in `typewriter-style characters`, and explanations are in *italics*.

```
        Establish a connection:  dial a phone or turn on a switch as necessary.
        Your system should say
        login: you                    Type your name, then press RETURN
        Password:                     Your password won't be echoed as you type it
        You have mail.                There's mail to be read after you log in
        $                             The system is now ready for your commands
        $                             Press RETURN a couple of times
        $ date                        What's the date and time?
        Sun Sep 25 23:02:57 EDT 1983
        $ who                         Who's using the machine?
        jlb       tty0     Sep 25 13:59
        you       tty2     Sep 25 23:01
        mary      tty4     Sep 25 19:03
        doug      tty5     Sep 25 19:22
        egb       tty7     Sep 25 17:17
        bob       tty8     Sep 25 20:48
        $ mail                        Read your mail
        From doug Sun Sep 25 20:53 EDT 1983
        give me a call sometime monday

        ?                             RETURN moves on to the next message
        From mary Sun Sep 25 19:07 EDT 1983    Next message
        Lunch at noon tomorrow?

        ? d                           Delete this message
        $                             No more mail
        $ mail mary                   Send mail to mary
        lunch at 12 is fine
        ctl-d                         End of mail
        $                             Hang up phone or turn off terminal
                                      and that's the end
```

Sometimes that's all there is to a session, though occasionally people do some work too. The rest of this section will discuss the session above, plus other programs that make it possible to do useful things.

Logging in

You must have a login name and password, which you can get from your system administrator. The UNIX system is capable of dealing with a wide variety of terminals, but it is strongly oriented towards devices with *lower case*; case distinctions matter! If your terminal produces only upper case (like some video and portable terminals), life will be so difficult that you should look for another terminal.

Be sure the switches are set appropriately on your device: upper and lower case, full duplex, and any other settings that local experts advise, such as the speed, or *baud rate*. Establish a connection using whatever magic is needed for your terminal; this may involve dialing a telephone or merely flipping a switch. In either case, the system should type

```
login:
```

If it types garbage, you may be at the wrong speed; check the speed setting and other switches. If that fails, press the BREAK or INTERRUPT key a few times, slowly. If nothing produces a login message, you will have to get help.

When you get the `login:` message, type your login name *in lower case*. Follow it by pressing RETURN. If a password is required, you will be asked for it, and printing will be turned off while you type it.

The culmination of your login efforts is a *prompt*, usually a single character, indicating that the system is ready to accept commands from you. The prompt is most likely to be a dollar sign $ or a percent sign %, but you can change it to anything you like; we'll show you how a little later. The prompt is actually printed by a program called the *command interpreter* or *shell*, which is your main interface to the system.

There may be a message of the day just before the prompt, or a notification that you have mail. You may also be asked what kind of terminal you are using; your answer helps the system to use any special properties the terminal might have.

Typing commands

Once you receive the prompt, you can type *commands*, which are requests that the system do something. We will use *program* as a synonym for command. When you see the prompt (let's assume it's $), type `date` and press RETURN. The system should reply with the date and time, then print another prompt, so the whole transaction will look like this on your terminal:

```
$ date
Mon Sep 26 12:20:57 EDT 1983
$
```

Don't forget RETURN, and don't type the $. If you think you're being ignored, press RETURN; something should happen. RETURN won't be mentioned again, but you need it at the end of every line.

The next command to try is who, which tells you everyone who is currently logged in:

```
$ who
rlm        tty0      Sep 26  11:17
pjw        tty4      Sep 26  11:30
gerard     tty7      Sep 26  10:27
mark       tty9      Sep 26  07:59
you        ttya      Sep 26  12:20
$
```

The first column is the user name. The second is the system's name for the connection being used ("tty" stands for "teletype," an archaic synonym for "terminal"). The rest tells when the user logged on. You might also try

```
$ who am i
you        ttya      Sep 26  12:20
$
```

If you make a mistake typing the name of a command, and refer to a non-existent command, you will be told that no command of that name can be found:

```
$ whom                           Misspelled command name ...
whom: not found                      ... so system didn't know how to run it
$
```

Of course, if you inadvertently type the name of an actual command, it will run, perhaps with mysterious results.

Strange terminal behavior

Sometimes your terminal will act strangely, for example, each letter may be typed twice, or RETURN may not put the cursor at the first column of the next line. You can usually fix this by turning the terminal off and on, or by logging out and logging back in. Or you can read the description of the command stty ("set terminal options") in Section 1 of the manual. To get intelligent treatment of tab characters if your terminal doesn't have tabs, type the command

```
$ stty -tabs
```

and the system will convert tabs into the right number of spaces. If your terminal does have computer-settable tab stops, the command tabs will set them correctly for you. (You may actually have to say

```
$ tabs terminal-type
```

to make it work — see the tabs command description in the manual.)

Mistakes in typing

If you make a typing mistake, and see it before you have pressed RETURN, there are two ways to recover: *erase* characters one at a time or *kill* the whole line and re-type it.

If you type the *line kill* character, by default an at-sign @, it causes the whole line to be discarded, just as if you'd never typed it, and starts you over on a new line:

```
$ ddtae@                        Completely botched; start over
date                              on a new line
Mon Sep 26 12:23:39 EDT 1983
$
```

The sharp character # erases the last character typed; each # erases one more character, back to the beginning of the line (but not beyond). So if you type badly, you can correct as you go:

```
$ dd#atte##e                    Fix it as you go
Mon Sep 26 12:24:02 EDT 1983
$
```

The particular erase and line kill characters are *very* system dependent. On many systems (including the one we use), the erase character has been changed to backspace, which works nicely on video terminals. You can quickly check which is the case on your system:

```
$ datee←                        Try ←
datee←: not found               It's not ←
$ datee#                        Try #
Mon Sep 26 12:26:08 EDT 1983    It is #
$
```

(We printed the backspace as ← so you can see it.) Another common choice is *ctl*-u for line kill.

We will use the sharp as the erase character for the rest of this section because it's visible, but make the mental adjustment if your system is different. Later on, in "tailoring the environment," we will tell you how to set the erase and line kill characters to whatever you like, once and for all.

What if you must enter an erase or line kill character as part of the text? If you precede either # or @ by a backslash \, it loses its special meaning. So to enter a # or @, type \# or \@. The system may advance the terminal's cursor to the next line after your @, even if it was preceded by a backslash. Don't worry — the at-sign has been recorded.

The backslash, sometimes called the *escape character*, is used extensively to indicate that the following character is in some way special. To erase a backslash, you have to type two erase characters: \##. Do you see why?

The characters you type are examined and interpreted by a sequence of programs before they reach their destination, and exactly how they are interpreted depends not only on where they end up but how they got there.

Every character you type is immediately echoed to the terminal, unless echoing is turned off, which is rare. Until you press RETURN, the characters are held temporarily by the kernel, so typing mistakes can be corrected with the erase and line kill characters. When an erase or line kill character is preceded by a backslash, the kernel discards the backslash and holds the following character without interpretation.

When you press RETURN, the characters being held are sent to the program that is reading from the terminal. That program may in turn interpret the characters in special ways; for example, the shell turns off any special interpretation of a character if it is preceded by a backslash. We'll come back to this in Chapter 3. For now, you should remember that the kernel processes erase and line kill, and backslash only if it precedes erase or line kill; whatever characters are left after that may be interpreted by other programs as well.

Exercise 1-1. Explain what happens with

```
$ date\@
```

□

Exercise 1-2. Most shells (though not the 7th Edition shell) interpret # as introducing a comment, and ignore all text from the # to the end of the line. Given this, explain the following transcript, assuming your erase character is also #:

```
$ date
Mon Sep 26 12:39:56 EDT 1983
$ #date
Mon Sep 26 12:40:21 EDT 1983
$ \#date
$ \\#date
#date: not found
$
```

□

Type-ahead

The kernel reads what you type as you type it, even if it's busy with something else, so you can type as fast as you want, whenever you want, even when some command is printing at you. If you type while the system is printing, your input characters will appear intermixed with the output characters, but they will be stored away and interpreted in the correct order. You can type commands one after another without waiting for them to finish or even to begin.

Stopping a program

You can stop most commands by typing the character DELETE. The BREAK key found on most terminals may also work, although this is system dependent. In a few programs, like text editors, DELETE stops whatever the program is doing but leaves you in that program. Turning off the terminal or hanging up the phone will stop most programs.

If you just want output to pause, for example to keep something critical from disappearing off the screen, type *ctl*-s. The output will stop almost immediately; your program is suspended until you start it again. When you want to resume, type *ctl*-q.

Logging out

The proper way to log out is to type *ctl*-d instead of a command; this tells the shell that there is no more input. (How this actually works will be explained in the next chapter.) You can usually just turn off the terminal or hang up the phone, but whether this really logs you out depends on your system.

Mail

The system provides a postal system for communicating with other users, so some day when you log in, you will see the message

```
You have mail.
```

before the first prompt. To read your mail, type

```
$ mail
```

Your mail will be printed, one message at a time, most recent first. After each item, mail waits for you to say what to do with it. The two basic responses are d, which deletes the message, and RETURN, which does not (so it will still be there the next time you read your mail). Other responses include p to reprint a message, s *filename* to save it in the file you named, and q to quit from mail. (If you don't know what a file is, think of it as a place where you can store information under a name of your choice, and retrieve it later. Files are the topic of Section 1.2 and indeed of much of this book.)

mail is one of those programs that is likely to differ from what we describe here; there are many variants. Look in your manual for details.

Sending mail to someone is straightforward. Suppose it is to go to the person with the login name nico. The easiest way is this:

```
$ mail nico
Now type in the text of the letter
on as many lines as you like ...
After the last line of the letter
type a control-d.
ctl-d
$
```

The *ctl*-d signals the end of the letter by telling the mail command that there is no more input. If you change your mind half-way through composing the letter, press DELETE instead of *ctl*-d. The half-formed letter will be stored in a file called dead.letter instead of being sent.

For practice, send mail to yourself, then type `mail` to read it. (This isn't as aberrant as it might sound — it's a handy reminder mechanism.)

There are other ways to send mail — you can send a previously prepared letter, you can mail to a number of people all at once, and you may be able to send mail to people on other machines. For more details see the description of the `mail` command in Section 1 of the *UNIX Programmer's Manual*. Henceforth we'll use the notation `mail(1)` to mean the page describing `mail` in Section 1 of the manual. All of the commands discussed in this chapter are found in Section 1.

There may also be a calendar service (see `calendar(1)`); we'll show you in Chapter 4 how to set one up if it hasn't been done already.

Writing to other users

If your UNIX system has multiple users, someday, out of the blue, your terminal will print something like

```
Message from mary tty7...
```

accompanied by a startling beep. Mary wants to write to you, but unless you take explicit action you won't be able to write back. To respond, type

```
$ write mary
```

This establishes a two-way communication path. Now the lines that Mary types on her terminal will appear on yours and vice versa, although the path is slow, rather like talking to the moon.

If you are in the middle of something, you have to get to a state where you can type a command. Normally, whatever program you are running has to stop or be stopped, but some programs, such as the editor and `write` itself, have a '!' command to escape temporarily to the shell — see Table 2 in Appendix 1.

The `write` command imposes no rules, so a protocol is needed to keep what you type from getting garbled up with what Mary types. One convention is to take turns, ending each turn with (o), which stands for "over," and to signal your intent to quit with (oo), for "over and out."

Mary's terminal:	*Your terminal:*
`$ write you`	
	`$ Message from mary tty7...`
	`write mary`
`Message from you ttya...`	
`did you forget lunch? (o)`	
	`did you forget lunch? (o)`
	`five@`
	`ten minutes (o)`
`ten minutes (o)`	
`ok (oo)`	
	`ok (oo)`
	`ctl-d`
`EOF`	
`ctl-d`	
	`$ EOF`
`$`	

You can also exit from `write` by pressing DELETE. Notice that your typing errors do not appear on Mary's terminal.

If you try to write to someone who isn't logged in, or who doesn't want to be disturbed, you'll be told. If the target is logged in but doesn't answer after a decent interval, the person may be busy or away from the terminal; simply type *ctl*-d or DELETE. If *you* don't want to be disturbed, use `mesg`(1).

News

Many UNIX systems provide a news service, to keep users abreast of interesting and not so interesting events. Try typing

    $ news

There is also a large network of UNIX systems that keep in touch through telephone calls; ask a local expert about `netnews` and USENET.

The manual

The UNIX *Programmer's Manual* describes most of what you need to know about the system. Section 1 deals with commands, including those we discuss in this chapter. Section 2 describes the system calls, the subject of Chapter 7, and Section 6 has information about games. The remaining sections talk about functions for use by C programmers, file formats, and system maintenance. (The numbering of these sections varies from system to system.) Don't forget the permuted index at the beginning; you can skim it quickly for commands that might be relevant to what you want to do. There is also an introduction to the system that gives an overview of how things work.

Often the manual is kept on-line so that you can read it on your terminal. If you get stuck on something, and can't find an expert to help, you can print any manual page on your terminal with the command `man` *command-name*.

Thus to read about the who command, type

```
$ man who
```

and, of course,

```
$ man man
```

tells about the man command.

Computer-aided instruction

Your system may have a command called learn, which provides computer-aided instruction on the file system and basic commands, the editor, document preparation, and even C programming. Try

```
$ learn
```

If learn exists on your system, it will tell you what to do from there. If that fails, you might also try teach.

Games

It's not always admitted officially, but one of the best ways to get comfortable with a computer and a terminal is to play games. The UNIX system comes with a modest supply of games, often supplemented locally. Ask around, or see Section 6 of the manual.

1.2 Day-to-day use: files and common commands

Information in a UNIX system is stored in *files*, which are much like ordinary office files. Each file has a name, contents, a place to keep it, and some administrative information such as who owns it and how big it is. A file might contain a letter, or a list of names and addresses, or the source statements of a program, or data to be used by a program, or even programs in their executable form and other non-textual material.

The UNIX file system is organized so you can maintain your own personal files without interfering with files belonging to other people, and keep people from interfering with you too. There are myriad programs that manipulate files, but for now, we will look at only the more frequently used ones. Chapter 2 contains a systematic discussion of the file system, and introduces many of the other file-related commands.

Creating files — the editor

If you want to type a paper or a letter or a program, how do you get the information stored in the machine? Most of these tasks are done with a *text editor*, which is a program for storing and manipulating information in the computer. Almost every UNIX system has a *screen editor*, an editor that takes advantage of modern terminals to display the effects of your editing changes in context as you make them. Two of the most popular are vi and emacs. We won't describe any specific screen editor here, however, partly because of typographic limitations, and partly because there is no standard one.

There is, however, an older editor called ed that is certain to be available on your system. It takes no advantage of special terminal features, so it will work on any terminal. It also forms the basis of other essential programs (including some screen editors), so it's worth learning eventually. Appendix 1 contains a concise description.

No matter what editor you prefer, you'll have to learn it well enough to be able to create files. We'll use ed here to make the discussion concrete, and to ensure that you can make our examples run on your system, but by all means use whatever editor you like best.

To use ed to create a file called junk with some text in it, do the following:

```
$ ed                              Invokes the text editor
a                                 ed command to add text
now type in
whatever text you want ...
                                  Type a '.' by itself to stop adding text
.
w junk                            Write your text into a file called junk
39                                ed prints number of characters written
q                                 Quit ed
$
```

The command a ("append") tells ed to start collecting text. The "." that signals the end of the text must be typed at the beginning of a line by itself. Don't forget it, for until it is typed, no other ed commands will be recognized — everything you type will be treated as text to be added.

The editor command w ("write") stores the information that you typed; "w junk" stores it in a file called junk. The filename can be any word you like; we picked junk to suggest that this file isn't very important.

ed responds with the number of characters it put in the file. Until the w command, nothing is stored permanently, so if you hang up and go home the information is not stored in the file. (If you hang up while editing, the data you were working on is saved in a file called ed.hup, which you can continue with at your next session.) If the system crashes (i.e., stops unexpectedly because of software or hardware failure) while you are editing, your file will contain only what the last write command placed there. But after w the information is recorded permanently; you can access it again later by typing

```
$ ed junk
```

Of course, you can edit the text you typed in, to correct spelling mistakes, change wording, rearrange paragraphs and the like. When you're done, the q command ("quit") leaves the editor.

What files are out there?

Let's create two files, junk and temp, so we know what we have:

```
$ ed
a
To be or not to be
.
w junk
19
q
$ ed
a
That is the question.
.
w temp
22
q
$
```

The character counts from ed include the character at the end of each line, called *newline*, which is how the system represents RETURN.

The ls command lists the names (not contents) of files:

```
$ ls
junk
temp
$
```

which are indeed the two files just created. (There might be others as well that you didn't create yourself.) The names are sorted into alphabetical order automatically.

ls, like most commands, has *options* that may be used to alter its default behavior. Options follow the command name on the command line, and are usually made up of an initial minus sign '-' and a single letter meant to suggest the meaning. For example, ls -t causes the files to be listed in "time" order: the order in which they were last changed, most recent first.

```
$ ls -t
temp
junk
$
```

The -l option gives a "long" listing that provides more information about each file:

```
$ ls -l
total 2
-rw-r--r-- 1 you          19 Sep 26 16:25 junk
-rw-r--r-- 1 you          22 Sep 26 16:26 temp
$
```

"`total 2`" tells how many blocks of disc space the files occupy; a block is usually either 512 or 1024 characters. The string `-rw-r--r--` tells who has permission to read and write the file; in this case, the owner (`you`) can read and write, but others can only read it. The "`1`" that follows is the number of links to the file; ignore it until Chapter 2. "`you`" is the owner of the file, that is, the person who created it. `19` and `22` are the number of characters in the corresponding files, which agree with the numbers you got from `ed`. The date and time tell when the file was last changed.

Options can be grouped: `ls -lt` gives the same data as `ls -l`, but sorted with most recent files first. The `-u` option gives information on when files were used: `ls -lut` gives a long (`-l`) listing in the order of most recent use. The option `-r` reverses the order of the output, so `ls -rt` lists in order of least recent use. You can also name the files you're interested in, and `ls` will list the information about them only:

```
$ ls -l junk
-rw-r--r-- 1 you         19 Sep 26 16:25 junk
$
```

The strings that follow the program name on the command line, such as `-l` and `junk` in the example above, are called the program's *arguments*. Arguments are usually options or names of files to be used by the command.

Specifying options by a minus sign and a single letter, such as `-t` or the combined `-lt`, is a common convention. In general, if a command accepts such optional arguments, they precede any filename arguments, but may otherwise appear in any order. But UNIX programs are capricious in their treatment of multiple options. For example, standard 7th Edition `ls` won't accept

```
$ ls -l -t                         Doesn't work in 7th Edition
```

as a synonym for `ls -lt`, while other programs *require* multiple options to be separated.

As you learn more, you will find that there is little regularity or system to optional arguments. Each command has its own idiosyncrasies, and its own choices of what letter means what (often different from the same function in other commands). This unpredictable behavior is disconcerting and is often cited as a major flaw of the system. Although the situation is improving — new versions often have more uniformity — all we can suggest is that you try to do better when you write your own programs, and in the meantime keep a copy of the manual handy.

Printing files — cat *and* pr

Now that you have some files, how do you look at their contents? There are many programs to do that, probably more than are needed. One possibility is to use the editor:

```
$ ed junk
19                          ed reports 19 characters in junk
1,$p                        Print lines 1 through last
To be or not to be          File has only one line
q                           All done
$
```

ed begins by reporting the number of characters in junk; the command 1,$p tells it to print all the lines in the file. After you learn how to use the editor, you can be selective about the parts you print.

There are times when it's not feasible to use an editor for printing. For example, there is a limit — several thousand lines — on how big a file ed can handle. Furthermore, it will only print one file at a time, and sometimes you want to print several, one after another without pausing. So here are a couple of alternatives.

First is cat, the simplest of all the printing commands. cat prints the *contents* of all the files named by its arguments:

```
$ cat junk
To be or not to be
$ cat temp
That is the question.
$ cat junk temp
To be or not to be
That is the question.
$
```

The named file or files are catenated† (hence the name "cat") onto the terminal one after another with nothing between.

There's no problem with short files, but for long ones, if you have a high-speed connection to your computer, you have to be quick with *ctl*-s to stop output from cat before it flows off your screen. There is no "standard" command to print a file on a video terminal one screenful at a time, though almost every UNIX system has one. Your system might have one called pg or more. Ours is called p; we'll show you its implementation in Chapter 6.

Like cat, the command pr prints the contents of all the files named in a list, but in a form suitable for line printers: every page is 66 lines (11 inches) long, with the date and time that the file was changed, the page number, and the filename at the top of each page, and extra lines to skip over the fold in the paper. Thus, to print junk neatly, then skip to the top of a new page and print temp neatly:

---

† "Catenate" is a slightly obscure synonym for "concatenate."

```
$ pr junk temp


Sep 26 16:25 1983   junk Page 1


To be or not to be
        (60 more blank lines)


Sep 26 16:26 1983   temp Page 1


That is the question.
        (60 more blank lines)
$
```

pr can also produce multi-column output:

```
$ pr -3 filenames
```

prints each file in 3-column format. You can use any reasonable number in place of "3" and pr will do its best. (The word *filenames* is a place-holder for a list of names of files.) pr -m will print a set of files in parallel columns. See pr(1).

It should be noted that pr is *not* a formatting program in the sense of re-arranging lines and justifying margins. The true formatters are nroff and troff, which are discussed in Chapter 9.

There are also commands that print files on a high-speed printer. Look in your manual under names like lp and lpr, or look up "printer" in the per-muted index. Which to use depends on what equipment is attached to your machine. pr and lpr are often used together; after pr formats the informa-tion properly, lpr handles the mechanics of getting it to the line printer. We will return to this a little later.

Moving, copying, removing files — mv, cp, rm

Let's look at some other commands. The first thing is to change the name of a file. Renaming a file is done by "moving" it from one name to another, like this:

```
$ mv junk precious
```

This means that the file that used to be called junk is now called precious; the contents are unchanged. If you run ls now, you will see a different list: junk is not there but precious is.

```
$ ls
precious
temp
$ cat junk
cat: can't open junk
$
```

Beware that if you move a file to another one that already exists, the target file is replaced.

To make a *copy* of a file (that is, to have two versions of something), use the cp command:

```
$ cp precious precious.save
```

makes a duplicate copy of precious in precious.save.

Finally, when you get tired of creating and moving files, the rm command removes all the files you name:

```
$ rm temp junk
rm: junk nonexistent
$
```

You will get a warning if one of the files to be removed wasn't there, but otherwise rm, like most UNIX commands, does its work silently. There is no prompting or chatter, and error messages are curt and sometimes unhelpful. Brevity can be disconcerting to newcomers, but experienced users find talkative commands annoying.

What's in a filename?

So far we have used filenames without ever saying what a legal name is, so it's time for a couple of rules. First, filenames are limited to 14 characters. Second, although you can use almost any character in a filename, common sense says you should stick to ones that are visible, and that you should avoid characters that might be used with other meanings. We have already seen, for example, that in the ls command, ls -t means to list in time order. So if you had a file whose name was -t, you would have a tough time listing it by name. (How would you do it?) Besides the minus sign as a first character, there are other characters with special meaning. To avoid pitfalls, you would do well to use only letters, numbers, the period and the underscore until you're familiar with the situation. (The period and the underscore are conventionally used to divide filenames into chunks, as in precious.save above.) Finally, don't forget that case distinctions matter — junk, Junk, and JUNK are three different names.

A handful of useful commands

Now that you have the rudiments of creating files, listing their names, and printing their contents, we can look at a half-dozen file-processing commands.

To make the discussion concrete, we'll use a file called poem that contains a familiar verse by Augustus De Morgan. Let's create it with ed:

```
$ ed
a
Great fleas have little fleas
   upon their backs to bite 'em,
And little fleas have lesser fleas,
   and so ad infinitum.
And the great fleas themselves, in turn,
   have greater fleas to go on;
While these again have greater still,
   and greater still, and so on.
.
w poem
263
q
$
```

The first command counts the lines, words and characters in one or more files; it is named wc after its word-counting function:

```
$ wc poem
      8     46     263 poem
$
```

That is, poem has 8 lines, 46 words, and 263 characters. The definition of a "word" is very simple: any string of characters that doesn't contain a blank, tab or newline.

wc will count more than one file for you (and print the totals), and it will also suppress any of the counts if requested. See wc(1).

The second command is called grep; it searches files for lines that match a pattern. (The name comes from the ed command g/*regular-expression*/p, which is explained in Appendix 1.) Suppose you want to look for the word "fleas" in poem:

```
$ grep fleas poem
Great fleas have little fleas
And little fleas have lesser fleas,
And the great fleas themselves, in turn,
   have greater fleas to go on;
$
```

grep will also look for lines that *don't* match the pattern, when the option -v is used. (It's named 'v' after the editor command; you can think of it as inverting the sense of the match.)

```
$ grep -v fleas poem
  upon their backs to bite 'em,
  and so ad infinitum.
While these again have greater still,
  and greater still, and so on.
$
```

grep can be used to search several files; in that case it will prefix the filename to each line that matches, so you can tell where the match took place. There are also options for counting, numbering, and so on. grep will also handle much more complicated patterns than just words like "fleas," but we will defer consideration of that until Chapter 4.

The third command is sort, which sorts its input into alphabetical order line by line. This isn't very interesting for the poem, but let's do it anyway, just to see what it looks like:

```
$ sort poem
  and greater still, and so on.
  and so ad infinitum.
  have greater fleas to go on;
  upon their backs to bite 'em,
And little fleas have lesser fleas,
And the great fleas themselves, in turn,
Great fleas have little fleas
While these again have greater still,
$
```

The sorting is line by line, but the default sorting order puts blanks first, then upper case letters, then lower case, so it's not strictly alphabetical.

sort has zillions of options to control the order of sorting — reverse order, numerical order, dictionary order, ignoring leading blanks, sorting on fields within the line, etc. — but usually one has to look up those options to be sure of them. Here are a handful of the most common:

sort -r	*Reverse normal order*
sort -n	*Sort in numeric order*
sort -nr	*Sort in reverse numeric order*
sort -f	*Fold upper and lower case together*
sort +n	*Sort starting at $n+1$-st field*

Chapter 4 has more information about sort.

Another file-examining command is tail, which prints the last 10 lines of a file. That's overkill for our eight-line poem, but it's good for larger files. Furthermore, tail has an option to specify the number of lines, so to print the last line of poem:

```
$ tail -1 poem
  and greater still, and so on.
$
```

`tail` can also be used to print a file starting at a specified line:

```
$ tail +3 filename
```

starts printing with the 3rd line. (Notice the natural inversion of the minus sign convention for arguments.)

The final pair of commands is for comparing files. Suppose that we have a variant of poem in the file new_poem:

```
$ cat poem
Great fleas have little fleas
  upon their backs to bite 'em,
And little fleas have lesser fleas,
  and so ad infinitum.
And the great fleas themselves, in turn,
  have greater fleas to go on;
While these again have greater still,
  and greater still, and so on.
$ cat new_poem
Great fleas have little fleas
  upon their backs to bite them,
And little fleas have lesser fleas,
  and so on ad infinitum.
And the great fleas themselves, in turn,
  have greater fleas to go on;
While these again have greater still,
  and greater still, and so on.
$
```

There's not much difference between the two files; in fact you'll have to look hard to find it. This is where file comparison commands come in handy. `cmp` finds the first place where two files differ:

```
$ cmp poem new_poem
poem new_poem differ: char 58, line 2
$
```

This says that the files are different in the second line, which is true enough, but it doesn't say what the difference is, nor does it identify any differences beyond the first.

The other file comparison command is `diff`, which reports on all lines that are changed, added or deleted:

```
$ diff poem new_poem
2c2
<     upon their backs to bite 'em,
---
>     upon their backs to bite them,
4c4
<     and so ad infinitum.
---
>     and so on ad infinitum.
$
```

This says that line 2 in the first file (poem) has to be changed into line 2 of the second file (new_poem), and similarly for line 4.

Generally speaking, cmp is used when you want to be sure that two files really have the same contents. It's fast and it works on any kind of file, not just text. diff is used when the files are expected to be somewhat different, and you want to know exactly which lines differ. diff works only on files of text.

A summary of file system commands

Table 1.1 is a brief summary of the commands we've seen so far that deal with files.

1.3 More about files: directories

The system distinguishes your file called junk from anyone else's of the same name. The distinction is made by grouping files into *directories*, rather in the way that books are placed on shelves in a library, so files in different directories can have the same name without any conflict.

Generally each user has a personal or *home directory*, sometimes called login directory, that contains only the files that belong to him or her. When you log in, you are "in" your home directory. You may change the directory you are working in — often called your working or *current directory* — but your home directory is always the same. Unless you take special action, when you create a new file it is made in your current directory. Since this is initially your home directory, the file is unrelated to a file of the same name that might exist in someone else's directory.

A directory can contain other directories as well as ordinary files ("Great directories have lesser directories ..."). The natural way to picture this organization is as a tree of directories and files. It is possible to move around within this tree, and to find any file in the system by starting at the root of the tree and moving along the proper branches. Conversely, you can start where you are and move toward the root.

Let's try the latter first. Our basic tool is the command pwd ("print working directory"), which prints the name of the directory you are currently in:

Table 1.1: Common File System Commands

`ls`	list names of all files in current directory
`ls` *filenames*	list only the named files
`ls -t`	list in time order, most recent first.
`ls -l`	list long: more information; also `ls -lt`
`ls -u`	list by time last used; also `ls -lu`, `ls -lut`
`ls -r`	list in reverse order; also `-rt`, `-rlt`, etc.
`ed` *filename*	edit named file
`cp` *file1 file2*	copy *file1* to *file2*, overwrite old *file2* if it exists
`mv` *file1 file2*	move *file1* to *file2*, overwrite old *file2* if it exists
`rm` *filenames*	remove named files, irrevocably
`cat` *filenames*	print contents of named files
`pr` *filenames*	print contents with header, 66 lines per page
`pr` *-n filenames*	print in *n* columns
`pr` *-m filenames*	print named files side by side (multiple columns)
`wc` *filenames*	count lines, words and characters for each file
`wc -l` *filenames*	count lines for each file
`grep` *pattern filenames*	print lines matching *pattern*
`grep -v` *pattern files*	print lines not matching *pattern*
`sort` *filenames*	sort files alphabetically by line
`tail` *filename*	print last 10 lines of file
`tail` *-n filename*	print last *n* lines of file
`tail` *+n filename*	start printing file at line *n*
`cmp` *file1 file2*	print location of first difference
`diff` *file1 file2*	print all differences between files

```
$ pwd
/usr/you
$
```

This says that you are currently in the directory you, in the directory usr, which in turn is in the *root directory*, which is conventionally called just '/'. The / characters separate the components of the name; the limit of 14 characters mentioned above applies to each component of such a name. On many systems, /usr is a directory that contains the directories of all the normal users of the system. (Even if your home directory is not /usr/you, pwd will print something analogous, so you should be able to follow what happens below.)

If you now type

```
$ ls /usr/you
```

you should get exactly the same list of file names as you get from a plain `ls`. When no arguments are provided, `ls` lists the contents of the current directory; given the name of a directory, it lists the contents of that directory.

Next, try

```
$ ls /usr
```

This should print a long series of names, among which is your own login directory `you`.

The next step is to try listing the root itself. You should get a response similar to this:

```
$ ls /
bin
boot
dev
etc
lib
tmp
unix
usr
$
```

(Don't be confused by the two meanings of `/`: it's both the name of the root and a separator in filenames.) Most of these are directories, but `unix` is actually a file containing the executable form of the UNIX kernel. More on this in Chapter 2.

Now try

```
$ cat /usr/you/junk
```

(if `junk` is still in your directory). The name

```
/usr/you/junk
```

is called the *pathname* of the file. "Pathname" has an intuitive meaning: it represents the full name of the path from the root through the tree of directories to a particular file. It is a universal rule in the UNIX system that wherever you can use an ordinary filename, you can use a pathname.

The file system is structured like a genealogical tree; here is a picture that may make it clearer.

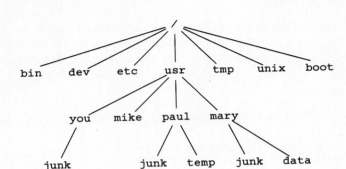

Your file named junk is unrelated to Paul's or to Mary's.

Pathnames aren't too exciting if all the files of interest are in your own directory, but if you work with someone else or on several projects concurrently, they become handy indeed. For example, your friends can print your junk by saying

```
$ cat /usr/you/junk
```

Similarly, you can find out what files Mary has by saying

```
$ ls /usr/mary
data
junk
$
```

or make your own copy of one of her files by

```
$ cp /usr/mary/data data
```

or edit her file:

```
$ ed /usr/mary/data
```

If Mary doesn't want you poking around in her files, or vice versa, privacy can be arranged. Each file and directory has read-write-execute permissions for the owner, a group, and everyone else, which can be used to control access. (Recall ls -l.) In our local systems, most users most of the time find openness of more benefit than privacy, but policy may be different on your system, so we'll get back to this in Chapter 2.

As a final set of experiments with pathnames, try

```
$ ls /bin /usr/bin
```

Do some of the names look familiar? When you run a command by typing its name after the prompt, the system looks for a file of that name. It normally looks first in your current directory (where it probably doesn't find it), then in /bin, and finally in /usr/bin. There is nothing special about commands

like `cat` or `ls`, except that they have been collected into a couple of directories to be easy to find and administer. To verify this, try to execute some of
these programs by using their full pathnames:

```
$ /bin/date
Mon Sep 26 23:29:32 EDT 1983
$ /bin/who
srm        tty1     Sep 26 22:20
cvw        tty4     Sep 26 22:40
you        tty5     Sep 26 23:04
$
```

Exercise 1-3. Try

```
$ ls /usr/games
```

and do whatever comes naturally. Things might be more fun outside of normal working
hours. □

Changing directory — cd

If you work regularly with Mary on information in her directory, you can
say "I want to work on Mary's files instead of my own." This is done by
changing your current directory with the `cd` command:

```
$ cd /usr/mary
```

Now when you use a filename (without /'s) as an argument to `cat` or `pr`, it
refers to the file in Mary's directory. Changing directories doesn't affect any
permissions associated with a file — if you couldn't access a file from your
own directory, changing to another directory won't alter that fact.

It is usually convenient to arrange your own files so that all the files related
to one thing are in a directory separate from other projects. For example, if
you want to write a book, you might want to keep all the text in a directory
called `book`. The command `mkdir` makes a new directory.

```
$ mkdir book          Make a directory
$ cd book             Go to it
$ pwd                 Make sure you're in the right place
/usr/you/book

...                   Write the book (several minutes pass)

$ cd ..               Move up one level in file system
$ pwd
/usr/you
$
```

'`..`' refers to the parent of whatever directory you are currently in, the directory one level closer to the root. '`.`' is a synonym for the current directory.

```
$ cd                  Return to home directory
```

all by itself will take you back to your home directory, the directory where you log in.

Once your book is published, you can clean up the files. To remove the directory `book`, remove all the files in it (we'll show a fast way shortly), then `cd` to the parent directory of `book` and type

```
$ rmdir book
```

`rmdir` will only remove an empty directory.

1.4 The shell

When the system prints the prompt `$` and you type commands that get executed, it's not the kernel that is talking to you, but a go-between called the command interpreter or *shell*. The shell is just an ordinary program like `date` or `who`, although it can do some remarkable things. The fact that the shell sits between you and the facilities of the kernel has real benefits, some of which we'll talk about here. There are three main ones:

- Filename shorthands: you can pick up a whole set of filenames as arguments to a program by specifying a pattern for the names — the shell will find the filenames that match your pattern.
- Input-output redirection: you can arrange for the output of any program to go into a file instead of onto the terminal, and for the input to come from a file instead of the terminal. Input and output can even be connected to other programs.
- Personalizing the environment: you can define your own commands and shorthands.

Filename shorthand

Let's begin with filename patterns. Suppose you're typing a large document like a book. Logically this divides into many small pieces, like chapters and perhaps sections. Physically it should be divided too, because it is cumbersome to edit large files. Thus you should type the document as a number of files. You might have separate files for each chapter, called `ch1`, `ch2`, etc. Or, if each chapter were broken into sections, you might create files called

```
ch1.1
ch1.2
ch1.3
...
ch2.1
ch2.2
...
```

which is the organization we used for this book. With a systematic naming convention, you can tell at a glance where a particular file fits into the whole.

What if you want to print the whole book? You could say

```
$ pr ch1.1 ch1.2 ch1.3 ...
```

but you would soon get bored typing filenames and start to make mistakes. This is where filename shorthand comes in. If you say

```
$ pr ch*
```

the shell takes the * to mean "any string of characters," so ch* is a pattern that matches all filenames in the current directory that begin with ch. The shell creates the list, in alphabetical† order, and passes the list to pr. The pr command never sees the *; the pattern match that the shell does in the current directory generates a list of strings that are passed to pr.

The crucial point is that filename shorthand is not a property of the pr command, but a service of the shell. Thus you can use it to generate a sequence of filenames for *any* command. For example, to count the words in the first chapter:

```
$ wc ch1.*
     113     562    3200 ch1.0
     935    4081   22435 ch1.1
     974    4191   22756 ch1.2
     378    1561    8481 ch1.3
    1293    5298   28841 ch1.4
      33     194    1190 ch1.5
      75     323    2030 ch1.6
    3801   16210   88933 total
$
```

There is a program called echo that is especially valuable for experimenting with the meaning of the shorthand characters. As you might guess, echo does nothing more than echo its arguments:

```
$ echo hello world
hello world
$
```

But the arguments can be generated by pattern-matching:

```
$ echo ch1.*
```

lists the names of all the files in Chapter 1,

```
$ echo *
```

lists *all* the filenames in the current directory in alphabetical order,

```
$ pr *
```

prints all your files (in alphabetical order), and

---

† Again, the order is not strictly alphabetical, in that upper case letters come before lower case letters. See ascii(7) for the ordering of the characters used in the sort.

```
$ rm *
```

removes *all files* in your current directory. (You had better be *very* sure that's
what you wanted to say!)

The * is not limited to the last position in a filename — *'s can be anywhere and can occur several times. Thus

```
$ rm *.save
```

removes all files that end with .save.

Notice that the filenames are sorted alphabetically, which is not the same as
numerically. If your book has ten chapters, the order might not be what you
intended, since ch10 comes before ch2:

```
$ echo *
ch1.1 ch1.2 ... ch10.1 ch10.2 ... ch2.1 ch2.2 ...
$
```

The * is not the only pattern-matching feature provided by the shell,
although it's by far the most frequently used. The pattern [...] matches any
of the characters inside the brackets. A range of consecutive letters or digits
can be abbreviated:

```
$ pr ch[12346789]*      Print chapters 1,2,3,4,6,7,8,9 but not 5
$ pr ch[1-46-9]*        Same thing
$ rm temp[a-z]          Remove any of tempa, ..., tempz that exist
```

The ? pattern matches any single character:

```
$ ls ?                  List files with single-character names
$ ls -1 ch?.1           List ch1.1 ch2.1 ch3.1, etc. but not ch10.1
$ rm temp?              Remove files temp1, ..., tempa, etc.
```

Note that the patterns match only *existing* filenames. In particular, you cannot
make up new filenames by using patterns. For example, if you want to expand
ch to chapter in each filename, you cannot do it this way:

```
$ mv ch.* chapter.*      Doesn't work!
```

because chapter.* matches no existing filenames.

Pattern characters like * can be used in pathnames as well as simple
filenames; the match is done for each component of the path that contains a
special character. Thus /usr/mary/* performs the match in /usr/mary,
and /usr/*/calendar generates a list of pathnames of all user calendar
files.

If you should ever have to turn off the special meaning of *, ?, etc.,
enclose the entire argument in single quotes, as in

```
$ ls '?'
```

You can also precede a special character with a backslash:

```
$ ls \?
```

(Remember that because ? is not the erase or line kill character, this backslash is interpreted by the shell, not by the kernel.) Quoting is treated at length in Chapter 3.

Exercise 1-4. What are the differences among these commands?

```
$ ls junk            $ echo junk
$ ls /               $ echo /
$ ls                 $ echo
$ ls *               $ echo *
$ ls '*'             $ echo '*'
```

□

Input-output redirection

Most of the commands we have seen so far produce output on the terminal; some, like the editor, also take their input from the terminal. It is nearly universal that the terminal can be replaced by a file for either or both of input and output. As one example,

```
$ ls
```

makes a list of filenames on your terminal. But if you say

```
$ ls >filelist
```

that same list of filenames will be placed in the file `filelist` instead. The symbol > means "put the output in the following file, rather than on the terminal." The file will be created if it doesn't already exist, or the previous contents overwritten if it does. Nothing is produced on your terminal. As another example, you can combine several files into one by capturing the output of `cat` in a file:

```
$ cat f1 f2 f3 >temp
```

The symbol >> operates much as > does, except that it means "add to the end of." That is,

```
$ cat f1 f2 f3 >>temp
```

copies the contents of `f1`, `f2` and `f3` onto the end of whatever is already in `temp`, instead of overwriting the existing contents. As with >, if `temp` doesn't exist, it will be created initially empty for you.

In a similar way, the symbol < means to take the input for a program from the following file, instead of from the terminal. Thus, you can prepare a letter in file `let`, then send it to several people with

```
$ mail mary joe tom bob <let
```

In all of these examples, blanks are optional on either side of > or <, but our formatting is traditional.

Given the capability of redirecting output with >, it becomes possible to combine commands to achieve effects not possible otherwise. For example, to print an alphabetical list of users,

```
$ who >temp
$ sort <temp
```

Since who prints one line of output per logged-on user, and wc -1 counts lines (suppressing the word and character counts), you can count users with

```
$ who >temp
$ wc -1 <temp
```

You can count the files in the current directory with

```
$ ls >temp
$ wc -1 <temp
```

though this includes the filename temp itself in the count. You can print the filenames in three columns with

```
$ ls >temp
$ pr -3 <temp
```

And you can see if a particular user is logged on by combining who and grep:

```
$ who >temp
$ grep mary <temp
```

In all of these examples, as with filename pattern characters like *, it's important to remember that the interpretation of > and < is being done by the shell, not by the individual programs. Centralizing the facility in the shell means that input and output redirection can be used with any program; the program itself isn't aware that something unusual has happened.

This brings up an important convention. The command

```
$ sort <temp
```

sorts the contents of the file temp, as does

```
$ sort temp
```

but there is a difference. Because the string <temp is interpreted by the shell, sort does not see the filename temp as an argument; it instead sorts its *standard input*, which the shell has redirected so it comes from the file. The latter example, however, passes the name temp as an argument to sort, which reads the file and sorts it. sort can be given a list of filenames, as in

```
$ sort temp1 temp2 temp3
```

but if no filenames are given, it sorts its standard input. This is an essential property of most commands: if no filenames are specified, the standard input is processed. This means that you can simply type at commands to see how they work. For example,

```
$ sort
ghi
abc
def
ctl-d
abc
def
ghi
$
```

In the next section, we will see how this principle is exploited.

Exercise 1-5. Explain why

```
$ ls >ls.out
```

causes ls.out to be included in the list of names. □

Exercise 1-6. Explain the output from

```
$ wc temp >temp
```

If you misspell a command name, as in

```
$ woh >temp
```

what happens? □

Pipes

All of the examples at the end of the previous section rely on the same trick: putting the output of one program into the input of another via a temporary file. But the temporary file has no other purpose; indeed, it's clumsy to have to use such a file. This observation leads to one of the fundamental contributions of the UNIX system, the idea of a *pipe*. A pipe is a way to connect the output of one program to the input of another program without any temporary file; a *pipeline* is a connection of two or more programs through pipes.

Let us revise some of the earlier examples to use pipes instead of temporaries. The vertical bar character ¦ tells the shell to set up a pipeline:

```
$ who ¦ sort          Print sorted list of users
$ who ¦ wc -l         Count users
$ ls ¦ wc -l          Count files
$ ls ¦ pr -3          3-column list of filenames
$ who ¦ grep mary     Look for particular user
```

Any program that reads from the terminal can read from a pipe instead; any program that writes on the terminal can write to a pipe. This is where the convention of reading the standard input when no files are named pays off: any program that adheres to the convention can be used in pipelines. grep, pr, sort and wc are all used that way in the pipelines above.

You can have as many programs in a pipeline as you wish:

```
$ ls | pr -3 | lpr
```

creates a 3-column list of filenames on the line printer, and

```
$ who | grep mary | wc -l
```

counts how many times Mary is logged in.

The programs in a pipeline actually run at the same time, not one after another. This means that the programs in a pipeline can be interactive; the kernel looks after whatever scheduling and synchronization is needed to make it all work.

As you probably suspect by now, the shell arranges things when you ask for a pipe; the individual programs are oblivious to the redirection. Of course, programs have to operate sensibly if they are to be combined this way. Most commands follow a common design, so they will fit properly into pipelines at any position. Normally a command invocation looks like

command   optional-arguments   optional-filenames

If no filenames are given, the command reads its standard input, which is by default the terminal (handy for experimenting) but which can be redirected to come from a file or a pipe. At the same time, on the output side, most commands write their output on the *standard output*, which is by default sent to the terminal. But it too can be redirected to a file or a pipe.

Error messages from commands have to be handled differently, however, or they might disappear into a file or down a pipe. So each command has a *standard error* output as well, which is normally directed to your terminal. Or, as a picture:

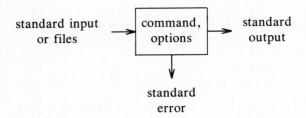

Almost all of the commands we have talked about so far fit this model; the only exceptions are commands like date and who that read no input, and a few like cmp and diff that have a fixed number of file inputs. (But look at the '-' option on these.)

Exercise 1-7. Explain the difference between

```
$ who | sort
```

and

```
$ who >sort
```

☐

Processes

The shell does quite a few things besides setting up pipes. Let us turn briefly to the basics of running more than one program at a time, since we have already seen a bit of that with pipes. For example, you can run two programs with one command line by separating the commands with a semicolon; the shell recognizes the semicolon and breaks the line into two commands:

```
$ date; who
Tue Sep 27 01:03:17 EDT 1983
ken       tty0    Sep 27 00:43
dmr       tty1    Sep 26 23:45
rob       tty2    Sep 26 23:59
bwk       tty3    Sep 27 00:06
jj        tty4    Sep 26 23:31
you       tty5    Sep 26 23:04
ber       tty7    Sep 26 23:34
$
```

Both commands are executed (in sequence) before the shell returns with a prompt character.

You can also have more than one program running simultaneously if you wish. For example, suppose you want to do something time-consuming like counting the words in your book, but you don't want to wait for wc to finish before you start something else. Then you can say

```
$ wc ch* >wc.out &
6944                    Process-id printed by the shell
$
```

The ampersand & at the end of a command line says to the shell "start this command running, then take further commands from the terminal immediately," that is, don't wait for it to complete. Thus the command will begin, but you can do something else while it's running. Directing the output into the file wc.out keeps it from interfering with whatever you're doing at the same time.

An instance of a running program is called a *process*. The number printed by the shell for a command initiated with & is called the *process-id*; you can use it in other commands to refer to a specific running program.

It's important to distinguish between programs and processes. wc is a program; each time you run the program wc, that creates a new process. If several instances of the same program are running at the same time, each is a separate process with a different process-id.

If a pipeline is initiated with &, as in

```
$ pr ch* | lpr &
6951                      Process-id of lpr
$
```

the processes in it are all started at once — the & applies to the whole pipeline.
Only one process-id is printed, however, for the last process in the sequence.
    The command

```
$ wait
```

waits until all processes initiated with & have finished. If it doesn't return
immediately, you have commands still running. You can interrupt `wait` with
DELETE.
    You can use the process-id printed by the shell to stop a process initiated
with &:

```
$ kill 6944
```

If you forget the process-id, you can use the command `ps` to tell you about
everything you have running. If you are desperate, `kill 0` will kill all your
processes except your login shell. And if you're curious about what other users
are doing, `ps -ag` will tell you about *all* processes that are currently running.
Here is some sample output:

```
$ ps -ag
   PID TTY TIME CMD
    36 co  6:29 /etc/cron
  6423 5   0:02 -sh
  6704 1   0:04 -sh
  6722 1   0:12 vi paper
  4430 2   0:03 -sh
  6612 7   0:03 -sh
  6628 7   1:13 rogue
  6843 2   0:02 write dmr
  6949 4   0:01 login bimmler
  6952 5   0:08 pr ch1.1 ch1.2 ch1.3 ch1.4
  6951 5   0:03 lpr
  6959 5   0:02 ps -ag
  6844 1   0:02 write rob
$
```

`PID` is the process-id; `TTY` is the terminal associated with the process (as in
`who`); `TIME` is the processor time used in minutes and seconds; and the rest is
the command being run. `ps` is one of those commands that is different on different versions of the system, so your output may not be formatted like this.
Even the arguments may be different — see the manual page ps(1).
    Processes have the same sort of hierarchical structure that files do: each
process has a parent, and may well have children. Your shell was created by a
process associated with whatever terminal line connects you to the system. As

you run commands, those processes are the direct children of your shell. If you run a program from within one of those, for example with the ! command to escape from `ed`, that creates its own child process which is thus a grandchild of the shell.

Sometimes a process takes so long that you would like to start it running, then turn off the terminal and go home without waiting for it to finish. But if you turn off your terminal or break your connection, the process will normally be killed even if you used &. The command `nohup` ("no hangup") was created to deal with this situation: if you say

        $ *nohup command* &

the command will continue to run if you log out. Any output from the command is saved in a file called `nohup.out`. There is no way to `nohup` a command retroactively.

If your process will take a lot of processor resources, it is kind to those who share your system to run your job with lower than normal priority; this is done by another program called `nice`:

        $ *nice expensive-command* &

`nohup` automatically calls `nice`, because if you're going to log out you can afford to have the command take a little longer.

Finally, you can simply tell the system to start your process at some wee hour of the morning when normal people are asleep, not computing. The command is called `at(1)`:

        $ *at time*
        whatever commands
        you want ...
        ctl-d
        $

This is the typical usage, but of course the commands could come from a file:

        $ *at 3am <file*
        $

Times can be written in 24-hour style like `2130`, or 12-hour style like `930pm`.

Tailoring the environment

One of the virtues of the UNIX system is that there are several ways to bring it closer to your personal taste or the conventions of your local computing environment. For example, we mentioned earlier the problem of different standards for the erase and line kill characters, which by default are usually # and @. You can change these any time you want with

        $ *stty erase e kill k*

where *e* is whatever character you want for erase and *k* is for line kill. But it's a bother to have to type this every time you log in.

The shell comes to the rescue. If there is a file named `.profile` in your login directory, the shell will execute the commands in it when you log in, before printing the first prompt. So you can put commands into `.profile` to set up your environment as you like it, and they will be executed every time you log in.

The first thing most people put in their `.profile` is

```
stty erase ←
```

We're using ← here so you can see it, but you could put a literal backspace in your `.profile`. `stty` also understands the notation `^x` for *ctl-x*, so you can get the same effect with

```
stty erase '^h'
```

because *ctl-h* is backspace. (The ^ character is an obsolete synonym for the pipe operator ¦, so you must protect it with quotes.)

If your terminal doesn't have sensible tab stops, you can add `-tabs` to the `stty` line:

```
stty erase '^h' -tabs
```

If you like to see how busy the system is when you log in, add

```
who ¦ wc -l
```

to count the users. If there's a news service, you can add **news**. Some people like a fortune cookie:

```
/usr/games/fortune
```

After a while you may decide that it is taking too long to log in, and cut your `.profile` back to the bare necessities.

Some of the properties of the shell are actually controlled by so-called *shell variables*, with values that you can access and set yourself. For example, the prompt string, which we have been showing as `$`, is actually stored in a shell variable called `PS1`, and you can set it to anything you like, like this:

```
PS1='Yes dear? '
```

The quotes are necessary since there are spaces in the prompt string. Spaces are not permitted around the = in this construction.

The shell also treats the variables `HOME` and `MAIL` specially. `HOME` is the name of your home directory; it is normally set properly without having to be in `.profile`. The variable `MAIL` names the standard file where your mail is kept. If you define it for the shell, you will be notified after each command if new mail has arrived:†

---

† This is implemented badly in the shell. Looking at the file after every command adds perceptibly to the system load. Also, if you are working in an editor for a long time you won't learn about

```
MAIL=/usr/spool/mail/you
```

(The mail file may be different on your system; `/usr/mail/you` is also common.)

Probably the most useful shell variable is the one that controls where the shell looks for commands. Recall that when you type the name of a command, the shell normally looks for it first in the current directory, then in `/bin`, and then in `/usr/bin`. This sequence of directories is called the *search path*, and is stored in a shell variable called `PATH`. If the default search path isn't what you want, you can change it, again usually in your `.profile`. For example, this line sets the path to the standard one plus `/usr/games`:

```
PATH=.:/bin:/usr/bin:/usr/games        One way ...
```

The syntax is a bit strange: a sequence of directory names separated by colons. Remember that '.' is the current directory. You can omit the '.'; a null component in `PATH` means the current directory.

An alternate way to set `PATH` in this specific case is simply to augment the previous value:

```
PATH=$PATH:/usr/games                        ... Another way
```

You can obtain the value of any shell variable by prefixing its name with a `$`. In the example above, the expression `$PATH` retrieves the current value, to which the new part is added, and the result is assigned back to `PATH`. You can verify this with `echo`:

```
$ echo PATH is $PATH
PATH is :/bin:/usr/bin:/usr/games
$ echo $HOME              Your login directory
/usr/you
$
```

If you have some of your own commands, you might want to collect them in a directory of your own and add that to your search path as well. In that case, your `PATH` might look like this:

```
PATH=:$HOME/bin:/bin:/usr/bin:/usr/games
```

We'll talk about writing your own commands in Chapter 3.

Another variable, often used by text editors fancier than `ed`, is `TERM`, which names the kind of terminal you are using. That information may make it possible for programs to manage your screen more effectively. Thus you might add something like

---

new mail because you aren't running new commands with your login shell. A better design is to look every few minutes, instead of after every command. Chapters 5 and 7 show how to implement this kind of mail checker. A third possibility, not available to everyone, is to have the `mail` program notify you itself: it certainly knows when mail comes for you.

```
TERM=adm3
```

to your .profile file.

It is also possible to use variables for abbreviation. If you find yourself frequently referring to some directory with a long name, it might be worthwhile
adding a line like

> d=/horribly/long/directory/name

to your profile, so that you can say things like

```
$ cd $d
```

Personal variables like d are conventionally spelled in lower case to distinguish
them from those used by the shell itself, like PATH.

Finally, it's necessary to tell the shell that you intend to use the variables in
other programs; this is done with the command export, to which we will
return in Chapter 3:

```
export MAIL PATH TERM
```

To summarize, here is what a typical .profile file might look like:

```
$ cat .profile
stty erase '^h' -tabs
MAIL=/usr/spool/mail/you
PATH=:$HOME/bin:/bin:/usr/bin:/usr/games
TERM=adm3
b=$HOME/book
export MAIL PATH TERM b
date
who | wc -l
$
```

We have by no means exhausted the services that the shell provides. One
of the most useful is that you can create your own commands by packaging
existing commands into a file to be processed by the shell. It is remarkable
how much can be achieved by this fundamentally simple mechanism. Our discussion of it begins in Chapter 3.

1.5 The rest of the UNIX system

There's much more to the UNIX system than we've addressed in this
chapter, but then there's much more to this book. By now, you should feel
comfortable with the system and, particularly, with the manual. When you
have specific questions about when or how to use commands, the manual is the
place to look.

It is also worth browsing in the manual occasionally, to refresh your
knowledge of familiar commands and to discover new ones. The manual
describes many programs we won't illustrate, including compilers for languages

like FORTRAN 77; calculator programs such as bc(1); cu(1) and uucp(1) for
inter-machine communication; graphics packages; statistics programs; and eso-
terica such as units(1).

As we've said before, this book does not replace the manual, it supplements
it. In the chapters that follow we will look at pieces and programs of the UNIX
system, starting from the information in the manual but following the threads
that connect the components. Although the program interrelationships are
never made explicit in the manual, they form the fabric of the UNIX programming environment.

History and bibliographic notes

The original UNIX paper is by D. M. Ritchie and K. L. Thompson: "The
UNIX Time-sharing System," *Communications of the ACM*, July, 1974, and
reprinted in *CACM*, January, 1983. (Page 89 of the reprint is in the March
1983 issue.) This overview of the system for people interested in operating
systems is worth reading by anyone who programs.

The Bell System Technical Journal (*BSTJ*) special issue on the UNIX system
(July, 1978) contains many papers describing subsequent developments, and
some retrospective material, including an update of the original *CACM* paper
by Ritchie and Thompson. A second special issue of the BSTJ, containing new
UNIX papers, is scheduled to be published in 1984.

"The UNIX Programming Environment," by B. W. Kernighan and J. R.
Mashey (*IEEE Computer Magazine*, April, 1981), attempts to convey the essential features of the system for programmers.

The *UNIX Programmer's Manual*, in whatever version is appropriate for your
system, lists commands, system routines and interfaces, file formats, and
maintenance procedures. You can't live without this for long, although you
will probably only need to read parts of Volume 1 until you start programming. Volume 1 of the 7th Edition manual is published by Holt, Rinehart and
Winston.

Volume 2 of the *UNIX Programmer's Manual* is called "Documents for Use
with the UNIX Time-sharing System" and contains tutorials and reference
manuals for major commands. In particular, it describes document preparation
programs and program development tools at some length. You will want to
read most of this eventually.

A UNIX Primer, by Ann and Nico Lomuto (Prentice-Hall, 1983), is a good
introduction for raw beginners, especially non-programmers.

CHAPTER 2: **THE FILE SYSTEM**

Everything in the UNIX system is a file. That is less of an oversimplification than you might think. When the first version of the system was being designed, before it even had a name, the discussions focused on the structure of a file system that would be clean and easy to use. The file system is central to the success and convenience of the UNIX system. It is one of the best examples of the "keep it simple" philosophy, showing the power achieved by careful implementation of a few well-chosen ideas.

To talk comfortably about commands and their interrelationships, we need a good background in the structure and outer workings of the file system. This chapter covers most of the details of using the file system — what files are, how they are represented, directories and the file system hierarchy, permissions, inodes (the system's internal record of files) and device files. Because most use of the UNIX system deals with manipulating files, there are many commands for file investigation or rearrangement; this chapter introduces the more commonly used ones.

2.1 The basics of files

A file is a sequence of bytes. (A byte is a small chunk of information, typically 8 bits long. For our purposes, a byte is equivalent to a character.) No structure is imposed on a file by the system, and no meaning is attached to its contents — the meaning of the bytes depends solely on the programs that interpret the file. Furthermore, as we shall see, this is true not just of disc files but of peripheral devices as well. Magnetic tapes, mail messages, characters typed on the keyboard, line printer output, data flowing in pipes — each of these files is just a sequence of bytes as far as the system and the programs in it are concerned.

The best way to learn about files is to play with them, so start by creating a small file:

```
$ ed
a
now is the time
for all good people
.
w junk
36
q
$ ls -l junk
-rw-r--r-- 1 you              36 Sep 27 06:11 junk
$
```

junk is a file with 36 bytes — the 36 characters you typed while appending (except, of course, for correction of any typing mistakes). To see the file,

```
$ cat junk
now is the time
for all good people
$
```

cat shows what the file looks like. The command od (octal dump) prints a visible representation of all the bytes of a file:

```
$ od -c junk
0000000   n   o   w       i   s       t   h   e       t   i   m   e  \n
0000020   f   o   r       a   l   l       g   o   o   d       p   e   o
0000040   p   l   e  \n
0000044
$
```

The −c option means "interpret bytes as characters." Turning on the −b option will show the bytes as octal (base 8) numbers† as well:

```
$ od -cb junk
0000000   n   o   w       i   s       t   h   e       t   i   m   e  \n
        156 157 167 040 151 163 040 164 150 145 040 164 151 155 145 012
0000020   f   o   r       a   l   l       g   o   o   d       p   e   o
        146 157 162 040 141 154 154 040 147 157 157 144 040 160 145 157
0000040   p   l   e  \n
        160 154 145 012
0000044
$
```

The 7-digit numbers down the left side are positions in the file, that is, the

---

† Each byte in a file contains a number large enough to encode a printable character. The encoding on most UNIX systems is called ASCII (American Standard Code for Information Interchange), but some machines, particularly those manufactured by IBM, use an encoding called EBCDIC (Extended Binary-Coded-Decimal Interchange Code). Throughout this book, we will assume the ASCII encoding; cat /usr/pub/ascii or read ascii(7) to see the octal values of all the characters.

ordinal number of the next character shown, in octal. By the way, the emphasis on octal numbers is a holdover from the PDP-11, for which octal was the preferred notation. Hexadecimal is better suited for other machines; the -x option tells od to print in hex.

Notice that there is a character after each line, with octal value 012. This is the ASCII *newline* character; it is what the system places in the input when you press the RETURN key. By a convention borrowed from C, the character representation of a newline is \n, but this is only a convention used by programs like od to make it easy to read — the value stored in the file is the single byte 012.

Newline is the most common example of a *special character*. Other characters associated with some terminal control operation include backspace (octal value 010, printed as \b), tab (011, \t), and carriage return (015, \r).

It is important in each case to distinguish between how the character is stored in a file and how it is interpreted in various situations. For example, when you type a backspace on your keyboard (and assuming that your erase character is backspace), the kernel interprets it to mean that you want to discard whatever character you typed previously. Both that character and the backspace disappear, but the backspace is echoed to your terminal, where it makes the cursor move one position backwards.

If you type the sequence

        \←

(i.e., \ followed by a backspace), however, the kernel interprets that to mean that you want a literal backspace in your input, so the \ is discarded and the byte 010 winds up in your file. When the backspace is echoed on your terminal, it moves the cursor to sit on top of the \.

When you *print* a file that contains a backspace, the backspace is passed uninterpreted to your terminal, which again will move the cursor one position backwards. When you use od to display a file that contains a backspace, it appears as a byte with value 010, or, with the -c option, as \b.

The story for tabs is much the same: on input, a tab character is echoed to your terminal and sent to the program that is reading; on output, the tab is simply sent to the terminal for interpretation there. There is a difference, though — you can tell the kernel that you want *it* to interpret tabs for you on output; in that case, each tab that would be printed is replaced by the right number of blanks to get to the next tab stop. Tab stops are set at columns 9, 17, 25, etc. The command

        $ stty -tabs

causes tabs to be replaced by spaces *when printed on your terminal*. See stty(1).

The treatment of RETURN is analogous. The kernel echoes RETURN as a carriage return and a newline, but stores only the newline in the input. On output, the newline is expanded into carriage return and newline.

The UNIX system is unusual in its approach to representing control information, particularly its use of newlines to terminate lines. Many systems instead provide "records," one per line, each of which contains not only your data but also a count of the number of characters in the line (and no newline). Other systems terminate each line with a carriage return *and* a newline, because that sequence is necessary for output on most terminals. (The word "linefeed" is a synonym for newline, so this sequence is often called "CRLF," which is nearly pronounceable.)

The UNIX system does neither — there are no records, no record counts, and no bytes in any file that you or your programs did not put there. A newline is expanded into a carriage return and a newline when sent to a terminal, but programs need only deal with the single newline character, because that is all they see. For most purposes, this simple scheme is exactly what is wanted. When a more complicated structure is needed, it can easily be built on top of this; the converse, creating simplicity from complexity, is harder to achieve.

Since the end of a line is marked by a newline character, you might expect a file to be terminated by another special character, say \e for "end of file." Looking at the output of od, though, you will see no special character at the end of the file — it just stops. Rather than using a special code, the system signifies the end of a file by simply saying there is no more data in the file. The kernel keeps track of file lengths, so a program encounters end-of-file when it has processed all the bytes in a file.

Programs retrieve the data in a file by a system call (a subroutine in the kernel) called read. Each time read is called, it returns the next part of a file — the next line of text typed on the terminal, for example. read also says how many bytes of the file were returned, so end of file is assumed when a read says "zero bytes are being returned." If there were any bytes left, read would have returned some of them. Actually, it makes sense not to represent end of file by a special byte value, because, as we said earlier, the meaning of the bytes depends on the interpretation of the file. But *all* files must end, and since all files must be accessed through read, returning zero is an interpretation-independent way to represent the end of a file without introducing a new special character.

When a program reads from your terminal, each input line is given to the program by the kernel only when you type its newline (i.e, press RETURN). Therefore if you make a typing mistake, you can back up and correct it if you realize the mistake before you type newline. If you type newline before realizing the error, the line has been read by the system and you cannot correct it.

We can see how this line-at-a-time input works using cat. cat normally saves up or *buffers* its output to write in large chunks for efficiency, but cat -u "unbuffers" the output, so it is printed immediately as it is read:

```
    $ cat                        Buffered output from cat
    123
    456
    789
    ctl-d
    123
    456
    789
    $ cat -u                     Unbuffered output from cat
    123
    123
    456
    456
    789
    789
    ctl-d
    $
```

cat receives each line when you press RETURN; without buffering, it prints
the data as it is received.

   Now try something different: type some characters and then a *ctl*-d rather
than a RETURN:

```
    $ cat -u
    123ctl-d123
```

cat prints the characters out immediately. *ctl*-d says, "immediately send the
characters I have typed to the program that is reading from my terminal." The
ctl-d itself is not sent to the program, unlike a newline. Now type a second
ctl-d, with no other characters:

```
    $ cat -u
    123ctl-d123ctl-d$
```

The shell responds with a prompt, because cat read no characters, decided
that meant end of file, and stopped. *ctl*-d sends whatever you have typed to
the program that is reading from the terminal. If you haven't typed anything,
the program will therefore read no characters, and that looks like the end of
the file. That is why typing *ctl*-d logs you out — the shell sees no more input.
Of course, *ctl*-d is usually used to signal an end-of-file but it is interesting that
it has a more general function.

Exercise 2-1. What happens when you type *ctl*-d to ed? Compare this to the command

```
    $ ed <file
```

□

2.2 What's in a file?

The format of a file is determined by the programs that use it; there is a wide variety of file types, perhaps because there is a wide variety of programs. But since file types are not determined by the file system, the kernel can't tell you the type of a file: it doesn't know it. The `file` command makes an educated guess (we'll explain how shortly):

```
$ file /bin /bin/ed /usr/src/cmd/ed.c /usr/man/man1/ed.1
/bin:    directory
/bin/ed:         pure executable
/usr/src/cmd/ed.c:      c program text
/usr/man/man1/ed.1:     roff, nroff, or eqn input text
$
```

These are four fairly typical files, all related to the editor: the directory in which it resides (`/bin`), the "binary" or runnable program itself (`/bin/ed`), the "source" or C statements that define the program (`/usr/src/cmd/ed.c`) and the manual page (`/usr/man/man1/ed.1`).

To determine the types, `file` didn't pay attention to the names (although it could have), because naming conventions are just conventions, and thus not perfectly reliable. For example, files suffixed `.c` are almost always C source, but there is nothing to prevent you from creating a `.c` file with arbitrary contents. Instead, `file` reads the first few hundred bytes of a file and looks for clues to the file type. (As we will show later on, files with special system properties, such as directories, can be identified by asking the system, but `file` could identify a directory by reading it.)

Sometimes the clues are obvious. A runnable program is marked by a binary "magic number" at its beginning. `od` with no options dumps the file in 16-bit, or 2-byte, words and makes the magic number visible:

```
$ od /bin/ed
0000000 000410 025000 000462 011444 000000 000000 000000 000001
0000020 170011 016600 000002 005060 177776 010600 162706 000004
0000040 016616 000004 005720 010066 000002 005720 001376 020076
...
$
```

The octal value `410` marks a pure executable program, one for which the executing code may be shared by several processes. (Specific magic numbers are system dependent.) The bit pattern represented by `410` is not ASCII text, so this value could not be created inadvertently by a program like an editor. But you could certainly create such a file by running a program of your own, and the system understands the convention that such files are program binaries.

For text files, the clues may be deeper in the file, so `file` looks for words like `#include` to identify C source, or lines beginning with a period to identify `nroff` or `troff` input.

You might wonder why the system doesn't track file types more carefully, so that, for example, `sort` is never given `/bin/ed` as input. One reason is to avoid foreclosing some useful computation. Although

```
$ sort /bin/ed
```

doesn't make much sense, there are many commands that can operate on any file at all, and there's no reason to restrict their capabilities. `od`, `wc`, `cp`, `cmp`, `file` and many others process files regardless of their contents. But the formatless idea goes deeper than that. If, say, `nroff` input were distinguished from C source, the editor would be forced to make the distinction when it created a file, and probably when it read in a file for editing again. And it would certainly make it harder for us to typeset the C programs in Chapters 6 through 8!

Instead of creating distinctions, the UNIX system tries to efface them. All text consists of lines terminated by newline characters, and most programs understand this simple format. Many times while writing this book, we ran commands to create text files, processed them with commands like those listed above, and used an editor to merge them into the `troff` input for the book. The transcripts you see on almost every page are made by commands like

```
$ od -c junk >temp
$ ed ch2.1
1534
r temp
168
...
```

`od` produces text on its standard output, which can then be used anywhere text can be used. This uniformity is unusual; most systems have several file formats, even for text, and require negotiation by a program or a user to create a file of a particular type. In UNIX systems there is just one kind of file, and all that is required to access a file is its name.†

The lack of file formats is an advantage overall — programmers needn't worry about file types, and all the standard programs will work on any file — but there are a handful of drawbacks. Programs that sort and search and edit really expect text as input: `grep` can't examine binary files correctly, nor can `sort` sort them, nor can any standard editor manipulate them.

There are implementation limitations with most programs that expect text as input. We tested a number of programs on a 30,000 byte text file containing no newlines, and surprisingly few behaved properly, because most programs make unadvertised assumptions about the maximum length of a line of text (for an exception, see the BUGS section of `sort(1)`).

---

† There's a good test of file system uniformity, due originally to Doug McIlroy, that the UNIX file system passes handily. Can the output of a FORTRAN program be used as input to the FORTRAN compiler? A remarkable number of systems have trouble with this test.

Non-text files definitely have their place. For example, very large data-bases usually need extra address information for rapid access; this has to be binary for efficiency. But every file format that is not text must have its own family of support programs to do things that the standard tools could perform if the format were text. Text files may be a little less efficient in machine cycles, but this must be balanced against the cost of extra software to maintain more specialized formats. If you design a file format, you should think care-fully before choosing a non-textual representation. (You should also think about making your programs robust in the face of long input lines.)

2.3 Directories and filenames

All the files you own have unambiguous names, starting with /usr/you, but if the only file you have is junk, and you type ls, it doesn't print /usr/you/junk; the filename is printed without any prefix:

```
$ ls
junk
$
```

That is because each running program, that is, each process, has a *current directory*, and all filenames are implicitly assumed to start with the name of that directory, unless they begin directly with a slash. Your login shell, and ls, therefore have a current directory. The command pwd (print working directory) identifies the current directory:

```
$ pwd
/usr/you
$
```

The current directory is an attribute of a process, not a person or a program — people have login directories, processes have current directories. If a pro-cess creates a child process, the child inherits the current directory of its parent. But if the child then changes to a new directory, the parent is unaf-fected — its current directory remains the same no matter what the child does.

The notion of a current directory is certainly a notational convenience, because it can save a lot of typing, but its real purpose is organizational. Related files belong together in the same directory. /usr is often the top directory of the user file system. (user is abbreviated to usr in the same spirit as cmp, ls, etc.) /usr/you is your login directory, your current direc-tory when you first log in. /usr/src contains source for system programs, /usr/src/cmd contains source for UNIX commands, /usr/src/cmd/sh contains the source files for the shell, and so on. Whenever you embark on a new project, or whenever you have a set of related files, say a set of recipes, you could create a new directory with mkdir and put the files there.

```
$ pwd
/usr/you
$ mkdir recipes
$ cd recipes
$ pwd
/usr/you/recipes
$ mkdir pie cookie
$ ed pie/apple
. . .
$ ed cookie/choc.chip
. . .
$
```

Notice that it is simple to refer to subdirectories. `pie/apple` has an obvious meaning: the apple pie recipe, in directory `/usr/you/recipes/pie`. You could instead have put the recipe in, say, `recipes/apple.pie`, rather than in a subdirectory of `recipes`, but it seems better organized to put all the pies together, too. For example, the crust recipe could be kept in `recipes/pie/crust` rather than duplicating it in each pie recipe.

Although the file system is a powerful organizational tool, you can forget where you put a file, or even what files you've got. The obvious solution is a command or two to rummage around in directories. The `ls` command is certainly helpful for finding files, but it doesn't look in sub-directories.

```
$ cd
$ ls
junk
recipes
$ file *
junk:     ascii text
recipes:          directory
$ ls recipes
cookie
pie
$ ls recipes/pie
apple
crust
$
```

This piece of the file system can be shown pictorially as:

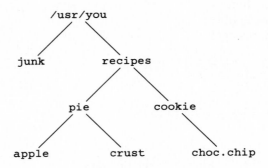

The command du (disc usage) was written to tell how much disc space is consumed by the files in a directory, including all its subdirectories.

```
$ du
6           ./recipes/pie
4           ./recipes/cookie
11          ./recipes
13          .
$
```

The filenames are obvious; the numbers are the number of disc blocks — typically 512 or 1024 bytes each — of storage for each file. The value for a directory indicates how many blocks are consumed by all the files in that directory and its subdirectories, including the directory itself.

du has an option -a, for "all," that causes it to print out all the files in a directory. If one of those is a directory, du processes that as well:

```
$ du -a
2           ./recipes/pie/apple
3           ./recipes/pie/crust
6           ./recipes/pie
3           ./recipes/cookie/choc.chip
4           ./recipes/cookie
11          ./recipes
1           ./junk
13          .
$
```

The output of du -a can be piped through grep to look for specific files:

```
$ du -a ¦ grep choc
3           ./recipes/cookie/choc.chip
$
```

Recall from Chapter 1 that the name '.' is a directory entry that refers to the directory itself; it permits access to a directory without having to know the full name. `du` looks in a directory for files; if you don't tell it which directory, it assumes '`.`', the directory you are in now. Therefore, `junk` and `./junk` are names for the same file.

Despite their fundamental properties inside the kernel, directories sit in the file system as ordinary files. They can be read as ordinary files. But they can't be created or written as ordinary files — to preserve its sanity and the users' files, the kernel reserves to itself all control over the contents of directories.

The time has come to look at the bytes in a directory:

```
$ od -cb .
0000000   4   ;   .  \0  \0  \0  \0  \0  \0  \0  \0  \0  \0  \0  \0  \0
        064 073 056 000 000 000 000 000 000 000 000 000 000 000 000 000
0000020 273   (   .   .  \0  \0  \0  \0  \0  \0  \0  \0  \0  \0  \0  \0
        273 050 056 056 000 000 000 000 000 000 000 000 000 000 000 000
0000040 252   ;   r   e   c   i   p   e   s  \0  \0  \0  \0  \0  \0  \0
        252 073 162 145 143 151 160 145 163 000 000 000 000 000 000 000
0000060 230   =   j   u   n   k  \0  \0  \0  \0  \0  \0  \0  \0  \0  \0
        230 075 152 165 156 153 000 000 000 000 000 000 000 000 000 000
0000100
$
```

See the filenames buried in there? The directory format is a combination of binary and textual data. A directory consists of 16-byte chunks, the last 14 bytes of which hold the filename, padded with ASCII NUL's (which have value 0) and the first two of which tell the system where the administrative information for the file resides — we'll come back to that. Every directory begins with the two entries '`.`' ("dot") and '`..`' ("dot-dot").

```
$ cd                        Home
$ cd recipes
$ pwd
/usr/you/recipes
$ cd ..; pwd                Up one level
/usr/you
$ cd ..; pwd                Up another level
/usr
$ cd ..; pwd                Up another level
/
$ cd ..; pwd                Up another level
/                           Can't go any higher
$
```

The directory `/` is called the *root* of the file system. Every file in the system is in the root directory or one of its subdirectories, and the root is its own parent directory.

Exercise 2-2. Given the information in this section, you should be able to understand roughly how the `ls` command operates. Hint: `cat . >foo; ls -f foo`. □

Exercise 2-3. (Harder) How does the `pwd` command operate? □

Exercise 2-4. `du` was written to monitor disc usage. Using it to find files in a directory hierarchy is at best a strange idiom, and perhaps inappropriate. As an alternative, look at the manual page for `find(1)`, and compare the two commands. In particular, compare the command `du -a ¦ grep ...` with the corresponding invocation of `find`. Which runs faster? Is it better to build a new tool or use a side effect of an old one? □

2.4 Permissions

Every file has a set of *permissions* associated with it, which determine who can do what with the file. If you're so organized that you keep your love letters on the system, perhaps hierarchically arranged in a directory, you probably don't want other people to be able to read them. You could therefore change the permissions on each letter to frustrate gossip (or only on some of the letters, to encourage it), or you might just change the permissions on the directory containing the letters, and thwart snoopers that way.

But we must warn you: there is a special user on *every* UNIX system, called the *super-user*, who can read or modify *any* file on the system. The special login name `root` carries super-user privileges; it is used by system administrators when they do system maintenance. There is also a command called `su` that grants super-user status if you know the `root` password. Thus anyone who knows the super-user password can read your love letters, so don't keep sensitive material in the file system.

If you need more privacy, you can change the data in a file so that even the super-user cannot read (or at least understand) it, using the `crypt` command (`crypt(1)`). Of course, even `crypt` isn't perfectly secure. A super-user can change the `crypt` command itself, and there are cryptographic attacks on the `crypt` algorithm. The former requires malfeasance and the latter takes hard work, however, so `crypt` is in practice fairly secure.

In real life, most security breaches are due to passwords that are given away or easily guessed. Occasionally, system administrative lapses make it possible for a malicious user to gain super-user permission. Security issues are discussed further in some of the papers cited in the bibliography at the end of this chapter.

When you log in, you type a name and then verify that you are that person by typing a password. The name is your login identification, or *login-id*. But the system actually recognizes you by a number, called your user-id, or *uid*. In fact different login-id's may have the same uid, making them indistinguishable to the system, although that is relatively rare and perhaps undesirable for security reasons. Besides a uid, you are assigned a group identification, or *group-id*, which places you in a class of users. On many systems, all ordinary users (as opposed to those with login-id's like `root`) are placed in a single group called `other`, but your system may be different. The file system, and therefore the UNIX system in general, determines what you can do by the permissions granted to your uid and group-id.

The file /etc/passwd is the *password file*; it contains all the login information about each user. You can discover your uid and group-id, as does the system, by looking up your name in /etc/passwd:

```
$ grep you /etc/passwd
you:gkmbCTrJ04COM:604:1:Y.O.A.People:/usr/you:
$
```

The fields in the password file are separated by colons and are laid out like this (as seen in passwd(5)):

> *login-id*:*encrypted-password*:*uid*:*group-id*:*miscellany*:*login-directory*:*shell*

The file is ordinary text, but the field definitions and separator are a convention agreed upon by the programs that use the information in the file.

The shell field is often empty, implying that you use the default shell, /bin/sh. The miscellany field may contain anything; often, it has your name and address or phone number.

Note that your password appears here in the second field, but only in an encrypted form. Anybody can read the password file (you just did), so if your password itself were there, anyone would be able to use it to masquerade as you. When you give your password to login, it encrypts it and compares the result against the encrypted password in /etc/passwd. If they agree, it lets you log in. The mechanism works because the encryption algorithm has the property that it's easy to go from the clear form to the encrypted form, but very hard to go backwards. For example, if your password is ka-boom, it might be encrypted as gkmbCTrJ04COM, but given the latter, there's no easy way to get back to the original.

The kernel decided that you should be allowed to read /etc/passwd by looking at the permissions associated with the file. There are three kinds of permissions for each file: read (i.e., examine its contents), write (i.e., change its contents), and execute (i.e., run it as a program). Furthermore, different permissions can apply to different people. As file owner, you have one set of read, write and execute permissions. Your "group" has a separate set. Everyone else has a third set.

The -1 option of ls prints the permissions information, among other things:

```
$ ls -l /etc/passwd
-rw-r--r-- 1 root         5115 Aug 30 10:40 /etc/passwd
$ ls -lg /etc/passwd
-rw-r--r-- 1 adm          5115 Aug 30 10:40 /etc/passwd
$
```

These two lines may be collectively interpreted as: /etc/passwd is owned by login-id root, group adm, is 5115 bytes long, was last modified on August 30 at 10:40 AM, and has one link (one name in the file system; we'll discuss links in the next section). Some versions of ls give both owner and group in one invocation.

The string -rw-r--r-- is how ls represents the permissions on the file. The first - indicates that it is an ordinary file. If it were a directory, there would be a d there. The next three characters encode the file owner's (based on uid) read, write and execute permissions. rw- means that root (the owner) may read or write, but not execute the file. An executable file would have an x instead of a dash.

The next three characters (r--) encode group permissions, in this case that people in group adm, presumably the system administrators, can read the file but not write or execute it. The next three (also r--) define the permissions for everyone else — the rest of the users on the system. On this machine, then, only root can change the login information for a user, but anybody may read the file to discover the information. A plausible alternative would be for group adm to also have write permission on /etc/passwd.

The file /etc/group encodes group names and group-id's, and defines which users are in which groups. /etc/passwd identifies only your login group; the newgrp command changes your group permissions to another group.

Anybody can say

```
$ ed /etc/passwd
```

and edit the password file, but only root can write back the changes. You might therefore wonder how you can change your password, since that involves editing the password file. The program to change passwords is called passwd; you will probably find it in /bin:

```
$ ls -l /bin/passwd
-rwsr-xr-x 1 root       8454 Jan  4  1983 /bin/passwd
$
```

(Note that /etc/passwd is the text file containing the login information, while /bin/passwd, in a different directory, is a file containing an executable program that lets you change the password information.) The permissions here state that anyone may execute the command, but only root can change the passwd command. But the s instead of an x in the execute field for the file owner states that, when the command is run, it is to be given the permissions corresponding to the file owner, in this case root. Because /bin/passwd is "set-uid" to root, any user can run the passwd command to edit the password file.

The set-uid bit is a simple but elegant idea† that solves a number of security problems. For example, the author of a game program can make the program set-uid to the owner, so that it can update a score file that is otherwise

---

† The set-uid bit is patented by Dennis Ritchie.

protected from other users' access. But the set-uid concept is potentially dangerous. /bin/passwd has to be correct; if it were not, it could destroy system information under root's auspices. If it had the permissions -rwsrwxrwx, it could be overwritten by *any* user, who could therefore replace the file with a program that does anything. This is particularly serious for a set-uid program, because root has access permissions to every file on the system. (Some UNIX systems turn the set-uid bit off whenever a file is modified, to reduce the danger of a security hole.)

The set-uid bit is powerful, but used primarily for a few system programs such as passwd. Let's look at a more ordinary file.

```
$ ls -l /bin/who
-rwxrwxr-x 1 root        6348 Mar 29  1983 /bin/who
$
```

who is executable by everybody, and writable by root and the owner's group. What "executable" means is this: when you type

```
$ who
```

to the shell, it looks in a set of directories, one of which is /bin, for a file named "who." If it finds such a file, and if the file has execute permission, the shell calls the kernel to run it. The kernel checks the permissions, and, if they are valid, runs the program. Note that a program is just a file with execute permission. In the next chapter we will show you programs that are just text files, but that can be executed as commands because they have execute permission set.

Directory permissions operate a little differently, but the basic idea is the same.

```
$ ls -ld .
drwxrwxr-x 3 you          80 Sep 27 06:11 .
$
```

The -d option of ls asks it to tell you about the directory itself, rather than its contents, and the leading d in the output signifies that '.' is indeed a directory. An r field means that you can read the directory, so you can find out what files are in it with ls (or od, for that matter). A w means that you can create and delete files in this directory, because that requires modifying and therefore writing the directory file.

Actually, you cannot simply write in a directory — even root is forbidden to do so.

```
$ who >.                    Try to overwrite '.'
.: cannot create            You can't
$
```

Instead there are system calls that create and remove files, and only through them is it possible to change the contents of a directory. The permissions idea, however, still applies: the w fields tell who can use the system routines to modify the directory.

Permission to remove a file is independent of the file itself. If you have write permission in a directory, you may remove files there, even files that are protected against writing. The rm command asks for confirmation before removing a protected file, however, to check that you really want to do so — one of the rare occasions that a UNIX program double-checks your intentions. (The -f flag to rm forces it to remove files without question.)

The x field in the permissions on a directory does not mean execution; it means "search." Execute permission on a directory determines whether the directory may be searched for a file. It is therefore possible to create a directory with mode --x for other users, implying that users may access any file that they know about in that directory, but may not run ls on it or read it to see what files are there. Similarly, with directory permissions r--, users can see (ls) but not use the contents of a directory. Some installations use this device to turn off /usr/games during busy hours.

The chmod (change mode) command changes permissions on files.

> $ *chmod permissions filenames ...*

The syntax of the *permissions* is clumsy, however. They can be specified in two ways, either as octal numbers or by symbolic description. The octal numbers are easier to use, although the symbolic descriptions are sometimes convenient because they can specify relative changes in the permissions. It would be nice if you could say

> $ *chmod rw-rw-rw- junk*   *Doesn't work this way!*

rather than

> $ *chmod 666 junk*

but you cannot. The octal modes are specified by adding together a 4 for read, 2 for write and 1 for execute permission. The three digits specify, as in ls, permissions for the owner, group and everyone else. The symbolic codes are difficult to explain; you must look in chmod(1) for a proper description. For our purposes, it is sufficient to note that + turns a permission on and that - turns it off. For example

> $ *chmod +x command*

allows everyone to execute command, and

> $ *chmod -w file*

turns off write permission for everyone, including the file's owner. Except for the usual disclaimer about super-users, only the owner of a file may change the permissions on a file, regardless of the permissions themselves. Even if somebody else allows you to write a file, the system will not allow you to change its permission bits.

```
$ ls -ld /usr/mary
drwxrwxrwx 5 mary              704 Sep 25 10:18 /usr/mary
$ chmod 444 /usr/mary
chmod: can't change /usr/mary
$
```

If a directory is writable, however, people can remove files in it regardless of the permissions on the files themselves. If you want to make sure that you or your friends never delete files from a directory, remove write permission from it:

```
$ cd
$ date >temp
$ chmod -w .                         Make directory unwritable
$ ls -ld .
dr-xr-xr-x 3 you           80 Sep 27 11:48 .
$ rm temp
rm: temp not removed                 Can't remove file
$ chmod 775 .                        Restore permission
$ ls -ld .
drwxrwxr-x 3 you           80 Sep 27 11:48 .
$ rm temp
$                                    Now you can
```

temp is now gone. Notice that changing the permissions on the directory didn't change its modification date. The modification date reflects changes to the file's contents, not its modes. The permissions and dates are not stored in the file itself, but in a system structure called an index node, or *i-node*, the subject of the next section.

Exercise 2-5. Experiment with chmod. Try different simple modes, like 0 and 1. Be careful not to damage your login directory! □

2.5 Inodes

A file has several components: a name, contents, and administrative information such as permissions and modification times. The administrative information is stored in the inode (over the years, the hyphen fell out of "i-node"), along with essential system data such as how long it is, where on the disc the contents of the file are stored, and so on.

There are three times in the inode: the time that the contents of the file were last modified (written); the time that the file was last used (read or executed); and the time that the inode itself was last changed, for example to set the permissions.

```
$ date
Tue Sep 27 12:07:24 EDT 1983
$ date >junk
$ ls -l junk
-rw-rw-rw- 1 you            29 Sep 27 12:07 junk
$ ls -lu junk
-rw-rw-rw- 1 you            29 Sep 27 06:11 junk
$ ls -lc junk
-rw-rw-rw- 1 you            29 Sep 27 12:07 junk
$
```

Changing the contents of a file does not affect its usage time, as reported by
ls -lu, and changing the permissions affects only the inode change time, as
reported by ls -lc.

```
$ chmod 444 junk
$ ls -lu junk
-r--r--r-- 1 you            29 Sep 27 06:11 junk
$ ls -lc junk
-r--r--r-- 1 you            29 Sep 27 12:11 junk
$ chmod 666 junk
$
```

The -t option to ls, which sorts the files according to time, by default that
of last modification, can be combined with -c or -u to report the order in
which inodes were changed or files were read:

```
$ ls recipes
cookie
pie
$ ls -lut
total 2
drwxrwxrwx 4 you            64 Sep 27 12:11 recipes
-rw-rw-rw- 1 you            29 Sep 27 06:11 junk
$
```

recipes is most recently used, because we just looked at its contents.

It is important to understand inodes, not only to appreciate the options on
ls, but because in a strong sense the inodes *are* the files. All the directory
hierarchy does is provide convenient names for files. The system's internal
name for a file is its *i-number*: the number of the inode holding the file's information. ls -i reports the i-number in decimal:

```
$ date >x
$ ls -i
15768 junk
15274 recipes
15852 x
$
```

It is the i-number that is stored in the first two bytes of a directory, before the name. `od -d` will dump the data in decimal by byte pairs rather than octal by bytes and thus make the i-number visible.

```
$ od -c .
0000000   4   ;   .  \0  \0  \0  \0  \0  \0  \0  \0  \0  \0  \0  \0  \0
0000020 273   (   .   .  \0  \0  \0  \0  \0  \0  \0  \0  \0  \0  \0  \0
0000040 252   ;   r   e   c   i   p   e   s  \0  \0  \0  \0  \0  \0  \0
0000060 230   =   j   u   n   k  \0  \0  \0  \0  \0  \0  \0  \0  \0  \0
0000100 354   =   x  \0  \0  \0  \0  \0  \0  \0  \0  \0  \0  \0  \0  \0
0000120
$ od -d .
0000000 15156 00046 00000 00000 00000 00000 00000 00000
0000020 10427 11822 00000 00000 00000 00000 00000 00000
0000040 15274 25970 26979 25968 00115 00000 00000 00000
0000060 15768 30058 27502 00000 00000 00000 00000 00000
0000100 15852 00120 00000 00000 00000 00000 00000 00000
0000120
$
```

The first two bytes in each directory entry are the only connection between the name of a file and its contents. A filename in a directory is therefore called a *link*, because it links a name in the directory hierarchy to the inode, and hence to the data. The same i-number can appear in more than one directory. The `rm` command does not actually remove inodes; it removes directory entries or links. Only when the last link to a file disappears does the system remove the inode, and hence the file itself.

If the i-number in a directory entry is zero, it means that the link has been removed, but not necessarily the contents of the file — there may still be a link somewhere else. You can verify that the i-number goes to zero by removing the file:

```
$ rm x
$ od -d .
0000000 15156 00046 00000 00000 00000 00000 00000 00000
0000020 10427 11822 00000 00000 00000 00000 00000 00000
0000040 15274 25970 26979 25968 00115 00000 00000 00000
0000060 15768 30058 27502 00000 00000 00000 00000 00000
0000100 00000 00120 00000 00000 00000 00000 00000 00000
0000120
$
```

The next file created in this directory will go into the unused slot, although it will probably have a different i-number.

The `ln` command makes a link to an existing file, with the syntax

```
$ ln old-file new-file
```

The purpose of a link is to give two names to the same file, often so it can appear in two different directories. On many systems there is a link to `/bin/ed` called `/bin/e`, so that people can call the editor `e`. Two links to a file point to the same inode, and hence have the same i-number:

```
$ ln junk linktojunk
$ ls -li
total 3
15768 -rw-rw-rw- 2 you        29 Sep 27 12:07 junk
15768 -rw-rw-rw- 2 you        29 Sep 27 12:07 linktojunk
15274 drwxrwxrwx 4 you        64 Sep 27 09:34 recipes
$
```

The integer printed between the permissions and the owner is the number of links to the file. Because each link just points to the inode, each link is equally important — there is no difference between the first link and subsequent ones. (Notice that the total disc space computed by ls is wrong because of double counting.)

When you change a file, access to the file by any of its names will reveal the changes, since all the links point to the same file.

```
$ echo x >junk
$ ls -l
total 3
-rw-rw-rw- 2 you         2 Sep 27 12:37 junk
-rw-rw-rw- 2 you         2 Sep 27 12:37 linktojunk
drwxrwxrwx 4 you        64 Sep 27 09:34 recipes
$ rm linktojunk
$ ls -l
total 2
-rw-rw-rw- 1 you         2 Sep 27 12:37 junk
drwxrwxrwx 4 you        64 Sep 27 09:34 recipes
$
```

After linktojunk is removed the link count goes back to one. As we said before, rm'ing a file just breaks a link; the file remains until the last link is removed. In practice, of course, most files only have one link, but again we see a simple idea providing great flexibility.

A word to the hasty: once the last link to a file is gone, the data is irretrievable. Deleted files go into the incinerator, rather than the waste basket, and there is no way to call them back from the ashes. (There is a faint hope of resurrection. Most large UNIX systems have a formal backup procedure that periodically copies changed files to some safe place like magnetic tape, from which they can be retrieved. For your own protection and peace of mind, you should know just how much backup is provided on your system. If there is none, watch out — some mishap to the discs could be a catastrophe.)

Links to files are handy when two people wish to share a file, but sometimes you really want a *separate* copy — a different file with the same information. You might copy a document before making extensive changes to it, for example, so you can restore the original if you decide you don't like the changes. Making a link wouldn't help, because when the data changed, both links would reflect the change. cp makes copies of files:

```
$ cp junk copyofjunk
$ ls -li
total 3
15850 -rw-rw-rw- 1 you              2 Sep 27 13:13 copyofjunk
15768 -rw-rw-rw- 1 you              2 Sep 27 12:37 junk
15274 drwxrwxrwx 4 you             64 Sep 27 09:34 recipes
$
```

The i-numbers of junk and copyofjunk are different, because they are different files, even though they currently have the same contents. It's often a good idea to change the permissions on a backup copy so it's harder to remove it accidentally.

```
$ chmod -w copyofjunk            Turn off write permission
$ ls -li
total 3
15850 -r--r--r-- 1 you              2 Sep 27 13:13 copyofjunk
15768 -rw-rw-rw- 1 you              2 Sep 27 12:37 junk
15274 drwxrwxrwx 4 you             64 Sep 27 09:34 recipes
$ rm copyofjunk
rm: copyofjunk 444 mode n          No! It's precious
$ date >junk
$ ls -li
total 3
15850 -r--r--r-- 1 you              2 Sep 27 13:13 copyofjunk
15768 -rw-rw-rw- 1 you             29 Sep 27 13:16 junk
15274 drwxrwxrwx 4 you             64 Sep 27 09:34 recipes
$ rm copyofjunk
rm: copyofjunk 444 mode y          Well, maybe not so precious
$ ls -li
total 2
15768 -rw-rw-rw- 1 you             29 Sep 27 13:16 junk
15274 drwxrwxrwx 4 you             64 Sep 27 09:34 recipes
$
```

Changing the copy of a file doesn't change the original, and removing the copy has no effect on the original. Notice that because copyofjunk had write permission turned off, rm asked for confirmation before removing the file.

There is one more common command for manipulating files: mv moves or renames files, simply by rearranging the links. Its syntax is the same as cp and ln:

```
$ mv junk sameoldjunk
$ ls -li
total 2
15274 drwxrwxrwx 4 you          64 Sep 27 09:34 recipes
15768 -rw-rw-rw- 1 you          29 Sep 27 13:16 sameoldjunk
$
```

sameoldjunk is the same file as our old junk, right down to the i-number; only its name — the directory entry associated with inode 15768 — has been changed.

We have been doing all this file shuffling in one directory, but it also works across directories. ln is often used to put links with the same name in several directories, such as when several people are working on one program or document. mv can move a file or directory from one directory to another. In fact, these are common enough idioms that mv and cp have special syntax for them:

```
$ mv (or cp) file1 file2 ... directory
```

moves (or copies) one or more files to the directory which is the last argument. The links or copies are made with the same filenames. For example, if you wanted to try your hand at beefing up the editor, you might begin by saying

```
$ cp /usr/src/cmd/ed.c .
```

to get your own copy of the source to play with. If you were going to work on the shell, which is in a number of different source files, you would say

```
$ mkdir sh
$ cp /usr/src/cmd/sh/* sh
```

and cp would duplicate all of the shell's source files in your subdirectory sh (assuming no subdirectory structure in /usr/src/cmd/sh — cp is not very clever). On some systems, ln also accepts multiple file arguments, again with a directory as the last argument. And on some systems, mv, cp and ln are themselves links to a single file that examines its name to see what service to perform.

Exercise 2-6. Why does ls -l report 4 links to recipes? Hint: try

```
$ ls -ld /usr/you
```

Why is this useful information? □

Exercise 2-7. What is the difference between

```
$ mv junk junk1
```

and

```
$ cp junk junk1
$ rm junk
```

Hint: make a link to junk, then try it. □

Exercise 2-8. cp doesn't copy subdirectories, it just copies files at the first level of a hierarchy. What does it do if one of the argument files is a directory? Is this kind or even sensible? Discuss the relative merits of three possibilities: an option to cp to descend directories, a separate command rcp (recursive copy) to do the job, or just having cp copy a directory recursively when it finds one. See Chapter 7 for help on providing this facility. What other programs would profit from the ability to traverse the directory tree? □

2.6 The directory hierarchy

In Chapter 1, we looked at the file system hierarchy rather informally, starting from /usr/you. We're now going to investigate it in a more orderly way, starting from the top of the tree, the root.

The top directory is /.

```
$ ls /
bin
boot
dev
etc
lib
tmp
unix
usr
$
```

/unix is the program for the UNIX kernel itself: when the system starts, /unix is read from disc into memory and started. Actually, the process occurs in two steps: first the file /boot is read; it then reads in /unix. More information about this "bootstrap" process may be found in boot(8). The rest of the files in /, at least here, are directories, each a somewhat self-contained section of the total file system. In the following brief tour of the hierarchy, play along with the text: explore a bit in the directories mentioned. The more familiar you are with the layout of the file system, the more effectively you will be able to use it. Table 2.1 suggests good places to look, although some of the names are system dependent.

/bin (binaries) we have seen before: it is the directory where the basic programs such as who and ed reside.

/dev (devices) we will discuss in the next section.

/etc (*et cetera*) we have also seen before. It contains various administrative files such as the password file and some system programs such as /etc/getty, which initializes a terminal connection for /bin/login. /etc/rc is a file of shell commands that is executed after the system is bootstrapped. /etc/group lists the members of each group.

/lib (library) contains primarily parts of the C compiler, such as /lib/cpp, the C preprocessor, and /lib/libc.a, the C subroutine library.

/tmp (temporaries) is a repository for short-lived files created during the

Table 2.1: Interesting Directories (see also `hier`(7))	
`/`	root of the file system
`/bin`	essential programs in executable form ("binaries")
`/dev`	device files
`/etc`	system miscellany
`/etc/motd`	login message of the day
`/etc/passwd`	password file
`/lib`	essential libraries, etc.
`/tmp`	temporary files; cleaned when system is restarted
`/unix`	executable form of the operating system
`/usr`	user file system
`/usr/adm`	system administration: accounting info., etc.
`/usr/bin`	user binaries: `troff`, etc.
`/usr/dict`	dictionary (`words`) and support for `spell`(1)
`/usr/games`	game programs
`/usr/include`	header files for C programs, e.g. `math.h`
`/usr/include/sys`	system header files for C programs, e.g. `inode.h`
`/usr/lib`	libraries for C, FORTRAN, etc.
`/usr/man`	on-line manual
`/usr/man/man1`	manual pages for section 1 of manual
`/usr/mdec`	hardware diagnostics, bootstrap programs, etc.
`/usr/news`	community service messages
`/usr/pub`	public oddments: see `ascii`(7) and `eqnchar`(7)
`/usr/src`	source code for utilities and libraries
`/usr/src/cmd`	source for commands in `/bin` and `/usr/bin`
`/usr/src/lib`	source code for subroutine libraries
`/usr/spool`	working directories for communications programs
`/usr/spool/lpd`	line printer temporary directory
`/usr/spool/mail`	mail in-boxes
`/usr/spool/uucp`	working directory for the `uucp` programs
`/usr/sys`	source for the operating system kernel
`/usr/tmp`	alternate temporary directory (little used)
`/usr/you`	your login directory
`/usr/you/bin`	your personal programs

execution of a program. When you start up the editor `ed`, for example, it creates a file with a name like `/tmp/e00512` to hold its copy of the file you are editing, rather than working with the original file. It could, of course, create the file in your current directory, but there are advantages to placing it in `/tmp`: although it is unlikely, you might already have a file called `e00512` in your directory; `/tmp` is cleaned up automatically when the system starts, so your directory doesn't get an unwanted file if the system crashes; and often `/tmp` is arranged on the disc for fast access.

There is a problem, of course, when several programs create files in /tmp at once: they might interfere with each other's files. That is why ed's temporary file has a peculiar name: it is constructed in such a way as to guarantee that no other program will choose the same name for its temporary file. In Chapters 5 and 6 we will see ways to do this.

/usr is called the "user file system," although it may have little to do with the actual users of the system. On our machine, our login directories are /usr/bwk and /usr/rob, but on your machine the /usr part might be different, as explained in Chapter 1. Whether or not your personal files are in a subdirectory of /usr, there are a number of things you are likely to find there (although local customs vary in this regard, too). Just as in /, there are directories called /usr/bin, /usr/lib and /usr/tmp. These directories have functions similar to their namesakes in /, but contain programs less critical to the system. For example, nroff is usually in /usr/bin rather than /bin, and the FORTRAN compiler libraries live in /usr/lib. Of course, just what is deemed "critical" varies from system to system. Some systems, such as the distributed 7th Edition, have all the programs in /bin and do away with /usr/bin altogether; others split /usr/bin into two directories according to frequency of use.

Other directories in /usr are /usr/adm, containing accounting information and /usr/dict, which holds a modest dictionary (see spell(1)). The on-line manual is kept in /usr/man — see /usr/man/man1/spell.1, for example. If your system has source code on-line, you will probably find it in /usr/src.

It is worth spending a little time exploring the file system, especially /usr, to develop a feeling for how the file system is organized and where you might expect to find things.

2.7 Devices

We skipped over /dev in our tour, because the files there provide a nice review of files in general. As you might guess from the name, /dev contains device files.

One of the prettiest ideas in the UNIX system is the way it deals with *peripherals* — discs, tape drives, line printers, terminals, etc. Rather than having special system routines to, for example, read magnetic tape, there is a file called /dev/mt0 (again, local customs vary). Inside the kernel, references to that file are converted into hardware commands to access the tape, so if a program reads /dev/mt0, the contents of a tape mounted on the drive are returned. For example,

```
$ cp /dev/mt0 junk
```

copies the contents of the tape to a file called junk. cp has no idea there is anything special about /dev/mt0; it is just a file — a sequence of bytes.

The device files are something of a zoo, each creature a little different, but the basic ideas of the file system apply to each. Here is a significantly shortened list of our /dev:

```
$ ls -l /dev
crw--w--w- 1 root       0,  0 Sep 27 23:09 console
crw-r--r-- 1 root       3,  1 Sep 27 14:37 kmem
crw-r--r-- 1 root       3,  0 May  6  1981 mem
brw-rw-rw- 1 root       1, 64 Aug 24 17:41 mt0
crw-rw-rw- 1 root       3,  2 Sep 28 02:03 null
crw-rw-rw- 1 root       4, 64 Sep  9 15:42 rmt0
brw-r----- 1 root       2,  0 Sep  8 08:07 rp00
brw-r----- 1 root       2,  1 Sep 27 23:09 rp01
crw-r----- 1 root      13,  0 Apr 12  1983 rrp00
crw-r----- 1 root      13,  1 Jul 28 15:18 rrp01
crw-rw-rw- 1 root       2,  0 Jul  5 08:04 tty
crw--w--w- 1 you        1,  0 Sep 28 02:38 tty0
crw--w--w- 1 root       1,  1 Sep 27 23:09 tty1
crw--w--w- 1 root       1,  2 Sep 27 17:33 tty2
crw--w--w- 1 root       1,  3 Sep 27 18:48 tty3
$
```

The first things to notice are that instead of a byte count there is a pair of small integers, and that the first character of the mode is always a 'b' or a 'c'. This is how ls prints the information from an inode that specifies a device rather than a regular file. The inode of a regular file contains a list of disc blocks that store the file's contents. For a device file, the inode instead contains the internal name for the device, which consists of its type — *character* (c) or *block* (b) — and a pair of numbers, called the *major* and *minor* device numbers. Discs and tapes are block devices; everything else — terminals, printers, phone lines, etc. — is a character device. The major number encodes the type of device, while the minor number distinguishes different instances of the device. For example, /dev/tty0 and /dev/tty1 are two ports on the same terminal controller, so they have the same major device number but different minor numbers.

Disc files are usually named after the particular hardware variant they represent. /dev/rp00 and /dev/rp01 are named after the DEC RP06 disc drive attached to the system. There is just one drive, divided logically into two file systems. If there were a second drive, its associated files would be named /dev/rp10 and /dev/rp11. The first digit specifies the physical drive, and the second which portion of the drive.

You might wonder why there are several disc device files, instead of just one. For historical reasons and for ease of maintenance, the file system is divided into smaller subsystems. The files in a subsystem are accessible through a directory in the main system. The program /etc/mount reports the correspondence between device files and directories:

```
$ /etc/mount
rp01 on /usr
$
```

In our case, the root system occupies /dev/rp00 (although this isn't reported by /etc/mount) while the user file system — the files in /usr and its sub-directories — reside on /dev/rp01.

The root file system has to be present for the system to execute. /bin, /dev and /etc are always kept on the root system, because when the system starts only files in the root system are accessible, and some files such as /bin/sh are needed to run at all. During the bootstrap operation, all the file systems are checked for self-consistency (see icheck(8) or fsck(8)), and attached to the root system. This attachment operation is called mounting, the software equivalent of mounting a new disc pack in a drive; it can normally be done only by the super-user. After /dev/rp01 has been mounted as /usr, the files in the user file system are accessible exactly as if they were part of the root system.

For the average user, the details of which file subsystem is mounted where are of little interest, but there are a couple of relevant points. First, because the subsystems may be mounted and dismounted, it is illegal to make a link to a file in another subsystem. For example, it is impossible to link programs in /bin to convenient names in private bin directories, because /usr is in a different file subsystem from /bin:

```
$ ln /bin/mail /usr/you/bin/m
ln: Cross-device link
$
```

There would also be a problem because inode numbers are not unique in different file systems.

Second, each subsystem has fixed upper limits on size (number of blocks available for files) and inodes. If a subsystem fills up, it will be impossible to enlarge files in that subsystem until some space is reclaimed. The df (disc free space) command reports the available space on the mounted file subsystems:

```
$ df
/dev/rp00 1989
/dev/rp01 21257
$
```

/usr has 21257 free blocks. Whether this is ample space or a crisis depends on how the system is used; some installations need more file space headroom than others. By the way, of all the commands, df probably has the widest variation in output format. Your df output may look quite different.

Let's turn now to some more generally useful things. When you log in, you get a terminal line and therefore a file in /dev through which the characters

you type and receive are sent. The `tty` command tells you which terminal you
are using:

```
$ who am i
you        tty0      Sep 28 01:02
$ tty
/dev/tty0
$ ls -l /dev/tty0
crw--w--w- 1 you        1, 12 Sep 28 02:40 /dev/tty0
$ date >/dev/tty0
Wed Sep 28 02:40:51 EDT 1983
$
```

Notice that you own the device, and that only you are permitted to read it. In
other words, no one else can directly read the characters you are typing. Anyone may write on your terminal, however. To prevent this, you could `chmod`
the device, thereby preventing people from using `write` to contact you, or you
could just use `mesg`.

```
$ mesg n                          Turn off messages
$ ls -l /dev/tty0
crw------- 1 you        1, 12 Sep 28 02:41 /dev/tty0
$ mesg y                          Restore
$
```

It is often useful to be able to refer by name to the terminal you are using,
but it's inconvenient to determine which one it is. The device `/dev/tty` is a
synonym for your login terminal, whatever terminal you are actually using.

```
$ date >/dev/tty
Wed Sep 28 02:42:23 EDT 1983
$
```

`/dev/tty` is particularly useful when a program needs to interact with a user
even though its standard input and output are connected to files rather than the
terminal. `crypt` is one program that uses `/dev/tty`. The "clear text"
comes from the standard input, and the encrypted data goes to the standard
output, so `crypt` reads the encryption key from `/dev/tty`:

```
$ crypt <cleartext >cryptedtext
Enter key:                        Type encryption key
$
```

The use of `/dev/tty` isn't explicit in this example, but it is there. If `crypt`
read the key from the standard input, it would read the first line of the clear
text. So instead `crypt` opens `/dev/tty`, turns off automatic character echoing so your encryption key doesn't appear on the screen, and reads the key. In
Chapters 5 and 6 we will come across several other uses of `/dev/tty`.

Occasionally you want to run a program but don't care what output is produced. For example, you may have already seen today's news, and don't want

to read it again. Redirecting `news` to the file `/dev/null` causes its output to be thrown away:

```
$ news >/dev/null
$
```

Data written to `/dev/null` is discarded without comment, while programs that read from `/dev/null` get end-of-file immediately, because reads from `/dev/null` always return zero bytes.

One common use of `/dev/null` is to throw away regular output so that diagnostic messages are visible. For example, the `time` command (`time(1)`) reports the CPU usage of a program. The information is printed on the standard error, so you can time commands that generate copious output by sending the standard output to `/dev/null`:

```
$ ls -l /usr/dict/words
-r--r--r-- 1 bin      196513 Jan 20  1979 /usr/dict/words
$ time grep e /usr/dict/words >/dev/null

real      13.0
user       9.0
sys        2.7
$ time egrep e /usr/dict/words >/dev/null

real       8.0
user       3.9
sys        2.8
$
```

The numbers in the output of `time` are elapsed clock time, CPU time spent in the program and CPU time spent in the kernel while the program was running. `egrep` is a high-powered variant of `grep` that we will discuss in Chapter 4; it's about twice as fast as `grep` when searching through large files. If output from `grep` and `egrep` had not been sent to `/dev/null` or a real file, we would have had to wait for hundreds of thousands of characters to appear on the terminal before finding out the timing information we were after.

Exercise 2-9. Find out about the other files in `/dev` by reading Section 4 of the manual. What is the difference between `/dev/mt0` and `/dev/rmt0`? Comment on the potential advantages of having subdirectories in `/dev` for discs, tapes, etc. □

Exercise 2-10. Tapes written on non-UNIX systems often have different block sizes, such as 800 bytes — ten 80-character card images — but the tape device `/dev/mt0` expects 512-byte blocks. Look up the `dd` command (`dd(1)`) to see how to read such a tape. □

Exercise 2-11. Why isn't `/dev/tty` just a link to your login terminal? What would happen if it were mode `rw--w--w-` like your login terminal? □

Exercise 2-12. How does `write(1)` work? Hint: see `utmp(5)`. □

Exercise 2-13. How can you tell if a user has been active at the terminal recently? □

History and bibliographic notes

The file system forms one part of the discussion in "UNIX implementation," by Ken Thompson (*BSTJ*, July, 1978). A paper by Dennis Ritchie, entitled "The evolution of the UNIX time-sharing system" (Symposium on Language Design and Programming Methodology, Sydney, Australia, Sept. 1979) is an fascinating description of how the file system was designed and implemented on the original PDP-7 UNIX system, and how it grew into its present form.

The UNIX file system adapts some ideas from the MULTICS file system. *The MULTICS System: An Examination of its Structure*, by E. I. Organick (MIT Press, 1972) provides a comprehensive treatment of MULTICS.

"Password security: a case history," by Bob Morris and Ken Thompson, is an entertaining comparison of password mechanisms on a variety of systems; it can be found in Volume 2B of the *UNIX Programmer's Manual*.

In the same volume, the paper "On the security of UNIX," by Dennis Ritchie, explains how the security of a system depends more on the care taken with its administration than with the details of programs like `crypt`.

CHAPTER 3: **USING THE SHELL**

The shell — the program that interprets your requests to run programs — is the most important program for most UNIX users; with the possible exception of your favorite text editor, you will spend more time working with the shell than any other program. In this chapter and in Chapter 5, we will spend a fair amount of time on the shell's capabilities. The main point we want to make is that you can accomplish a lot without much hard work, and certainly without resorting to programming in a conventional language like C, if you know how to use the shell.

We have divided our coverage of the shell into two chapters. This chapter goes one step beyond the necessities covered in Chapter 1 to some fancier but commonly used shell features, such as metacharacters, quoting, creating new commands, passing arguments to them, the use of shell variables, and some elementary control flow. These are topics you should know for your own use of the shell. The material in Chapter 5 is heavier going — it is intended for writing serious shell programs, ones that are bullet-proofed for use by others. The division between the two chapters is somewhat arbitrary, of course, so both should be read eventually.

3.1 Command line structure

To proceed, we need a slightly better understanding of just what a command is, and how it is interpreted by the shell. This section is a more formal coverage, with some new information, of the shell basics introduced in the first chapter.

The simplest command is a single *word*, usually naming a file for execution (later we will see some other types of commands):

```
$ who                              Execute the file /bin/who
you      tty2     Sep 28 07:51
jpl      tty4     Sep 28 08:32
$
```

A command usually ends with a newline, but a semicolon ; is also a *command terminator*:

71

```
$ date;
Wed Sep 28 09:07:15 EDT 1983
$ date; who
Wed Sep 28 09:07:23 EDT 1983
you        tty2      Sep 28 07:51
jpl        tty4      Sep 28 08:32
$
```

Although semicolons can be used to terminate commands, as usual nothing happens until you type RETURN. Notice that the shell only prints one prompt after multiple commands, but except for the prompt,

```
$ date; who
```

is identical to typing the two commands on different lines. In particular, who doesn't run until date has finished.

Try sending the output of "date; who" through a pipe:

```
$ date; who | wc
Wed Sep 28 09:08:48 EDT 1983
         2       10       60
$
```

This might not be what you expected, because only the output of who goes to wc. Connecting who and wc with a pipe forms a single command, called a *pipeline*, that runs after date. The precedence of | is higher than that of ';' as the shell parses your command line.

Parentheses can be used to group commands:

```
$ (date; who)
Wed Sep 28 09:11:09 EDT 1983
you        tty2      Sep 28 07:51
jpl        tty4      Sep 28 08:32
$ (date; who) | wc
         3       16       89
$
```

The outputs of date and who are concatenated into a single stream that can be sent down a pipe.

Data flowing through a pipe can be tapped and placed in a file (but not another pipe) with the tee command, which is not part of the shell, but is nonetheless handy for manipulating pipes. One use is to save intermediate output in a file:

```
$ (date; who) | tee save | wc
        3       16      89                              Output from wc
$ cat save
Wed Sep 28 09:13:22 EDT 1983
you        tty2      Sep 28 07:51
jpl        tty4      Sep 28 08:32
$ wc <save
        3       16      89
$
```

tee copies its input to the named file or files, as well as to its output, so wc receives the same data as if tee weren't in the pipeline.

Another command terminator is the ampersand &. It's exactly like the semicolon or newline, except that it tells the shell not to wait for the command to complete. Typically, & is used to run a long-running command "in the background" while you continue to type interactive commands:

```
$ long-running-command &
5273                                    Process-id of long-running-command
$                                       Prompt appears immediately
```

Given the ability to group commands, there are some more interesting uses of background processes. The command sleep waits the specified number of seconds before exiting:

```
$ sleep 5
$                                       Five seconds pass before prompt
$ (sleep 5; date) & date
5278
Wed Sep 28 09:18:20 EDT 1983            Output from second date
$ Wed Sep 28 09:18:25 EDT 1983          Prompt appears, then date 5 sec. later
```

The background process starts but immediately sleeps; meanwhile, the second date command prints the current time and the shell prompts for a new command. Five seconds later, the sleep exits and the first date prints the new time. It's hard to represent the passage of time on paper, so you should try this example. (Depending on how busy your machine is and other such details, the difference between the two times might not be exactly five seconds.) This is an easy way to run a command in the future; consider

```
$ (sleep 300; echo Tea is ready) &      Tea will be ready in 5 minutes
5291
$
```

as a handy reminder mechanism. (A *ctl*-g in the string to be echoed will ring the terminal's bell when it's printed.) The parentheses are needed in these examples, since the precedence of & is higher than that of ';'.

The & terminator applies to commands, and since pipelines are commands you don't need parentheses to run pipelines in the background:

```
$ pr file | lpr &
```

arranges to print the file on the line printer without making you wait for the command to finish. Parenthesizing the pipeline has the same effect, but requires more typing:

```
$ (pr file | lpr) &                    Same as last example
```

Most programs accept *arguments* on the command line, such as file (an argument to pr) in the above example. Arguments are words, separated by blanks and tabs, that typically name files to be processed by the command, but they are strings that may be interpreted any way the program sees fit. For example, pr accepts names of files to print, echo echoes its arguments without interpretation, and grep's first argument specifies a text pattern to search for. And, of course, most programs also have options, indicated by arguments beginning with a minus sign.

The various special characters interpreted by the shell, such as <, >, |, ; and &, are *not* arguments to the programs the shell runs. They instead control how the shell runs them. For example,

```
$ echo Hello >junk
```

tells the shell to run echo with the single argument Hello, and place the output in the file junk. The string >junk is not an argument to echo; it is interpreted by the shell and never seen by echo. In fact, it need not be the last string in the command:

```
$ >junk echo Hello
```

is identical, but less obvious.

Exercise 3-1. What are the differences among the following three commands?

```
$ cat file | pr
$ pr <file
$ pr file
```

(Over the years the redirection operator < has lost some ground to pipes; people seem to find "cat file |" more natural than "<file".) □

3.2 Metacharacters

The shell recognizes a number of other characters as special; the most commonly used is the asterisk * which tells the shell to search the directory for filenames in which any string of characters occurs in the position of the *. For example,

```
$ echo *
```

is a poor facsimile of ls. Something we didn't mention in Chapter 1 is that the filename-matching characters do not look at filenames beginning with a

dot, to avoid problems with the names '.' and '..' that are in every directory.
The rule is: the filename-matching characters only match filenames beginning
with a period if the period is explicitly supplied in the pattern. As usual, a
judicious echo or two will clarify what happens:

```
$ ls
.profile
junk
temp
$ echo *
junk temp
$ echo .*
.  ..  .profile
$
```

Characters like * that have special properties are known as *metacharacters*.
There are a lot of them: Table 3.1 is the complete list, although a few of them
won't be discussed until Chapter 5.

Given the number of shell metacharacters, there has to be some way to say
to the shell, "Leave it alone." The easiest and best way to protect special
characters from being interpreted is to enclose them in single quote characters:

```
$ echo '***'
***
$
```

It's also possible to use the double quotes "...", but the shell actually peeks
inside these quotes to look for $, `...`, and \, so don't use "..." unless you
intend some processing of the quoted string.

A third possibility is to put a backslash \ in front of *each* character that you
want to protect from the shell, as in

```
$ echo \*\*\*
```

Although *** isn't much like English, the shell terminology for it is still a
word, which is any single string the shell accepts as a unit, including blanks if
they are quoted.

Quotes of one kind protect quotes of the other kind:

```
$ echo "Don't do that!"
Don't do that!
$
```

and they don't have to surround the whole argument:

```
$ echo x'*'y
x*y
$ echo '*'A'?'
*A?
$
```

Table 3.1: Shell Metacharacters

>	*prog* >*file* direct standard output to *file*
>>	*prog* >>*file* append standard output to *file*
<	*prog* <*file* take standard input from *file*
¦	p_1¦p_2 connect standard output of p_1 to standard input of p_2
<<*str*	*here document*: standard input follows, up to next *str* on a line by itself
*	match any string of zero or more characters in filenames
?	match any single character in filenames
[*ccc*]	match any single character from *ccc* in filenames; ranges like 0-9 or a-z are legal
;	command terminator: p_1;p_2 does p_1, then p_2
&	like ; but doesn't wait for p_1 to finish
`...`	run command(s) in ...; output replaces `...`
(...)	run command(s) in ... in a sub-shell
{...}	run command(s) in ... in current shell (rarely used)
$1, $2 *etc.*	$0...$9 replaced by arguments to shell file
$*var*	value of shell variable *var*
${*var*}	value of *var*; avoids confusion when concatenated with text; see also Table 5.3
\	\c take character *c* literally, *newline* discarded
'...'	take ... literally
"..."	take ... literally after $, `...` and \ interpreted
#	if # starts word, rest of line is a comment (not in 7th Ed.)
var=value	assign to variable *var*
p_1 && p_2	run p_1; if successful, run p_2
p_1 ¦¦ p_2	run p_1; if unsuccessful, run p_2

In this last example, because the quotes are discarded after they've done their job, echo sees a single argument containing no quotes.

Quoted strings can contain newlines:

```
$ echo 'hello
> world'
hello
world
$
```

The string '> ' is a *secondary prompt* printed by the shell when it expects you to type more input to complete a command. In this example the quote on the first line has to be balanced with another. The secondary prompt string is stored in the shell variable PS2, and can be modified to taste.

In all of these examples, the quoting of a metacharacter prevents the shell from trying to interpret it. The command

```
$ echo x*y
```

echoes all the filenames beginning x and ending y. As always, echo knows nothing about files or shell metacharacters; the interpretation of *, if any, is supplied by the shell.

What happens if no files match the pattern? The shell, rather than complaining (as it did in early versions), passes the string on as though it had been quoted. It's usually a bad idea to depend on this behavior, but it can be exploited to learn of the existence of files matching a pattern:

```
$ ls x*y
x*y not found            Message from ls: no such files exist
$ >xyzzy                 Create xyzzy
$ ls x*y
xyzzy                    File xyzzy matches x*y
$ ls 'x*y'
x*y not found            ls doesn't interpret the *
$
```

A backslash at the end of a line causes the line to be continued; this is the way to present a very long line to the shell.

```
$ echo abc\
> def\
> ghi
abcdefghi
$
```

Notice that the newline is discarded when preceded by backslash, but is retained when it appears in quotes.

The metacharacter # is almost universally used for shell comments; if a shell word begins with #, the rest of the line is ignored:

```
$ echo hello # there
hello
$ echo hello#there
hello#there
$
```

The # was not part of the original 7th Edition, but it has been adopted very widely, and we will use it in the rest of the book.

Exercise 3-2. Explain the output produced by

```
$ ls .*
```

□

A digression on echo

Even though it isn't explicitly asked for, a final newline is provided by echo. A sensible and perhaps cleaner design for echo would be to print only what is requested. This would make it easy to issue prompts from the shell:

```
$ pure-echo Enter a command:
Enter a command:$              No trailing newline
```

but has the disadvantage that the most common case — providing a newline —
is not the default and takes extra typing:

```
$ pure-echo 'Hello!
> '
Hello!
$
```

Since a command should by default execute its most commonly used function,
the real echo appends the final newline automatically.

But what if it isn't desired? The 7th Edition echo has a single option, -n,
to suppress the last newline:

```
$ echo -n Enter a command:
Enter a command:$              Prompt on same line
$ echo -
-                              Only -n is special
$
```

The only tricky case is echoing -n followed by a newline:

```
$ echo -n '-n
> '
-n
$
```

It's ugly, but it works, and this is a rare situation anyway.

A different approach, taken in System V, is for echo to interpret C-like
backslash sequences, such as \b for backspace and \c (which isn't actually in
the C language) to suppress the last newline:

```
$ echo 'Enter a command:\c'        System V version
Enter a command:$
```

Although this mechanism avoids confusion about echoing a minus sign, it has
other problems. echo is often used as a diagnostic aid, and backslashes are
interpreted by so many programs that having echo look at them too just adds
to the confusion.

Still, both designs of echo have good and bad points. We shall use the 7th
Edition version (-n), so if your local echo obeys a different convention, a
couple of our programs will need minor revision.

Another question of philosophy is what echo should do if given *no* arguments — specifically, should it print a blank line or nothing at all? All the
current echo implementations we know print a blank line, but past versions
didn't, and there were once great debates on the subject. Doug McIlroy
imparted the right feelings of mysticism in his discussion of the topic:

The UNIX and the Echo

There dwelt in the land of New Jersey the UNIX, a fair maid whom savants traveled far to admire. Dazzled by her purity, all sought to espouse her, one for her virginal grace, another for her polished civility, yet another for her agility in performing exacting tasks seldom accomplished even in much richer lands. So large of heart and accommodating of nature was she that the UNIX adopted all but the most insufferably rich of her suitors. Soon many offspring grew and prospered and spread to the ends of the earth.

Nature herself smiled and answered to the UNIX more eagerly than to other mortal beings. Humbler folk, who knew little of more courtly manners, delighted in her *echo,* so precise and crystal clear they scarce believed she could be answered by the same rocks and woods that so garbled their own shouts into the wilderness. And the compliant UNIX obliged with perfect echoes of whatever she was asked.

When one impatient swain asked the UNIX, 'Echo nothing,' the UNIX obligingly opened her mouth, echoed nothing, and closed it again.

'Whatever do you mean,' the youth demanded, 'opening your mouth like that? Henceforth never open your mouth when you are supposed to echo nothing!' And the UNIX obliged.

'But I want a perfect performance, even when you echo nothing,' pleaded a sensitive youth, 'and no perfect echoes can come from a closed mouth.' Not wishing to offend either one, the UNIX agreed to say different nothings for the impatient youth and for the sensitive youth. She called the sensitive nothing '\n.'

Yet now when she said '\n,' she was really not saying nothing so she had to open her mouth twice, once to say '\n,' and once to say nothing, and so she did not please the sensitive youth, who said forthwith, 'The \n sounds like a perfect nothing to me, but the second one ruins it. I want you to take back one of them.' So the UNIX, who could not abide offending, agreed to undo some echoes, and called that '\c.' Now the sensitive youth could hear a perfect echo of nothing by asking for '\n' and '\c' together. But they say that he died of a surfeit of notation before he ever heard one.

Exercise 3-3. Predict what each of the following `grep` commands will do, then verify your understanding.

```
grep \$                  grep \\
grep \\$                 grep \\\\
grep \\\$                grep "\$"
grep '\$'                grep '"$'
grep '\'$'               grep "$"
```

A file containing these commands themselves makes a good test case if you want to experiment. □

Exercise 3-4. How do you tell `grep` to search for a pattern beginning with a '-'? Why doesn't quoting the argument help? Hint: investigate the -e option. □

Exercise 3-5. Consider

```
$ echo */*
```

Does this produce all names in all directories? In what order do the names appear? □

Exercise 3-6. (Trick question) How do you get a / into a filename (i.e., a / that doesn't separate components of the path)? □

Exercise 3-7. What happens with

```
$ cat x y >y
```

and with

```
$ cat x >>x
```

Think before rushing off to try them. □

Exercise 3-8. If you type

```
$ rm *
```

why can't rm warn you that you're about to delete all your files? □

3.3 Creating new commands

It's now time to move on to something that we promised in Chapter 1 —
how to create new commands out of old ones.

Given a sequence of commands that is to be repeated more than a few
times, it would be convenient to make it into a "new" command with its own
name, so you can use it like a regular command. To be specific, suppose you
intend to count users frequently with the pipeline

```
$ who | wc -1
```

that was mentioned in Chapter 1, and you want to make a new program nu to
do that.

The first step is to create an ordinary file that contains 'who | wc -1'.
You can use a favorite editor, or you can get creative:

```
$ echo 'who | wc -1' >nu
```

(Without the quotes, what would appear in nu?)

As we said in Chapter 1, the shell is a program just like an editor or who or
wc; its name is sh. And since it's a program, you can run it and redirect *its*
input. So run the shell with its input coming from the file nu instead of the
terminal:

```
$ who
you       tty2      Sep 28 07:51
rhh       tty4      Sep 28 10:02
moh       tty5      Sep 28 09:38
ava       tty6      Sep 28 10:17
$ cat nu
who | wc -1
$ sh <nu
       4
$
```

The output is the same as it would have been if you had typed who | wc -1
at the terminal.

Again like most other programs, the shell takes its input from a file if one is named as an argument; you could have written

```
$ sh nu
```

for the same result. But it's a nuisance to have to type "sh" in either case: it's longer, and it creates a distinction between programs written in, say, C and ones written by connecting programs with the shell.† Therefore, if a file is executable and if it contains text, then the shell assumes it to be a file of shell commands. Such a file is called a *shell file*. All you have to do is to make nu executable, once:

```
$ chmod +x nu
```

and thereafter you can invoke it with

```
$ nu
```

From now on, users of nu cannot tell, just by running it, that you implemented it in this easy way.

The way the shell actually runs nu is to create a new shell process exactly as if you had typed

```
$ sh nu
```

This child shell is called a *sub-shell* — a shell process invoked by your current shell. sh nu is not the same as sh <nu, because its standard input is still connected to the terminal.

As it stands, nu works only if it's in your current directory (provided, of course, that the current directory is in your PATH, which we will assume from now on). To make nu part of your repertoire regardless of what directory you're in, move it to your private bin directory, and add /usr/you/bin to your search path:

```
$ pwd
/usr/you
$ mkdir bin                         Make a bin if you haven't already
$ echo $PATH                        Check PATH for sure
:/usr/you/bin:/bin:/usr/bin         Should look like this
$ mv nu bin                         Install nu
$ ls nu
nu not found                        It's really gone from current directory
$ nu
        4                           But it's found by the shell
$
```

Of course, your PATH should be set properly by your .profile, so you don't have to reset it every time you log in.

There are other simple commands that you might create this way to tailor

---

† Nonetheless, it is a distinction made on most other operating systems.

your environment to your own taste. Some that we have found convenient include

- cs, which echoes the proper sequence of mysterious characters to clear the screen on your terminal (24 newlines is a fairly general implementation);
- what, which runs who and ps -a to tell who's logged on and what they are doing;
- where, which prints the identifying name of the UNIX system you're using — it's handy if you use several regularly. (Setting PS1 serves a similar purpose.)

Exercise 3-9. Look in /bin and /usr/bin to see how many commands are actually shell files. Can you do it with one command? Hint: file(1). How accurate are guesses based on file length? □

3.4 Command arguments and parameters

Although nu is adequate as it stands, most shell programs interpret arguments, so that, for example, filenames and options can be specified when the program is run.

Suppose we want to make a program called cx to change the mode of a file to executable, so

```
$ cx nu
```

is a shorthand for

```
$ chmod +x nu
```

We already know almost enough to do this. We need a file called cx whose contents are

```
chmod +x filename
```

The only new thing we need to know is how to tell cx what the name of the file is, since it will be different each time cx is run.

When the shell executes a file of commands, each occurrence of $1 is replaced by the first argument, each $2 is replaced by the second argument, and so on through $9. So if the file cx contains

```
chmod +x $1
```

when the command

```
$ cx nu
```

is run, the sub-shell replaces "$1" by its first argument, "nu."

Let's look at the whole sequence of operations:

```
$ echo 'chmod +x $1' >cx          Create cx originally
$ sh cx cx                        Make cx itself executable
$ echo echo Hi, there! >hello     Make a test program
$ hello                           Try it
hello: cannot execute
$ cx hello                        Make it executable
$ hello                           Try again
Hi, there!                        It works
$ mv cx /usr/you/bin              Install cx
$ rm hello                        Clean up
$
```

Notice that we said

```
$ sh cx cx
```

exactly as the shell would have automatically done if cx were already executable and we typed

```
$ cx cx
```

What if you want to handle more than one argument, for example to make
a program like cx handle several files at once? A crude first cut is to put nine
arguments into the shell program, as in

```
chmod +x $1 $2 $3 $4 $5 $6 $7 $8 $9
```

(It only works up to $9, because the string $10 is parsed as "first argument,
$1, followed by a 0"!) If the user of this shell file provides fewer than nine
arguments, the missing ones are null strings; the effect is that only the arguments that were actually provided are passed to chmod by the sub-shell. So
this implementation works, but it's obviously unclean, and it fails if more than
nine arguments are provided.

Anticipating this problem, the shell provides a shorthand $* that means "all
the arguments." The proper way to define cx, then, is

```
chmod +x $*
```

which works regardless of how many arguments are provided.

With $* added to your repertoire, you can make some convenient shell
files, such as lc or m:

```
$ cd /usr/you/bin
$ cat lc
# lc: count number of lines in files
wc -l $*
$ cat m
# m: a concise way to type mail
mail $*
$
```

Both can sensibly be used without arguments. If there are no arguments, $*

will be null, and no arguments at all will be passed to wc or mail. With or
without arguments, the command is invoked properly:

```
$ lc /usr/you/bin/*
        1 /usr/you/bin/cx
        2 /usr/you/bin/lc
        2 /usr/you/bin/m
        1 /usr/you/bin/nu
        2 /usr/you/bin/what
        1 /usr/you/bin/where
        9 total
$ ls /usr/you/bin | lc
        6
$
```

These commands and the others in this chapter are examples of *personal*
programs, the sort of things you write for yourself and put in your bin, but
are unlikely to make publicly available because they are too dependent on personal taste. In Chapter 5 we will address the issues of writing shell programs
suitable for public use.

The arguments to a shell file need not be filenames. For example, consider
searching a personal telephone directory. If you have a file named
/usr/you/lib/phone-book that contains lines like

```
dial-a-joke   212-976-3838
dial-a-prayer 212-246-4200
dial santa    212-976-3636
dow jones report  212-976-4141
```

then the grep command can be used to search it. (Your own lib directory is
a good place to store such personal data bases.) Since grep doesn't care about
the format of information, you can search for names, addresses, zip codes or
anything else that you like. Let's make a directory assistance program, which
we'll call 411 in honor of the telephone directory assistance number where we
live:

```
$ echo 'grep $* /usr/you/lib/phone-book' >411
$ cx 411
$ 411 joke
dial-a-joke   212-976-3838
$ 411 dial
dial-a-joke   212-976-3838
dial-a-prayer 212-246-4200
dial santa    212-976-3636
$ 411 'dow jones'
grep: can't open jones               Something is wrong
$
```

The final example is included to show a potential problem: even though dow
jones is presented to 411 as a single argument, it contains a space and is no

longer in quotes, so the sub-shell interpreting the 411 command converts it into two arguments to grep: it's as if you had typed

```
$ grep dow jones /usr/you/lib/phone-book
```

and that's obviously wrong.

One remedy relies on the way the shell treats double quotes. Although anything quoted with '...' is inviolate, the shell looks inside "..." for $'s, \'s, and `...`'s. So if you revise 411 to look like

```
grep "$*" /usr/you/lib/phone-book
```

the $* will be replaced by the arguments, but it will be passed to grep as a single argument even if it contains spaces.

```
$ 411 dow jones
dow jones report  212-976-4141
$
```

By the way, you can make grep (and thus 411) case-independent with the -y option:

```
$ grep -y pattern ...
```

with -y, lower case letters in *pattern* will also match upper case letters in the input. (This option is in 7th Edition grep, but is absent from some other systems.)

There are fine points about command arguments that we are skipping over until Chapter 5, but one is worth noting here. The argument $0 is the name of the program being executed — in cx, $0 is "cx." A novel use of $0 is in the implementation of the programs 2, 3, 4, ..., which print their output in that many columns:

```
$ who | 2
drh        tty0      Sep 28 21:23        cvw        tty5      Sep 28 21:09
dmr        tty6      Sep 28 22:10        scj        tty7      Sep 28 22:11
you        tty9      Sep 28 23:00        jlb        ttyb      Sep 28 19:58
$
```

The implementations of 2, 3, ... are identical; in fact they are links to the same file:

```
$ ln 2 3; ln 2 4; ln 2 5; ln 2 6
$ ls -li [1-9]
16722 -rwxrwxrwx 5 you        51 Sep 28 23:21 2
16722 -rwxrwxrwx 5 you        51 Sep 28 23:21 3
16722 -rwxrwxrwx 5 you        51 Sep 28 23:21 4
16722 -rwxrwxrwx 5 you        51 Sep 28 23:21 5
16722 -rwxrwxrwx 5 you        51 Sep 28 23:21 6
```

```
$ ls /usr/you/bin | 5
2                 3                4              411            5
6                 cx               lc             m              nu
what              where
$ cat 5
# 2, 3, ...:  print in n columns
pr -$0 -t -11 $*
$
```

The -t option turns off the heading at the top of the page and the -1*n* option sets the page length to *n* lines. The name of the program becomes the number-of-columns argument to pr, so the output is printed a row at a time in the number of columns specified by $0.

3.5 Program output as arguments

Let us turn now from command arguments within a shell file to the generation of arguments. Certainly filename expansion from metacharacters like * is the most common way to generate arguments (other than by providing them explicitly), but another good way is by running a program. The output of any program can be placed in a command line by enclosing the invocation in backquotes `...`:

```
$ echo At the tone the time will be `date`.
At the tone the time will be Thu Sep 29 00:02:15 EDT 1983.
$
```

A small change illustrates that `...` is interpreted inside double quotes "...":

```
$ echo "At the tone
> the time will be `date`."
At the tone
the time will be Thu Sep 29 00:03:07 EDT 1983.
$
```

As another example, suppose you want to send mail to a list of people whose login names are in the file mailinglist. A clumsy way to handle this is to edit mailinglist into a suitable mail command and present it to the shell, but it's far easier to say

```
$ mail `cat mailinglist` <letter
```

This runs cat to produce the list of user names, and those become the arguments to mail. (When interpreting output in backquotes as arguments, the shell treats newlines as word separators, not command-line terminators; this subject is discussed fully in Chapter 5.) Backquotes are easy enough to use that there's really no need for a separate mailing-list option to the mail command.

A slightly different approach is to convert the file mailinglist from just a list of names into a program that prints the list of names:

```
$ cat mailinglist                          New version
echo don whr ejs mb
$ cx mailinglist
$ mailinglist
don whr ejs mb
$
```

Now mailing the letter to the people on the list becomes

```
$ mail `mailinglist` <letter
```

With the addition of one more program, it's even possible to modify the user list interactively. The program is called `pick`:

```
$ pick arguments ...
```

presents the *arguments* one at a time and waits after each for a response. The output of `pick` is those arguments selected by `y` (for "yes") responses; any other response causes the argument to be discarded. For example,

```
$ pr `pick *.c` | lpr
```

presents each filename that ends in `.c`; those selected are printed with `pr` and `lpr`. (`pick` is not part of the 7th Edition, but it's so easy and useful that we've included versions of it in Chapters 5 and 6.)

Suppose you have the second version of `mailinglist`. Then

```
$ mail `pick \`mailinglist\`` <letter
don? y
whr?
ejs?
mb? y
$
```

sends the letter to don and mb. Notice that there are nested backquotes; the backslashes prevent the interpretation of the inner `` `...` `` during the parsing of the outer one.

Exercise 3-10. If the backslashes are omitted in

```
$ echo `echo \`date\``
```

what happens? □

Exercise 3-11. Try

```
$ `date`
```

and explain the result. □

Exercise 3-12.

```
$ grep -l pattern filenames
```

lists the filenames in which there was a match of *pattern*, but produces no other output. Try some variations on

```
$ command `grep -l pattern filenames`
```

□

3.6 Shell variables

The shell has variables, like those in most programming languages, which in shell jargon are sometimes called *parameters*. Strings such as $1 are *positional parameters* — variables that hold the arguments to a shell file. The digit indicates the position on the command line. We have seen other shell variables: PATH is the list of directories to search for commands, HOME is your login directory, and so on. Unlike variables in a regular language, the argument variables cannot be changed; although PATH is a variable whose value is $PATH, there is no variable 1 whose value is $1. $1 is nothing more than a compact notation for the first argument.

Leaving positional parameters aside, shell variables can be created, accessed and modified. For example,

```
$ PATH=:/bin:/usr/bin
```

is an assignment that changes the search path. There must be no spaces around the equals sign, and the assigned value must be a single word, which means it must be quoted if it contains shell metacharacters that should not be interpreted. The value of a variable is extracted by preceding the name by a dollar sign:

```
$ PATH=$PATH:/usr/games
$ echo $PATH
:/usr/you/bin:/bin:/usr/bin:/usr/games
$ PATH=:/usr/you/bin:/bin:/usr/bin        Restore it
$
```

Not all variables are special to the shell. You can create new variables by assigning them values; traditionally, variables with special meaning are spelled in upper case, so ordinary names are in lower case. One of the common uses of variables is to remember long strings such as pathnames:

```
$ pwd
/usr/you/bin
$ dir=`pwd`              Remember where we are
$ cd /usr/mary/bin       Go somewhere else
$ ln $dir/cx .           Use the variable in a filename
$ ...                    Work for a while
$ cd $dir                Return
$ pwd
/usr/you/bin
$
```

The shell built-in command set displays the values of all your defined variables. To see just one or two variables, echo is more appropriate.

```
$ set
HOME=/usr/you
IFS=

PATH=:/usr/you/bin:/bin:/usr/bin
PS1=$
PS2=>
dir=/usr/you/bin
$ echo $dir
/usr/you/bin
$
```

The value of a variable is associated with the shell that creates it, and is not automatically passed to the shell's children.

```
$ x=Hello                    Create x
$ sh                         New shell
$ echo $x

                             Newline only: x undefined in the sub-shell
$ ctl-d                      Leave this shell
$                            Back in original shell
$ echo $x
Hello                        x still defined
$
```

This means that a shell file cannot change the value of a variable, because the shell file is run by a sub-shell:

```
$ echo 'x="Good Bye"         Make a two-line shell file ...
> echo $x' >setx             ... to set and print x
$ cat setx
x="Good Bye"
echo $x
$ echo $x
Hello                        x is Hello in original shell
$ sh setx
Good Bye                     x is Good Bye in sub-shell...
$ echo $x
Hello                        ...but still Hello in this shell
$
```

There are times when using a shell file to change shell variables would be useful, however. An obvious example is a file to add a new directory to your PATH. The shell therefore provides a command '.' (dot) that executes the commands in a file in the current shell, rather than in a sub-shell. This was originally invented so people could conveniently re-execute their .profile files without having to log in again, but it has other uses:

```
$ cat /usr/you/bin/games
PATH=$PATH:/usr/games                    Append /usr/games to PATH
$ echo $PATH
:/usr/you/bin:/bin:/usr/bin
$ . games
$ echo $PATH
:/usr/you/bin:/bin:/usr/bin:/usr/games
$
```

The file for the '.' command is searched for with the PATH mechanism, so it can be placed in your bin directory.

When a file is executing with '.', it is only superficially like running a shell file. The file is not "executed" in the usual sense of the word. Instead, the commands in it are interpreted exactly as if you had typed them interactively — the standard input of the shell is temporarily redirected to come from the file. Since the file is read but not executed, it need not have execute permissions. Another difference is that the file does not receive command line arguments; instead, $1, $2 and the rest are empty. It would be nice if arguments were passed, but they are not.

The other way to set the value of a variable in a sub-shell is to assign to it explicitly on the command line *before* the command itself:

```
$ echo 'echo $x' >echox
$ cx echox
$ echo $x
Hello                                    As before
$ echox
                                         x not set in sub-shell
$ x=Hi echox
Hi                                       Value of x passed to sub-shell
$
```

(Originally, assignments anywhere in the command line were passed to the command, but this interfered with dd(1).)

The '.' mechanism should be used to change the value of a variable permanently, while in-line assignments should be used for temporary changes. As an example, consider again searching /usr/games for commands, with the directory not in your PATH:

```
$ ls /usr/games | grep fort
fortune                                  Fortune cookie command
$ fortune
fortune: not found
$ echo $PATH
:/usr/you/bin:/bin:/usr/bin              /usr/games not in PATH
$ PATH=/usr/games fortune
Ring the bell; close the book; quench the candle.
```

```
$ echo $PATH
:/usr/you/bin:/bin:/usr/bin          PATH unchanged
$ cat /usr/you/bin/games
PATH=$PATH:/usr/games                games command still there
$ . games
$ fortune
Premature optimization is the root of all evil - Knuth
$ echo $PATH
:/usr/you/bin:/bin:/usr/bin:/usr/games    PATH changed this time
$
```

It's possible to exploit both these mechanisms in a single shell file. A slightly different games command can be used to run a single game without changing PATH, or can set PATH permanently to include /usr/games:

```
$ cat /usr/you/bin/games
PATH=$PATH:/usr/games $*          Note the $*
$ cx /usr/you/bin/games
$ echo $PATH
:/usr/you/bin:/bin:/usr/bin          Doesn't have /usr/games
$ games fortune
I'd give my right arm to be ambidextrous.
$ echo $PATH
:/usr/you/bin:/bin:/usr/bin          Still doesn't
$ . games
$ echo $PATH
:/usr/you/bin:/bin:/usr/bin:/usr/games    Now it does
$ fortune
He who hesitates is sometimes saved.
$
```

The first call to games ran the shell file in a sub-shell, where PATH was temporarily modified to include /usr/games. The second example instead interpreted the file in the current shell, with $* the empty string, so there was no command on the line, and PATH was modified. Using games in these two ways is tricky, but results in a facility that is convenient and natural to use.

When you want to make the value of a variable accessible in sub-shells, the shell's export command should be used. (You might think about why there is no way to export the value of a variable from a sub-shell to its parent.) Here is one of our earlier examples, this time with the variable exported:

```
$ x=Hello
$ export x
$ sh                              New shell
$ echo $x
Hello                             x known in sub-shell
```

```
$ x='Good Bye'                          Change its value
$ echo $x
Good Bye
$ ctl-d                                 Leave this shell
$                                       Back in original shell
$ echo $x
Hello                                   x still Hello
$
```

export has subtle semantics, but for day-to-day purposes at least, a rule of thumb suffices: don't export temporary variables set for short-term convenience, but always export variables you want set in all your shells and sub-shells (including, for example, shells started with the ed's ! command). Therefore, variables special to the shell, such as PATH and HOME, should be exported.

Exercise 3-13. Why do we always include the current directory in PATH? Where should it be placed? □

3.7 More on I/O redirection

The standard error was invented so that error messages would always appear on the terminal:

```
$ diff file1 fiel2 >diff.out
diff: fiel2: No such file or directory
$
```

It's certainly desirable that error messages work this way — it would be most unfortunate if they disappeared into diff.out, leaving you with the impression that the erroneous diff command had worked properly.

Every program has three default files established when it starts, numbered by small integers called *file descriptors* (which we will return to in Chapter 7). The standard input, 0, and the standard output, 1, which we are already familiar with, are often redirected from and into files and pipes. The last, numbered 2, is the *standard error* output, and normally finds its way to your terminal.

Sometimes programs produce output on the standard error even when they work properly. One common example is the program time, which runs a command and then reports on the standard error how much time it took.

```
$ time wc ch3.1
     931    4288    22691 ch3.1

real         1.0
user         0.4
sys          0.4
```

```
$ time wc ch3.1 >wc.out

real        2.0
user        0.4
sys         0.3
$ time wc ch3.1 >wc.out 2>time.out
$ cat time.out

real        1.0
user        0.4
sys         0.3
$
```

The construction 2>*filename* (no spaces are allowed between the 2 and the >)
directs the standard error output into the file; it's syntactically graceless but it
does the job. (The times produced by time are not very accurate for such a
short test as this one, but for a sequence of longer tests the numbers are useful
and reasonably trustworthy, and you might well want to save them for further
analysis; see, for example, Table 8.1.)

It is also possible to merge the two output streams:

```
$ time wc ch3.1 >wc.out 2>&1
$ cat wc.out
    931    4288    22691 ch3.1

real        1.0
user        0.4
sys         0.3
$
```

The notation 2>&1 tells the shell to put the standard error on the same stream
as the standard output. There is not much mnemonic value to the ampersand;
it's simply an idiom to be learned. You can also use 1>&2 to add the standard
output to the standard error:

```
echo ... 1>&2
```

prints on the standard error. In shell files, it prevents the messages from van-
ishing accidentally down a pipe or into a file.

The shell provides a mechanism so you can put the standard input for a
command along with the command, rather than in a separate file, so the shell
file can be completely self-contained. Our directory information program 411
could be written

```
$ cat 411
grep "$*" <<End
dial-a-joke   212-976-3838
dial-a-prayer   212-246-4200
dial santa   212-976-3636
dow jones report   212-976-4141
End
$
```

The shell jargon for this construction is a *here document*; it means that the
input is right here instead of in a file somewhere. The << signals the construction; the word that follows (End in our example) is used to delimit the input,
which is taken to be everything up to an occurrence of that word on a line by
itself. The shell substitutes for $, `...`, and \ in a here document, unless
some part of the word is quoted with quotes or a backslash; in that case, the
whole document is taken literally.

We'll return to here documents at the end of the chapter, with a much more
interesting example.

Table 3.2 lists the various input-output redirections that the shell understands.

Exercise 3-14. Compare the here-document version of 411 with the original. Which is
easier to maintain? Which is a better basis for a general service? □

Table 3.2: Shell I/O Redirections	
>*file*	direct standard output to *file*
>>*file*	append standard output to *file*
<*file*	take standard input from *file*
p_1 ┆ p_2	connect standard output of program p_1 to input of p_2
^	obsolete synonym for ┆
n>*file*	direct output from file descriptor *n* to *file*
n>>*file*	append output from file descriptor *n* to *file*
n>&*m*	merge output from file descriptor *n* with file descriptor *m*
n<&*m*	merge input from file descriptor *n* with file descriptor *m*
<<*s*	here document: take standard input until next *s* at beginning of a line; substitute for $, `...`, and \
<<*s*	here document with no substitution
<<'*s*'	here document with no substitution

3.8 Looping in shell programs

The shell is actually a programming language: it has variables, loops,
decision-making, and so on. We will discuss basic looping here, and talk more
about control flow in Chapter 5.

Looping over a set of filenames is very common, and the shell's `for` statement is the only shell control-flow statement that you might commonly type at
the terminal rather than putting in a file for later execution. The syntax is:

```
for var in list of words
do
            commands
done
```

For example, a `for` statement to echo filenames one per line is just

```
$ for i in *
> do
>        echo $i
> done
```

The "i" can be any shell variable, although i is traditional. Note that the
variable's value is accessed by `$i`, but that the `for` loop refers to the variable
as `i`. We used `*` to pick up all the files in the current directory, but any other
list of arguments can be used. Normally you want to do something more
interesting than merely printing filenames. One thing we do frequently is to
compare a set of files with previous versions. For example, to compare the old
version of Chapter 2 (kept in directory `old`) with the current one:

```
$ ls ch2.* | 5
ch2.1          ch2.2          ch2.3          ch2.4          ch2.5
ch2.6          ch2.7
$ for i in ch2.*
> do
>        echo $i:
>        diff -b old/$i $i
>        echo                        Add a blank line for readability
> done | pr -h "diff `pwd`/old `pwd`" | lpr &
3712                                   Process-id
$
```

We piped the output into `pr` and `lpr` just to illustrate that it's possible: the
standard output of the programs within a `for` goes to the standard output of
the `for` itself. We put a fancy heading on the output with the `-h` option of
`pr`, using two embedded calls of `pwd`. And we set the whole sequence running
asynchronously (`&`) so we wouldn't have to wait for it; the `&` applies to the
entire loop and pipeline.

We prefer to format a `for` statement as shown, but you can compress it
somewhat. The main limitations are that `do` and `done` are only recognized as
keywords when they appear right after a newline or semicolon. Depending on
the size of the `for`, it's sometimes better to write it all on one line:

```
for i in list; do commands; done
```

You should use the `for` loop for multiple commands, or where the built-in

argument processing in individual commands is not suitable. But don't use it
when the individual command will already loop over filenames:

```
# Poor idea:
for i in $*
do
        chmod +x $i
done
```

is inferior to

```
chmod +x $*
```

because the `for` loop executes a separate `chmod` for each file, which is more
expensive in computer resources. (Be sure that you understand the difference
between

```
for i in *
```

which loops over all filenames in the current directory, and

```
for i in $*
```

which loops over all arguments to the shell file.)

The argument list for a `for` most often comes from pattern matching on
filenames, but it can come from anything. It could be

```
$ for i in `cat ...`
```

or arguments could just be typed. For example, earlier in this chapter we
created a group of programs for multi-column printing, called 2, 3, and so on.
These are just links to a single file that can be made, once the file 2 has been
written, by

```
$ for i in 3 4 5 6; do ln 2 $i; done
$
```

As a somewhat more interesting use of the `for`, we could use `pick` to
select which files to compare with those in the backup directory:

```
$ for i in `pick ch2.*`
> do
>         echo $i:
>         diff old/$i $i
> done | pr | lpr
ch2.1? y
ch2.2?
ch2.3?
ch2.4? y
ch2.5? y
ch2.6?
ch2.7?
$
```

It's obvious that this loop should be placed in a shell file to save typing next time: if you've done something twice, you're likely to do it again.

Exercise 3-15. If the `diff` loop were placed in a shell file, would you put the `pick` in the shell file? Why or why not? □

Exercise 3-16. What happens if the last line of the loop above is

```
> done | pr | lpr &
```

that is, ends with an ampersand? See if you can figure it out, then try it. □

3.9 `bundle`: **putting it all together**

To give something of the flavor of how shell files develop, let's work through a larger example. Pretend you have received mail from a friend on another machine, say `somewhere!bob`,† who would like copies of the shell files in your `bin`. The simplest way to send them is by return mail, so you might start by typing

```
$ cd /usr/you/bin
$ for i in `pick *`
> do
>         echo ============ This is file $i ============
>         cat $i
> done | mail somewhere!bob
$
```

But look at it from `somewhere!bob`'s viewpoint: he's going to get a mail message with all the files clearly demarcated, but he'll need to use an editor to break them into their component files. The flash of insight is that a properly-constructed mail message could automatically unpack itself so the recipient needn't do any work. That implies it should be a shell file containing both the

---

† There are several notations for remote machine addresses. The form *machine!person* is most common. See `mail(1)`.

files and the instructions to unpack it.

A second insight is that the shell's here documents are a convenient way to combine a command invocation and the data for the command. The rest of the job is just getting the quotes right. Here's a working program, called `bundle`, that groups the files together into a self-explanatory shell file on its standard output:

```
$ cat bundle
# bundle:  group files into distribution package

echo '# To unbundle, sh this file'
for i
do
        echo "echo $i 1>&2"
        echo "cat >$i <<'End of $i'"
        cat $i
        echo "End of $i"
done
$
```

Quoting "End of $i" ensures that any shell metacharacters in the files will be ignored.

Naturally, you should try it out before inflicting it on somewhere!bob:

```
$ bundle cx lc >junk                    Make a trial bundle
$ cat junk
# To unbundle, sh this file
echo cx 1>&2
cat >cx <<'End of cx'
chmod +x $*
End of cx
echo lc 1>&2
cat >lc <<'End of lc'
# lc: count number of lines in files
wc -l $*
End of lc
$ mkdir test
$ cd test
$ sh ../junk                            Try it out
cx
lc
$ ls
cx
lc
```

```
$ cat cx
chmod +x $*
$ cat lc
# lc: count number of lines in files
wc -l $*                                          Looks good
$ cd ..
$ rm junk test/*; rmdir test                      Clean up
$ pwd
/usr/you/bin
$ bundle `pick *` | mail somewhere!bob            Send the files
```

There's a problem if one of the files you're sending happens to contain a line of the form

End of *filename*

but it's a low-probability event. To make bundle utterly safe, we need a thing or two from later chapters, but it's eminently usable and convenient as it stands.

bundle illustrates much of the flexibility of the UNIX environment: it uses shell loops, I/O redirection, here documents and shell files, it interfaces directly to mail, and, perhaps most interesting, it is a program that creates a program. It's one of the prettiest shell programs we know — a few lines of code that do something simple, useful and elegant.

Exercise 3-17. How would you use bundle to send all the files in a directory and its subdirectories? Hint: shell files can be recursive. □

Exercise 3-18. Modify bundle so it includes with each file the information garnered from ls -l, particularly permissions and date of last change. Contrast the facilities of bundle with the archive program ar(1). □

3.10 Why a programmable shell?

The UNIX shell isn't typical of command interpreters: although it lets you run commands in the usual way, because it is a programming language it can accomplish much more. It's worth a brief look back at what we've seen, in part because there's a lot of material in this chapter but more because we promised to talk about "commonly used features" and then wrote about 30 pages of shell programming examples. But when using the shell you write little one-line programs all the time: a pipeline is a program, as is our "Tea is ready" example. The shell works like that: you program it constantly, but it's so easy and natural (once you're familiar with it) that you don't think of it as programming.

The shell does some things, like looping, I/O redirection with < and >, and filename expansion with *, so that no program need worry about them, and more importantly, so that the application of these facilities is uniform across all programs. Other features, such as shell files and pipes, are really provided by the kernel, but the shell gives a natural syntax for creating them. They go beyond convenience, to actually increasing the capabilities of the system.

Much of the power and convenience of the shell derives from the UNIX kernel underneath it; for example, although the shell sets up pipes, the kernel actually moves the data through them. The way the system treats executable files makes it possible to write shell files so that they are run exactly like compiled programs. The user needn't be aware that they are command files — they aren't invoked with a special command like RUN. Also, the shell is a program itself, not part of the kernel, so it can be tuned, extended and used like any other program. This idea is not unique to the UNIX system, but it has been exploited better there than anywhere else.

In Chapter 5, we'll return to the subject of shell programming, but you should keep in mind that whatever you're doing with the shell, you're programming it — that's largely why it works so well.

History and bibliographic notes

The shell has been programmable from earliest times. Originally there were separate commands for `if`, `goto`, and labels, and the `goto` command operated by scanning the input file from the beginning looking for the right label. (Because it is not possible to re-read a pipe, it was not possible to pipe into a shell file that had any control flow).

The 7th Edition shell was written originally by Steve Bourne with some help and ideas from John Mashey. It contains everything needed for programming, as we shall see in Chapter 5. In addition, input and output are rationalized: it is possible to redirect I/O into and out of shell programs without limit. The parsing of filename metacharacters is also internal to this shell; it had been a separate program in earlier versions, which had to live on very small machines.

One other major shell that you may run into (you may already be using it by preference) is `csh`, the so-called "C shell" developed at Berkeley by Bill Joy by building on the 6th Edition shell. The C shell has gone further than the Bourne shell in the direction of helping interaction — most notably, it provides a history mechanism that permits shorthand repetition (perhaps with slight editing) of previously issued commands. The syntax is also somewhat different. But because it is based on an earlier shell, it has less of the programming convenience; it is more an interactive command interpreter than a programming language. In particular, it is not possible to pipe into or out of control flow constructs.

`pick` was invented by Tom Duff, and `bundle` was invented independently by Alan Hewett and James Gosling.

There is a large family of UNIX programs that read some input, perform a simple transformation on it, and write some output. Examples include `grep` and `tail` to select part of the input, `sort` to sort it, `wc` to count it, and so on. Such programs are called *filters*.

This chapter discusses the most frequently used filters. We begin with `grep`, concentrating on patterns more complicated than those illustrated in Chapter 1. We will also present two other members of the `grep` family, `egrep` and `fgrep`.

The next section briefly describes a few other useful filters, including `tr` for character transliteration, `dd` for dealing with data from other systems, and `uniq` for detecting repeated text lines. `sort` is also presented in more detail than in Chapter 1.

The remainder of the chapter is devoted to two general purpose "data transformers" or "programmable filters." They are called programmable because the particular transformation is expressed as a program in a simple programming language. Different programs can produce very different transformations.

The programs are `sed`, which stands for *stream editor*, and `awk`, named after its authors. Both are derived from a generalization of `grep`:

$ *program pattern-action filenames ...*

scans the files in sequence, looking for lines that match a pattern; when one is found a corresponding action is performed. For `grep`, the pattern is a regular expression as in `ed`, and the default action is to print each line that matches the pattern.

`sed` and `awk` generalize both the patterns and the actions. `sed` is a derivative of `ed` that takes a "program" of editor commands and streams data from the files past them, doing the commands of the program on every line. `awk` is not as convenient for text substitution as `sed` is, but it includes arithmetic, variables, built-in functions, and a programming language that looks quite a bit like C. This chapter doesn't have the complete story on either program; Volume 2B of the UNIX *Programmer's Manual* has tutorials on both.

4.1 The `grep` family

We mentioned `grep` briefly in Chapter 1, and have used it in examples since then.

```
$ grep pattern filenames...
```

searches the named files or the standard input and prints each line that contains an instance of the *pattern*. `grep` is invaluable for finding occurrences of variables in programs or words in documents, or for selecting parts of the output of a program:

```
$ grep -n variable *.[ch]          Locate variable in C source
$ grep From $MAIL                  Print message headers in mailbox
$ grep From $MAIL | grep -v mary   Headers that didn't come from mary
$ grep -y mary $HOME/lib/phone-book   Find mary's phone number
$ who | grep mary                  See if mary is logged in
$ ls | grep -v temp                Filenames that don't contain temp
```

The option `-n` prints line numbers, `-v` inverts the sense of the test, and `-y` makes lower case letters in the pattern match letters of either case in the file (upper case still matches only upper case).

In all the examples we've seen so far, `grep` has looked for ordinary strings of letters and numbers. But `grep` can actually search for much more complicated patterns: `grep` interprets expressions in a simple language for describing strings.

Technically, the patterns are a slightly restricted form of the string specifiers called *regular expressions*. `grep` interprets the same regular expressions as `ed`; in fact, `grep` was originally created (in an evening) by straightforward surgery on `ed`.

Regular expressions are specified by giving special meaning to certain characters, just like the `*`, etc., used by the shell. There are a few more metacharacters, and, regrettably, differences in meanings. Table 4.1 shows all the regular expression metacharacters, but we will review them briefly here.

The metacharacters `^` and `$` "anchor" the pattern to the beginning (`^`) or end (`$`) of the line. For example,

```
$ grep From $MAIL
```

locates lines containing `From` in your mailbox, but

```
$ grep '^From' $MAIL
```

prints lines that *begin* with `From`, which are more likely to be message header lines. Regular expression metacharacters overlap with shell metacharacters, so it's always a good idea to enclose `grep` patterns in single quotes.

`grep` supports *character classes* much like those in the shell, so `[a-z]` matches any lower case letter. But there are differences; if a `grep` character class begins with a circumflex `^`, the pattern matches any character *except*

those in the class. Therefore, [^0-9] matches any non-digit. Also, in the
shell a backslash protects] and - in a character class, but grep and ed
require that these characters appear where their meaning is unambiguous. For
example, [][-] (sic) matches either an opening or closing square bracket or a
minus sign.

A period '.' is equivalent to the shell's ?: it matches any character. (The
period is probably the character with the most different meanings to different
UNIX programs.) Here are a couple of examples:

```
$ ls -l | grep '^d'                 List subdirectory names
$ ls -l | grep '^.......rw'         List files others can read and write
```

The '^' and seven periods match any seven characters at the beginning of the
line, which when applied the output of ls -l means any permission string.

The *closure* operator * applies to the previous character or metacharacter
(including a character class) in the expression, and collectively they match any
number of successive matches of the character or metacharacter. For example,
x* matches a sequence of x's as long as possible, [a-zA-Z]* matches an
alphabetic string, .* matches anything up to a newline, and .*x matches anything up to and including the *last* x on the line.

There are a couple of important things to note about closures. First, closure applies to only one character, so xy* matches an x followed by y's, not a
sequence like xyxyxy. Second, "any number" includes zero, so if you want at
least one character to be matched, you must duplicate it. For example, to
match a string of letters the correct expression is [a-zA-Z][a-zA-Z]* (a
letter followed by zero or more letters). The shell's * filename matching character is similar to the regular expression .*.

No grep regular expression matches a newline; the expressions are applied
to each line individually.

With regular expressions, grep is a simple programming language. For
example, recall that the second field of the password file is the encrypted password. This command searches for users without passwords:

```
$ grep '^[^:]*::' /etc/passwd
```

The pattern is: beginning of line, any number of non-colons, double colon.

grep is actually the oldest of a family of programs, the other members of
which are called fgrep and egrep. Their basic behavior is the same, but
fgrep searches for many literal strings simultaneously, while egrep interprets
true regular expressions — the same as grep, but with an "or" operator and
parentheses to group expressions, explained below.

Both fgrep and egrep accept a -f option to specify a file from which to
read the pattern. In the file, newlines separate patterns to be searched for in
parallel. If there are words you habitually misspell, for example, you could
check your documents for their occurrence by keeping them in a file, one per
line, and using fgrep:

```
$ fgrep -f common-errors document
```

The regular expressions interpreted by `egrep` (also listed in Table 4.1) are the same as in `grep`, with a couple of additions. Parentheses can be used to group, so `(xy)*` matches any of the empty string, `xy`, `xyxy`, `xyxyxy` and so on. The vertical bar `|` is an "or" operator; `today|tomorrow` matches either `today` or `tomorrow`, as does `to(day|morrow)`. Finally, there are two other closure operators in `egrep`, `+` and `?`. The pattern `x+` matches one or more `x`'s, and `x?` matches zero or one `x`, but no more.

  `egrep` is excellent at word games that involve searching the dictionary for words with special properties. Our dictionary is Webster's Second International, and is stored on-line as the list of words, one per line, without definitions. Your system may have `/usr/dict/words`, a smaller dictionary intended for checking spelling; look at it to check the format. Here's a pattern to find words that contain all five vowels in alphabetical order:

```
$ cat alphvowels
^[^aeiou]*a[^aeiou]*e[^aeiou]*i[^aeiou]*o[^aeiou]*u[^aeiou]*$
$ egrep -f alphvowels /usr/dict/web2 | 3
abstemious          abstemiously        abstentious
acheilous           acheirous           acleistous
affectious          annelidous          arsenious
arterious           bacterious          caesious
facetious           facetiously         fracedinous
majestious
$
```

The pattern is not enclosed in quotes in the file `alphvowels`. When quotes are used to enclose `egrep` patterns, the shell protects the commands from interpretation but strips off the quotes; `egrep` never sees them. Since the file is not examined by the shell, however, quotes are *not* used around its contents. We could have used `grep` for this example, but because of the way `egrep` works, it is much faster when searching for patterns that include closures, especially when scanning large files.

  As another example, to find all words of six or more letters that have the letters in alphabetical order:

```
$ cat monotonic
^a?b?c?d?e?f?g?h?i?j?k?l?m?n?o?p?q?r?s?t?u?v?w?x?y?z?$
$ egrep -f monotonic /usr/dict/web2 | grep '......' | 5
abdest      acknow      adipsy      agnosy      almost
befist      behint      beknow      bijoux      biopsy
chintz      dehors      dehort      deinos      dimpsy
egilops     ghosty
$
```

(Egilops is a disease that attacks wheat.) Notice the use of `grep` to filter the output of `egrep`.

Why are there three `grep` programs? `fgrep` interprets no metacharacters, but can look efficiently for thousands of words in parallel (once initialized, its running time is independent of the number of words), and thus is used primarily for tasks like bibliographic searches. The size of typical `fgrep` patterns is beyond the capacity of the algorithms used in `grep` and `egrep`. The distinction between `grep` and `egrep` is harder to justify. `grep` came much earlier, uses the regular expressions familiar from `ed`, and has tagged regular expressions and a wider set of options. `egrep` interprets more general expressions (except for tagging), and runs significantly faster (with speed independent of the pattern), but the standard version takes longer to start when the expression is complicated. A newer version exists that starts immediately, so `egrep` and `grep` could now be combined into a single pattern matching program.

Table 4.1: `grep` and `egrep` Regular Expressions (decreasing order of precedence)	
c	any non-special character *c* matches itself
c	turn off any special meaning of character *c*
^	beginning of line
$	end of line
.	any single character
[...]	any one of characters in ...; ranges like `a-z` are legal
[^...]	any single character not in ...; ranges are legal
n	what the *n*'th \\(...\\) matched (`grep` only)
r∗	zero or more occurrences of *r*
r+	one or more occurrences of *r* (`egrep` only)
r?	zero or one occurrences of *r* (`egrep` only)
r1r2	*r1* followed by *r2*
r1¦*r2*	*r1* or *r2* (`egrep` only)
\\(*r*\\)	tagged regular expression *r* (`grep` only); can be nested
(*r*)	regular expression *r* (`egrep` only); can be nested
No regular expression matches a newline.	

Exercise 4-1. Look up tagged regular expressions (\\(and \\)) in Appendix 1 or `ed`(1), and use `grep` to search for palindromes — words spelled the same backwards as forwards. Hint: write a different pattern for each length of word. □

Exercise 4-2. The structure of `grep` is to read a single line, check for a match, then loop. How would `grep` be affected if regular expressions could match newlines? □

4.2 Other filters

The purpose of this section is to alert you to the existence and possibilities of the rich set of small filters provided by the system, and to give a few examples of their use. This list is by no means all-inclusive — there are many more that were part of the 7th Edition, and each installation creates some of its own. All of the standard ones are described in Section 1 of the manual.

We begin with `sort`, which is probably the most useful of all. The basics of `sort` were covered in Chapter 1: it sorts its input by line in ASCII order. Although this is the obvious thing to do by default, there are lots of other ways that one might want data sorted, and `sort` tries to cater to them by providing lots of different options. For example, the `-f` option causes upper and lower case to be "folded," so case distinctions are eliminated. The `-d` option (dictionary order) ignores all characters except letters, digits and blanks in comparisons.

Although alphabetic comparisons are most common, sometimes a numeric comparison is needed. The `-n` option sorts by numeric value, and the `-r` option reverses the sense of any comparison. So,

```
$ ls ! sort -f           Sort filenames in alphabetic order
$ ls -s ! sort -n        Sort with smallest files first
$ ls -s ! sort -nr       Sort with largest files first
```

`sort` normally sorts on the entire line, but it can be told to direct its attention only to specific fields. The notation *+m* means that the comparison skips the first *m* fields; +0 is the beginning of the line. So, for example,

```
$ ls -l ! sort +3nr      Sort by byte count, largest first
$ who ! sort +4n         Sort by time of login, oldest first
```

Other useful `sort` options include `-o`, which specifies a filename for the output (it can be one of the input files), and `-u`, which suppresses all but one of each group of lines that are identical in the sort fields.

Multiple sort keys can be used, as illustrated by this cryptic example from the manual page `sort(1)`:

```
$ sort +0f +0 -u filenames
```

`+0f` sorts the line, folding upper and lower case together, but lines that are identical may not be adjacent. So `+0` is a secondary key that sorts the equal lines from the first sort into normal ASCII order. Finally, `-u` discards any adjacent duplicates. Therefore, given a list of words, one per line, the command prints the unique words. The index for this book was prepared with a similar `sort` command, using even more of `sort`'s capabilities. See `sort(1)`.

The command `uniq` is the inspiration for the `-u` flag of `sort`: it discards all but one of each group of adjacent duplicate lines. Having a separate program for this function allows it to do tasks unrelated to sorting. For example, `uniq` will remove multiple blank lines whether its input is sorted or not.

Options invoke special ways to process the duplications: `uniq -d` prints only those lines that are duplicated; `uniq -u` prints only those that are unique (i.e., not duplicated); and `uniq -c` counts the number of occurrences of each line. We'll see an example shortly.

The `comm` command is a file comparison program. Given two *sorted* input files `f1` and `f2`, `comm` prints three columns of output: lines that occur only in `f1`, lines that occur only in `f2`, and lines that occur in both files. Any of these columns can be suppressed by an option:

```
$ comm -12 f1 f2
```

prints only those lines that are in both files, and

```
$ comm -23 f1 f2
```

prints the lines that are in the first file but not in the second. This is useful for comparing directories and for comparing a word list with a dictionary.

The `tr` command transliterates the characters in its input. By far the most common use of `tr` is case conversion:

```
$ tr a-z A-Z          Map lower case to upper
$ tr A-Z a-z          Map upper case to lower
```

The `dd` command is rather different from all of the other commands we have looked at. It is intended primarily for processing tape data from other systems — its very name is a reminder of OS/360 job control language. `dd` will do case conversion (with a syntax very different from `tr`); it will convert from ASCII to EBCDIC and vice versa; and it will read or write data in the fixed size records with blank padding that characterize non-UNIX systems. In practice, `dd` is often used to deal with raw, unformatted data, whatever the source; it encapsulates a set of facilities for dealing with binary data.

To illustrate what can be accomplished by combining filters, consider the following pipeline, which prints the 10 most frequent words in its input:

```
cat $* |
tr -sc A-Za-z '\012' |      Compress runs of non-letters into newline
sort |
uniq -c |
sort -n |
tail |
5
```

`cat` collects the files, since `tr` only reads its standard input. The `tr` command is from the manual: it compresses adjacent non-letters into newlines, thus converting the input into one word per line. The words are then sorted and `uniq -c` compresses each group of identical words into one line prefixed by a count, which becomes the sort field for `sort -n`. (This combination of two `sort`s around a `uniq` occurs often enough to be called an idiom.) The result is the unique words in the document, sorted in increasing frequency. `tail` selects the 10 most common words (the end of the sorted list) and 5 prints them in five columns.

By the way, notice that ending a line with ¦ is a valid way to continue it.

Exercise 4-3. Use the tools in this section to write a simple spelling checker, using `/usr/dict/words`. What are its shortcomings, and how would you address them? □

Exercise 4-4. Write a word-counting program in your favorite programming language and compare its size, speed and maintainability with the word-counting pipeline. How easily can you convert it into a spelling checker? □

4.3 The stream editor `sed`

Let us now turn to `sed`. Since it is derived directly from `ed`, it should be easy to learn, and it will consolidate your knowledge of `ed`.

The basic idea of `sed` is simple:

```
$ sed 'list of ed commands' filenames ...
```

reads lines one at a time from the input files; it applies the commands from the list, in order, to each line and writes its edited form on the standard output. So, for instance, you can change UNIX to UNIX(TM) everywhere it occurs in a set of files with

```
$ sed 's/UNIX/UNIX(TM)/g' filenames ... >output
```

Do not misinterpret what happens here. `sed` does *not* alter the contents of its input files. It writes on the standard output, so the original files are not changed. By now you have enough shell experience to realize that

```
$ sed '...' file >file
```

is a bad idea: to replace the contents of files, you must use a temporary file, or another program. (We will talk later about a program to encapsulate the idea of overwriting an existing file; look at `overwrite` in Chapter 5.)

`sed` outputs each line automatically, so no p was needed after the substitution command above; indeed, if there had been one, each modified line would have been printed twice. Quotes are almost always necessary, however, since so many `sed` metacharacters mean something to the shell as well. For example, consider using `du -a` to generate a list of filenames. Normally, `du` prints the size and the filename:

```
$ du -a ch4.*
18      ch4.1
13      ch4.2
14      ch4.3
17      ch4.4
2       ch4.9
$
```

You can use `sed` to discard the size part, but the editing command needs quotes to protect a * and a tab from being interpreted by the shell:

```
$ du -a ch4.* | sed 's/.*→//'
ch4.1
ch4.2
ch4.3
ch4.4
ch4.9
$
```

The substitution deletes all characters (. *) up to and including the rightmost tab (shown in the pattern as →).

In a similar way, you could select the user names and login times from the output of who:

```
$ who
lr          tty1      Sep 29 07:14
ron         tty3      Sep 29 10:31
you         tty4      Sep 29 08:36
td          tty5      Sep 29 08:47
$ who | sed 's/ .* / /'
lr 07:14
ron 10:31
you 08:36
td 08:47
$
```

The s command replaces a blank and everything that follows it (as much as possible, including more blanks) up to another blank by a single blank. Again, quotes are needed.

Almost the same sed command can be used to make a program getname that will return your user name:

```
$ cat getname
who am i | sed 's/ .*//'
$ getname
you
$
```

Another sed sequence is used so frequently that we have made it into a shell file called ind. The ind command indents its input one tab stop; it is handy for moving something over to fit better onto line-printer paper.

The implementation of ind is easy — stick a tab at the front of each line:

```
sed 's/^/→/' $*                           Version 1 of ind
```

This version even puts a tab on each empty line, which seems unnecessary. A better version uses sed's ability to select the lines to be modified. If you prefix a pattern to the command, only the lines that match the pattern will be affected:

```
        sed '/./s/^/→/' $*                      Version 2 of ind
```

The pattern `/./` matches any line that has at least one character on it other than a newline; the `s` command is done for those lines but not for empty lines. Remember that `sed` outputs all lines regardless of whether they were changed, so the empty lines are still produced as they should be.

There's yet another way that `ind` could be written. It is possible to do the commands only on lines that *don't* match the selection pattern, by preceding the command with an exclamation mark '`!`'. In

```
        sed '/^$/!s/^/→/' $*                    Version 3 of ind
```

the pattern `/^$/` matches empty lines (the end of the line immediately follows the beginning), so `/^$/!` says, "don't do the command on empty lines."

As we said above, `sed` prints each line automatically, regardless of what was done to it (unless it was deleted). Furthermore, most `ed` commands can be used. So it's easy to write a `sed` program that will print the first three (say) lines of its input, then quit:

```
        sed 3q
```

Although `3q` is not a legal `ed` command, it makes sense in `sed`: copy lines, then quit after the third one.

You might want to do other processing to the data, such as indent it. One way is to run the output from `sed` through `ind`, but since `sed` accepts multiple commands, it can be done with a single (somewhat unlikely) invocation of `sed`:

```
        sed 's/^/→/
             3q'
```

Notice where the quotes and the newline are: the commands have to be on separate lines, but `sed` ignores leading blanks and tabs.

With these ideas, it might seem sensible to write a program, called `head`, to print the first few lines of each filename argument. But `sed 3q` (or `10q`) is so easy to type that we've never felt the need. We do, however, have an `ind`, since its equivalent `sed` command is harder to type. (In the process of writing this book we replaced the existing 30-line C program by version 2 of the one-line implementations shown earlier). There is no clear criterion for when it's worth making a separate command from a complicated command line; the best rule we've found is to put it in your `bin` and see if you actually use it.

It's also possible to put `sed` commands in a file and execute them from there, with

```
        $ sed -f cmdfile ...
```

You can use line selectors other than numbers like 3:

```
$ sed '/pattern/q'
```

prints its input up to and including the first line matching *pattern*, and

```
$ sed '/pattern/d'
```

deletes every line that contains *pattern*; the deletion happens before the line is automatically printed, so deleted lines are discarded. Although automatic printing is usually convenient, sometimes it gets in the way. It can be turned off by the −n option; in that case, only lines explicitly printed with a p command appear in the output. For example,

```
$ sed -n '/pattern/p'
```

does what grep does. Since the matching condition can be inverted by following it with !,

```
$ sed -n '/pattern/!p'
```

is grep −v. (So is sed '*/pattern/*d'.)

Why do we have both sed and grep? After all, grep is just a simple special case of sed. Part of the reason is history — grep came well before sed. But grep survives, and indeed thrives, because for the particular job that they both do, it is significantly easier to use than sed is: it does the common case about as succinctly as possible. (It also does a few things that sed won't; look at the −b option, for instance.) Programs do die, however. There was once a program called gres that did simple substitution, but it expired almost immediately when sed was born.

Newlines can be inserted with sed, using the same syntax as in ed:

```
$ sed 's/$/\
> /'
```

adds a newline to the end of each line, thus double-spacing its input, and

```
$ sed 's/[ →][ →]*/\
> /g'
```

replaces each string of blanks or tabs with a newline and thus splits its input into one word per line. (The regular expression '[→]' matches a blank or tab; '[→]*' matches zero or more of these, so the whole pattern matches one or more blanks and/or tabs.)

You can also use pairs of regular expressions or line numbers to select a *range* of lines over which any one of the commands will operate.

```
$ sed -n '20,30p'          Print only lines 20 through 30
$ sed '1,10d'              Delete lines 1 through 10 (= tail +11)
$ sed '1,/^$/d'            Delete up to and including first blank line
$ sed -n '/^$/,/^end/p'    Print each group of lines from
                              an empty line to line starting with end
$ sed '$d'                 Delete last line
```

Line numbers go from the beginning of the input; they do not reset at the beginning of a new file.

There is a fundamental limitation of sed that is not shared by ed, however: relative line numbers are not supported. In particular, + and − are not understood in line number expressions, so it is impossible to reach backwards in the input:

```
$ sed '$-1d'                       Illegal: can't refer backward
Unrecognized command: $-1d
$
```

Once a line is read, the previous line is gone forever: there is no way to identify the next-to-last line, which is what this command requires. (In fairness, there is a way to handle this with sed, but it is pretty advanced. Look up the "hold" command in the manual.) There is also no way to do relative addressing forward:

```
$ sed '/thing/+1d'                 Illegal:  can't refer forward
```

sed provides the ability to write on multiple output files. For example,

```
$ sed -n '/pat/w file1
>           /pat/!w file2' filenames ...
$
```

writes lines matching *pat* on file1 and lines not matching *pat* on file2. Or, to revisit our first example,

```
$ sed 's/UNIX/UNIX(TM)/gw u.out' filenames ... >output
```

writes the entire output to file output as before, but also writes just the changed lines to file u.out.

Sometimes it's necessary to cooperate with the shell to get shell file arguments into the middle of a sed command. One example is the program newer, which lists all files in a directory that are newer than a specified one.

```
$ cat newer
# newer f:  list files newer than f
ls -t | sed '/^'$1'$/q'
$
```

The quotes protect the various special characters aimed at sed, while leaving the $1 exposed so the shell will replace it by the filename. An alternate way to write the argument is

Table 4.2: Summary of `sed` Commands

`a\`	append lines to output until one not ending in `\`
`b` *label*	branch to command : *label*
`c\`	change lines to following text as in `a`
`d`	delete line; read next input line
`i\`	insert following text before next output
`l`	list line, making all non-printing characters visible
`p`	print line
`q`	quit
`r` *file*	read *file*, copy contents to output
`s/`*old*`/`*new*`/`*f*	substitute *new* for *old*. If *f*=`g`, replace all occurrences; *f*=`p`, print; *f*=`w` *file*, write to *file*
`t` *label*	test: branch to *label* if substitution made to current line
`w` *file*	write line to *file*
`y/`*str1*`/`*str2*`/`	replace each character from *str1* with corresponding character from *str2* (no ranges allowed)
`=`	print current input line number
`!`*cmd*	do `sed` *cmd* only if line is not selected
`:` *label*	set label for `b` and `t` commands
`{`	treat commands up to matching `}` as a group

```
"/^$1\$/q"
```

since the `$1` will be replaced by the argument while the `\$` becomes just `$`.

In the same way, we can write `older`, which lists all the files older than the named one:

```
$ cat older
# older f:  list files older than f
ls -tr | sed '/^'$1'$/q'
$
```

The only difference is the `-r` option on `ls`, to reverse the order.

Although `sed` will do much more than we have illustrated, including testing conditions, looping and branching, remembering previous lines, and of course many of the `ed` commands described in Appendix 1, most of the use of `sed` is similar to what we have shown here — one or two simple editing commands — rather than long or complicated sequences. Table 4.2 summarizes some of `sed`'s capabilities, although it omits the multi-line functions.

`sed` is convenient because it will handle arbitrarily long inputs, because it is fast, and because it is so similar to `ed` with its regular expressions and line-at-a-time processing. On the other side of the coin, however, `sed` provides a relatively limited form of memory (it's hard to remember text from one line to another), it only makes one pass over the data, it's not possible to go backwards, there's no way to do forward references like /.../+1, and it provides no facilities for manipulating numbers — it is purely a text editor.

Exercise 4-5. Modify `older` and `newer` so they don't include the argument file in their output. Change them so the files are listed in the opposite order. □

Exercise 4-6. Use `sed` to make `bundle` robust. Hint: in here documents, the end-marking word is recognized only when it matches the line exactly. □

4.4 The `awk` pattern scanning and processing language

Some of the limitations of `sed` are remedied by `awk`. The idea in `awk` is much the same as in `sed`, but the details are based more on the C programming language than on a text editor. Usage is just like `sed`:

    $ awk 'program' filenames ...

but the *program* is different:

        pattern { action }
        pattern { action }
        . . .

`awk` reads the input in the *filenames* one line at a time. Each line is compared with each *pattern* in order; for each *pattern* that matches the line, the corresponding *action* is performed. Like `sed`, `awk` does not alter its input files.

The patterns can be regular expressions exactly as in `egrep`, or they can be more complicated conditions reminiscent of C. As a simple example, though,

    $ awk '/regular expression/ { print }' filenames ...

does what `egrep` does: it prints every line that matches the *regular expression*.

Either the pattern or the action is optional. If the action is omitted, the default action is to print matched lines, so

    $ awk '/regular expression/' filenames ...

does the same job as the previous example. Conversely, if the pattern is omitted, then the action part is done for *every* input line. So

    $ awk '{ print }' filenames ...

does what `cat` does, albeit more slowly.

One final note before we get on to interesting examples. As with `sed`, it is possible to present the *program* to `awk` from a file:

    $ awk -f cmdfile filenames ...

Fields

awk splits each input line automatically into *fields*, that is, strings of non-blank characters separated by blanks or tabs. By this definition, the output of who has five fields:

```
$ who
you        tty2      Sep 29 11:53
jim        tty4      Sep 29 11:27
$
```

awk calls the fields $1, $2, ..., $NF, where NF is a variable whose value is set to the number of fields. In this case, NF is 5 for both lines. (Note the difference between NF, the number of fields, and $NF, the last field on the line. In awk, unlike the shell, only fields begin with a $; variables are unadorned.) For example, to discard the file sizes produced by du -a,

```
$ du -a | awk '{ print $2 }'
```

and to print the names of the people logged in and the time of login, one per line:

```
$ who | awk '{ print $1, $5 }'
you 11:53
jim 11:27
$
```

To print the name and time of login sorted by time:

```
$ who | awk '{ print $5, $1 }' | sort
11:27 jim
11:53 you
$
```

These are alternatives to the sed versions shown earlier in this chapter. Although awk is easier to use than sed for operations like these, it is usually slower, both getting started and in execution when there's a lot of input.

awk normally assumes that white space (any number of blanks and tabs) separates fields, but the separator can be changed to any single character. One way is with the -F (upper case) command-line option. For example, the fields in the password file /etc/passwd are separated by colons:

```
$ sed 3q /etc/passwd
root:3D.fHR5KoB.3s:0:1:S.User:/:
ken:y.68wd1.ijayz:6:1:K.Thompson:/usr/ken:
dmr:z4u3dJWbg7wCk:7:1:D.M.Ritchie:/usr/dmr:
$
```

To print the user names, which come from the first field,

```
$ sed 3q /etc/passwd | awk -F: '{ print $1 }'
root
ken
dmr
$
```

The handling of blanks and tabs is intentionally special. By default, both blanks and tabs are separators, and leading separators are discarded. If the separator is set to anything other than blank, however, then leading separators are counted in determining the fields. In particular, if the separator is a tab, then blanks are not separator characters, leading blanks are part of the field, and each tab defines a field.

Printing

awk keeps track of other interesting quantities besides the number of input fields. The built-in variable NR is the number of the current input "record" or line. So to add line numbers to an input stream, use this:

```
$ awk '{ print NR, $0 }'
```

The field $0 is the entire input line, unchanged. In a print statement items separated by commas are printed separated by the output field separator, which is by default a blank.

The formatting that print does is often acceptable, but if it isn't, you can use a statement called printf for complete control of your output. For example, to print line numbers in a field four digits wide, you might use the following:

```
$ awk '{ printf "%4d %s\n", NR, $0 }'
```

%4d specifies a decimal integer (NR) in a field four digits wide, %s a string of characters ($0), and \n a newline character, since printf doesn't print any spaces or newlines automatically. The printf statement in awk is like the C function; see printf(3).

We could have written the first version of ind (from early in this chapter) as

```
awk '{ printf "\t%s\n", $0 }' $*
```

which prints a tab (\t) and the input record.

Patterns

Suppose you want to look in /etc/passwd for people who have no passwords. The encrypted password is the second field, so the program is just a pattern:

```
$ awk -F: '$2 == ""' /etc/passwd
```

The pattern asks if the second field is an empty string ('==' is the equality test operator). You can write this pattern in a variety of ways:

```
$2 == ""              2nd field is empty
$2 ~ /^$/             2nd field matches empty string
$2 !~ /./             2nd field doesn't match any character
length($2) == 0       Length of 2nd field is zero
```

The symbol ~ indicates a regular expression match, and !~ means "does not match." The regular expression itself is enclosed in slashes.

length is an awk built-in function that produces the length of a string of characters. A pattern can be preceded by ! to negate it, as in

```
!($2 == "")
```

The '!' operator is like that in C, but opposite to sed, where the ! follows the pattern.

One common use of patterns in awk is for simple data validation tasks. Many of these amount to little more than looking for lines that fail to meet some criterion; if there is no output, the data is acceptable ("no news is good news"). For example, the following pattern makes sure that every input record has an even number of fields, using the operator % to compute the remainder:

```
NF % 2 != 0     # print if odd number of fields
```

Another prints excessively long lines, using the built-in function length:

```
length($0) > 72 # print if too long
```

awk uses the same comment convention as the shell does: a # marks the beginning of a comment.

You can make the output somewhat more informative by printing a warning and part of the too-long line, using another built-in function, substr:

```
length($0) > 72 { print "Line", NR, "too long:", substr($0,1,60) }
```

substr(s,m,n) produces the substring of s that begins at position m and is n characters long. (The string begins at position 1.) If n is omitted, the substring from m to the end is used. substr can also be used for extracting fixed-position fields, for instance, selecting the hour and minute from the output of date:

```
$ date
Thu Sep 29 12:17:01 EDT 1983
$ date | awk '{ print substr($4, 1, 5) }'
12:17
$
```

Exercise 4-7. How many awk programs can you write that copy input to output as cat does? Which is the shortest? □

The BEGIN *and* END *patterns*

awk provides two special patterns, BEGIN and END. BEGIN actions are performed before the first input line has been read; you can use the BEGIN pattern to initialize variables, to print headings or to set the field separator by assigning to the variable FS:

```
$ awk 'BEGIN { FS = ":" }
>        $2 == "" ' /etc/passwd
$                        No output: we all use passwords
```

END actions are done after the last line of input has been processed:

```
$ awk 'END { print NR }' ...
```

prints the number of lines of input.

Arithmetic and variables

The examples so far have involved only simple text manipulation. awk's real strength lies in its ability to do calculations on the input data as well; it is easy to count things, compute sums and averages, and the like. A common use of awk is to sum columns of numbers. For example, to add up all the numbers in the first column:

```
         { s = s + $1 }
END      { print s }
```

Since the number of values is available in the variable NR, changing the last line to

```
END      { print s, s/NR }
```

prints both sum and average.

This example also illustrates the use of variables in awk. s is not a built-in variable, but one defined by being used. Variables are initialized to zero by default so you usually don't have to worry about initialization.

awk also provides the same shorthand arithmetic operators that C does, so the example would normally be written

```
         { s += $1 }
END      { print s }
```

s += $1 is the same as s = s + $1, but notationally more compact.

You can generalize the example that counts input lines like this:

```
         { nc += length($0) + 1   # number of chars, 1 for \n
           nw += NF               # number of words
         }
END      { print NR, nw, nc }
```

This counts the lines, words and characters in its input, so it does the same job as wc (although it doesn't break the totals down by file).

As another example of arithmetic, this program computes the number of

66-line pages that will be produced by running a set of files through `pr`. This can be wrapped up in a command called `prpages`:

```
$ cat prpages
# prpages:  compute number of pages that pr will print
wc $* |
awk '!/ total$/ { n += int(($1+55) / 56) }
      END           { print n }'
$
```

`pr` puts 56 lines of text on each page (a fact determined empirically). The number of pages is rounded up, then truncated to an integer with the built-in function `int`, for each line of `wc` output that does not match `total` at the end of a line.

```
$ wc ch4.*
    753    3090   18129 ch4.1
    612    2421   13242 ch4.2
    637    2462   13455 ch4.3
    802    2986   16904 ch4.4
     50     213    1117 ch4.9
   2854   11172   62847 total
$ prpages ch4.*
53
$
```

To verify this result, run `pr` into `awk` directly:

```
$ pr ch4.* | awk 'END { print NR/66 }'
53
$
```

Variables in `awk` also store strings of characters. Whether a variable is to be treated as a number or as a string of characters depends on the context. Roughly speaking, in an arithmetic expression like `s+=$1`, the numeric value is used; in a string context like `x="abc"`, the string value is used; and in an ambiguous case like `x>y`, the string value is used unless the operands are clearly numeric. (The rules are stated precisely in the `awk` manual.) String variables are initialized to the empty string. Coming sections will put strings to good use.

`awk` itself maintains a number of built-in variables of both types, such as `NR` and `FS`. Table 4.3 gives the complete list. Table 4.4 lists the operators.

Exercise 4-8. Our test of `prpages` suggests alternate implementations. Experiment to see which is fastest. □

Control flow

It is remarkably easy (speaking from experience) to create adjacent duplicate words accidentally when editing a big document, and it is obvious that that almost never happens intentionally. To prevent such problems, one of the

Table 4.3: awk Built-in Variables

FILENAME	name of current input file
FS	field separator character (default blank & tab)
NF	number of fields in input record
NR	number of input record
OFMT	output format for numbers (default %g; see printf(3))
OFS	output field separator string (default blank)
ORS	output record separator string (default newline)
RS	input record separator character (default newline)

Table 4.4: awk Operators (increasing order of precedence)

= += -= *= /= %=	assignment; v op= expr is v = v op (expr)
¦¦	OR: expr1 ¦¦ expr2 true if either is; expr2 not evaluated if expr1 is true
&&	AND: expr1 && expr2 true if both are; expr2 not evaluated if expr1 is false
!	negate value of expression
> >= < <= == != ~ !~	relational operators; ~ and !~ are match and non-match
nothing	string concatenation
+ -	plus, minus
* / %	multiply, divide, remainder
++ --	increment, decrement (prefix or postfix)

the components of the Writer's Workbench family of programs, called double, looks for pairs of identical adjacent words. Here is an implementation of double in awk:

```
$ cat double
awk '
FILENAME != prevfile {    # new file
    NR = 1                # reset line number
    prevfile = FILENAME
}
NF > 0 {
    if ($1 == lastword)
        printf "double %s, file %s, line %d\n",$1,FILENAME,NR
    for (i = 2; i <= NF; i++)
        if ($i == $(i-1))
            printf "double %s, file %s, line %d\n",$i,FILENAME,NR
    if (NF > 0)
        lastword = $NF
}' $*
$
```

The operator ++ increments its operand, and the operator -- decrements.

The built-in variable FILENAME contains the name of the current input file. Since NR counts lines from the beginning of the input, we reset it every time the filename changes so an offending line is properly identified.

The if statement is just like that in C:

```
if (condition)
        statement1
else
        statement2
```

If *condition* is true, then *statement1* is executed; if it is false, and if there is an else part, then *statement2* is executed. The else part is optional.

The for statement is a loop like the one in C, but different from the shell's:

```
for (expression1; condition; expression2)
        statement
```

The for is identical to the following while statement, which is also valid in awk:

```
expression1
while (condition) {
        statement
        expression2
}
```

For example,

```
        for (i = 2; i <= NF; i++)
```

runs the loop with i set in turn to 2, 3, ..., up to the number of fields, NF.

The break statement causes an immediate exit from the enclosing while or `for`; the `continue` statement causes the next iteration to begin (at *condition* in the `while` and *expression2* in the `for`). The `next` statement causes the next input line to be read and pattern matching to resume at the beginning of the `awk` program. The `exit` statement causes an immediate transfer to the END pattern.

Arrays

`awk` provides arrays, as do most programming languages. As a trivial example, this `awk` program collects each line of input in a separate array element, indexed by line number, then prints them out in reverse order:

```
$ cat backwards
# backwards:  print input in backward line order
awk '   { line[NR] = $0 }
END     { for (i = NR; i > 0; i--) print line[i] } ' $*
$
```

Notice that, like variables, arrays don't have to be declared; the size of an array is limited only by the memory available on your machine. Of course if a very large file is being read into an array, it may eventually run out of memory. To print the end of a large file in reverse order requires cooperation with `tail`:

```
$ tail -5 /usr/dict/web2 | backwards
zymurgy
zymotically
zymotic
zymosthenic
zymosis
$
```

`tail` takes advantage of a file system operation called *seeking*, to advance to the end of a file without reading the intervening data. Look at the discussion of `lseek` in Chapter 7. (Our local version of `tail` has an option `-r` that prints the lines in reverse order, which supersedes `backwards`.)

Normal input processing splits each input line into fields. It is possible to perform the same field-splitting operation on any string with the built-in function `split`:

n = `split`(*s*, *arr*, *sep*)

splits the string *s* into fields that are stored in elements 1 through n of the array *arr*. If a separator character *sep* is provided, it is used; otherwise the current value of `FS` is used. For example, `split($0,a,":")` splits the input line on colons, which is suitable for processing `/etc/passwd`, and `split("9/29/83",date,"/")` splits a date on slashes.

```
$ sed 1q /etc/passwd | awk '{split($0,a,":"); print a[1]}'
root
$ echo 9/29/83 | awk '{split($0,date,"/"); print date[3]}'
83
$
```

Table 4.5 lists the awk built-in functions.

Table 4.5: awk Built-in Functions	
cos(*expr*)	cosine of *expr*
exp(*expr*)	exponential of *expr*: e^{expr}
getline()	reads next input line; returns 0 if end of file, 1 if not
index(*s1*,*s2*)	position of string *s2* in *s1*; returns 0 if not present
int(*expr*)	integer part of *expr*; truncates toward 0
length(*s*)	length of string *s*
log(*expr*)	natural logarithm of *expr*
sin(*expr*)	sine of *expr*
split(*s*,*a*,*c*)	split *s* into *a*[1]...*a*[*n*] on character *c*; return *n*
sprintf(*fmt*, ...)	format ... according to specification *fmt*
substr(*s*,*m*,*n*)	*n*-character substring of *s* beginning at position *m*

Associative arrays

A standard problem in data processing is to accumulate values for a set of name-value pairs. That is, from input like

```
Susie    400
John     100
Mary     200
Mary     300
John     100
Susie    100
Mary     100
```

we want to compute the total for each name:

```
John     200
Mary     600
Susie    500
```

awk provides a neat way to do this, the *associative array*. Although one normally thinks of array subscripts as integers, in awk any value can be used as a subscript. So

```
        { sum[$1] += $2 }
END     { for (name in sum) print name, sum[name] }
```

is the complete program for adding up and printing the sums for the name-value pairs like those above, whether or not they are sorted. Each name ($1) is used as a subscript in sum; at the end, a special form of the for statement is used to cycle through all the elements of sum, printing them out. Syntactically, this variant of the for statement is

```
for (var in array)
      statement
```

Although it might look superficially like the for loop in the shell, it's unrelated. It loops over the subscripts of *array*, not the elements, setting *var* to each subscript in turn. The subscripts are produced in an unpredictable order, however, so it may be necessary to sort them. In the example above, the output can be piped into sort to list the people with the largest values at the top.

```
$ awk '...' | sort +1nr
```

The implementation of associative memory uses a hashing scheme to ensure that access to any element takes about the same time as to any other, and that (at least for moderate array sizes) the time doesn't depend on how many elements are in the array.

The associative memory is effective for tasks like counting all the words in the input:

```
$ cat wordfreq
awk '    { for (i = 1; i <= NF; i++) num[$i]++ }
END      { for (word in num) print word, num[word] }
' $*
$ wordfreq ch4.* | sort +1 -nr | sed 20q | 4
the 372         .CW 345         of 220          is 185
to 175          a 167           in 109          and 100
.P1 94          .P2 94          .PP 90          $ 87
awk 87          sed 83          that 76         for 75
The 63          are 61          line 55         print 52
$
```

The first for loop looks at each word in the input line, incrementing the element of array num subscripted by the word. (Don't confuse awk's $i, the i'th field of the input line, with any shell variables.) After the file has been read, the second for loop prints, in arbitrary order, the words and their counts.

Exercise 4-9. The output from wordfreq includes text formatting commands like .CW, which is used to print words in this font. How would you get rid of such nonwords? How would you use tr to make wordfreq work properly regardless of the case of its input? Compare the implementation and performance of wordfreq to the pipeline from Section 4.2 and to this one:

```
sed 's/[ →][ →]*/\
/g' $* | sort | uniq -c | sort -nr
```

□

Strings

Although both sed and awk are used for tiny jobs like selecting a single field, only awk is used to any extent for tasks that really require programming. One example is a program that folds long lines to 80 columns. Any line that exceeds 80 characters is broken after the 80th; a \ is appended as a warning, and the residue is processed. The final section of a folded line is right-justified, not left-justified, since this produces more convenient output for program listings, which is what we most often use fold for. As an example, using 20-character lines instead of 80,

```
$ cat test
A short line.
A somewhat longer line.
This line is quite a bit longer than the last one.
$ fold test
A short line.
A somewhat longer li\
                  ne.
This line is quite a\
 bit longer than the\
              last one.
$
```

Strangely enough, the 7th Edition provides no program for adding or removing tabs, although pr in System V will do both. Our implementation of fold uses sed to convert tabs into spaces so that awk's character count is right. This works properly for leading tabs (again typical of program source) but does not preserve columns for tabs in the middle of a line.

```
# fold:  fold long lines
sed 's/→/          /g' $* |   # convert tabs to 8 spaces
awk '
BEGIN {
    N = 80       # folds at column 80
    for (i = 1; i <= N; i++)    # make a string of blanks
        blanks = blanks " "
}
{   if ((n = length($0)) <= N)
        print
    else {
        for (i = 1; n > N; n -= N) {
            printf "%s\\\n", substr($0,i,N)
            i += N;
        }
        printf "%s%s\n", substr(blanks,1,N-n), substr($0,i)
    }
} '
```

In awk there is no explicit string concatenation operator; strings are

concatenated when they are adjacent. Initially, blanks is a null string. The
loop in the BEGIN part creates a long string of blanks by concatenation: each
trip around the loop adds one more blank to the end of blanks. The second
loop processes the input line in chunks until the remaining part is short
enough. As in C, an assignment statement can be used as an expression, so
the construction

```
if ((n = length($0)) <= N) ...
```

assigns the length of the input line to n before testing the value. Notice the
parentheses.

Exercise 4-10. Modify fold so that it will fold lines at blanks or tabs rather than splitting a word. Make it robust for long words. □

Interaction with the shell

Suppose you want to write a program field *n* that will print the *n*-th field
from each line of input, so that you could say, for example,

```
$ who | field 1
```

to print only the login names. awk clearly provides the field selection capability; the main problem is passing the field number *n* to an awk program. Here
is one implementation:

```
awk '{ print $'$1' }'
```

The $1 is exposed (it's not inside any quotes) and thus becomes the field
number seen by awk. Another approach uses double quotes:

```
awk "{ print \$$1 }"
```

In this case, the argument is interpreted by the shell, so the \$ becomes a $
and the $1 is replaced by the value of *n*. We prefer the single-quote style
because so many extra \'s are needed with the double-quote style in a typical
awk program.

A second example is addup *n*, which adds up the numbers in the *n*-th field:

```
awk '{ s += $'$1' }
     END { print s }'
```

A third example forms separate sums of each of *n* columns, plus a grand
total:

```
awk '
BEGIN { n = '$1' }
{       for (i = 1; i <= n; i++)
                sum[i] += $i
}
END {   for (i = 1; i <= n; i++) {
                printf "%6g ", sum[i]
                total += sum[i]
        }
        printf "; total = %6g\n", total
} '
```

We use a BEGIN to insert the value of *n* into a variable, rather than cluttering up the rest of the program with quotes.

The main problem with all these examples is not keeping track of whether one is inside or outside of the quotes (though that is a bother), but that as currently written, such programs can read only their standard input; there is no way to pass them both the parameter *n* and an arbitrarily long list of filenames. This requires some shell programming that we'll address in the next chapter.

A calendar service based on awk

Our final example uses associative arrays; it is also an illustration of how to interact with the shell, and demonstrates a bit about program evolution.

The task is to have the system send you mail every morning that contains a reminder of upcoming events. (There may already be such a calendar service; see calendar(1). This section shows an alternate approach.) The basic service should tell you of events happening today; the second step is to give a day of warning — events of tomorrow as well as today. The proper handling of weekends and holidays is left as an exercise.

The first requirement is a place to keep the calendar. For that, a file called calendar in /usr/you seems easiest.

```
$ cat calendar
Sep 30  mother's birthday
Oct 1   lunch with joe, noon
Oct 1   meeting 4pm
$
```

Second, you need a way to scan the calendar for a date. There are many choices here; we will use awk because it is best at doing the arithmetic necessary to get from "today" to "tomorrow," but other programs like sed or egrep can also serve. The lines selected from the calendar are shipped off by mail, of course.

Third, you need a way to have calendar scanned reliably and automatically every day, probably early in the morning. This can be done with at, which we mentioned briefly in Chapter 1.

If we restrict the format of calendar so each line begins with a month
name and a day as produced by date, the first draft of the calendar program
is easy:

```
$ date
Thu Sep 29 15:23:12 EDT 1983
$ cat bin/calendar
# calendar:  version 1 -- today only
awk <$HOME/calendar '
        BEGIN { split("'"`date`"'", date) }
        $1 == date[2] && $2 == date[3]
' | mail $NAME
$
```

The BEGIN block splits the date produced by date into an array; the second
and third elements of the array are the month and the day. We are assuming
that the shell variable NAME contains your login name.

The remarkable sequence of quote characters is required to capture the date
in a string in the middle of the awk program. An alternative that is easier to
understand is to pass the date in as the first line of input:

```
$ cat bin/calendar
# calendar:  version 2 -- today only, no quotes
(date; cat $HOME/calendar) |
awk '
  NR == 1    { mon = $2; day = $3 } # set the date
  NR > 1 && $1 == mon && $2 == day  # print calendar lines
' | mail $NAME
$
```

The next step is to arrange for calendar to look for tomorrow as well as
today. Most of the time all that is needed is to take today's date and add 1 to
the day. But at the end of the month, we have to get the next month and set
the day back to 1. And of course each month has a different number of days.

This is where the associative array comes in handy. Two arrays, days and
nextmon, whose subscripts are month names, hold the number of days in the
month and the name of the next month. Then days["Jan"] is 31, and
nextmon["Jan"] is Feb. Rather than create a whole sequence of statements
like

```
days["Jan"] = 31; nextmon["Jan"] = "Feb"
days["Feb"] = 28; nextmon["Feb"] = "Mar"
...
```

we will use split to convert a convenient data structure into the one really
needed:

```
$ cat calendar
# calendar:   version 3 -- today and tomorrow
awk <$HOME/calendar '
BEGIN {
    x = "Jan 31 Feb 28 Mar 31 Apr 30 May 31 Jun 30 " \
        "Jul 31 Aug 31 Sep 30 Oct 31 Nov 30 Dec 31 Jan 31"
    split(x, data)
    for (i = 1; i < 24; i += 2) {
        days[data[i]] = data[i+1]
        nextmon[data[i]] = data[i+2]
    }
    split("'"`date`"'", date)
    mon1 = date[2]; day1 = date[3]
    mon2 = mon1; day2 = day1 + 1
    if (day1 >= days[mon1]) {
        day2 = 1
        mon2 = nextmon[mon1]
    }
}
$1 == mon1 && $2 == day1 || $1 == mon2 && $2 == day2
' | mail $NAME
$
```

Notice that Jan appears twice in the data; a "sentinel" data value like this sim-
plifies processing for December.

The final stage is to arrange for the calendar program to be run every day.
What you want is for someone to wake up every morning at around 5 AM and
run calendar. You can do this yourself by remembering to say (every day!)

```
$ at 5am
calendar
ctl-d
$
```

but that's not exactly automatic or reliable. The trick is to tell at not only to
run the calendar, but also to schedule the next run as well.

```
$ cat early.morning
calendar
echo early.morning | at 5am
$
```

The second line schedules another at command for the next day, so once
started, this sequence is self-perpetuating. The at command sets your PATH,
current directory and other parameters for the commands it processes, so you
needn't do anything special.

Exercise 4-11. Modify calendar so it knows about weekends: on Friday, "tomorrow"
includes Saturday, Sunday and Monday. Modify calendar to handle leap years.
Should calendar know about holidays? How would you arrange it? □

Exercise 4-12. Should `calendar` know about dates inside a line, not just at the beginning? How about dates expressed in other formats, like 10/1/83? □

Exercise 4-13. Why doesn't `calendar` use `getname` instead of `$NAME`? □

Exercise 4-14. Write a personal version of `rm` that moves files to a temporary directory rather than deleting them, with an `at` command to clean out the directory while you are sleeping. □

Loose ends

`awk` is an ungainly language, and it's impossible to show all its capabilities in a chapter of reasonable size. Here are some other things to look at in the manual:

- Redirecting the output of `print` into files and pipes: any `print` or `printf` statement can be followed by > and a filename (as a quoted string or in a variable); the output will be sent to that file. As with the shell, >> appends instead of overwriting. Printing into a pipe uses ¦ instead of >.
- Multi-line records: if the record separator `RS` is set to newline, then input records will be separated by an empty line. In this way, several input lines can be treated as a single record.
- "Pattern, pattern" as a selector: as in `ed` and `sed`, a range of lines can be specified by a pair of patterns. This matches lines from an occurrence of the first pattern until the next occurrence of the second. A simple example is

```
NR == 10, NR == 20
```

which matches lines 10 through 20 inclusive.

4.5 Good files and good filters

Although the last few `awk` examples are self-contained commands, many uses of `awk` are simple one- or two-line programs to do some filtering as part of a larger pipeline. This is true of most filters — sometimes the problem at hand can be solved by the application of a single filter, but more commonly it breaks down into subproblems solvable by filters joined together into a pipeline. This use of tools is often cited as the heart of the UNIX programming environment. That view is overly restrictive; nevertheless, the use of filters pervades the system, and it is worth observing why it works.

The output produced by UNIX programs is in a format understood as input by other programs. Filterable files contain lines of text, free of decorative headers, trailers or blank lines. Each line is an object of interest — a filename, a word, a description of a running process — so programs like `wc` and `grep` can count interesting items or search for them by name. When more information is present for each object, the file is still line-by-line, but columnated into fields separated by blanks or tabs, as in the output of `ls -l`. Given data divided into such fields, programs like `awk` can easily select, process or rearrange the information.

Filters share a common design. Each writes on its standard output the result of processing the argument files, or the standard input if no arguments are given. The arguments specify *input*, never output,† so the output of a command can always be fed to a pipeline. Optional arguments (or non-filename arguments such as the `grep` pattern) precede any filenames. Finally, error messages are written on the standard error, so they will not vanish down a pipe.

These conventions have little effect on the individual commands, but when uniformly applied to all programs result in a simplicity of interconnection, illustrated by many examples throughout this book, but perhaps most spectacularly by the word-counting example at the end of Section 4.2. If any of the programs demanded a named input or output file, required interaction to specify parameters, or generated headers and trailers, the pipeline wouldn't work. And of course, if the UNIX system didn't provide pipes, someone would have to write a conventional program to do the job. But there are pipes, and the pipeline works, and is even easy to write if you are familiar with the tools.

Exercise 4-15. `ps` prints an explanatory header, and `ls -l` announces the total number of blocks in the files. Comment.

History and bibliographic notes

A good review of pattern matching algorithms can be found in the paper "Pattern matching in strings" (Proceedings of the Symposium on Formal Language Theory, Santa Barbara, 1979) by Al Aho, author of `egrep`.

`sed` was designed and implemented by Lee McMahon, using `ed` as a base.

`awk` was designed and implemented by Al Aho, Peter Weinberger and Brian Kernighan, by a much less elegant process. Naming a language after its authors also shows a certain poverty of imagination. A paper by the implementors, "AWK — a pattern scanning and processing language," *Software—Practice and Experience*, July 1978, discusses the design. `awk` has its origins in several areas, but has certainly stolen good ideas from SNOBOL4, from `sed`, from a validation language designed by Marc Rochkind, from the language tools `yacc` and `lex`, and of course from C. Indeed, the similarity between `awk` and C is a source of problems — the language looks like C but it's not. Some constructions are missing; others differ in subtle ways.

An article by Doug Comer entitled "The flat file system FFG: a database system consisting of primitives" (*Software—Practice and Experience*, November, 1982) discusses the use of the shell and `awk` to create a database system.

---

† An early UNIX file system was destroyed by a maintenance program that violated this rule, because a harmless-looking command scribbled all over the disc.

CHAPTER 5: **SHELL PROGRAMMING**

Although most users think of the shell as an interactive command interpreter, it is really a programming language in which each statement runs a
command. Because it must satisfy both the interactive and programming
aspects of command execution, it is a strange language, shaped as much by history as by design. The range of its application leads to an unsettling quantity
of detail in the language, but you don't need to understand every nuance to use
it effectively. This chapter explains the basics of shell programming by showing the evolution of some useful shell programs. It is *not* a manual for the
shell. That is in the manual page sh(1) of the *Unix Programmer's Manual*,
which you should have handy while you are reading.

With the shell, as with most commands, the details of behavior can often be
most quickly discovered by experimentation. The manual can be cryptic, and
there is nothing better than a good example to clear things up. For that reason, this chapter is organized around examples rather than shell features; it is a
guide to *using* the shell for programming, rather than an encyclopedia of its
capabilities. We will talk not only about what the shell can do, but also about
developing and writing shell programs, with an emphasis on testing ideas
interactively.

When you've written a program, in the shell or any other language, it may
be helpful enough that other people on your system would like to use it. But
the standards other people expect of a program are usually more rigorous than
those you apply for yourself. A major theme in shell programming is therefore
making programs robust so they can handle improper input and give helpful
information when things go wrong.

5.1 Customizing the cal command

One common use of a shell program is to enhance or to modify the user
interface to a program. As an example of a program that could stand enhance-
ment, consider the cal(1) command:

133

```
$ cal
usage: cal [month] year        Good so far
$ cal october 1983
Bad argument                   Not so good
$ cal 10 1983
    October 1983
 S   M Tu  W Th   F   S
                      1
 2   3  4  5  6   7   8
 9  10 11 12 13  14  15
16  17 18 19 20  21  22
23  24 25 26 27  28  29
30  31
$
```

It's a nuisance that the month has to be provided numerically. And, as it turns out, `cal 10` prints out the calendar for the entire year 10, rather than for the current October, so you must always specify the year to get a calendar for a single month.

The important point here is that no matter what interface the `cal` command provides, you can change it without changing `cal` itself. You can place a command in your private `bin` directory that converts a more convenient argument syntax into whatever the real `cal` requires. You can even call your version `cal`, which means one less thing for you to remember.

The first issue is design: what should `cal` do? Basically, we want `cal` to be reasonable. It should recognize a month by name. With two arguments, it should behave just as the old `cal` does, except for converting month names into numbers. Given one argument, it should print the month or year's calendar as appropriate, and given zero arguments, it should print the *current* month's calendar, since that is certainly the most common use of a `cal` command. So the problem is to decide how many arguments there are, then map them to what the standard `cal` wants.

The shell provides a `case` statement that is well suited for making such decisions:

```
case word in
pattern)    commands ;;
pattern)    commands ;;
   ...
esac
```

The `case` statement compares *word* to the *pattern*s from top to bottom, and performs the *commands* associated with the first, and only the first, *pattern* that matches. The patterns are written using the shell's pattern matching rules, slightly generalized from what is available for filename matching. Each action is terminated by the double semicolon ``;;``. (The ``;;`` may be left off the last case but we often leave it in for easy editing.)

Our version of cal decides how many arguments are present, processes alphabetic month names, then calls the real cal. The shell variable $# holds the number of arguments that a shell file was called with; other special shell variables are listed in Table 5.1.

```
$ cat cal
# cal:   nicer interface to /usr/bin/cal

case $# in
0)        set `date`; m=$2; y=$6 ;;    # no args: use today
1)        m=$1; set `date`; y=$6 ;;    # 1 arg: use this year
*)        m=$1; y=$2 ;;                # 2 args: month and year
esac

case $m in
jan*|Jan*)        m=1 ;;
feb*|Feb*)        m=2 ;;
mar*|Mar*)        m=3 ;;
apr*|Apr*)        m=4 ;;
may*|May*)        m=5 ;;
jun*|Jun*)        m=6 ;;
jul*|Jul*)        m=7 ;;
aug*|Aug*)        m=8 ;;
sep*|Sep*)        m=9 ;;
oct*|Oct*)        m=10 ;;
nov*|Nov*)        m=11 ;;
dec*|Dec*)        m=12 ;;
[1-9]|10|11|12)   ;;               # numeric month
*)                y=$m; m="" ;;    # plain year
esac

/usr/bin/cal $m $y              # run the real one
$
```

The first case checks the number of arguments, $#, and chooses the appropriate action. The final * pattern in the first case is a catch-all: if the number of arguments is neither 0 nor 1, the last case will be executed. (Since patterns are scanned in order, the catch-all must be last.) This sets m and y to the month and year — given two arguments, our cal is going to act the same as the original.

The first case statement has a couple of tricky lines containing

```
set `date`
```

Although not obvious from appearance, it is easy to see what this statement does by trying it:

Table 5.1:   Shell Built-in Variables

`$#`	the number of arguments
`$*`	all arguments to shell
`$@`	similar to `$*`; see Section 5.7
`$-`	options supplied to the shell
`$?`	return value of the last command executed
`$$`	process-id of the shell
`$!`	process-id of the last command started with `&`
`$HOME`	default argument for `cd` command
`$IFS`	list of characters that separate words in arguments
`$MAIL`	file that, when changed, triggers "you have mail" message
`$PATH`	list of directories to search for commands
`$PS1`	prompt string, default '`$` '
`$PS2`	prompt string for continued command line, default '`>` '

```
$ date
Sat Oct  1 06:05:18 EDT 1983
$ set `date`
$ echo $1
Sat
$ echo $4
06:05:20
$
```

`set` is a shell built-in command that does too many things. With no arguments, it shows the values of variables in the environment, as we saw in Chapter 3. Ordinary arguments reset the values of `$1`, `$2`, and so on. So `set` `date` sets `$1` to the day of the week, `$2` to the name of the month, and so on. The first `case` in `cal`, therefore, sets the month and year from the current date if there are no arguments; if there's one argument, it's used as the month and the year is taken from the current date.

`set` also recognizes several options, of which the most often used are `-v` and `-x`; they turn on echoing of commands as they are being processed by the shell. These are indispensable for debugging complicated shell programs.

The remaining problem is to convert the month, if it is in textual form, into a number. This is done by the second `case` statement, which should be largely self-explanatory. The only twist is that the `|` character in `case` statement patterns, as in `egrep`, indicates an alternative: `big|small` matches either `big` or `small`. Of course, these cases could also be written as `[jJ]an*` and so on. The program accepts month names either in all lower case, because most commands accept lower case input, or with first letter capitalized, because that is the format printed by `date`. The rules for shell pattern matching are given in Table 5.2.

```
┌─────────────────────────────────────────────────────────────────┐
│              Table 5.2:   Shell Pattern Matching Rules            │
│                                                                   │
│   *       match any string, including the null string             │
│   ?       match any single character                              │
│   [ccc]   match any of the characters in ccc.                     │
│              [a-d0-3] is equivalent to [abcd0123]                 │
│   "..."   match ... exactly; quotes protect special characters. Also '...' │
│   \c      match c literally                                       │
│   a¦b     in case expressions only, matches either a or b         │
│   /       in filenames, matched only by an explicit / in the expression; │
│              in case, matched like any other character            │
│   .       as the first character of a filename, is matched only by an │
│              explicit . in the expression                         │
└─────────────────────────────────────────────────────────────────┘
```

The last two cases in the second case statement deal with a single argument that could be a year; recall that the first case statement assumed it was a month. If it is a number that could be a month, it is left alone. Otherwise, it is assumed to be a year.

Finally, the last line calls /usr/bin/cal (the real cal) with the converted arguments. Our version of cal works as a newcomer might expect:

```
$ date
Sat Oct   1 06:09:55 EDT  1983
$ cal
    October 1983
 S   M Tu  W Th   F   S
                      1
 2   3  4  5  6   7   8
 9  10 11 12 13  14  15
16  17 18 19 20  21  22
23  24 25 26 27  28  29
30  31
$ cal dec
    December 1983
 S   M Tu  W Th   F   S
               1   2   3
 4   5  6  7  8   9  10
11  12 13 14 15  16  17
18  19 20 21 22  23  24
25  26 27 28 29  30  31

$
```

And cal 1984 prints out the calendar for all of 1984.

Our enhanced cal program does the same job as the original, but in a simpler, easier-to-remember way. We therefore chose to call it cal, rather than `calendar` (which is already a command) or something less mnemonic like `ncal`. Leaving the name alone also has the advantage that users don't have to develop a new set of reflexes for printing a calendar.

Before we leave the `case` statement, it's worth a brief comment on why the shell's pattern matching rules are different from those in `ed` and its derivatives. After all, two kinds of patterns means two sets of rules to learn and two pieces of code to process them. Some of the differences are simply bad choices that were never fixed — for example, there is no reason except compatibility with a past now lost that `ed` uses '.' and the shell uses '?' for "match any character." But sometimes the patterns do different jobs. Regular expressions in the editor search for a string that can occur anywhere in a line; the special characters ^ and $ are needed to *anchor* the search to the beginning and end of the line. For filenames, however, we want the search anchored by default, since that is the most common case; having to write something like

```
$ ls ^?*.c$                        Doesn't work this way
```

instead of

```
$ ls *.c
```

would be a great nuisance.

Exercise 5-1. If users prefer your version of `cal`, how do you make it globally accessible? What has to be done to put it in `/usr/bin`? □

Exercise 5-2. Is it worth fixing `cal` so `cal 83` prints the calendar for 1983? If so, how would you print the calendar for year 83? □

Exercise 5-3. Modify `cal` to accept more than one month, as in

```
$ cal oct nov
```

or perhaps a range of months:

```
$ cal oct - dec
```

If it's now December, and you ask for `cal jan`, should you get this year's January or next year's? When should you have stopped adding features to `cal`? □

5.2 Which command is `which`?

There are problems with making private versions of commands such as `cal`. The most obvious is that if you are working with Mary and type `cal` while logged in as `mary`, you will get the standard `cal` instead of the new one, unless of course Mary has linked the new `cal` into her `bin` directory. This can be confusing — recall that the error messages from the original `cal` are not very helpful — but is just an example of a general problem. Since the shell searches for commands in a set of directories specified by `PATH`, it is always possible to get a version of a command other than the one you expect. For instance, if you type a command, say `echo`, the pathname of the file that is actually run could be `./echo` or `/bin/echo` or `/usr/bin/echo` or something else, depending on the components of your `PATH` and where the files are. It can be very confusing if there happens to be an executable file with the right name but the wrong behavior earlier in your search path than you expect. Perhaps the most common is the `test` command, which we will discuss later: its name is such an obvious one for a temporary version of a program that the wrong `test` program gets called annoyingly often.† A command that reports which version of a program will be executed would provide a useful service.

One implementation is to loop over the directories named in `PATH`, searching each for an executable file of the given name. In Chapter 3, we used the `for` to loop over filenames and arguments. Here, we want a loop that says

```
for i in each component of PATH
do
            if given name is in directory i
                      print its full pathname
done
```

Because we can run any command inside backquotes `` `...` ``, the obvious solution is to run `sed` over `$PATH`, converting colons into spaces. We can test it out with our old friend `echo`:

```
$ echo $PATH
:/usr/you/bin:/bin:/usr/bin                              4 components
$ echo $PATH | sed 's/:/ /g'
 /usr/you/bin /bin /usr/bin                              Only 3 printed!
$ echo `echo $PATH | sed 's/:/ /g'`
/usr/you/bin /bin /usr/bin                               Still only 3
$
```

There is clearly a problem. A null string in `PATH` is a synonym for '.'. Converting the colons in `PATH` to blanks is therefore not good enough — the information about null components will be lost. To generate the correct list of directories, we must convert a null component of `PATH` into a dot. The null component could be in the middle or at either end of the string, so it takes a little work to catch all the cases:

```
$ echo $PATH | sed 's/^:/.:/
>                   s/::/:.:/g
>                   s/:$/:./
>                   s/:/ /g'
. /usr/you/bin /bin /usr/bin
$
```

We could have written this as four separate `sed` commands, but since `sed` does the substitutions in order, one invocation can do it all.

---

† Later we will see how to avoid this problem in shell files, where `test` is usually used.

Once we have the directory components of `PATH`, the `test(1)` command we've mentioned can tell us whether a file exists in each directory. The `test` command is actually one of the clumsier UNIX programs. For example, `test -r file` tests if `file` exists and can be read, and `test -w file` tests if `file` exists and can be written, but the 7th Edition provides no `test -x` (although the System V and other versions do) which would otherwise be the one for us. We'll settle for `test -f`, which tests that the file exists and is not a directory, in other words, is a regular file. You should look over the manual page for `test` on your system, however, since there are several versions in circulation.

Every command returns an *exit status* — a value returned to the shell to indicate what happened. The exit status is a small integer; by convention, 0 means "true" (the command ran successfully) and non-zero means "false" (the command ran unsuccessfully). Note that this is opposite to the values of true and false in C.

Since many different values can all represent "false," the reason for failure is often encoded in the "false" exit status. For example, `grep` returns 0 if there was a match, 1 if there was no match, and 2 if there was an error in the pattern or filenames. Every program returns a status, although we usually aren't interested in its value. `test` is unusual because its *sole* purpose is to return an exit status. It produces no output and changes no files.

The shell stores the exit status of the last program in the variable `$?`:

```
$ cmp /usr/you/.profile /usr/you/.profile
$                                           No output; they're the same
$ echo $?
0                                           Zero implies ran O.K.: files identical
$ cmp /usr/you/.profile /usr/mary/.profile
/usr/you/.profile /usr/mary/.profile differ: char 6, line 3
$ echo $?
1                                           Non-zero means files were different
$
```

A few commands, such as `cmp` and `grep`, have an option `-s` that causes them to exit with an appropriate status but suppress all output.

The shell's `if` statement runs commands based on the exit status of a command, as in

```
if command
then
        commands if condition true
else
        commands if condition false
fi
```

The location of the newlines is important: `fi`, `then` and `else` are recognized only after a newline or a semicolon. The `else` part is optional.

The `if` statement always runs a command — the condition — whereas the `case` statement does pattern matching directly in the shell. In some UNIX versions, including System V, `test` is a shell built-in function so an `if` and a `test` will run as fast as a `case`. If `test` isn't built in, `case` statements are more efficient than `if` statements, and should be used for any pattern matching:

```
case "$1" in
hello)   command
esac
```

will be faster than

```
if test "$1" = hello                    Slower unless test is a shell built-in
then
        command
fi
```

That is one reason why we sometimes use `case` statements in the shell for testing things that would be done with an `if` statement in most programming languages. A `case` statement, on the other hand, can't easily determine whether a file has read permissions; that is better done with a `test` and an `if`.

So now the pieces are in place for the first version of the command `which`, to report which file corresponds to a command:

```
$ cat which
# which cmd:  which cmd in PATH is executed, version 1

case $# in
0)      echo 'Usage: which command' 1>&2; exit 2
esac
for i in `echo $PATH | sed 's/^:/.:/
                            s/::/:.:/g
                            s/:$/:./
                            s/:/ /g'`
do
        if test -f $i/$1        # use test -x if you can
        then
                echo $i/$1
                exit 0          # found it
        fi
done
exit 1          # not found
$
```

Let's test it:

```
$ cx which                              Make it executable
$ which which
./which
$ which ed
/bin/ed
$ mv which /usr/you/bin
$ which which
/usr/you/bin/which
$
```

The initial `case` statement is just error-checking. Notice the redirection `1>&2` on the `echo` so the error message doesn't vanish down a pipe. The shell built-in command `exit` can be used to return an exit status. We wrote `exit 2` to return an error status if the command didn't work, `exit 1` if it couldn't find the file, and `exit 0` if it found one. If there is no explicit `exit` statement, the exit status from a shell file is the status of the last command executed.

What happens if you have a program called `test` in the current directory? (We're assuming that `test` is not a shell built-in.)

```
$ echo 'echo hello' >test            Make a fake test
$ cx test                            Make it executable
$ which which                        Try which now
hello                                Fails!
./which
$
```

More error-checking is called for. You could run `which` (if there weren't a `test` in the current directory!) to find out the full pathname for `test`, and specify it explicitly. But that is unsatisfactory: `test` may be in different directories on different systems, and `which` also depends on `sed` and `echo`, so we should specify their pathnames too. There is a simpler solution: fix `PATH` in the shell file, so it only looks in `/bin` and `/usr/bin` for commands. Of course, for the `which` command only, you have to save the old `PATH` for determining the sequence of directories to be searched.

```
$ cat which
# which cmd:  which cmd in PATH is executed, final version

opath=$PATH
PATH=/bin:/usr/bin

case $# in
0)      echo 'Usage: which command' 1>&2; exit 2
esac
for i in `echo $opath | sed 's/^:/.:/
                             s/::/:.:/g
                             s/:$/:./
                             s/:/ /g'`
do
        if test -f $i/$1        # this is /bin/test
        then                    # or /usr/bin/test only
                echo $i/$1
                exit 0          # found it
        fi
done
exit 1          # not found
$
```

which now works even if there is a spurious test (or sed or echo) along
the search path.

```
$ ls -l test
-rwxrwxrwx 1 you           11 Oct  1 06:55 test     Still there
$ which which
/usr/you/bin/which
$ which test
./test
$ rm test
$ which test
/bin/test
$
```

The shell provides two other operators for combining commands, || and
&&, that are often more compact and convenient than the if statement. For
example, || can replace some if statements:

    test -f *filename* || echo file *filename* does not exist

is equivalent to

```
if test ! -f filename                    The ! negates the condition
then
        echo file filename does not exist
fi
```

The operator ||, despite appearances, has nothing to do with pipes — it is a

conditional operator meaning OR. The command to the left of ¦¦ is executed.
If its exit status is zero (success), the command to the right of ¦¦ is ignored.
If the left side returns non-zero (failure), the right side is executed and the
value of the entire expression is the exit status of the right side. In other
words, ¦¦ is a conditional OR operator that does not execute its right-hand
command if the left one succeeds. The corresponding && conditional is AND;
it executes its right-hand command only if the left one succeeds.

Exercise 5-4. Why doesn't which reset PATH to opath before exiting? □

Exercise 5-5. Since the shell uses esac to terminate a case, and fi to terminate an
if, why does it use done to terminate a do? □

Exercise 5-6. Add an option -a to which so it prints all files in PATH, rather than
quitting after the first. Hint: match='exit 0'. □

Exercise 5-7. Modify which so it knows about shell built-ins like exit. □

Exercise 5-8. Modify which to check for execute permissions on the files. Change it
to print an error message when a file cannot be found. □

5.3 while and until loops: watching for things

In Chapter 3, the for loop was used for a number of simple iterative programs. Usually, a for loops over a set of filenames, as in 'for i in *.c', or
all the arguments to a shell program, as in 'for i in $*'. But shell loops are
more general than these idioms would suggest; consider the for loop in
which.

There are three loops: for, while and until. The for is by far the
most commonly used. It executes a set of commands — the loop body — once
for each element of a set of words. Most often these are just filenames. The
while and until use the exit status from a command to control the execution
of the commands in the body of the loop. The loop body is executed until the
condition command returns a non-zero status (for the while) or zero (for the
until). while and until are identical except for the interpretation of the
exit status of the command.

Here are the basic forms of each loop:

```
      for i in list of words
      do
                  loop body, $i set to successive elements of list
      done

      for i                   (List is implicitly all arguments to shell file, i.e., $*)
      do
                  loop body, $i set to successive arguments
      done
```

```
while command
do
            loop body executed as long as command returns true
done

until command
do
            loop body executed as long as command returns false
done
```

The second form of the `for`, in which an empty list implies `$*`, is a convenient shorthand for the most common usage.

The conditional command that controls a `while` or `until` can be any command. As a trivial example, here is a `while` loop to watch for someone (say Mary) to log in:

```
while sleep 60
do
            who | grep mary
done
```

The `sleep`, which pauses for 60 seconds, will always execute normally (unless interrupted) and therefore return "success," so the loop will check once a minute to see if Mary has logged in.

This version has the disadvantage that if Mary is already logged in, you must wait 60 seconds to find out. Also, if Mary stays logged in, you will be told about her once a minute. The loop can be turned inside out and written with an `until`, to provide the information once, without delay, if Mary is on now:

```
until who | grep mary
do
            sleep 60
done
```

This is a more interesting condition. If Mary is logged in, 'who | grep mary' prints out her entry in the who listing and returns "true," because `grep` returns a status to indicate whether it found something, and the exit status of a pipeline is the exit status of the last element.

Finally, we can wrap up this command, give it a name and install it:

```
$ cat watchfor
# watchfor:  watch for someone to log in

PATH=/bin:/usr/bin

case $# in
0)        echo 'Usage: watchfor person' 1>&2; exit 1
esac

until who | egrep "$1"
do
          sleep 60
done
$ cx watchfor
$ watchfor you
you       tty0     Oct  1 08:01        It works
$ mv watchfor /usr/you/bin             Install it
$
```

We changed grep to egrep so you can type

```
$ watchfor 'joe|mary'
```

to watch for more than one person.

As a more complicated example, we could watch *all* people logging in and
out, and report as people come and go — a sort of incremental who. The basic
structure is simple: once a minute, run who, compare its output to that from a
minute ago, and report any differences. The who output will be kept in a file,
so we will store it in the directory /tmp. To distinguish our files from those
belonging to other processes, the shell variable $$ (the process id of the shell
command), is incorporated into the filenames; this is a common convention.
Encoding the command name in the temporary files is done mostly for the sys-
tem administrator. Commands (including this version of watchwho) often
leave files lying around in /tmp, and it's nice to know which command is
doing it.

```
$ cat watchwho
# watchwho:  watch who logs in and out

PATH=/bin:/usr/bin
new=/tmp/wwho1.$$
old=/tmp/wwho2.$$
>$old            # create an empty file

while :          # loop forever
do
        who >$new
        diff $old $new
        mv $new $old
        sleep 60
done | awk '/>/ { $1 = "in:     "; print }
            /</ { $1 = "out:    "; print }'
$
```

":" is a shell built-in command that does nothing but evaluate its arguments and return "true." Instead, we could have used the command true, which merely returns a true exit status. (There is also a false command.) But ':' is more efficient than true because it does not execute a command from the file system.

diff output uses < and > to distinguish data from the two files; the awk program processes this to report the changes in an easier-to-understand format. Notice that the entire while loop is piped into awk, rather than running a fresh awk once a minute. sed is unsuitable for this processing, because its output is always behind its input by one line: there is always a line of input that has been processed but not printed, and this would introduce an unwanted delay.

Because old is created empty, the first output from watchwho is a list of all users currently logged in. Changing the command that initially creates old to who >$old will cause watchwho to print only the changes; it's a matter of taste.

Another looping program is one that watches your mailbox periodically; whenever the mailbox changes, the program prints "You have mail." This is a useful alternative to the shell's built-in mechanism using the variable MAIL. We have implemented it with shell variables instead of files, to illustrate a different way of doing things.

```
$ cat checkmail
# checkmail:  watch mailbox for growth

PATH=/bin:/usr/bin
MAIL=/usr/spool/mail/`getname`   # system dependent

t=${1-60}

x="`ls -l $MAIL`"
while :
do
        y="`ls -l $MAIL`"
        echo $x $y
        x="$y"
        sleep $t
done | awk '$4 < $12 { print "You have mail" }'
$
```

We have used awk again, this time to ensure that the message is printed only
when the mailbox grows, not merely when it changes. Otherwise, you'll get a
message right after you delete mail. (The shell's built-in version suffers from
this drawback.)

The time interval is normally set to 60 seconds, but if there is a parameter
on the command line, as in

```
$ checkmail 30
```

that is used instead. The shell variable t is set to the time if one is supplied,
and to 60 if no value was given, by the line

```
t=${1-60}
```

This introduces another feature of the shell.

${var} is equivalent to $var, and can be used to avoid problems with
variables inside strings containing letters or numbers:

```
$ var=hello
$ varx=goodbye
$ echo $var
hello
$ echo $varx
goodbye
$ echo ${var}x
hellox
$
```

Certain characters inside the braces specify special processing of the variable.
If the variable is undefined, and the name is followed by a question mark, then
the string after the ? is printed and the shell exits (unless it's interactive). If
the message is not provided, a standard one is printed:

```
$ echo ${var?}
hello                                O.K.; var is set
$ echo ${junk?}
junk: parameter not set              Default message
$ echo ${junk?error!}
junk: error!                         Message provided
$
```

Note that the message generated by the shell always contains the name of the undefined variable.

Another form is `${var-thing}` which evaluates to `$var` if it is defined, and thing if it is not. `${var=thing}` is similar, but also sets `$var` to thing:

```
$ echo ${junk-'Hi there'}
Hi there
$ echo ${junk?}
junk: parameter not set              junk unaffected
$ echo ${junk='Hi there'}
Hi there
$ echo ${junk?}
Hi there                             junk set to Hi there
$
```

The rules for evaluating variables are given in Table 5.3.

Returning to our original example,

```
t=${1-60}
```

sets t to `$1`, or if no argument is provided, to 60.

Table 5.3: Evaluation of Shell Variables	
`$var`	value of var; nothing if var undefined
`${var}`	same; useful if alphanumerics follow variable name
`${var-thing}`	value of var if defined; otherwise thing. $var unchanged.
`${var=thing}`	value of var if defined; otherwise thing. If undefined, $var set to thing
`${var?message}`	if defined, $var. Otherwise, print message and exit shell. If message empty, print: var: parameter not set
`${var+thing}`	thing if $var defined, otherwise nothing

Exercise 5-9. Look at the implementation of `true` and `false` in `/bin` or `/usr/bin`. (How would you find out where they are?) □

Exercise 5-10. Change `watchfor` so that multiple arguments are treated as different people, rather than requiring the user to type `'joe!mary'`. □

Exercise 5-11. Write a version of `watchwho` that uses `comm` instead of `awk` to compare the old and new data. Which version do you prefer? □

Exercise 5-12. Write a version of `watchwho` that stores the `who` output in shell variables instead of files. Which version do you prefer? Which version runs faster? Should `watchwho` and `checkmail` do & automatically? □

Exercise 5-13. What is the difference between the shell `:` do-nothing command and the `#` comment character? Are both needed? □

5.4 Traps: catching interrupts

If you hit DEL or hang up the phone while `watchwho` is running, one or two temporary files are left in `/tmp`. `watchwho` should remove the temporary files before it exits. We need a way to detect when such events happen, and a way to recover.

When you type DEL, an *interrupt signal* is sent to all the processes that you are running on that terminal. Similarly, when you hang up, a *hangup signal* is sent. There are other signals as well. Unless a program has taken explicit action to deal with signals, the signal will terminate it. The shell protects programs run with & from interrupts but not from hangups.

Chapter 7 discusses signals in detail, but you needn't know much to be able to handle them in the shell. The shell built-in command `trap` sets up a sequence of commands to be executed when a signal occurs:

    `trap` *sequence-of-commands list of signal numbers*

The *sequence-of-commands* is a single argument, so it must almost always be quoted. The *signal numbers* are small integers that identify the signal. For example, 2 is the signal generated by pressing the DEL key, and 1 is generated by hanging up the phone. The signal numbers most often useful to shell programmers are listed in Table 5.4.

Table 5.4: Shell Signal Numbers	
0	shell exit (for any reason, including end of file)
1	hangup
2	interrupt (DEL key)
3	quit (*ctl-*; causes program to produce core dump)
9	kill (cannot be caught or ignored)
15	terminate, default signal generated by `kill(1)`

So to clean up the temporary files in `watchwho`, a `trap` call should go just before the loop, to catch hangup, interrupt and terminate:

```
    ...
    trap 'rm -f $new $old; exit 1' 1 2 15

    while :
    ...
```

The command sequence that forms the first argument to `trap` is like a subroutine call that occurs immediately when the signal happens. When it finishes, the program that was running will resume where it was unless the signal killed it. Therefore, the `trap` command sequence must explicitly invoke `exit`, or the shell program will continue to execute after the interrupt. Also, the command sequence will be read twice: once when the `trap` is set and once when it is invoked. Therefore, the command sequence is best protected with single quotes, so variables are evaluated only when the `trap` routines are executed. It makes no difference in this case, but we will see one later in which it matters. By the way, the `-f` option tells `rm` not to ask questions.

`trap` is sometimes useful interactively, most often to prevent a program from being killed by the hangup signal generated by a broken phone connection:

```
$ (trap '' 1; long-running-command) &
2134
$
```

The null command sequence means "ignore interrupts" in this process and its children. The parentheses cause the `trap` and command to be run together in a background sub-shell; without them, the `trap` would apply to the login shell as well as to `long-running-command`.

The nohup(1) command is a short shell program to provide this service. Here is the 7th Edition version, in its entirety:

```
$ cat `which nohup`
trap "" 1 15
if test -t 2>&1
then
        echo "Sending output to 'nohup.out'"
        exec nice -5 $* >>nohup.out 2>&1
else
        exec nice -5 $* 2>&1
fi
$
```

`test -t` tests whether the standard output is a terminal, to see if the output should be saved. The background program is run with `nice` to give it a lower priority than interactive programs. (Notice that nohup doesn't set PATH. Should it?)

The `exec` is just for efficiency; the command would run just as well without it. `exec` is a shell built-in that replaces the process running this shell by the named program, thereby saving one process — the shell that would normally wait for the program to complete. We could have used `exec` in several other places, such as at the end of the enhanced `cal` program when it invokes `/usr/bin/cal`.

By way, the signal 9 is one that can't be caught or ignored: it always kills. From the shell, it is sent as

```
$ kill -9 process id ...
```

`kill -9` is not the default because a process killed that way is given no chance to put its affairs in order before dying.

Exercise 5-14. The version of `nohup` above combines the standard error of the command with the standard output. Is this a good design? If not, how would you separate them cleanly? □

Exercise 5-15. Look up the `times` shell built-in, and add a line to your `.profile` so that when you log off the shell prints out how much CPU time you have used. □

Exercise 5-16. Write a program that will find the next available user-id in `/etc/passwd`. If you are enthusiastic (and have permission), make it into a command that will add a new user to the system. What permissions does it need? How should it handle interrupts? □

5.5 Replacing a file: `overwrite`

The `sort` command has an option `-o` to overwrite a file:

```
$ sort file1 -o file2
```

is equivalent to

```
$ sort file1 >file2
```

If `file1` and `file2` are the same file, redirection with `>` will truncate the input file before it is sorted. The `-o` option, however, works correctly, because the input is sorted and saved in a temporary file before the output file is created.

Many other commands could also use a `-o` option. For example, `sed` could edit a file in place:

```
$ sed 's/UNIX/UNIX(TM)/g' ch2 -o ch2        Doesn't work this way!
```

It would be impractical to modify all such commands to add the option. Furthermore, it would be bad design: it is better to centralize functions, as the shell does with the `>` operator. We will provide a program `overwrite` to do the job. The first design is like this:

```
$ sed 's/UNIX/UNIX(TM)/g' ch2 | overwrite ch2
```

The basic implementation is straightforward — just save away the input until end of file, then copy the data to the argument file:

```
# overwrite:  copy standard input to output after EOF
# version 1.  BUG here

PATH=/bin:/usr/bin

case $# in
1)       ;;
*)       echo 'Usage: overwrite file' 1>&2; exit 2
esac

new=/tmp/overwr.$$
trap 'rm -f $new; exit 1' 1 2 15

cat >$new                  # collect the input
cp $new $1                 # overwrite the input file
rm -f $new
```

cp is used instead of mv so the permissions and owner of the output file aren't changed if it already exists.

Appealingly simple as this version is, it has a fatal flaw: if the user types DEL during the cp, the original input file will be ruined. We must prevent an interrupt from stopping the overwriting of the input file:

```
# overwrite:  copy standard input to output after EOF
# version 2.  BUG here too

PATH=/bin:/usr/bin

case $# in
1)       ;;
*)       echo 'Usage: overwrite file' 1>&2; exit 2
esac

new=/tmp/overwr1.$$
old=/tmp/overwr2.$$
trap 'rm -f $new $old; exit 1' 1 2 15

cat >$new                  # collect the input
cp $1 $old                 # save original file

trap '' 1 2 15             # we are committed; ignore signals
cp $new $1                 # overwrite the input file

rm -f $new $old
```

If a DEL happens before the original file is touched, then the temporary files are removed and the file is left alone. After the backup is made, signals are ignored so the last cp won't be interrupted — once the cp starts, overwrite is committed to changing the original file.

There is still a subtle problem. Consider:

```
$ sed 's/UNIX/UNIX(TM)g' precious | overwrite precious
command garbled: s/UNIX/UNIX(TM)g
$ ls -l precious
-rw-rw-rw- 1 you                   0 Oct   1 09:02 precious        #$%@*!
$
```

If the program providing input to overwrite gets an error, its output will be empty and overwrite will dutifully and reliably destroy the argument file.

A number of solutions are possible. overwrite could ask for confirmation before replacing the file, but making overwrite interactive would negate much of its merit. overwrite could check that its input is non-empty (by test -z), but that is ugly and not right, either: some output might be generated before an error is detected.

The best solution is to run the data-generating program under overwrite's control so its exit status can be checked. This is against tradition and intuition — in a pipeline, overwrite would normally go at the end. But to work properly it must go first. overwrite produces nothing on its standard output, however, so no generality is lost. And its syntax isn't unheard of: time, nice and nohup are all commands that take another command as arguments.

Here is the safe version:

```
# overwrite:  copy standard input to output after EOF
# final version

opath=$PATH
PATH=/bin:/usr/bin

case $# in
0|1)    echo 'Usage: overwrite file cmd [args]' 1>&2; exit 2
esac

file=$1; shift
new=/tmp/overwr1.$$; old=/tmp/overwr2.$$
trap 'rm -f $new $old; exit 1' 1 2 15   # clean up files

if PATH=$opath "$@" >$new               # collect input
then
        cp $file $old    # save original file
        trap '' 1 2 15   # we are committed; ignore signals
        cp $new $file
else
        echo "overwrite: $1 failed, $file unchanged" 1>&2
        exit 1
fi
rm -f $new $old
```

The shell built-in command `shift` moves the entire argument list one position to the left: `$2` becomes `$1`, `$3` becomes `$2`, etc. `"$@"` provides all the arguments (after the `shift`), like `$*`, but uninterpreted; we'll come back to it in Section 5.7.

Notice that `PATH` is restored to run the user's command; if it weren't, commands that were not in `/bin` or `/usr/bin` would be inaccessible to `overwrite`.

`overwrite` now works (if somewhat clumsily):

```
$ cat notice
UNIX is a Trademark of Bell Laboratories
$ overwrite notice sed 's/UNIXUNIX(TM)/g' notice
command garbled: s/UNIXUNIX(TM)/g
overwrite: sed failed, notice unchanged
$ cat notice
UNIX is a Trademark of Bell Laboratories          Unchanged
$ overwrite notice sed 's/UNIX/UNIX(TM)/g' notice
$ cat notice
UNIX(TM) is a Trademark of Bell Laboratories
$
```

Using `sed` to replace all occurrences of one word with another is a common thing to do. With `overwrite` in hand, a shell file to automate the task is easy:

```
$ cat replace
# replace:  replace str1 in files with str2, in place

PATH=/bin:/usr/bin

case $# in
0|1|2)   echo 'Usage: replace str1 str2 files' 1>&2; exit 1
esac

left="$1"; right="$2"; shift; shift

for i
do
        overwrite $i sed "s@$left@$right@g" $i
done
$ cat footnote
UNIX is not an acronym
$ replace UNIX Unix footnote
$ cat footnote
Unix is not an acronym
$
```

(Recall that if the list on a `for` statement is empty, it defaults to `$*`.) We used @ instead of / to delimit the substitute command, since @ is somewhat less likely to conflict with an input string.

`replace` sets `PATH` to `/bin:/usr/bin`, excluding `$HOME/bin`. This means that `overwrite` must be in `/usr/bin` for `replace` to work. We made this assumption for simplicity; if you can't install `overwrite` in `/usr/bin`, you will have to put `$HOME/bin` in `PATH` inside `replace`, or give `overwrite`'s pathname explicitly. From now on, we will assume that the commands we are writing reside in `/usr/bin`; they are meant to.

Exercise 5-17. Why doesn't `overwrite` use signal code 0 in the `trap` so the files are removed when it exits? Hint: Try typing DEL while running the following program:

```
trap "echo exiting; exit 1" 0 2
sleep 10
```

□

Exercise 5-18. Add an option `-v` to `replace` to print all changed lines on `/dev/tty`. Strong hint: `s/$left/$right/g$vflag`. □

Exercise 5-19. Fix `replace` so it works regardless of the characters in the substitution strings. □

Exercise 5-20. Can `replace` be used to change the variable `i` to `index` everywhere in a program? How could you change things to make this work? □

Exercise 5-21. Is `replace` convenient and powerful enough to belong in `/usr/bin`? Is it preferable to simply typing the correct `sed` commands when needed? Why or why not? □

Exercise 5-22. (Hard)

```
$ overwrite file 'who ¦ sort'
```

doesn't work. Explain why not, and fix it. Hint: see `eval` in sh(1). How does your solution affect the interpretation of metacharacters in the command? □

5.6 `zap`: killing processes by name

The `kill` command only terminates processes specified by process-id. When a specific background process needs to be killed, you must usually run `ps` to find the process-id and then laboriously re-type it as an argument to `kill`. But it's silly to have one program print a number that you immediately transcribe manually to another. Why not write a program, say `zap`, to automate the job?

One reason is that killing processes is dangerous, and care must be taken to kill the right processes. A safeguard is always to run `zap` interactively, and use `pick` to select the victims.

A quick reminder about `pick`: it prints each of its arguments in turn and asks the user for a response; if the response is `y`, the argument is printed. (`pick` is the subject of the next section.) `zap` uses `pick` to verify that the processes chosen by name are the ones the user wants to kill:

```
$ cat zap
# zap pattern:  kill all processes matching pattern
# BUG in this version

PATH=/bin:/usr/bin

case $# in
0)      echo 'Usage: zap pattern' 1>&2; exit 1
esac

kill `pick \`ps -ag | grep "$*"\` | awk '{print $1}'`
$
```

Note the nested backquotes, protected by backslashes. The `awk` program
selects the process-id from the `ps` output selected by the `pick`:

```
$ sleep 1000 &
22126
$ ps -ag
   PID TTY TIME CMD
...
 22126 0    0:00 sleep 1000
...
$ zap sleep
22126?
0? q                        What's going on?
$
```

The problem is that the output of `ps` is being broken into words, which are
seen by `pick` as individual arguments rather than being processed a line at a
time. The shell's normal behavior is to break strings into arguments at
blank/non-blank boundaries, as in

```
for i in 1 2 3 4 5
```

In this program we must control the shell's division of strings into arguments,
so that only newlines separate adjacent "words."

The shell variable `IFS` (internal field separator) is a string of characters
that separate words in argument lists such as backquotes and `for` statements.
Normally, `IFS` contains a blank, a tab and a newline, but we can change it to
anything useful, such as just a newline:

```
$ echo 'echo $#' >nargs
$ cx nargs
$ who
you        tty0      Oct   1 05:59
pjw        tty2      Oct   1 11:26
$ nargs `who`
10                                          Ten blank and newline-separated fields
$ IFS='
'                                           Just a newline
$ nargs `who`
2                                           Two lines, two fields
$
```

With IFS set to newline, zap works fine:

```
$ cat zap
# zap pat:  kill all processes matching pat
# final version

PATH=/bin:/usr/bin
IFS='
'                          # just a newline
case $1 in
"")     echo 'Usage: zap [-2] pattern' 1>&2; exit 1 ;;
-*)     SIG=$1; shift
esac

echo '  PID TTY    TIME CMD'
kill $SIG `pick \`ps -ag | egrep "$*"\` | awk '{print $1}'`
$ ps -ag
   PID TTY TIME CMD
...
 22126 0    0:00 sleep 1000
...
$ zap sleep
   PID TTY TIME CMD
 22126 0    0:00 sleep 1000? y
 23104 0    0:02 egrep sleep? n
$
```

We added a couple of wrinkles: an optional argument to specify the signal (note that SIG will be undefined, and therefore treated as a null string if the argument is not supplied) and the use of egrep instead of grep to permit more complicated patterns such as 'sleep¦date'. An initial echo prints out the column headers for the ps output.

You might wonder why this command is called zap instead of just kill. The main reason is that, unlike our cal example, we aren't really providing a new kill command: zap is necessarily interactive, for one thing — and we want to retain kill for the real one. zap is also annoyingly slow — the overhead of all the extra programs is appreciable, although `ps` (which must be run anyway) is the most expensive. In the next chapter we will provide a more efficient implementation.

Exercise 5-23. Modify `zap` to print out the `ps` header from the pipeline so that it is insensitive to changes in the format of `ps` output. How much does this complicate the program? □

5.7 The `pick` command: blanks vs. arguments

We've encountered most of what we need to write a `pick` command in the shell. The only new thing needed is a mechanism to read the user's input. The shell built-in `read` reads one line of text from the standard input and assigns the text (without the newline) as the value of the named variable:

```
$ read greeting
hello, world                    Type new value for greeting
$ echo $greeting
hello, world
$
```

The most common use of `read` is in `.profile` to set up the environment when logging in, primarily to set shell variables like `TERM`.

`read` can only read from the standard input; it can't even be redirected. None of the shell built-in commands (as opposed to the control flow primitives like `for`) can be redirected with `>` or `<`:

```
$ read greeting </etc/passwd
goodbye                         Must type a value anyway
illegal io                      Now shell reports error
$ echo $greeting
goodbye                         greeting has typed value, not one from file
$
```

This might be described as a bug in the shell, but it is a fact of life. Fortunately, it can usually be circumvented by redirecting the loop surrounding the `read`. This is the key to our implementation of the `pick` command:

```
# pick:   select arguments

PATH=/bin:/usr/bin

for i                                   # for each argument
do
        echo -n "$i? " >/dev/tty
        read response
        case $response in
        y*)     echo $i ;;
        q*)     break
        esac
done </dev/tty
```

echo -n suppresses the final newline, so the response can be typed on the same line as the prompt. And, of course, the prompts are printed on /dev/tty because the standard output is almost certainly not the terminal.

The break statement is borrowed from C: it terminates the innermost enclosing loop. In this case it breaks out of the for loop when a q is typed. We let q terminate selection because it's easy to do, potentially convenient, and consistent with other programs.

It's interesting to play with blanks in the arguments to pick:

```
$ pick '1 2' 3
1 2?
3?
$
```

If you want to see how pick is reading its arguments, run it and just press RETURN after each prompt. It's working fine as it stands: for i handles the arguments properly. We could have written the loop other ways:

```
$ grep for pick             See what this version does
for i in $*
$ pick '1 2' 3
1?
2?
3?
$
```

This form doesn't work, because the operands of the loop are rescanned, and the blanks in the first argument cause it to become two arguments. Try quoting the $*:

```
$ grep for pick             Try a different version
for i in "$*"
$ pick '1 2' 3
1 2 3?
$
```

This doesn't work either, because `"$*"` is a single word formed from all the arguments joined together, separated by blanks.

Of course there is a solution, but it is almost black magic: the string `"$@"` is treated specially by the shell, and converted into exactly the arguments to the shell file:

```
$ grep for pick              Try a third version
for i in "$@"
$ pick '1 2' 3
1 2?
3?
$
```

If `$@` is not quoted, it is identical to `$*`; the behavior is special only when it is enclosed in double quotes. We used it in `overwrite` to preserve the arguments to the user's command.

In summary, here are the rules:

- `$*` and `$@` expand into the arguments, and are rescanned; blanks in arguments will result in multiple arguments.
- `"$*"` is a single word composed of all the arguments to the shell file joined together with spaces.
- `"$@"` is identical to the arguments received by the shell file: blanks in arguments are ignored, and the result is a list of words identical to the original arguments.

If `pick` has no arguments, it should probably read its standard input, so we could say

```
$ pick <mailinglist
```

instead of

```
$ pick `cat mailinglist`
```

But we won't investigate this version of `pick`: it involves some ugly complications and is significantly harder than the same program written in C, which we will present in the next chapter.

The first two of the following exercises are difficult, but educational to the advanced shell programmer.

Exercise 5-24. Try writing a `pick` that reads its arguments from the standard input if none are supplied on the command line. It should handle blanks properly. Does a `q` response work? If not, try the next exercise. ☐

Exercise 5-25. Although shell built-ins like `read` and `set` cannot be redirected, the shell itself can be temporarily redirected. Read the section of `sh(1)` that describes `exec` and work out how to `read` from `/dev/tty` without calling a sub-shell. (It might help to read Chapter 7 first.) ☐

Exercise 5-26. (Much easier) Use `read` in your `.profile` to initialize `TERM` and whatever else depends on it, such as tab stops. ☐

5.8 The news command: community service messages

In Chapter 1 we mentioned that your system might have a news command
to report messages of general interest to the user community. Although the
name and details of the command differ, most systems provide a news service.
Our reason for presenting a news command is not to replace your local command, but to show how easily such a program can be written in the shell. It
might be interesting to compare the implementation of our news command to
your local version.

The basic idea of such programs is usually that individual news items are
stored, one per file, in a special directory like /usr/news. news (that is, our
news program) operates by comparing the modification times of the files in
/usr/news with that of a file in your home directory (.news_time) that
serves as a time stamp. For debugging, we can use '.' as the directory for
both the news files and .news_time; it can be changed to /usr/news when
the program is ready for general use.

```
$ cat news
# news:  print news files, version 1

HOME=.             # debugging only
cd .               # place holder for /usr/news
for i in `ls -t * $HOME/.news_time`
do
        case $i in
        */.news_time)    break ;;
        *)               echo news: $i
        esac
done
touch $HOME/.news_time
$ touch .news_time
$ touch x
$ touch y
$ news
news: y
news: x
$
```

touch changes the last-modified time of its argument file to the present
time, without actually modifying the file. For debugging, we just echo the
names of the news files, rather than printing them. The loop terminates when
it discovers .news_time, thereby listing only those files that are newer. Note
that the * in case statements can match a /, which it cannot in filename patterns.

What happens if .news_time doesn't exist?

```
$ rm .news_time
$ news
$
```

This silence is unexpected, and wrong. It happens because if ls can't find a file, it reports the problem on its standard output, before printing any information about existing files. This is undeniably a bug — the diagnostic should be printed on the standard error — but we can get around it by recognizing the problem in the loop and redirecting standard error to standard output so all versions work the same. (This problem has been fixed in newer versions of the system, but we've left it as is to illustrate how you can often cope with minor botches.)

```
$ cat news
# news:  print news files, version 2

HOME=.            # debugging only
cd .              # place holder for /usr/news
IFS='
'                 # just a newline
for i in  `ls -t * $HOME/.news_time 2>&1`
do
        case $i in
        *' not found')   ;;
        */.news_time)    break ;;
        *)               echo news: $i ;;
        esac
done
touch $HOME/.news_time
$ rm .news_time
$ news
news: news
news: y
news: x
$
```

We must set IFS to newline so the message

```
./.news_time not found
```

is not parsed as three words.

   news must next print the news files, rather than echoing their names. It's useful to know who posted a message and when, so we use the set command and ls -1 to print a header before the message itself:

```
$ ls -l news
-rwxrwxrwx 1 you             208 Oct  1 12:05 news
$ set `ls -l news`
-rwxrwxrwx: bad option(s)                        Something is wrong!
$
```

Here is one example where the interchangeability of program and data in the shell gets in the way. set complains because its argument ("-rwxrwxrwx") begins with a minus sign and thus looks like an option. An easy (if inelegant) fix is to prefix the argument by an ordinary character:

```
$ set X`ls -l news`
$ echo "news: ($3) $5 $6 $7"
news: (you) Oct 1 12:05
$
```

This is a reasonable format, showing the author and date of the message along with the filename.

Here is the final version of the news command:

```
# news:  print news files, final version

PATH=/bin:/usr/bin
IFS='
'                                 # just a newline
cd /usr/news

for i in `ls -t * $HOME/.news_time 2>&1`
do
        IFS=' '
        case $i in
        *' not found')   ;;
        */.news_time)    break ;;
        *)          set X`ls -l $i`
                    echo "
$i: ($3) $5 $6 $7
"
                    cat $i
        esac
done
touch $HOME/.news_time
```

The extra newlines in the header separate the news items as they are printed. The first value of IFS is just a newline, so the not found message (if any) from the first ls is treated as a single argument. The second assignment to IFS resets it to a blank, so the output of the second ls is split into multiple arguments.

Exercise 5-27. Add an option -n (notify) to news to report but not print the news items, and not touch .news_time. This might be placed in your .profile. □

Exercise 5-28. Compare our design and implementation of news to the similar command on your system. □

5.9 get and put: tracking file changes

In this section, the last of a long chapter, we will show a larger, more complicated example that illustrates cooperation of the shell with awk and sed.

A program evolves as bugs are fixed and features are added. It is sometimes convenient to keep track of these versions, especially if people take the program to other machines — they will come back and ask "What has changed since we got our version?" or "How did you fix the such-and-such bug?" Also, always maintaining backup copies makes it safer to try out ideas: if something doesn't work out, it's painless to revert to the original program.

One solution is to keep copies of all the versions around, but that is difficult to organize and expensive in disc space. Instead, we will capitalize on the likelihood that successive versions have large portions in common, which need to be stored only once. The diff -e command

```
$ diff -e old new
```

generates a list of ed commands that will convert old into new. It is therefore possible to keep all the versions of a file in a single (different) file by maintaining one complete version and the set of editing commands to convert it into any other version.

There are two obvious organizations: keep the newest version intact and have editing commands go backwards in time, or keep the oldest version and have editing commands go forwards. Although the latter is slightly easier to program, the former is faster if there are many versions, because we are almost always interested in recent versions.

We chose the former organization. In a single file, which we'll call the *history file*, there is the current version followed by sets of editing commands that convert each version into the previous (i.e., next older) one. Each set of editing commands begins with a line that looks like

```
@@@ person date summary
```

The *summary* is a single line, provided by *person*, that describes the change.

There are two commands to maintain versions: get extracts a version from the history file, and put enters a new version into the history file after asking for a one-line summary of the changes.

Before showing the implementation, here is an example to show how get and put work and how the history file is maintained:

```
$ echo a line of text >junk
$ put junk
Summary: make a new file                 Type the description
get: no file junk.H                      History doesn't exist...
put: creating junk.H                     ... so put creates it
$ cat junk.H
a line of text
@@@ you Sat Oct  1 13:31:03 EDT 1983 make a new file
$ echo another line >>junk
$ put junk
Summary: one line added
$ cat junk.H
a line of text
another line
@@@ you Sat Oct  1 13:32:28 EDT 1983 one line added
2d
@@@ you Sat Oct  1 13:31:03 EDT 1983 make a new file
$
```

The "editing commands" consist of the single line 2d, which deletes line 2 of the file, turning the new version into the original.

```
$ rm junk
$ get junk                               Most recent version
$ cat junk
a line of text
another line
$ get -1 junk
$ cat junk                               Newest-but-one version
a line of text
$ get junk                               Most recent again
$ replace another 'a different' junk     Change it
$ put junk
Summary: second line changed
$ cat junk.H
a line of text
a different line
@@@ you Sat Oct  1 13:34:07 EDT 1983 second line changed
2c
another line
.
@@@ you Sat Oct  1 13:32:28 EDT 1983 one line added
2d
@@@ you Sat Oct  1 13:31:03 EDT 1983 make a new file
$
```

The editing commands run top to bottom throughout the history file to extract the desired version: the first set converts the newest to the second newest, the next converts that to the third newest, etc. Therefore, we are actually converting the new file into the old one a version at a time when running ed.

There will clearly be trouble if the file we are modifying contains lines
beginning with a triple at-sign, and the BUGS section of diff(1) warns about
lines that contain only a period. We chose @@@ to mark the editing commands
because it's an unlikely sequence for normal text.

Although it might be instructive to show how the get and put commands
evolved, they are relatively long and showing their various forms would
require too much discussion. We will therefore show you only their finished
forms. put is simpler:

```
# put:  install file into history

PATH=/bin:/usr/bin

case $# in
        1)      HIST=$1.H ;;
        *)      echo 'Usage: put file' 1>&2; exit 1 ;;
esac
if test ! -r $1
then
        echo "put: can't open $1" 1>&2
        exit 1
fi
trap 'rm -f /tmp/put.[ab]$$; exit 1' 1 2 15
echo -n 'Summary: '
read Summary

if get -o /tmp/put.a$$ $1                  # previous version
then                            # merge pieces
        cp $1 /tmp/put.b$$                  # current version
        echo "@@@ `getname` `date` $Summary" >>/tmp/put.b$$
        diff -e $1 /tmp/put.a$$ >>/tmp/put.b$$  # latest diffs
        sed -n '/^@@@/,$p' <$HIST >>/tmp/put.b$$ # old diffs
        overwrite $HIST cat /tmp/put.b$$        # put it back
else                            # make a new one
        echo "put: creating $HIST"
        cp $1 $HIST
        echo "@@@ `getname` `date` $Summary" >>$HIST
fi
rm -f /tmp/put.[ab]$$
```

After reading the one-line summary, put calls get to extract the previous version of the file from the history file. The −o option to get specifies an alternate output file. If get couldn't find the history file, it returns an error status
and put creates a new history file. If the history file does exist, the then
clause creates the new history in a temporary file from, in order, the newest
version, the @@@ line, the editor commands to convert from the newest version
to the previous, and the old editor commands and @@@ lines. Finally, the temporary file is copied onto the history file using overwrite.

get is more complicated than put, mostly because it has options.

```
# get:   extract file from history

PATH=/bin:/usr/bin

VERSION=0
while test "$1" != ""
do
    case "$1" in
        -i) INPUT=$2; shift ;;
        -o) OUTPUT=$2; shift ;;
        -[0-9]) VERSION=$1 ;;
        -*) echo "get: Unknown argument $i" 1>&2; exit 1 ;;
        *)  case "$OUTPUT" in
            "") OUTPUT=$1 ;;
            *)  INPUT=$1.H ;;
            esac
    esac
    shift
done
OUTPUT=${OUTPUT?"Usage: get [-o outfile] [-i file.H] file"}
INPUT=${INPUT-$OUTPUT.H}
test -r $INPUT || { echo "get: no file $INPUT" 1>&2; exit 1; }
trap 'rm -f /tmp/get.[ab]$$; exit 1' 1 2 15
# split into current version and editing commands
sed <$INPUT -n '1,/^@@@/w /tmp/get.a'$$'
                    /^@@@/,$w /tmp/get.b'$$
# perform the edits
awk </tmp/get.b$$ '
    /^@@@/   { count++ }
    !/^@@@/ && count > 0 && count <= - '$VERSION'
    END { print "$d"; print "w", "'$OUTPUT'" }
' | ed - /tmp/get.a$$
rm -f /tmp/get.[ab]$$
```

The options are fairly ordinary. -i and -o specify alternate input and output. -[0-9] selects a particular version: 0 is the newest version (the default), -1 the newest-but-one, etc. The loop over arguments is a while with a test and a shift, rather than a for, because some of the options (-i, -o) consume another argument and must therefore shift it out, and for loops and shifts do not cooperate properly if the shift is inside the for. The ed option '-' turns off the character count that normally accompanies reading or writing a file.

The line

```
test -r $INPUT || { echo "get: no file $INPUT" 1>&2; exit 1; }
```

is equivalent to

```
if test ! -r $INPUT
then
        echo "get: no file $INPUT" 1>&2
        exit 1
fi
```

(which is the form we used in put) but is shorter to write and clearer to programmers who are familiar with the ¦¦ operator. Commands between { and } are executed in the current shell, not a sub-shell; this is necessary here so the exit will exit from get and not just a sub-shell. The characters { and } are like do and done — they have special meaning only if they follow a semicolon, newline or other command terminator.

Finally, we come to the code in get that does the work. First, sed breaks the history file into two pieces: the most recent version and the set of edits. The awk program then processes the editing commands. @@@ lines are counted (but not printed), and as long as the count is not greater than the desired version, the editing commands are passed through (recall that the default awk action is to print the input line). Two ed commands are added after those from the history file: $d deletes the single @@@ line that sed left on the current version, and a w command writes the file to its final location. overwrite is unnecessary here because get changes only the version of the file, not the precious history file.

Exercise 5-29. Write a command version that does two things:

```
$ version -5 file
```

reports the summary, modification date and person making the modification of the selected version in the history file.

```
$ version sep 20 file
```

reports which version number was current on September 20. This would typically be used in:

```
$ get `version sep 20 file`
```

(version can echo the history filename for convenience.)   □

Exercise 5-30. Modify get and put so they manipulate the history file in a separate directory, rather than cluttering up the working directory with .H files.   □

Exercise 5-31. Not all versions of a file are worth remembering once things settle down. How can you arrange to delete versions from the middle of the history file?   □

5.10 A look back

When you're faced with writing a new program, there's a natural tendency to start thinking immediately about how to write it in your favorite programming language. In our case, that language is most often the shell.

Although it has some unusual syntax, the shell is an excellent programming language. It is certainly high-level; its operators are whole programs. Since it is interactive, programs can be developed interactively, and refined in small steps until they "work." After that, if they are intended for more than personal use, they can be polished and hardened for a wider user population. In those infrequent cases where a shell program turns out to be too inefficient, some or all of it can be rewritten in C, but with the design already proven and a working implementation in hand. (We'll follow this path a couple of times in the next chapter.)

This general approach is characteristic of the UNIX programming environment — build on what others have done instead of starting over from nothing; start with something small and let it evolve; use the tools to experiment with new ideas.

In this chapter, we've presented many examples that are easy to do with existing programs and the shell. Sometimes it's enough merely to rearrange arguments; that was the case with `cal`. Sometimes the shell provides a loop over a set of filenames or through a sequence of command executions, as in `watchfor` and `checkmail`. More complicated examples are still less work than they would be in C; for instance, our 20-line shell version of `news` replaces a 350-line [sic] version written in C.

But it's not enough to have a programmable command language. Nor is it enough to have a lot of programs. What matters is that all of the components *work together*. They share conventions about how information is represented and communicated. Each is designed to focus on one job and do it well. The shell then serves to bind them together, easily and efficiently, whenever you have a new idea. This cooperation is why the UNIX programming environment is so productive.

History and bibliographic notes

The idea for `get` and `put` comes from the Source Code Control System (SCCS) originated by Marc Rochkind ("The source code control system," *IEEE Trans. on Software Engineering*, 1975). SCCS is far more powerful and flexible than our simple programs; it is meant for maintenance of large programs in a production environment. The basis of SCCS is the same `diff` program, however.

CHAPTER 6: **PROGRAMMING WITH STANDARD I/O**

So far we have used existing tools to build new ones, but we are at the limit of what can be reasonably done with the shell, sed and awk. In this chapter we are going to write some simple programs in the C programming language. The basic philosophy of making things that work together will continue to dominate the discussion and the design of the programs — we want to create tools that others can use and build on. In each case, we will also try to show a sensible implementation strategy: start with the bare minimum that does something useful, then add features and options (only) if the need arises.

There are good reasons for writing new programs from scratch. It may be that the problem at hand just can't be solved with existing programs. This is often true when the program must deal with non-text files, for example — the majority of the programs we have shown so far really work well only on textual information. Or it may be too difficult to achieve adequate robustness or efficiency with just the shell and other general-purpose tools. In such cases, a shell version may be good for honing the definition and user interface of a program. (And if it works well enough, there's no point re-doing it.) The zap program from the last chapter is a good example: it took only a few minutes to write the first version in the shell, and the final version has an adequate user interface, but it's too slow.

We will be writing in C because it is the standard language of UNIX systems — the kernel and all user programs are written in C — and, realistically, no other language is nearly as well supported. We will assume that you know C, at least well enough to read along. If not, read *The C Programming Language*, by B. W. Kernighan and D. M. Ritchie (Prentice-Hall, 1978).

We will also be using the "standard I/O library," a collection of routines that provide efficient and portable I/O and system services for C programs. The standard I/O library is available on many non-UNIX systems that support C, so programs that confine their system interactions to its facilities can easily be transported.

The examples we have chosen for this chapter have a common property: they are small tools that we use regularly, but that were not part of the 7th Edition. If your system has similar programs, you may find it enlightening to

171

compare designs.   And if they are new to you, you may find them as useful as
we have.   In any case, they should help to make the point that no system is
perfect, and that often it is quite easy to improve things and to cover up
defects with modest effort.

6.1 Standard input and output: `vis`

Many programs read only one input and write one output; for such programs, I/O that uses only standard input and standard output may be entirely
adequate, and it is almost always enough to get started.

Let us illustrate with a program called `vis` that copies its standard input to
its standard output, except that it makes all non-printing characters visible by
printing them as *nnn*, where *nnn* is the octal value of the character. `vis` is
invaluable for detecting strange or unwanted characters that may have crept
into files.   For instance, `vis` will print each backspace as \010, which is the
octal value of the backspace character:

```
$ cat x
abc
$ vis <x
abc\010\010\010___
$
```

To scan multiple files with this rudimentary version of `vis`, you can use `cat`
to collect the files:

```
$ cat file1 file2 ... | vis
...
$ cat file1 file2 ... | vis | grep '\\'
...
```

and thus avoid learning how to access files from a program.

By the way, it might seem that you could do this job with `sed`, since the '1'
command displays non-printable characters in an understandable form:

```
$ sed -n l x
abc◄◄◄___
$
```

The `sed` output is probably clearer than that from `vis`.   But `sed` was never
meant for non-text files:

```
$ sed -n l /usr/you/bin
$                              Nothing at all!
```

(This was on a PDP-11; on one VAX system, `sed` aborted, probably because
the input looks like a very long line of text.)   So `sed` is inadequate, and we are
forced to write a new program.

The simplest input and output routines are called `getchar` and `putchar`.
Each call to `getchar` gets the next character from the standard input, which

may be a file or a pipe or the terminal (the default) — the program doesn't know which. Similarly, `putchar(c)` puts the character c on the standard output, which is also by default the terminal.

The function `printf`(3) does output format conversion. Calls to `printf` and `putchar` may be interleaved in any order; the output will appear in the order of the calls. There is a corresponding function `scanf`(3) for input format conversion; it will read the standard input and break it up into strings, numbers, etc., as desired. Calls to `scanf` and `getchar` may also be intermixed.

Here is the first version of `vis`:

```
/* vis:  make funny characters visible (version 1) */

#include <stdio.h>
#include <ctype.h>

main()
{
    int c;

    while ((c = getchar()) != EOF)
        if (isascii(c) &&
            (isprint(c) || c=='\n' || c=='\t' || c==' '))
            putchar(c);
        else
            printf("\\%03o", c);
    exit(0);
}
```

`getchar` returns the next byte from the input, or the value EOF when it encounters the end of file (or an error). By the way, EOF is *not* a byte from the file; recall the discussion of end of file in Chapter 2. The value of EOF is guaranteed to be different from any value that occurs in a single byte so it can be distinguished from real data; c is declared `int`, not `char`, so that it is big enough to hold the EOF value. The line

```
#include <stdio.h>
```

should appear at the beginning of each source file. It causes the C compiler to read a *header file* (`/usr/include/stdio.h`) of standard routines and symbols that includes the definition of EOF. We will use `<stdio.h>` as a shorthand for the full filename in the text.

The file `<ctype.h>` is another header file in `/usr/include` that defines machine-independent tests for determining the properties of characters. We used `isascii` and `isprint` here, to determine whether the input character is ASCII (i.e., value less than 0200) and printable; other tests are listed in Table 6.1. Notice that newline, tab and blank are not "printable" by the definitions in `<ctype.h>`.

The call to `exit` at the end of `vis` is not necessary to make the program work properly, but it ensures that any caller of the program will see a normal exit status (conventionally zero) from the program when it completes. An alternate way to return status is to leave `main` with `return 0`; the return value from `main` is the program's exit status. If there is no explicit `return` or `exit`, the exit status is unpredictable.

To compile a C program, put the source in a file whose name ends in `.c`, such as `vis.c`, compile it with `cc`, then run the result, which the compiler leaves in a file called `a.out` ('a' is for assembler):

```
$ cc vis.c
$ a.out
hello worldctl-g
hello world\007
ctl-d
$
```

Normally you would rename `a.out` once it's working, or use the `cc` option `-o` to do it directly:

```
$ cc -o vis vis.c                              Output in vis, not a.out
```

Exercise 6-1. We decided that tabs should be left alone, rather than made visible as `\011` or ➤ or `\t`, since our main use of `vis` is looking for truly anomalous characters. An alternate design is to identify *every* character of output unambiguously — tabs, non-graphics, blanks at line ends, etc. Modify `vis` so that characters like tab, backslash, backspace, formfeed, etc., are printed in their conventional C representations `\t`, `\\`, `\b`, `\f`, etc., and so that blanks at the ends of lines are marked. Can you do this unambiguously? Compare your design with

```
$ sed -n l
```

□

Exercise 6-2. Modify `vis` so that it folds long lines at some reasonable length. How does this interact with the unambiguous output required in the previous exercise? □

6.2 Program arguments: `vis` version 2

When a C program is executed, the command-line arguments are made available to the function `main` as a count `argc` and an array `argv` of pointers to character strings that contain the arguments. By convention, `argv[0]` is the command name itself, so `argc` is always greater than 0; the "useful" arguments are `argv[1]` ... `argv[argc-1]`. Recall that redirection with `<` and `>` is done by the shell, not by individual programs, so redirection has no effect on the number of arguments seen by the program.

To illustrate argument handling, let's modify `vis` by adding an optional argument: `vis -s` strips out any non-printing characters rather than displaying them prominently. This option is handy for cleaning up files from other systems, for example those that use CRLF (carriage return and line feed) instead

```
                Table 6.1:  <ctype.h> Character Test Macros
 isalpha(c)       alphabetic: a-z A-Z
 isupper(c)       upper case: A-Z
 islower(c)       lower case: a-z
 isdigit(c)       digit: 0-9
 isxdigit(c)      hexadecimal digit: 0-9 a-f A-F
 isalnum(c)       alphabetic or digit
 isspace(c)       blank, tab, newline, vertical tab, formfeed, return
 ispunct(c)       not alphanumeric or control or space
 isprint(c)       printable: any graphic
 iscntrl(c)       control character: 0 <= c < 040 ¦¦ c == 0177
 isascii(c)       ASCII character: 0 <= c <= 0177
```

of newline to terminate lines.

```
      /* vis:  make funny characters visible (version 2) */

      #include <stdio.h>
      #include <ctype.h>

      main(argc, argv)
          int argc;
          char *argv[];
      {
          int c, strip = 0;

          if (argc > 1 && strcmp(argv[1], "-s") == 0)
              strip = 1;
          while ((c = getchar()) != EOF)
              if (isascii(c) &&
                  (isprint(c) ¦¦ c=='\n' ¦¦ c=='\t' ¦¦ c==' '))
                  putchar(c);
              else if (!strip)
                  printf("\\%03o", c);
          exit(0);
      }
```

argv is a pointer to an array whose individual elements are pointers to arrays of characters; each array is terminated by the ASCII character NUL ('\0'), so it can be treated as a string. This version of vis starts by checking to see if there is an argument and if it is -s. (Invalid arguments are ignored.) The function strcmp(3) compares two strings, returning zero if they are the same.

Table 6.2 lists a set of string handling and general utility functions, of which strcmp is one. It's usually best to use these functions instead of writing your own, since they are standard, they are debugged, and they are often faster than what you can write yourself because they have been optimized for particular machines (sometimes by being written in assembly language).

Exercise 6-3. Change the `-s` argument so that `vis -s`*n* will print only strings of *n* or more consecutive printable characters, discarding non-printing characters and short sequences of printable ones. This is valuable for isolating the text parts of non-text files such as executable programs. Some versions of the system provide a `strings` program that does this. Is it better to have a separate program or an argument to `vis`? □

Exercise 6-4. The availability of the C source code is one of the strengths of the UNIX system — the code illustrates elegant solutions to many programming problems. Comment on the tradeoff between readability of the C source and the occasional optimizations obtained from rewriting in assembly language. □

Table 6.2: Standard String Functions	
`strcat(s,t)`	append string `t` to string `s`; return `s`
`strncat(s,t,n)`	append at most `n` characters of `t` to `s`
`strcpy(s,t)`	copy `t` to `s`; return `s`
`strncpy(s,t,n)`	copy exactly `n` characters; null pad if necessary
`strcmp(s,t)`	compare `s` and `t`, return <0, 0, >0 for <, ==, >
`strncmp(s,t,n)`	compare at most `n` characters
`strlen(s)`	return length of `s`
`strchr(s,c)`	return pointer to first `c` in `s`, NULL if none
`strrchr(s,c)`	return pointer to last `c` in `s`, NULL if none. These are `index` and `rindex` on older systems
`atoi(s)`	return integer value of `s`
`atof(s)`	return floating point value of `s`; needs declaration `double atof()`
`malloc(n)`	return pointer to `n` bytes of memory, NULL if can't
`calloc(n,m)`	return pointer to `n`×`m` bytes, set to 0, NULL if can't. `malloc` and `calloc` return `char *`
`free(p)`	free memory allocated by `malloc` or `calloc`

6.3 File access: `vis` version 3

The first two versions of `vis` read the standard input and write the standard output, which are both inherited from the shell. The next step is to modify `vis` to access files by their names, so that

```
$ vis file1 file2 ...
```

will scan the named files instead of the standard input. If there are no filename arguments, though, we still want `vis` to read its standard input.

The question is how to arrange for the files to be read — that is, how to connect the filenames to the I/O statements that actually read the data.

The rules are simple. Before it can be read or written a file must be *opened* by the standard library function fopen. fopen takes a filename (like temp or /etc/passwd), does some housekeeping and negotiation with the kernel, and returns an internal name to be used in subsequent operations on the file.

This internal name is actually a pointer, called a *file pointer*, to a structure that contains information about the file, such as the location of a buffer, the current character position in the buffer, whether the file is being read or written, and the like. One of the definitions obtained by including <stdio.h> is for a structure called FILE. The declaration for a file pointer is

```
FILE *fp;
```

This says that fp is a pointer to a FILE. fopen returns a pointer to a FILE; there is a type declaration for fopen in <stdio.h>.

The actual call to fopen in a program is

```
char *name, *mode;

fp = fopen(name, mode);
```

The first argument of fopen is the name of the file, as a character string. The second argument, also a character string, indicates how you intend to use the file; the legal modes are read ("r"), write ("w"), or append ("a").

If a file that you open for writing or appending does not exist, it is created, if possible. Opening an existing file for writing causes the old contents to be discarded. Trying to read a file that does not exist is an error, as is trying to read or write a file when you don't have permission. If there is any error, fopen will return the invalid pointer value NULL (which is defined, usually as (char *)0, in <stdio.h>).

The next thing needed is a way to read or write the file once it is open. There are several possibilities, of which getc and putc are the simplest. getc gets the next character from a file.

```
c = getc(fp)
```

places in c the next character from the file referred to by fp; it returns EOF when it reaches end of file. putc is analogous to getc:

```
putc(c, fp)
```

puts the character c on the file fp and returns c. getc and putc return EOF if an error occurs.

When a program is started, three files are open already, and file pointers are provided for them. These files are the standard input, the standard output, and the standard error output; the corresponding file pointers are called stdin, stdout, and stderr. These file pointers are declared in <stdio.h>; they may be used anywhere an object of type FILE * can be. They are constants, however, *not* variables, so you can't assign to them.

getchar() is the same as getc(stdin) and putchar(c) is the same as putc(c,stdout). In fact, all four of these "functions" are defined as macros in <stdio.h>, since they run faster by avoiding the overhead of a function call for each character. See Table 6.3 for some other definitions in <stdio.h>.

With some of the preliminaries out of the way, we can now write the third version of vis. If there are command-line arguments, they are processed in order. If there are no arguments, the standard input is processed.

```
/* vis:  make funny characters visible (version 3) */

#include <stdio.h>
#include <ctype.h>
int strip = 0;        /* 1 => discard special characters */

main(argc, argv)
    int argc;
    char *argv[];
{
    int i;
    FILE *fp;

    while (argc > 1 && argv[1][0] == '-') {
        switch (argv[1][1]) {
        case 's':   /* -s: strip funny chars */
            strip = 1;
            break;
        default:
            fprintf(stderr, "%s: unknown arg %s\n",
                argv[0], argv[1]);
            exit(1);
        }
        argc--;
        argv++;
    }
    if (argc == 1)
        vis(stdin);
    else
        for (i = 1; i < argc; i++)
            if ((fp=fopen(argv[i], "r")) == NULL) {
                fprintf(stderr, "%s: can't open %s\n",
                    argv[0], argv[i]);
                exit(1);
            } else {
                vis(fp);
                fclose(fp);
            }
    exit(0);
}
```

This code relies on the convention that optional arguments come first. After

```
              Table 6.3:  Some <stdio.h> Definitions
   stdin          standard input
   stdout         standard output
   stderr         standard error
   EOF            end of file; normally -1
   NULL           invalid pointer; normally 0
   FILE           used for declaring file pointers
   BUFSIZ         normal I/O buffer size (often 512 or 1024)

   getc(fp)       return one character from stream fp
   getchar()      getc(stdin)
   putc(c,fp)     put character c on stream fp
   putchar(c)     putc(c,stdout)
   feof(fp)       non-zero when end of file on stream fp
   ferror(fp)     non-zero when any error on stream fp
   fileno(fp)     file descriptor for stream fp;  see Chapter 7
```

each optional argument is processed, argc and argv are adjusted so the rest of the program is independent of the presence of that argument. Even though vis only recognizes a single option, we wrote the code as a loop to show one way to organize argument processing. In Chapter 1 we remarked on the disorderly way that UNIX programs handle optional arguments. One reason, aside from a taste for anarchy, is that it's obviously easy to write code to handle argument parsing for any variation. The function getopt(3) found on some systems is an attempt to rationalize the situation; you might investigate it before writing your own.

The routine vis prints a single file:

```
vis(fp) /* make chars visible in FILE *fp */
    FILE *fp;
{
    int c;

    while ((c = getc(fp)) != EOF)
        if (isascii(c) &&
            (isprint(c) || c=='\n' || c=='\t' || c==' '))
            putchar(c);
        else if (!strip)
            printf("\\%03o", c);
}
```

The function fprintf is identical to printf, except for a file pointer argument that specifies the file to be written.

The function fclose breaks the connection between the file pointer and the external name that was established by fopen, freeing the file pointer for another file. Since there is a limit (about 20) on the number of files that a program may have open simultaneously, it's best to free files when they are no longer needed. Normally, output produced with any of the standard library functions like `printf`, `putc`, etc., is buffered so it can be written in large chunks for efficiency. (The exception is output to a terminal, which is usually written as it is produced, or at least when a newline is printed.) Calling `fclose` on an output file also forces out any buffered output. `fclose` is also called automatically for each open file when a program calls `exit` or returns from `main`.

   `stderr` is assigned to a program in the same way that `stdin` and `stdout` are. Output written on `stderr` appears on the user's terminal even if the standard output is redirected. `vis` writes its diagnostics on `stderr` instead of `stdout` so that if one of the files can't be accessed for some reason, the message finds its way to the user's terminal instead of disappearing down a pipeline or into an output file. (The standard error was invented somewhat after pipes, after error messages *did* start disappearing into pipelines.)

   Somewhat arbitrarily, we decided that `vis` will quit if it can't open an input file; this is reasonable for a program most often used interactively, and with a single input file. You can argue for the other design as well, however.

Exercise 6-5. Write a program `printable` that prints the name of each argument file that contains only printable characters; if the file contains any non-printable character, the name is not printed. `printable` is useful in situations like this:

```
$ pr `printable *` | lpr
```

Add the option `-v` to invert the sense of the test, as in `grep`. What should `printable` do if there are no filename arguments? What status should `printable` return? □

6.4 A screen-at-a-time printer: `p`

   So far we have used `cat` to examine files. But if a file is long, and if you are connected to your system by a high-speed connection, `cat` produces the output too fast to be read, even if you are quick with *ctl*-s and *ctl*-q.

   There clearly should be a program to print a file in small, controllable chunks, but there isn't a standard one, probably because the original UNIX system was written in the days of hard-copy (paper) terminals and slow communications lines. So our next example is a program called p that will print a file a screenful at a time, waiting for a response from the user after each screen before continuing to the next. ("p" is a nice short name for a program that we use a lot.) As with other programs, p reads either from files named as arguments or from its standard input:

```
$ p vis.c
...
$ grep '#define' *.[ch] | p
...
$
```

This program is best written in C because it's easy in C, and hard otherwise; the standard tools are not good at mixing the input from a file or pipe with terminal input.

The basic, no-frills design is to print the input in small chunks. A suitable chunk size is 22 lines: that's slightly less than the 24-line screen of most video terminals, and one third of a standard 66-line page. A simple way for p to prompt the user is to not print the last newline of each 22-line chunk. The cursor will thus pause at the right end of the line rather than at the left margin. When the user presses RETURN, that will supply the missing newline and thus cause the next line to appear in the proper place. If the user types *ctl*-d or q at the end of a screen, p will exit.

We will take no special action for long lines. We will also not worry about multiple files: we'll merely skip from one to the next without comment. That way the behavior of

```
$ p filenames...
```

will be the same as

```
$ cat filenames... | p
```

If filenames are needed, they can be added with a for loop like

```
$ for i in filenames...
> do
>        echo $i:
>        cat $i
> done | p
```

Indeed, there are too many features that we can add to this program. It's better to make a stripped-down version, then let it evolve as experience dictates. That way, the features are the ones that people really want, not the ones we thought they would want.

The basic structure of p is the same as vis: the main routine cycles through the files, calling a routine print that does the work on each.

```
/* p:  print input in chunks (version 1) */

#include <stdio.h>
#define PAGESIZE    22
char    *progname;  /* program name for error message */

main(argc, argv)
    int argc;
    char *argv[];
{
    int i;
    FILE *fp, *efopen();

    progname = argv[0];
    if (argc == 1)
        print(stdin, PAGESIZE);
    else
        for (i = 1; i < argc; i++) {
            fp = efopen(argv[i], "r");
            print(fp, PAGESIZE);
            fclose(fp);
        }
    exit(0);
}
```

The routine efopen encapsulates a very common operation: try to open a file; if it's not possible, print an error message and exit. To encourage error messages that identify the offending (or offended) program, efopen refers to an external string progname containing the name of the program, which is set in main.

```
FILE *efopen(file, mode)    /* fopen file, die if can't */
    char *file, *mode;
{
    FILE *fp, *fopen();
    extern char *progname;

    if ((fp = fopen(file, mode)) != NULL)
        return fp;
    fprintf(stderr, "%s: can't open file %s mode %s\n",
        progname, file, mode);
    exit(1);
}
```

We tried a couple of other designs for efopen before settling on this. One was to have it return after printing the message, with a null pointer indicating failure. This gives the caller the option of continuing or exiting. Another design provided efopen with a third argument specifying whether it should return after failing to open the file. In almost all of our examples, however,

there's no point to continuing if a file can't be accessed, so the current version
of efopen is best for our use.

The real work of the p command is done in print:

```
print(fp, pagesize) /* print fp in pagesize chunks */
    FILE *fp;
    int pagesize;
{
    static int lines = 0;   /* number of lines so far */
    char buf[BUFSIZ];

    while (fgets(buf, sizeof buf, fp) != NULL)
        if (++lines < pagesize)
            fputs(buf, stdout);
        else {
            buf[strlen(buf)-1] = '\0';
            fputs(buf, stdout);
            fflush(stdout);
            ttyin();
            lines = 0;
        }
}
```

We used BUFSIZ, which is defined in <stdio.h>, as the size of the input
buffer. fgets(buf,size,fp) fetches the next line of input from fp, up to
and including a newline, into buf, and adds a terminating \0; at most size-1
characters are copied. It returns NULL at end of file. (fgets could be better
designed: it returns buf instead of a character count; furthermore it provides
no warning if the input line was too long. No characters are lost, but you have
to look at buf to see what really happened.)

The function strlen returns the length of a string; we use that to knock
the trailing newline off the last input line. fputs(buf,fp) writes the string
buf on file fp. The call to fflush at the end of the page forces out any buffered output.

The task of reading the response from the user after each page has been
printed is delegated to a routine called ttyin. ttyin can't read the standard
input, since p must work even when its input comes from a file or pipe. To
handle this, the program opens the file /dev/tty, which is the user's terminal
regardless of any redirection of standard input. We wrote ttyin to return the
first character of the response, but don't use that feature here.

```
ttyin() /* process response from /dev/tty (version 1) */
{
    char buf[BUFSIZ];
    FILE *efopen();
    static FILE *tty = NULL;

    if (tty == NULL)
        tty = efopen("/dev/tty", "r");
    if (fgets(buf, BUFSIZ, tty) == NULL || buf[0] == 'q')
        exit(0);
    else    /* ordinary line */
        return buf[0];
}
```

The file pointer devtty is declared static so that it retains its value from one call of ttyin to the next; the file /dev/tty is opened on the first call only.

There are obviously extra features that could be added to p without much work, but it is worth noting that our first version of this program did just what is described here: print 22 lines and wait. It was a long time before other things were added, and to this day only a few people use the extra features.

One easy extra is to make the number of lines per page a variable pagesize that can be set from the command line:

```
$ p -n ...
```

prints in n-line chunks. This requires only adding some familiar code at the beginning of main:

```
/* p:   print input in chunks (version 2) */
    ...
    int i, pagesize = PAGESIZE;

    progname = argv[0];
    if (argc > 1 && argv[1][0] == '-') {
        pagesize = atoi(&argv[1][1]);
        argc--;
        argv++;
    }
    ...
```

The function atoi converts a character string to an integer. (See atoi(3).)

Another addition to p is the ability to escape temporarily at the end of each page to do some other command. By analogy to ed and many other programs, if the user types a line that begins with an exclamation mark, the rest of that line is taken to be a command, and is passed to a shell for execution. This feature is also trivial, since there is a function called system(3) to do the work, but read the caveat below. The modified version of ttyin follows:

```
ttyin()  /* process response from /dev/tty (version 2) */
{
    char buf[BUFSIZ];
    FILE *efopen();
    static FILE *tty = NULL;

    if (tty == NULL)
        tty = efopen("/dev/tty", "r");
    for (;;) {
        if (fgets(buf,BUFSIZ,tty) == NULL || buf[0] == 'q')
            exit(0);
        else if (buf[0] == '!') {
            system(buf+1);   /* BUG here */
            printf("!\n");
        }
        else    /* ordinary line */
            return buf[0];
    }
}
```

Unfortunately, this version of `ttyin` has a subtle, pernicious bug. The command run by `system` inherits the standard input from p, so if p is reading from a pipe or a file, the command may interfere with its input:

```
$ cat /etc/passwd | p -1
root:3D.fHR5KoB.3s:0:1:S.User:/:!ed    Invoke ed from within p
?                                      ed reads /etc/passwd ...
!                                      ... is confused, and quits
```

The solution requires knowledge about how UNIX processes are controlled, and we will present it in Section 7.4. For now, be aware that the standard `system` in the library can cause trouble, but that `ttyin` works correctly if compiled with the version of `system` in Chapter 7.

We have now written two programs, `vis` and p, that might be considered variants of `cat`, with some embellishments. So should they all be part of `cat`, accessible by optional arguments like -v and -p? The question of whether to write a new program or to add features to an old one arises repeatedly as people have new ideas. We don't have a definitive answer, but there are some principles that help to decide.

The main principle is that a program should only do one basic job — if it does too many things, it gets bigger, slower, harder to maintain, and harder to use. Indeed, the features often lie unused because people can't remember the options anyway.

This suggests that `cat` and `vis` should *not* be combined. `cat` just copies its input, unchanged, while `vis` transforms it. Merging them makes a program that does two different things. It's almost as clear with `cat` and p. `cat` is meant for fast, efficient copying; p is meant for browsing. And p does transform its output: every 22nd newline is dropped. Three separate programs seems to be the proper design.

Exercise 6-6. Does p act sanely if `pagesize` is not positive? □

Exercise 6-7. What else could be done to p? Evaluate and implement (if appropriate) the ability to re-print parts of earlier input. (This is one extra feature that we enjoy.) Add a facility to permit printing less than a screenful of input after each pause. Add a facility to scan forward or backward for a line specified by number or content. □

Exercise 6-8. Use the file manipulation capabilities of the `exec` shell built-in (see sh(1)) to fix `ttyin`'s call to `system`. □

Exercise 6-9. If you forget to specify an input for p, it sits quietly waiting for input from the terminal. Is it worth detecting this probable error? If so, how? Hint: isatty(3). □

6.5 An example: `pick`

The version of `pick` in Chapter 5 was clearly stretching the capabilities of the shell. The C version that follows is somewhat different from the one in Chapter 5. If it has arguments, they are processed as before. But if the single argument '–' is specified, `pick` processes its standard input.

Why not just read the standard input if there are no arguments? Consider the second version of the `zap` command in Section 5.6:

```
kill $SIG `pick \`ps -ag ¦ egrep "$*"\` ¦ awk '{print $1}'`
```

What happens if the `egrep` pattern doesn't match anything? In that case, `pick` has no arguments and starts to read its standard input; the `zap` command fails in a mystifying way. Requiring an explicit argument is an easy way to disambiguate such situations, and the '–' convention from `cat` and other programs indicates how to specify it.

```
/* pick:   offer choice on each argument */

#include <stdio.h>
char     *progname;   /* program name for error message */

main(argc, argv)
    int argc;
    char *argv[];
{
    int i;
    char buf[BUFSIZ];

    progname = argv[0];
    if (argc == 2 && strcmp(argv[1],"-") == 0)   /* pick - */
        while (fgets(buf, sizeof buf, stdin) != NULL) {
            buf[strlen(buf)-1] = '\0';   /* drop newline */
            pick(buf);
        }
    else
        for (i = 1; i < argc; i++)
            pick(argv[i]);
    exit(0);
}

pick(s) /* offer choice of s */
    char *s;
{
    fprintf(stderr, "%s? ", s);
    if (ttyin() == 'y')
        printf("%s\n", s);
}
```

pick centralizes in one program a facility for interactively selecting arguments. This not only provides a useful service, but also reduces the need for "interactive" options on other commands.

Exercise 6-10. Given pick, is there a need for rm -i? □

6.6 On bugs and debugging

If you've ever written a program before, the notion of a bug will be familiar. There's no good solution to writing bug-free code except to take care to produce a clean, simple design, to implement it carefully, and to keep it clean as you modify it.

There are a handful of UNIX tools that will help you to find bugs, though none is really first-rate. To illustrate them, however, we need a bug, and all of the programs in this book are perfect. Therefore we'll create a typical bug. Consider the function pick shown above. Here it is again, this time containing an error. (No fair looking back at the original.)

```
pick(s) /* offer choice of s */
    char *s;
{
    fprintf("%s? ", s);
    if (ttyin() == 'y')
        printf("%s\n", s);
}
```

If we compile and run it, what happens?

```
$ cc pick.c -o pick
$ pick *.c                                Try it
Memory fault - core dumped                Disaster!
$
```

"Memory fault" means that your program tried to reference an area of memory that it was not allowed to. It usually means that a pointer points somewhere wild. "Bus error" is another diagnostic with a similar meaning, often caused by scanning a non-terminated string.

"Core dumped" means that the kernel saved the state of your executing program in a file called core in the current directory. You can also force a program to dump core by typing ctl-\ if it is running in the foreground, or by the command kill -3 if it is in the background.

There are two programs for poking around in the corpse, adb and sdb. Like most debuggers, they are arcane, complicated, and indispensable. adb is in the 7th Edition; sdb is available on more recent versions of the system. One or the other is sure to be there.

We have space here only for the absolute minimum use of each: printing a *stack trace*, that is, the function that was executing when the program died, the function that called it, and so on. The first function named in the stack trace is where the program was when it aborted.

To get a stack trace with adb, the command is $C:

```
$ adb pick core              Invoke adb
$C                           Stack trace request
~_strout(0175722,011,0,011200)
          adjust:      0
          fillch:      060542
__doprnt(0177345,0176176,011200)
~fprintf(011200,0177345)
          iop:         011200
          fmt:         0177345
          args:        0
~pick(0177345)
          s:           0177345
~main(035,0177234)
          argc:        035
          argv:        0177234
          i:           01
          buf:         0
ctl-d                        Quit
$
```

This says that `main` called `pick`, which called `fprintf`, which called
`_doprnt`, which called `_strout`. Since `_doprnt` isn't mentioned anywhere
in `pick.c`, our troubles must be somewhere in `fprintf` or above. (The lines
after each subroutine in the traceback show the values of local variables. `$c`
suppresses this information, as does `$C` itself on some versions of `adb`.)

Before revealing all, let's try the same thing with `sdb`:

```
$ sdb pick core
Warning: 'a.out' not compiled with -g
lseek: address 0xa64          Routine where program died
*t                            Stack trace request
lseek()
fprintf(6154,2147479154)
pick(2147479154)
main(30,2147478988,2147479112)
*q                            Quit
$
```

The information is formatted differently, but there's a common theme:
`fprintf`. (The traceback is different because this was run on a different
machine — a VAX-11/750 — which has a different implementation of the standard I/O library). And sure enough, if we look at the `fprintf` invocation in
the defective version of `pick`, it is wrong:

```
fprintf("%s? ", s);
```

There's no `stderr`, so the format string `"%s? "` is being used as a `FILE`
pointer, and of course chaos ensues.

We picked this error because it's common, a result of oversight rather than bad design. It's also possible to find errors like this, in which a function is called with the wrong arguments, by using the C verifier lint(1). lint examines C programs for potential errors, portability problems, and dubious constructions. If we run lint on the whole pick.c file, the error is identified:

```
$ lint pick.c
...
fprintf, arg. 1 used inconsistently "llib-lc"(69) :: "pick.c"(28)
...
$
```

In translation, this says that fprintf's first argument is different in the standard library definition from its use in line 28 of our program. That is a strong hint about what's wrong.

lint is a mixed success. It says exactly what's wrong with this program, but also produces a lot of irrelevant messages that we've elided above, and it takes some experience to know what to heed and what to ignore. It's worth the effort, though, because lint finds some errors that are almost impossible for people to see. It's always worth running lint after a long stretch of editing, making sure that you understand each warning that it gives.

6.7 An example: zap

zap, which selectively kills processes, is another program that we presented as a shell file in Chapter 5. The main problem with that version is speed: it creates so many processes that it runs slowly, which is especially undesirable for a program that kills errant processes. Rewriting zap in C will make it faster. We are not going to do the whole job, however: we will still use ps to find the process information. This is *much* easier than digging the information out of the kernel, and it is also portable. zap opens a pipe with ps on the input end, and reads from that instead of from a file. The function popen(3) is analogous to fopen, except that the first argument is a command instead of a filename. There is also a pclose that we don't need here.

```
/* zap:   interactive process killer */

#include <stdio.h>
#include <signal.h>
char     *progname;  /* program name for error message */
char     *ps = "ps -ag"; /* system dependent */

main(argc, argv)
    int argc;
    char *argv[];
{
    FILE *fin, *popen();
    char buf[BUFSIZ];
    int pid;

    progname = argv[0];
    if ((fin = popen(ps, "r")) == NULL) {
        fprintf(stderr, "%s: can't run %s\n", progname, ps);
        exit(1);
    }
    fgets(buf, sizeof buf, fin);     /* get header line */
    fprintf(stderr, "%s", buf);
    while (fgets(buf, sizeof buf, fin) != NULL)
        if (argc == 1 || strindex(buf, argv[1]) >= 0) {
            buf[strlen(buf)-1] = '\0'; /* suppress \n */
            fprintf(stderr, "%s? ", buf);
            if (ttyin() == 'y') {
                sscanf(buf, "%d", &pid);
                kill(pid, SIGKILL);
            }
        }
    exit(0);
}
```

We wrote the program to use ps -ag (the option is system dependent), but unless you're the super-user you can kill only your own processes.

The first call to fgets picks up the header line from ps; it's an interesting exercise to deduce what happens if you try to kill the "process" corresponding to that header line.

The function sscanf is a member of the scanf(3) family for doing input format conversion. It converts from a string instead of a file. The system call kill sends the specified signal to the process; signal SIGKILL, defined in <signal.h>, can't be caught or ignored. You may remember from Chapter 5 that its numeric value is 9, but it's better practice to use the symbolic constants from header files than to sprinkle your programs with magic numbers.

If there are no arguments, zap presents each line of the ps output for possible selection. If there is an argument, then zap offers only ps output lines that match it. The function strindex(s1,s2) tests whether the argument

matches any part of a line of ps output, using strncmp (see Table 6.2).
strindex returns the position in s1 where s2 occurs, or −1 if it does not.

```
strindex(s, t)   /* return index of t in s, -1 if none */
    char *s, *t;
{
    int i, n;

    n = strlen(t);
    for (i = 0; s[i] != '\0'; i++)
        if (strncmp(s+i, t, n) == 0)
            return i;
    return -1;
}
```

Table 6.4 summarizes the commonly-used functions from the standard I/O library.

Exercise 6-11. Modify zap so that any number of arguments can be supplied. As written, zap will normally echo the line corresponding to itself as one of the choices. Should it? If not, modify the program accordingly. Hint: getpid(2). □

Exercise 6-12. Build an fgrep(1) around strindex. Compare running times for complicated searches, say ten words in a document. Why does fgrep run faster? □

6.8 An interactive file comparison program: idiff

A common problem is to have two versions of a file, somewhat different, each containing part of a desired file; this often results when changes are made independently by two different people. diff will tell you how the files differ, but it's of no direct help if you want to select some parts of the first file and some of the second.

In this section, we will write a program idiff ("interactive diff") that presents each chunk of diff output and offers the user the option of choosing the "from" part, choosing the "to" part, or editing the parts. idiff produces the selected pieces in the proper order, in a file called idiff.out. That is, given these two files:

```
file1:                          file2:
This is                         This is
a test                          not a test
of                              of
your                            our
skill                           ability.
and comprehension.
```

diff produces

Table 6.4: Useful Standard I/O Functions

`fp=fopen(s,mode)`	open file s; mode `"r"`, `"w"`, `"a"` for read, write, append (returns `NULL` for error)
`c=getc(fp)`	get character; `getchar()` is `getc(stdin)`
`putc(c,fp)`	put character; `putchar(c)` is `putc(c,stdout)`
`ungetc(c,fp)`	put character back on input file `fp`; at most 1 char can be pushed back at one time
`scanf(fmt,a1,...)`	read characters from `stdin` into a1,... according to `fmt`. Each a_i must be a pointer. Returns `EOF` or number of fields converted.
`fscanf(fp,...)`	read from file `fp`
`sscanf(s,...)`	read from string s
`printf(fmt,a1,...)`	format a1,... according to `fmt`, print on `stdout`
`fprintf(fp,...)`	print ... on file `fp`
`sprintf(s,...)`	print ... into string s
`fgets(s,n,fp)`	read at most n characters into s from `fp`. Returns `NULL` at end of file
`fputs(s,fp)`	print string s on file `fp`
`fflush(fp)`	flush any buffered output on file `fp`
`fclose(fp)`	close file `fp`
`fp=popen(s,mode)`	open pipe to command s. See `fopen`.
`pclose(fp)`	close pipe `fp`
`system(s)`	run command s and wait for completion

```
$ diff file1 file2
2c2
< a test
---
> not a test
4,6c4,5
< your
< skill
< and comprehension.
---
> our
> ability.
$
```

A dialog with `idiff` might look like this:

```
$ idiff file1 file2
2c2                              The first difference
< a test
---
> not a test
? >                              User chooses second (>) version
4,6c4,5                          The second difference
< your
< skill
< and comprehension.
---
> our
> ability.
? <                              User chooses first (<) version
idiff output in file idiff.out
$ cat idiff.out                  Output put in this file
This is
not a test
of
your
skill
and comprehension.
$
```

If the response e is given instead of < or >, idiff invokes ed with the two
groups of lines already read in. If the second response had been e, the editor
buffer would look like this:

```
your
skill
and comprehension.
---
our
ability.
```

Whatever is written back into the file by ed is what goes into the final output.

Finally, any command can be executed from within idiff by escaping with
!cmd.

Technically, the hardest part of the job is diff, and that has already been
done for us. So the real job of idiff is parsing diff's output, and opening,
closing, reading and writing the proper files at the right time. The main routine of idiff sets up the files and runs the diff process:

```
/* idiff:  interactive diff */

#include <stdio.h>
#include <ctype.h>
char    *progname;
#define HUGE    10000    /* large number of lines */

main(argc, argv)
    int argc;
    char *argv[];
{
    FILE *fin, *fout, *f1, *f2, *efopen();
    char buf[BUFSIZ], *mktemp();
    char *diffout = "idiff.XXXXXX";

    progname = argv[0];
    if (argc != 3) {
        fprintf(stderr, "Usage: idiff file1 file2\n");
        exit(1);
    }
    f1 = efopen(argv[1], "r");
    f2 = efopen(argv[2], "r");
    fout = efopen("idiff.out", "w");
    mktemp(diffout);
    sprintf(buf,"diff %s %s >%s",argv[1],argv[2],diffout);
    system(buf);
    fin = efopen(diffout, "r");
    idiff(f1, f2, fin, fout);
    unlink(diffout);
    printf("%s output in file idiff.out\n", progname);
    exit(0);
}
```

The function mktemp(3) creates a file whose name is guaranteed to be different from any existing file. mktemp overwrites its argument: the six X's are replaced by the process-id of the idiff process and a letter. The system call unlink(2) removes the named file from the file system.

The job of looping through the changes reported by diff is handled by a function called idiff. The basic idea is simple enough: print a chunk of diff output, skip over the unwanted data in one file, then copy the desired version from the other. There is a lot of tedious detail, so the code is bigger than we'd like, but it's easy enough to understand in pieces.

```
idiff(f1, f2, fin, fout)      /* process diffs */
    FILE *f1, *f2, *fin, *fout;
{
    char *tempfile = "idiff.XXXXXX";
    char buf[BUFSIZ], buf2[BUFSIZ], *mktemp();
    FILE *ft, *efopen();
    int cmd, n, from1, to1, from2, to2, nf1, nf2;

    mktemp(tempfile);
    nf1 = nf2 = 0;
    while (fgets(buf, sizeof buf, fin) != NULL) {
        parse(buf, &from1, &to1, &cmd, &from2, &to2);
        n = to1-from1 + to2-from2 + 1; /* #lines from diff */
        if (cmd == 'c')
            n += 2;
        else if (cmd == 'a')
            from1++;
        else if (cmd == 'd')
            from2++;
        printf("%s", buf);
        while (n-- > 0) {
            fgets(buf, sizeof buf, fin);
            printf("%s", buf);
        }
        do {
            printf("? ");
            fflush(stdout);
            fgets(buf, sizeof buf, stdin);
            switch (buf[0]) {
            case '>':
                nskip(f1, to1-nf1);
                ncopy(f2, to2-nf2, fout);
                break;
            case '<':
                nskip(f2, to2-nf2);
                ncopy(f1, to1-nf1, fout);
                break;
            case 'e':
                ncopy(f1, from1-1-nf1, fout);
                nskip(f2, from2-1-nf2);
                ft = efopen(tempfile, "w");
                ncopy(f1, to1+1-from1, ft);
                fprintf(ft, "---\n");
                ncopy(f2, to2+1-from2, ft);
                fclose(ft);
                sprintf(buf2, "ed %s", tempfile);
                system(buf2);
                ft = efopen(tempfile, "r");
                ncopy(ft, HUGE, fout);
```

```
                 fclose(ft);
                 break;
            case '!':
                 system(buf+1);
                 printf("!\n");
                 break;
            default:
                 printf("< or > or e or !\n");
                 break;
            }
       } while (buf[0]!='<' && buf[0]!='>' && buf[0]!='e');
       nf1 = to1;
       nf2 = to2;
   }
   ncopy(f1, HUGE, fout);   /* can fail on very long files */
   unlink(tempfile);
}
```

The function `parse` does the mundane but tricky job of parsing the lines produced by `diff`, extracting the four line numbers and the command (one of a, c or d). `parse` is complicated a bit because `diff` can produce either one line number or two on either side of the command letter.

```
parse(s, pfrom1, pto1, pcmd, pfrom2, pto2)
    char *s;
    int *pcmd, *pfrom1, *pto1, *pfrom2, *pto2;
{
#define a2i(p) while (isdigit(*s)) p = 10*(p) + *s++ - '0'

    *pfrom1 = *pto1 = *pfrom2 = *pto2 = 0;
    a2i(*pfrom1);
    if (*s == ',') {
        s++;
        a2i(*pto1);
    } else
        *pto1 = *pfrom1;
    *pcmd = *s++;
    a2i(*pfrom2);
    if (*s == ',') {
        s++;
        a2i(*pto2);
    } else
        *pto2 = *pfrom2;
}
```

The macro `a2i` handles our specialized conversion from ASCII to integer in the four places it occurs.

`nskip` and `ncopy` skip over or copy the specified number of lines from a file:

```
nskip(fin, n)    /* skip n lines of file fin */
    FILE *fin;
{
    char buf[BUFSIZ];

    while (n-- > 0)
        fgets(buf, sizeof buf, fin);
}

ncopy(fin, n, fout) /* copy n lines from fin to fout */
    FILE *fin, *fout;
{
    char buf[BUFSIZ];

    while (n-- > 0) {
        if (fgets(buf, sizeof buf, fin) == NULL)
            return;
        fputs(buf, fout);
    }
}
```

As it stands, `idiff` doesn't quit gracefully if it is interrupted, since it leaves several files lying around in `/tmp`. In the next chapter, we will show how to catch interrupts to remove temporary files like those used here.

The crucial observation with both `zap` and `idiff` is that most of the hard work has been done by someone else. These programs merely put a convenient interface on another program that computes the right information. It's worth watching for opportunities to build on someone else's labor instead of doing it yourself — it's a cheap way to be more productive.

Exercise 6-13. Add the command q to `idiff`: the response q< will take all the rest of the '<' choices automatically; q> will take the all the rest of the '>' choices. □

Exercise 6-14. Modify `idiff` so that any `diff` arguments are passed on to `diff`; -b and -h are likely candidates. Modify `idiff` so that a different editor can be specified, as in

    $ idiff -e another-editor file1 file2

How do these two modifications interact? □

Exercise 6-15. Change `idiff` to use `popen` and `pclose` instead of a temporary file for the output of `diff`. What difference does it make in program speed and complexity? □

Exercise 6-16. `diff` has the property that if one of its arguments is a directory, it searches that directory for a file with the same name as the other argument. But if you try the same thing with `idiff`, it fails in a strange way. Explain what happens, then fix it. □

6.9 Accessing the environment

It is easy to access shell environment variables from a C program, and this can sometimes be used to make programs adapt to their environment without requiring much of their users. For example, suppose that you are using a terminal in which the screen size is bigger than the normal 24 lines. If you want to use p and take full advantage of your terminal's capabilities, what choices are open to you? It's a bother to have to specify the screen size each time you use p:

```
$ p -36 ...
```

You could always put a shell file in your bin:

```
$ cat /usr/you/bin/p
exec /usr/bin/p -36 $*
$
```

A third solution is to modify p to use an environment variable that defines the properties of your terminal. Suppose that you define the variable PAGESIZE in your .profile:

```
PAGESIZE=36
export PAGESIZE
```

The routine getenv("*var*") searches the environment for the shell variable *var* and returns its value as a string of characters, or NULL if the variable is not defined. Given getenv, it's easy to modify p. All that is needed is to add a couple of declarations and a call to getenv to the beginning of the main routine.

```
/* p:  print input in chunks (version 3) */
...
    char *p, *getenv();

    progname = argv[0];
    if ((p=getenv("PAGESIZE")) != NULL)
        pagesize = atoi(p);
    if (argc > 1 && argv[1][0] == '-') {
        pagesize = atoi(&argv[1][1]);
        argc--;
        argv++;
    }
...
```

Optional arguments are processed after the environment variable, so any explicit page size will still override an implicit one.

Exercise 6-17. Modify idiff to search the environment for the name of the editor to be used. Modify 2, 3, etc., to use PAGESIZE. □

History and bibliographic notes

The standard I/O library was designed by Dennis Ritchie, after Mike Lesk's portable I/O library. The intent of both packages was to provide enough standard facilities that programs could be moved from UNIX to non-UNIX systems without change.

Our design of p is based on a program by Henry Spencer.

adb was written by Steve Bourne, sdb by Howard Katseff, and lint by Steve Johnson.

idiff is loosely based on a program originally written by Joe Maranzano. diff itself is by Doug McIlroy, and is based on an algorithm invented independently by Harold Stone and by Wayne Hunt and Tom Szymanski. (See "A fast algorithm for computing longest common subsequences," by J. W. Hunt and T. G. Szymanski, *CACM*, May, 1977.) The diff algorithm is described in M. D. McIlroy and J. W. Hunt, "An algorithm for differential file comparison," Bell Labs Computing Science Technical Report 41, 1976. To quote McIlroy, "I had tried at least three completely different algorithms before the final one. diff is a quintessential case of not settling for mere competency in a program but revising it until it was right."

## CHAPTER 7

UNIX SYSTEM CALLS

This chapter concentrates on the lowest level of interaction with the UNIX operating system — the system calls. These are the entries to the kernel. They *are* the facilities that the operating system provides; everything else is built on top of them.

We will cover several major areas. First is the I/O system, the foundation beneath library routines like fopen and putc. We'll talk more about the file system as well, particularly directories and inodes. Next comes a discussion of processes — how to run programs from within a program. After that we will talk about signals and interrupts: what happens when you push the DELETE key, and how to handle that sensibly in a program.

As in Chapter 6, many of our examples are useful programs that were not part of the 7th Edition. Even if they are not directly helpful to you, you should learn something from reading them, and they might suggest similar tools that you could build for your system.

Full details on the system calls are in Section 2 of the *UNIX Programmer's Manual*; this chapter describes the most important parts, but makes no pretense of completeness.

7.1 Low-level I/O

The lowest level of I/O is a direct entry into the operating system. Your program reads or writes files in chunks of any convenient size. The kernel buffers your data into chunks that match the peripheral devices, and schedules operations on the devices to optimize their performance over all users.

File descriptors

All input and output is done by reading or writing files, because all peripheral devices, even your terminal, are files in the file system. This means that a single interface handles all communication between a program and peripheral devices.

In the most general case, before reading or writing a file, it is necessary to inform the system of your intent to do so, a process called *opening* the file. If you are going to write on a file, it may also be necessary to *create* it. The system checks your right to do so (Does the file exist? Do you have permission to access it?), and if all is well, returns a non-negative integer called a *file descriptor*. Whenever I/O is to be done on the file, the file descriptor is used instead of the name to identify the file. All information about an open file is maintained by the system; your program refers to the file only by the file descriptor. A `FILE` pointer as discussed in Chapter 6 points to a structure that contains, among other things, the file descriptor; the macro `fileno(fp)` defined in `<stdio.h>` returns the file descriptor.

There are special arrangements to make terminal input and output convenient. When it is started by the shell, a program inherits three open files, with file descriptors 0, 1, and 2, called the standard input, the standard output, and the standard error. All of these are by default connected to the terminal, so if a program only reads file descriptor 0 and writes file descriptors 1 and 2, it can do I/O without having to open files. If the program opens any other files, they will have file descriptors 3, 4, etc.

If I/O is redirected to or from files or pipes, the shell changes the default assignments for file descriptors 0 and 1 from the terminal to the named files. Normally file descriptor 2 remains attached to the terminal, so error messages can go there. Shell incantations such as 2>*filename* and 2>&1 will cause rearrangements of the defaults, but the file assignments are changed by the shell, not by the program. (The program itself can rearrange these further if it wishes, but this is rare.)

File I/O — read *and* write

All input and output is done by two system calls, `read` and `write`, which are accessed from C by functions of the same name. For both, the first argument is a file descriptor. The second argument is an array of bytes that serves as the data source or destination. The third argument is the number of bytes to be transferred.

```
int fd, n, nread, nwritten;
char buf[SIZE];

nread = read(fd, buf, n);
nwritten = write(fd, buf, n);
```

Each call returns a count of the number of bytes transferred. On reading, the number of bytes returned may be less than the number requested, because fewer than n bytes remained to be read. (When the file is a terminal, `read` normally reads only up to the next newline, which is usually less than what was requested.) A return value of zero implies end of file, and −1 indicates an error of some sort. For writing, the value returned is the number of bytes actually written; an error has occurred if this isn't equal to the number supposed to be written.

While the number of bytes to be read or written is not restricted, the two most common values are 1, which means one character at a time ("unbuf-fered"), and the size of a block on a disc, most often 512 or 1024 bytes. (The parameter BUFSIZ in <stdio.h> has this value.)

To illustrate, here is a program to copy its input to its output. Since the input and output can be redirected to any file or device, it will actually copy anything to anything: it's a bare-bones implementation of cat.

```
/* cat:  minimal version */
#define SIZE    512 /* arbitrary */

main()
{
    char buf[SIZE];
    int n;

    while ((n = read(0, buf, sizeof buf)) > 0)
        write(1, buf, n);
    exit(0);
}
```

If the file size is not a multiple of SIZE, some read will return a smaller number of bytes to be written by write; the next call to read after that will return zero.

Reading and writing in chunks that match the disc will be most efficient, but even character-at-a-time I/O is feasible for modest amounts of data, because the kernel buffers your data; the main cost is the system calls. ed, for example, uses one-byte reads to retrieve its standard input. We timed this version of cat on a file of 54000 bytes, for six values of SIZE:

	Time (user+system, sec.)	
SIZE	PDP-11/70	VAX-11/750
1	271.0	188.8
10	29.9	19.3
100	3.8	2.6
512	1.3	1.0
1024	1.2	0.6
5120	1.0	0.6

The disc block size is 512 bytes on the PDP-11 system and 1024 on the VAX.

It is quite legal for several processes to be accessing the same file at the same time; indeed, one process can be writing while another is reading. If this isn't what you wanted, it can be disconcerting, but it's sometimes useful. Even though one call to read returns 0 and thus signals end of file, if more data is written on that file, a subsequent read will find more bytes available. This observation is the basis of a program called readslow, which continues to read its input, regardless of whether it got an end of file or not. readslow is handy for watching the progress of a program:

```
$ slowprog >temp &
5213                                        Process-id
$ readslow <temp | grep something
```

In other words, a slow program produces output in a file; `readslow`, perhaps in collaboration with some other program, watches the data accumulate.

Structurally, `readslow` is identical to `cat` except that it loops instead of quitting when it encounters the current end of the input. It has to use low-level I/O because the standard library routines continue to report EOF after the first end of file.

```
/* readslow:  keep reading, waiting for more */
#define SIZE    512 /* arbitrary */

main()
{
    char buf[SIZE];
    int n;

    for (;;) {
        while ((n = read(0, buf, sizeof buf)) > 0)
            write(1, buf, n);
        sleep(10);
    }
}
```

The function `sleep` causes the program to be suspended for the specified number of seconds; it is described in `sleep`(3). We don't want `readslow` to bang away at the file continuously looking for more data; that would be too costly in CPU time. Thus this version of `readslow` copies its input up to the end of file, sleeps a while, then tries again. If more data arrives while it is asleep, it will be read by the next `read`.

Exercise 7-1. Add a *-n* argument to `readslow` so the default sleep time can be changed to *n* seconds. Some systems provide an option `-f` ("forever") for `tail` that combines the functions of `tail` with those of `readslow`. Comment on this design. □

Exercise 7-2. What happens to `readslow` if the file being read is truncated? How would you fix it? Hint: read about `fstat` in Section 7.3. □

File creation — open, creat, close, unlink

Other than the default standard input, output and error files, you must explicitly open files in order to read or write them. There are two system calls for this, `open` and `creat`.†

---

† Ken Thompson was once asked what he would do differently if he were redesigning the UNIX system. His reply: "I'd spell `creat` with an e."

open is rather like fopen in the previous chapter, except that instead of returning a file pointer, it returns a file descriptor, which is an int.

```
char *name;
int fd, rwmode;

fd = open(name, rwmode);
```

As with fopen, the name argument is a character string containing the filename. The access mode argument is different, however: rwmode is 0 for read, 1 for write, and 2 to open a file for both reading *and* writing. open returns −1 if any error occurs; otherwise it returns a valid file descriptor.

It is an error to try to open a file that does not exist. The system call creat is provided to create new files, or to rewrite old ones.

```
int perms;

fd = creat(name, perms);
```

creat returns a file descriptor if it was able to create the file called name, and −1 if not. If the file does not exist, creat creates it with the *permissions* specified by the perms argument. If the file already exists, creat will truncate it to zero length; it is not an error to creat a file that already exists. (The permissions will not be changed.) Regardless of perms, a created file is open for writing.

As described in Chapter 2, there are nine bits of protection information associated with a file, controlling read, write and execute permission, so a three-digit octal number is convenient for specifying them. For example, 0755 specifies read, write and execute permission for the owner, and read and execute permission for the group and everyone else. Don't forget the leading 0, which is how octal numbers are specified in C.

To illustrate, here is a simplified version of cp. The main simplification is that our version copies only one file, and does not permit the second argument to be a directory. Another blemish is that our version does not preserve the permissions of the source file; we will show how to remedy this later.

```
/* cp:   minimal version */
#include <stdio.h>
#define PERMS 0644 /* RW for owner, R for group, others */
char *progname;

main(argc, argv)      /* cp: copy f1 to f2 */
    int argc;
    char *argv[];
{
    int f1, f2, n;
    char buf[BUFSIZ];

    progname = argv[0];
    if (argc != 3)
        error("Usage: %s from to", progname);
    if ((f1 = open(argv[1], 0)) == -1)
        error("can't open %s", argv[1]);
    if ((f2 = creat(argv[2], PERMS)) == -1)
        error("can't create %s", argv[2]);

    while ((n = read(f1, buf, BUFSIZ)) > 0)
        if (write(f2, buf, n) != n)
            error("write error", (char *) 0);
    exit(0);
}
```

We will discuss `error` in the next sub-section.

There is a limit (typically about 20; look for NOFILE in <sys/param.h>) on the number of files that a program may have open simultaneously. Accordingly, any program that intends to process many files must be prepared to reuse file descriptors. The system call `close` breaks the connection between a filename and a file descriptor, freeing the file descriptor for use with some other file. Termination of a program via `exit` or return from the main program closes all open files.

The system call `unlink` removes a file from the file system.

Error processing — errno

The system calls discussed in this section, and in fact all system calls, can incur errors. Usually they indicate an error by returning a value of -1. Sometimes it is nice to know what specific error occurred; for this purpose all system calls, when appropriate, leave an error number in an external integer called `errno`. (The meanings of the various error numbers are listed in the introduction to Section 2 of the *UNIX Programmer's Manual*.) By using `errno`, your program can, for example, determine whether an attempt to open a file failed because it did not exist or because you lacked permission to read it. There is also an array of character strings `sys_errlist` indexed by `errno` that translates the numbers into a meaningful string. Our version of `error` uses these data structures:

```
error(s1, s2)    /* print error message and die */
    char *s1, *s2;
{
    extern int errno, sys_nerr;
    extern char *sys_errlist[], *progname;

    if (progname)
        fprintf(stderr, "%s: ", progname);
    fprintf(stderr, s1, s2);
    if (errno > 0 && errno < sys_nerr)
        fprintf(stderr, " (%s)", sys_errlist[errno]);
    fprintf(stderr, "\n");
    exit(1);
}
```

errno is initially zero, and should always be less than sys_nerr. It is not reset to zero when things go well, however, so you must reset it after each error if your program intends to continue.

Here is how error messages appear with this version of cp:

```
$ cp foo bar
cp: can't open foo (No such file or directory)
$ date >foo; chmod 0 foo          Make an unreadable file
$ cp foo bar
cp: can't open foo (Permission denied)
$
```

Random access — lseek

File I/O is normally sequential: each read or write takes place in the file right after the previous one. When necessary, however, a file can be read or written in an arbitrary order. The system call lseek provides a way to move around in a file without actually reading or writing:

```
int fd, origin;
long offset, pos, lseek();

pos = lseek(fd, offset, origin);
```

forces the current position in the file whose descriptor is fd to move to position offset, which is taken relative to the location specified by origin. Subsequent reading or writing will begin at that position. origin can be 0, 1, or 2 to specify that offset is to be measured from the beginning, from the current position, or from the end of the file. The value returned is the new absolute position, or -1 for an error. For example, to append to a file, seek to the end before writing:

```
lseek(fd, 0L, 2);
```

To get back to the beginning ("rewind"),

```
lseek(fd, 0L, 0);
```

To determine the current position,

```
pos = lseek(fd, 0L, 1);
```

Notice the 0L argument: the offset is a long integer. (The '1' in lseek stands for 'long,' to distinguish it from the 6th Edition seek system call that used short integers.)

With lseek, it is possible to treat files more or less like large arrays, at the price of slower access. For example, the following function reads any number of bytes from any place in a file.

```
get(fd, pos, buf, n)  /* read n bytes from position pos */
    int fd, n;
    long pos;
    char *buf;
{
    if (lseek(fd, pos, 0) == -1)     /* get to pos */
        return -1;
    else
        return read(fd, buf, n);
}
```

Exercise 7-3. Modify readslow to handle a filename argument if one is present. Add the option -e:

```
$ readslow -e
```

causes readslow to seek to the end of the input before beginning to read. What does lseek do on a pipe? □

Exercise 7-4. Rewrite efopen from Chapter 6 to call error. □

7.2 File system: directories

The next topic is how to walk through the directory hierarchy. This doesn't actually use any new system calls, just some old ones in a new context. We will illustrate by writing a function called spname that tries to cope with misspelled filenames. The function

```
n = spname(name, newname);
```

searches for a file with a name "close enough" to *name*. If one is found, it is copied into *newname*. The value n returned by spname is −1 if nothing close enough was found, 0 if there was an exact match, and 1 if a correction was made.

spname is a convenient addition to the p command: if you try to print a file but misspell the name, p can ask if you really meant something else:

```
$ p /urs/srx/ccmd/p/spnam.c          Horribly botched name
"/usr/src/cmd/p/spname.c"? y         Suggested correction accepted
/* spname:   return correctly spelled filename */
...
```

As we will write it, `spname` will try to correct, in each component of the
filename, mismatches in which a single letter has been dropped or added, or a
single letter is wrong, or a pair of letters exchanged; all of these are illustrated
above. This is a boon for sloppy typists.

Before writing the code, a short review of file system structure is in order.
A directory is a file containing a list of file names and an indication of where
they are located. The "location" is actually an index into another table called
the *inode table*. The inode for a file is where all information about the file
except its name is kept. A directory entry thus consists of only two items, an
inode number and the file name. The precise specification can be found in the
file `<sys/dir.h>`:

```
$ cat /usr/include/sys/dir.h
#define DIRSIZ   14  /* max length of file name */

struct direct    /* structure of directory entry */
{
     ino_t d_ino;     /* inode number */
     char  d_name[DIRSIZ];   /* file name */
};
$
```

The "type" `ino_t` is a `typedef` describing the index into the inode table.
It happens to be `unsigned short` on PDP-11 and VAX versions of the system, but this is definitely not the sort of information to embed in a program: it
might be different on a different machine. Hence the `typedef`. A complete
set of "system" types is found in `<sys/types.h>`, which must be included
before `<sys/dir.h>`.

The operation of `spname` is straightforward enough, although there are a
lot of boundary conditions to get right. Suppose the file name is */d1/d2/f*.
The basic idea is to peel off the first component (*/*), then search that directory
for a name close to the next component (*d1*), then search that directory for
something near *d2*, and so on, until a match has been found for each component. If at any stage there isn't a plausible candidate in the directory, the
search is abandoned.

We have divided the job into three functions. `spname` itself isolates the
components of the path and builds them into a "best match so far" filename.
It calls `mindist`, which searches a given directory for the file that is closest to
the current guess, using a third function, `spdist`, to compute the distance
between two names.

```
/* spname:  return correctly spelled filename */
/*
 * spname(oldname, newname)  char *oldname, *newname;
 *   returns -1 if no reasonable match to oldname,
 *           0 if exact match,
 *           1 if corrected.
 *   stores corrected name in newname.
 */

#include <sys/types.h>
#include <sys/dir.h>

spname(oldname, newname)
    char *oldname, *newname;
{
    char *p, guess[DIRSIZ+1], best[DIRSIZ+1];
    char *new = newname, *old = oldname;

    for (;;) {
        while (*old == '/')  /* skip slashes */
            *new++ = *old++;
        *new = '\0';
        if (*old == '\0')   /* exact or corrected */
            return strcmp(oldname,newname) != 0;
        p = guess;  /* copy next component into guess */
        for ( ; *old != '/' && *old != '\0'; old++)
            if (p < guess+DIRSIZ)
                *p++ = *old;
        *p = '\0';
        if (mindist(newname, guess, best) >= 3)
            return -1;  /* hopeless */
        for (p = best; *new = *p++; )  /* add to end */
            new++;                     /* of newname */
    }
}
```

```
mindist(dir, guess, best)    /* search dir for guess */
    char *dir, *guess, *best;
{
    /* set best, return distance 0..3 */
    int d, nd, fd;
    struct {
        ino_t ino;
        char  name[DIRSIZ+1];    /* 1 more than in dir.h */
    } nbuf;

    nbuf.name[DIRSIZ] = '\0';    /* +1 for terminal '\0' */
    if (dir[0] == '\0')    /* current directory */
        dir = ".";
    d = 3;  /* minimum distance */
    if ((fd=open(dir, 0)) == -1)
        return d;
    while (read(fd,(char *) &nbuf,sizeof(struct direct)) > 0)
        if (nbuf.ino) {
            nd = spdist(nbuf.name, guess);
            if (nd <= d && nd != 3) {
                strcpy(best, nbuf.name);
                d = nd;
                if (d == 0)       /* exact match */
                    break;
            }
        }
    close(fd);
    return d;
}
```

If the directory name given to `mindist` is empty, '.' is searched. `mindist` reads one directory entry at a time. Notice that the buffer for `read` is a structure, not an array of characters. We use `sizeof` to compute the number of bytes, and coerce the address to a character pointer.

If a slot in a directory is not currently in use (because a file has been removed), then the inode entry is zero, and this position is skipped. The distance test is

```
if (nd <= d ...)
```

instead of

```
if (nd < d ...)
```

so that any other single character is a better match than '.', which is always the first entry in a directory.

```
/* spdist:  return distance between two names */
/*
 * very rough spelling metric:
 * 0 if the strings are identical
 * 1 if two chars are transposed
 * 2 if one char wrong, added or deleted
 * 3 otherwise
 */

#define EQ(s,t) (strcmp(s,t) == 0)

spdist(s, t)
    char *s, *t;
{
    while (*s++ == *t)
        if (*t++ == '\0')
            return 0;          /* exact match */
    if (*--s) {
        if (*t) {
            if (s[1] && t[1] && *s == t[1]
              && *t == s[1] && EQ(s+2, t+2))
                return 1;   /* transposition */
            if (EQ(s+1, t+1))
                return 2;   /* 1 char mismatch */
        }
        if (EQ(s+1, t))
            return 2;       /* extra character */
    }
    if (*t && EQ(s, t+1))
        return 2;               /* missing character */
    return 3;
}
```

Once we have spname, integrating spelling correction into p is easy:

```
/* p:  print input in chunks (version 4) */

#include <stdio.h>
#define PAGESIZE    22
char    *progname;  /* program name for error message */

main(argc, argv)
    int argc;
    char *argv[];
{
    FILE *fp, *efopen();
    int i, pagesize = PAGESIZE;
    char *p, *getenv(), buf[BUFSIZ];

    progname = argv[0];
    if ((p=getenv("PAGESIZE")) != NULL)
        pagesize = atoi(p);
    if (argc > 1 && argv[1][0] == '-') {
        pagesize = atoi(&argv[1][1]);
        argc--;
        argv++;
    }
    if (argc == 1)
        print(stdin, pagesize);
    else
        for (i = 1; i < argc; i++)
            switch (spname(argv[i], buf)) {
            case -1:    /* no match possible */
                fp = efopen(argv[i], "r");
                break;
            case 1:     /* corrected */
                fprintf(stderr, "\"%s\"? ", buf);
                if (ttyin() == 'n')
                    break;
                argv[i] = buf;
                /* fall through... */
            case 0: /* exact match */
                fp = efopen(argv[i], "r");
                print(fp, pagesize);
                fclose(fp);
            }
    exit(0);
}
```

Spelling correction is not something to be blindly applied to every program
that uses filenames. It works well with p because p is interactive, but it's not
suitable for programs that might not be interactive.

Exercise 7-5. How much can you improve on the heuristic for selecting the best match
in spname? For example, it is foolish to treat a regular file as if it were a directory;

this can happen with the current version. □

Exercise 7-6. The name tx matches whichever of tc happens to come last in the directory, for any single character c. Can you invent a better distance measure? Implement
it and see how well it works with real users. □

Exercise 7-7. mindist reads the directory one entry at a time. Does p run perceptibly
faster if directory reading is done in bigger chunks? □

Exercise 7-8. Modify spname to return a name that is a prefix of the desired name if
no closer match can be found. How should ties be broken if there are several names
that all match the prefix? □

Exercise 7-9. What other programs could profit from spname? Design a standalone
program that would apply correction to its arguments before passing them along to
another program, as in

```
$ fix prog filenames...
```

Can you write a version of cd that uses spname? How would you install it? □

7.3 File system: inodes

In this section we will discuss system calls that deal with the file system and
in particular with the information about files, such as size, dates, permissions,
and so on. These system calls allow you to get at all the information we talked
about in Chapter 2.

Let's dig into the inode itself. Part of the inode is described by a structure
called stat, defined in <sys/stat.h>:

```
struct stat /* structure returned by stat */
{
     dev_t    st_dev;      /* device of inode */
     ino_t    st_ino;      /* inode number */
     short    st_mode;     /* mode bits */
     short    st_nlink;    /* number of links to file */
     short    st_uid;      /* owner's userid */
     short    st_gid;      /* owner's group id */
     dev_t    st_rdev;     /* for special files */
     off_t    st_size;     /* file size in characters */
     time_t   st_atime;    /* time file last read */
     time_t   st_mtime;    /* time file last written or created */
     time_t   st_ctime;    /* time file or inode last changed */
};
```

Most of the fields are explained by the comments. Types like dev_t and
ino_t are defined in <sys/types.h>, as discussed above. The st_mode
entry contains a set of flags describing the file; for convenience, the flag definitions are also part of the file <sys/stat.h>:

```
#define S_IFMT    0170000    /* type of file */
#define     S_IFDIR 0040000 /* directory */
#define     S_IFCHR 0020000 /* character special */
#define     S_IFBLK 0060000 /* block special */
#define     S_IFREG 0100000 /* regular */
#define S_ISUID   0004000    /* set user id on execution */
#define S_ISGID   0002000    /* set group id on execution */
#define S_ISVTX   0001000    /* save swapped text even after use */
#define S_IREAD   0000400    /* read permission, owner */
#define S_IWRITE  0000200    /* write permission, owner */
#define S_IEXEC   0000100    /* execute/search permission, owner */
```

The inode for a file is accessed by a pair of system calls named `stat` and
`fstat`. `stat` takes a filename and returns inode information for that file (or
−1 if there is an error). `fstat` does the same from a file descriptor for an
open file (not from a `FILE` pointer). That is,

```
char *name;
int fd;
struct stat stbuf;

stat(name, &stbuf);
fstat(fd, &stbuf);
```

fills the structure `stbuf` with the inode information for the file `name` or file
descriptor `fd`.

With all these facts in hand, we can start to write some useful code. Let us
begin with a C version of `checkmail`, a program that watches your mailbox.
If the file grows larger, `checkmail` prints "You have mail" and rings the
bell. (If the file gets shorter, that is presumably because you have just read
and deleted some mail, and no message is wanted.) This is entirely adequate
as a first step; you can get fancier once this works.

```
/* checkmail: watch user's mailbox */
#include <stdio.h>
#include <sys/types.h>
#include <sys/stat.h>
char *progname;
char *maildir = "/usr/spool/mail";   /* system dependent */

main(argc, argv)
    int argc;
    char *argv[];
{
    struct stat buf;
    char *name, *getlogin();
    int lastsize = 0;

    progname = argv[0];
    if ((name = getlogin()) == NULL)
        error("can't get login name", (char *) 0);
    if (chdir(maildir) == -1)
        error("can't cd to %s", maildir);
    for (;;) {
        if (stat(name, &buf) == -1) /* no mailbox */
            buf.st_size = 0;
        if (buf.st_size > lastsize)
            fprintf(stderr, "\nYou have mail\007\n");
        lastsize = buf.st_size;
        sleep(60);
    }
}
```

The function getlogin(3) returns your login name, or NULL if it can't.
checkmail changes to the mail directory with the system call chdir, so that
the subsequent stat calls will not have to search each directory from the root
to the mail directory. You might have to change maildir to be correct on
your system. We wrote checkmail to keep trying even if there is no mailbox, since most versions of mail remove the mailbox if it's empty.

We wrote this program in Chapter 5 in part to illustrate shell loops. That
version created several processes every time it looked at the mailbox, so it
might be more of a system load than you want. The C version is a single process that does a stat on the file every minute. How much does it cost to have
checkmail running in the background all the time? We measured it at well
under one second per hour, which is low enough that it hardly matters.

sv: An illustration of error handling

We are next going to write a program called sv, similar to cp, that will
copy a set of files to a directory, but change each target file only if it does not
exist or is older than the source. "sv" stands for "save"; the idea is that sv

will not overwrite something that appears to be more up to date. sv uses more
of the information in the inode than checkmail does.

The design we will use for sv is this:

   $ *sv file1 file2 ... dir*

copies file1 to dir/file1, file2 to dir/file2, etc., except that when a
target file is newer than its source file, no copy is made and a warning is
printed. To avoid making multiple copies of linked files, sv does not allow /'s
in any of the source filenames.

```
/* sv:   save new files */
#include <stdio.h>
#include <sys/types.h>
#include <sys/dir.h>
#include <sys/stat.h>
char *progname;

main(argc, argv)
    int argc;
    char *argv[];
{
    int i;
    struct stat stbuf;
    char *dir = argv[argc-1];

    progname = argv[0];
    if (argc <= 2)
        error("Usage: %s files... dir", progname);
    if (stat(dir, &stbuf) == -1)
        error("can't access directory %s", dir);
    if ((stbuf.st_mode & S_IFMT) != S_IFDIR)
        error("%s is not a directory", dir);
    for (i = 1; i < argc-1; i++)
        sv(argv[i], dir);
    exit(0);
}
```

The times in the inode are in seconds-since-long-ago (0:00 GMT, January 1,
1970), so older files have smaller values in their st_mtime field.

```
sv(file, dir)    /* save file in dir */
    char *file, *dir;
{
    struct stat sti, sto;
    int fin, fout, n;
    char target[BUFSIZ], buf[BUFSIZ], *index();

    sprintf(target, "%s/%s", dir, file);
    if (index(file, '/') != NULL)   /* strchr() in some systems */
        error("won't handle /'s in %s", file);
    if (stat(file, &sti) == -1)
        error("can't stat %s", file);
    if (stat(target, &sto) == -1)   /* target not present */
        sto.st_mtime = 0;    /* so make it look old */
    if (sti.st_mtime < sto.st_mtime)     /* target is newer */
        fprintf(stderr, "%s: %s not copied\n",
            progname, file);
    else if ((fin = open(file, 0)) == -1)
        error("can't open file %s", file);
    else if ((fout = creat(target, sti.st_mode)) == -1)
        error("can't create %s", target);
    else
        while ((n = read(fin, buf, sizeof buf)) > 0)
            if (write(fout, buf, n) != n)
                error("error writing %s", target);
    close(fin);
    close(fout);
}
```

We used `creat` instead of the standard I/O functions so that `sv` can preserve the mode of the input file. (Note that `index` and `strchr` are different names for the same routine; check your manual under `string`(3) to see which name your system uses.)

Although the `sv` program is rather specialized, it does indicate some important ideas. Many programs are not "system programs" but may still use information maintained by the operating system and accessed through system calls. For such programs, it is crucial that the representation of the information appear only in standard header files like `<stat.h>` and `<dir.h>`, and that programs include those files instead of embedding the actual declarations in themselves. Such code is much more likely to be portable from one system to another.

It is also worth noting that at least two thirds of the code in `sv` is error checking. In the early stages of writing a program, it's tempting to skimp on error handling, since it is a diversion from the main task. And once the program "works," it's hard to be enthusiastic about going back to put in the checks that convert a private program into one that works regardless of what happens.

sv isn't proof against all possible disasters — it doesn't deal with interrupts at awkward times, for instance — but it's more careful than most programs. To focus on just one point for a moment, consider the final `write` statement. It is rare that a `write` fails, so many programs ignore the possibility. But discs run out of space; users exceed quotas; communications lines break. All of these can cause write errors, and you are a lot better off if you hear about them than if the program silently pretends that all is well.

The moral is that error checking is tedious but important. We have been cavalier in most of the programs in this book because of space limitations and to focus on more interesting topics. But for real, production programs, you can't afford to ignore errors.

Exercise 7-10. Modify `checkmail` to identify the sender of the mail as part of the "You have mail" message. Hint: `sscanf`, `lseek`. □

Exercise 7-11. Modify `checkmail` so that it does not change to the mail directory before it enters its loop. Does this have a measurable effect on its performance? (Harder) Can you write a version of `checkmail` that only needs one process to notify all users? □

Exercise 7-12. Write a program `watchfile` that monitors a file and prints the file from the beginning each time it changes. When would you use it? □

Exercise 7-13. `sv` is quite rigid in its error handling. Modify it to continue even if it can't process some file. □

Exercise 7-14. Make `sv` recursive: if one of the source files is a directory, that directory and its files are processed in the same manner. Make `cp` recursive. Discuss whether `cp` and `sv` ought to be the same program, so that `cp -v` doesn't do the copy if the target is newer. □

Exercise 7-15. Write the program `random`:

```
$ random filename
```

produces one line chosen at random from the file. Given a file `people` of names, `random` can be used in a program called `scapegoat`, which is valuable for allocating blame:

```
$ cat scapegoat
echo "It's all `random people`'s fault!"
$ scapegoat
It's all Ken's fault!
$
```

Make sure that `random` is fair regardless of the distribution of line lengths. □

Exercise 7-16. There's other information in the inode as well, in particular, disc addresses where the file blocks are located. Examine the file `<sys/ino.h>`, then write a program `icat` that will read files specified by inode number and disc device. (It will work only if the disc in question is readable, of course.) Under what circumstances is `icat` useful? □

7.4 Processes

This section describes how to execute one program from within another. The easiest way is with the standard library routine `system`, mentioned but censured in Chapter 6. `system` takes one argument, a command line exactly as typed at the terminal (except for the newline at the end) and executes it in a sub-shell. If the command line has to be built from pieces, the in-memory formatting capabilities of `sprintf` may be useful. At the end of this section we will show a safer version of `system` for use by interactive programs, but first we must examine the pieces from which it is built.

Low-level process creation — `execlp` *and* `execvp`

The most basic operation is to execute another program *without returning*, by using the system call `execlp`. For example, to print the date as the last action of a running program, use

```
execlp("date", "date", (char *) 0);
```

The first argument to `execlp` is the filename of the command; `execlp` extracts the search path (i.e., `$PATH`) from your environment and does the same search as the shell does. The second and subsequent arguments are the command name and the arguments for the command; these become the `argv` array for the new program. The end of the list is marked by a 0 argument. (Read `exec`(2) for insight on the design of `execlp`.)

The `execlp` call overlays the existing program with the new one, runs that, then exits. The original program gets control back only when there is an error, for example if the file can't be found or is not executable:

```
execlp("date", "date", (char *) 0);
fprintf(stderr, "Couldn't execute 'date'\n");
exit(1);
```

A variant of `execlp` called `execvp` is useful when you don't know in advance how many arguments there are going to be. The call is

```
execvp(filename, argp);
```

where `argp` is an array of pointers to the arguments (such as `argv`); the last pointer in the array must be NULL so `execvp` can tell where the list ends. As with `execlp`, `filename` is the file in which the program is found, and `argp` is the `argv` array for the new program; `argp[0]` is the program name.

Neither of these routines provides expansion of metacharacters like `<`, `>`, `*`, quotes, etc., in the argument list. If you want these, use `execlp` to invoke the shell `/bin/sh`, which then does all the work. Construct a string `commandline` that contains the complete command as it would have been typed at the terminal, then say

```
execlp("/bin/sh", "sh", "-c", commandline, (char *) 0);
```

The argument -c says to treat the next argument as the whole command line, not a single argument.

As an illustration of exec, consider the program waitfile. The command

$ *waitfile* filename [command]

periodically checks the file named. If it is unchanged since last time, the *command* is executed. If no *command* is specified, the file is copied to the standard output. We use waitfile to monitor the progress of troff, as in

$ *waitfile troff.out echo troff done* &

The implementation of waitfile uses fstat to extract the time when the file was last changed.

```
/* waitfile:  wait until file stops changing */
#include <stdio.h>
#include <sys/types.h>
#include <sys/stat.h>
char *progname;

main(argc, argv)
    int argc;
    char *argv[];
{
    int fd;
    struct stat stbuf;
    time_t old_time = 0;

    progname = argv[0];
    if (argc < 2)
        error("Usage: %s filename [cmd]", progname);
    if ((fd = open(argv[1], 0)) == -1)
        error("can't open %s", argv[1]);
    fstat(fd, &stbuf);
    while (stbuf.st_mtime != old_time) {
        old_time = stbuf.st_mtime;
        sleep(60);
        fstat(fd, &stbuf);
    }
    if (argc == 2) {     /* copy file */
        execlp("cat", "cat", argv[1], (char *) 0);
        error("can't execute cat %s", argv[1]);
    } else {             /* run process */
        execvp(argv[2], &argv[2]);
        error("can't execute %s", argv[2]);
    }
    exit(0);
}
```

This illustrates both `execlp` and `execvp`.

We picked this design because it's useful, but other variations are plausible. For example, `waitfile` could simply return after the file has stopped changing.

Exercise 7-17. Modify `watchfile` (Exercise 7-12) so it has the same property as `waitfile`: if there is no *command*, it copies the file; otherwise it does the command. Could `watchfile` and `waitfile` share source code? Hint: `argv[0]`. □

Control of processes — `fork` and `wait`

The next step is to regain control after running a program with `execlp` or `execvp`. Since these routines simply overlay the new program on the old one, to save the old one requires that it first be split into two copies; one of these can be overlaid, while the other waits for the new, overlaying program to finish. The splitting is done by a system call named `fork`:

```
proc_id = fork();
```

splits the program into two copies, both of which continue to run. The only difference between the two is the value returned by `fork`, the *process-id*. In one of these processes (the *child*), `proc_id` is zero. In the other (the *parent*), `proc_id` is non-zero; it is the process-id of the child. Thus the basic way to call, and return from, another program is

```
if (fork() == 0)
    execlp("/bin/sh", "sh", "-c", commandline, (char *) 0);
```

And in fact, except for handling errors, this is sufficient. The `fork` makes two copies of the program. In the child, the value returned by `fork` is zero, so it calls `execlp`, which does the `commandline` and then dies. In the parent, `fork` returns non-zero so it skips the `execlp`. (If there is any error, `fork` returns -1.)

More often, the parent waits for the child to terminate before continuing itself. This is done with the system call `wait`:

```
int status;

if (fork() == 0)
    execlp(...);        /* child */
wait(&status);          /* parent */
```

This still doesn't handle any abnormal conditions, such as a failure of the `execlp` or `fork`, or the possibility that there might be more than one child running simultaneously. (`wait` returns the process-id of the terminated child, if you want to check it against the value returned by `fork`.) Finally, this fragment doesn't deal with any funny behavior on the part of the child. Still, these three lines are the heart of the standard `system` function.

The `status` returned by `wait` encodes in its low-order eight bits the system's idea of the child's exit status; it is 0 for normal termination and non-zero to indicate various kinds of problems. The next higher eight bits are taken from the argument of the call to `exit` or return from `main` that caused termination of the child process.

When a program is called by the shell, the three file descriptors 0, 1, and 2 are set up pointing at the right files, and all other file descriptors are available for use. When this program calls another one, correct etiquette suggests making sure the same conditions hold. Neither `fork` nor `exec` calls affect open files in any way; both parent and child have the same open files. If the parent is buffering output that must come out before output from the child, the parent must flush its buffers before the `execlp`. Conversely, if the parent buffers an input stream, the child will lose any information that has been read by the parent. Output can be flushed, but input cannot be put back. Both of these considerations arise if the input or output is being done with the standard I/O library discussed in Chapter 6, since it normally buffers both input and output.

It is the inheritance of file descriptors across an `execlp` that breaks `system`: if the calling program does not have its standard input and output connected to the terminal, neither will the command called by `system`. This may be what is wanted; in an `ed` script, for example, the input for a command started with an exclamation mark ! should probably come from the script. Even then `ed` must read its input one character at a time to avoid input buffering problems.

For interactive programs like `p`, however, `system` should reconnect standard input and output to the terminal. One way is to connect them to `/dev/tty`.

The system call `dup(fd)` duplicates the file descriptor `fd` on the lowest-numbered unallocated file descriptor, returning a new descriptor that refers to the same open file. This code connects the standard input of a program to a file:

```
int fd;

fd = open("file", 0);
close(0);
dup(fd);
close(fd);
```

The `close(0)` deallocates file descriptor 0, the standard input, but as usual doesn't affect the parent.

Here is our version of `system` for interactive programs; it uses `progname` for error messages. You should ignore the parts of the function that deal with signals; we will return to them in the next section.

```
/*
 * Safer version of system for interactive programs
 */
#include <signal.h>
#include <stdio.h>

system(s)   /* run command line s */
    char *s;
{
    int status, pid, w, tty;
    int (*istat)(), (*qstat)();
    extern char *progname;

    fflush(stdout);
    tty = open("/dev/tty", 2);
    if (tty == -1) {
        fprintf(stderr, "%s: can't open /dev/tty\n", progname);
        return -1;
    }
    if ((pid = fork()) == 0) {
        close(0); dup(tty);
        close(1); dup(tty);
        close(2); dup(tty);
        close(tty);
        execlp("sh", "sh", "-c", s, (char *) 0);
        exit(127);
    }
    close(tty);
    istat = signal(SIGINT, SIG_IGN);
    qstat = signal(SIGQUIT, SIG_IGN);
    while ((w = wait(&status)) != pid && w != -1)
        ;
    if (w == -1)
        status = -1;
    signal(SIGINT, istat);
    signal(SIGQUIT, qstat);
    return status;
}
```

Note that /dev/tty is opened with mode 2 — read and write — and then dup'ed to form the standard input and output. This is actually how the system assembles the standard input, output and error when you log in. Therefore, your standard input is writable:

```
$ echo hello 1>&0
hello
$
```

This means we could have dup'ed file descriptor 2 to reconnect the standard input and output, but opening /dev/tty is cleaner and safer. Even this system has potential problems: open files in the caller, such as tty in the routine ttyin in p, will be passed to the child process.

The lesson here is not that you should use our version of system for all your programs — it would break a non-interactive ed, for example — but that you should understand how processes are managed and use the primitives correctly; the meaning of "correctly" varies with the application, and may not agree with the standard implementation of system.

7.5 Signals and interrupts

This section is concerned with how to deal gracefully with signals (like interrupts) from the outside world, and with program faults. Program faults arise mainly from illegal memory references, execution of peculiar instructions, or floating point errors. The most common outside-world signals are *interrupt*, which is sent when the DEL character is typed; *quit*, generated by the FS character (*ctl-*); *hangup*, caused by hanging up the phone; and *terminate*, generated by the kill command. When one of these events occurs, the signal is sent to all processes that were started from the same terminal; unless other arrangements have been made, the signal terminates the process. For most signals, a core image file is written for potential debugging. (See adb(1) and sdb(1).)

The system call signal alters the default action. It has two arguments. The first is a number that specifies the signal. The second is either the address of a function, or a code which requests that the signal be ignored or be given the default action. The file <signal.h> contains definitions for the various arguments. Thus

```
#include <signal.h>
    ...
signal(SIGINT, SIG_IGN);
```

causes interrupts to be ignored, while

```
signal(SIGINT, SIG_DFL);
```

restores the default action of process termination. In all cases, signal returns the previous value of the signal. If the second argument to signal is the name of a function (which must have been declared already in the same source file), the function will be called when the signal occurs. Most commonly this facility is used to allow the program to clean up unfinished business before terminating, for example to delete a temporary file:

```
#include <signal.h>
char *tempfile = "temp.XXXXXX";

main()
{
    extern onintr();

    if (signal(SIGINT, SIG_IGN) != SIG_IGN)
        signal(SIGINT, onintr);
    mktemp(tempfile);

    /* Process ... */

    exit(0);
}

onintr()     /* clean up if interrupted */
{
    unlink(tempfile);
    exit(1);
}
```

Why the test and the double call to `signal` in `main`? Recall that signals are sent to *all* processes started from a particular terminal. Accordingly, when a program is to be run non-interactively (started by &), the shell arranges that the program will ignore interrupts, so it won't be stopped by interrupts intended for foreground processes. If this program began by announcing that all interrupts were to be sent to the `onintr` routine regardless, that would undo the shell's effort to protect it when run in the background.

The solution, shown above, is to test the state of interrupt handling, and to continue to ignore interrupts if they are already being ignored. The code as written depends on the fact that `signal` returns the previous state of a particular signal. If signals were already being ignored, the process should continue to ignore them; otherwise, they should be caught.

A more sophisticated program may wish to intercept an interrupt and interpret it as a request to stop what it is doing and return to its own command-processing loop. Think of a text editor: interrupting a long printout should not cause it to exit and lose the work already done. The code for this case can be written like this:

```
#include <signal.h>
#include <setjmp.h>
jmp_buf sjbuf;

main()
{
    int onintr();

    if (signal(SIGINT, SIG_IGN) != SIG_IGN)
        signal(SIGINT, onintr);
    setjmp(sjbuf);   /* save current stack position */

    for (;;) {
        /* main processing loop */
    }
    ...
}

onintr()     /* reset if interrupted */
{
    signal(SIGINT, onintr); /* reset for next interrupt */
    printf("\nInterrupt\n");
    longjmp(sjbuf, 0);       /* return to saved state */
}
```

The file <setjmp.h> declares the type jmp_buf as an object in which the
stack position can be saved; sjbuf is declared to be such an object. The function setjmp(3) saves a record of where the program was executing. The
values of variables are *not* saved. When an interrupt occurs, a call is forced to
the onintr routine, which can print a message, set flags, or whatever.
longjmp takes as argument an object stored into by setjmp, and restores
control to the location after the call to setjmp. So control (and the stack
level) will pop back to the place in the main routine where the main loop is
entered.

Notice that the signal is set again in onintr after an interrupt occurs.
This is necessary: signals are automatically reset to their default action when
they occur.

Some programs that want to detect signals simply can't be stopped at an
arbitrary point, for example in the middle of updating a complicated data structure. The solution is to have the interrupt routine set a flag and return instead
of calling exit or longjmp. Execution will continue at the exact point it was
interrupted, and the interrupt flag can be tested later.

There is one difficulty associated with this approach. Suppose the program
is reading the terminal when the interrupt is sent. The specified routine is duly
called; it sets its flag and returns. If it were really true, as we said above, that
execution resumes "at the exact point it was interrupted," the program would
continue reading the terminal until the user typed another line. This behavior

might well be confusing, since the user might not know that the program is reading, and presumably would prefer to have the signal take effect instantly. To resolve this difficulty, the system terminates the `read`, but with an error status that indicates what happened: `errno` is set to `EINTR`, defined in `<errno.h>`, to indicate an interrupted system call.

Thus programs that catch and resume execution after signals should be prepared for "errors" caused by interrupted system calls. (The system calls to watch out for are `read`s from a terminal, `wait`, and `pause`.) Such a program could use code like the following when it reads the standard input:

```
#include <errno.h>
extern int errno;

...
if (read(0, &c, 1) <= 0)      /* EOF or interrupted */
    if (errno == EINTR) {     /* EOF caused by interrupt */
        errno = 0;   /* reset for next time */
        ...
    } else {             /* true end of file */
        ...
    }
```

There is a final subtlety to keep in mind when signal-catching is combined with execution of other programs. Suppose a program catches interrupts, and also includes a method (like "!" in `ed`) whereby other programs can be executed. Then the code would look something like this:

```
if (fork() == 0)
    execlp(...);
signal(SIGINT, SIG_IGN);    /* parent ignores interrupts */
wait(&status);              /* until child is done */
signal(SIGINT, onintr);     /* restore interrupts */
```

Why is this? Signals are sent to all your processes. Suppose the program you call catches its own interrupts, as an editor does. If you interrupt the subprogram, it will get the signal and return to its main loop, and probably read your terminal. But the calling program will also pop out of its `wait` for the subprogram and read your terminal. Having two processes reading your terminal is very confusing, since in effect the system flips a coin to decide who should get each line of input. The solution is to have the parent program ignore interrupts until the child is done. This reasoning is reflected in the signal handling in `system`:

```
#include <signal.h>

system(s)    /* run command line s */
    char *s;
{
    int status, pid, w, tty;
    int (*istat)(), (*qstat)();

    ...
    if ((pid = fork()) == 0) {
        ...
        execlp("sh", "sh", "-c", s, (char *) 0);
        exit(127);
    }
    ...
    istat = signal(SIGINT, SIG_IGN);
    qstat = signal(SIGQUIT, SIG_IGN);
    while ((w = wait(&status)) != pid && w != -1)
        ;
    if (w == -1)
        status = -1;
    signal(SIGINT, istat);
    signal(SIGQUIT, qstat);
    return status;
}
```

As an aside on declarations, the function `signal` obviously has a rather strange second argument. It is in fact a pointer to a function delivering an integer, and this is also the type of the signal routine itself. The two values `SIG_IGN` and `SIG_DFL` have the right type, but are chosen so they coincide with no possible actual functions. For the enthusiast, here is how they are defined for the PDP-11 and VAX; the definitions should be sufficiently ugly to encourage use of `<signal.h>`.

```
#define SIG_DFL (int (*)())0
#define SIG_IGN (int (*)())1
```

Alarms

The system call `alarm(n)` causes a signal `SIGALRM` to be sent to your process *n* seconds later. The alarm signal can be used for making sure that something happens within the proper amount of time; if the something happens, the alarm signal can be turned off, but if it does not, the process can regain control by catching the alarm signal.

To illustrate, here is a program called `timeout` that runs another command; if that command has not finished by the specified time, it will be aborted when the alarm goes off. For example, recall the `watchfor` command from Chapter 5. Rather than having it run indefinitely, you might set a limit of an hour:

```
$ timeout -3600 watchfor dmg &
```

The code in `timeout` illustrates almost everything we have talked about in the past two sections. The child is created; the parent sets an alarm and then waits for the child to finish. If the alarm arrives first, the child is killed. An attempt is made to return the child's exit status.

```c
/* timeout:  set time limit on a process */
#include <stdio.h>
#include <signal.h>
int pid;          /* child process id */
char *progname;

main(argc, argv)
    int argc;
    char *argv[];
{
    int sec = 10, status, onalarm();

    progname = argv[0];
    if (argc > 1 && argv[1][0] == '-') {
        sec = atoi(&argv[1][1]);
        argc--;
        argv++;
    }
    if (argc < 2)
        error("Usage: %s [-10] command", progname);
    if ((pid=fork()) == 0) {
        execvp(argv[1], &argv[1]);
        error("couldn't start %s", argv[1]);
    }
    signal(SIGALRM, onalarm);
    alarm(sec);
    if (wait(&status) == -1 || (status & 0177) != 0)
        error("%s killed", argv[1]);
    exit((status >> 8) & 0377);
}

onalarm()    /* kill child when alarm arrives */
{
    kill(pid, SIGKILL);
}
```

Exercise 7-18. Can you infer how `sleep` is implemented? Hint: pause(2). Under what circumstances, if any, could `sleep` and `alarm` interfere with each other? □

History and bibliographic notes

There is no detailed description of the UNIX system implementation, in part because the code is proprietary. Ken Thompson's paper "UNIX implementation" (*BSTJ*, July, 1978) describes the basic ideas. Other papers that discuss related topics are "The UNIX system—a retrospective" in the same issue of *BSTJ*, and "The evolution of the UNIX time-sharing system" (Symposium on Language Design and Programming Methodology, Springer-Verlag *Lecture Notes in Computer Science #79*, 1979.) Both are by Dennis Ritchie.

The program `readslow` was invented by Peter Weinberger, as a low-overhead way for spectators to watch the progress of Belle, Ken Thompson and Joe Condon's chess machine, during chess tournaments. Belle recorded the status of its game in a file; onlookers polled the file with `readslow` so as not to steal too many precious cycles from Belle. (The newest version of the Belle hardware does little computing on its host machine, so the problem has gone away.)

Our inspiration for `spname` comes from Tom Duff. A paper by Ivor Durham, David Lamb and James Saxe entitled "Spelling correction in user interfaces," CACM, October, 1983, presents a somewhat different design for spelling correction, in the context of a mail program.

CHAPTER 8: **PROGRAM DEVELOPMENT**

The UNIX system was originally meant as a program development environment. In this chapter we'll talk about some of the tools that are particularly suited for developing programs. Our vehicle is a substantial program, an interpreter for a programming language comparable in power to BASIC. We chose to implement a language because it's representative of problems encountered in large programs. Furthermore, many programs can profitably be viewed as languages that convert a systematic input into a sequence of actions and outputs, so we want to illustrate the language development tools.

In this chapter, we will cover specific lessons about

- `yacc`, a parser generator, a program that generates a parser from a grammatical description of a language;
- `make`, a program for specifying and controlling the processes by which a complicated program is compiled;
- `lex`, a program analogous to `yacc`, for making lexical analyzers.

We also want to convey some notions of how to go about such a project — the importance of starting with something small and letting it grow; language evolution; and the use of tools.

We will describe the implementation of the language in six stages, each of which would be useful even if the development went no further. These stages closely parallel the way that we actually wrote the program.

(1) A four-function calculator, providing +, -, *, / and parentheses, that operates on floating point numbers. One expression is typed on each line; its value is printed immediately.

(2) Variables with names `a` through `z`. This version also has unary minus and some defenses against errors.

(3) Arbitrarily-long variable names, built-in functions for `sin`, `exp`, etc., useful constants like π (spelled `PI` because of typographic limitations), and an exponentiation operator.

(4) A change in internals: code is generated for each statement and subsequently interpreted, rather than being evaluated on the fly. No new features are added, but it leads to (5).

(5) Control flow: `if-else` and `while`, statement grouping with { and }, and

233

relational operators like >, <=, etc.

(6) Recursive functions and procedures, with arguments. We also added statements for input and for output of strings as well as numbers.

The resulting language is described in Chapter 9, where it serves as the main example in our presentation of the UNIX document preparation software. Appendix 2 is the reference manual.

This is a very long chapter, because there's a lot of detail involved in getting a non-trivial program written correctly, let alone presented. We are assuming that you understand C, and that you have a copy of the *UNIX Programmer's Manual*, Volume 2, close at hand, since we simply don't have space to explain every nuance. Hang in, and be prepared to read the chapter a couple of times. We have also included all of the code for the final version in Appendix 3, so you can see more easily how the pieces fit together.

By the way, we wasted a lot of time debating names for this language but never came up with anything satisfactory. We settled on hoc, which stands for "high-order calculator." The versions are thus hoc1, hoc2, etc.

8.1 Stage 1: A four-function calculator

This section describes the implementation of hoc1, a program that provides about the same capabilities as a minimal pocket calculator, and is substantially less portable. It has only four functions: +, -, *, and /, but it does have parentheses that can be nested arbitrarily deeply, which few pocket calculators provide. If you type an expression followed by RETURN, the answer will be printed on the next line:

```
$ hoc1
4*3*2
        24
(1+2) * (3+4)
        21
1/2
        0.5
355/113
        3.1415929
-3-4
hoc1: syntax error near line 4      It doesn't have unary minus yet
$
```

Grammars

Ever since Backus-Naur Form was developed for Algol, languages have been described by formal grammars. The grammar for hoc1 is small and simple in its abstract representation:

```
list:     expr \n
          list expr \n
expr:     NUMBER
          expr + expr
          expr - expr
          expr * expr
          expr / expr
          ( expr )
```

In other words, a `list` is a sequence of expressions, each followed by a new-line. An expression is a number, or a pair of expressions joined by an operator, or a parenthesized expression.

This is not complete. Among other things, it does not specify the normal precedence and associativity of the operators, nor does it attach a meaning to any construct. And although `list` is defined in terms of `expr`, and `expr` is defined in terms of `NUMBER`, `NUMBER` itself is nowhere defined. These details have to be filled in to go from a sketch of the language to a working program.

Overview of yacc

`yacc` is a *parser generator*,† that is, a program for converting a grammatical specification of a language like the one above into a parser that will parse statements in the language. `yacc` provides a way to associate meanings with the components of the grammar in such a way that as the parsing takes place, the meaning can be "evaluated" as well. The stages in using `yacc` are the following.

First, a grammar is written, like the one above, but more precise. This specifies the syntax of the language. `yacc` can be used at this stage to warn of errors and ambiguities in the grammar.

Second, each rule or *production* of the grammar can be augmented with an *action* — a statement of what to do when an instance of that grammatical form is found in a program being parsed. The "what to do" part is written in C, with conventions for connecting the grammar to the C code. This defines the semantics of the language.

Third, a *lexical analyzer* is needed, which will read the input being parsed and break it up into meaningful chunks for the parser. A `NUMBER` is an example of a lexical chunk that is several characters long; single-character operators like + and * are also chunks. A lexical chunk is traditionally called a *token*.

Finally, a controlling routine is needed, to call the parser that `yacc` built.

`yacc` processes the grammar and the semantic actions into a parsing function, named `yyparse`, and writes it out as a file of C code. If `yacc` finds no errors, the parser, the lexical analyzer, and the control routine can be

---

† `yacc` stands for "yet another compiler-compiler," a comment by its creator, Steve Johnson, on the number of such programs extant at the time it was being developed (around 1972). `yacc` is one of a handful that have flourished.

compiled, perhaps linked with other C routines, and executed. The operation of this program is to call repeatedly upon the lexical analyzer for tokens, recognize the grammatical (syntactic) structure in the input, and perform the semantic actions as each grammatical rule is recognized. The entry to the lexical analyzer must be named `yylex`, since that is the function that `yyparse` calls each time it wants another token. (All names used by `yacc` start with `y`.)

To be somewhat more precise, the input to `yacc` takes this form:

```
%{
C statements like #include, declarations, etc. This section is optional.
%}
yacc declarations: lexical tokens, grammar variables,
    precedence and associativity information
%%
grammar rules and actions
%%
more C statements (optional):
main() { ...; yyparse(); ... }
yylex() { ... }
...
```

This is processed by `yacc` and the result written into a file called `y.tab.c`, whose layout is like this:

```
C statements from between %{ and %}, if any
C statements from after second %%, if any:
main() { ...; yyparse(); ... }
yylex() { ... }
...
yyparse() { parser, which calls yylex() }
```

It is typical of the UNIX approach that `yacc` produces C instead of a compiled object (`.o`) file. This is the most flexible arrangement — the generated code is portable and amenable to other processing whenever someone has a good idea.

`yacc` itself is a powerful tool. It takes some effort to learn, but the effort is repaid many times over. `yacc`-generated parsers are small, efficient, and correct (though the semantic actions are your own responsibility); many nasty parsing problems are taken care of automatically. Language-recognizing programs are easy to build, and (probably more important) can be modified repeatedly as the language definition evolves.

Stage 1 program

The source code for `hoc1` consists of a grammar with actions, a lexical routine `yylex`, and a `main`, all in one file `hoc.y`. (`yacc` filenames traditionally end in `.y`, but this convention is not enforced by `yacc` itself, unlike `cc` and `.c`.) The grammar part is the first half of `hoc.y`:

```
$ cat hoc.y
%{
#define YYSTYPE double  /* data type of yacc stack */
%}
%token  NUMBER
%left   '+' '-'    /* left associative, same precedence */
%left   '*' '/'    /* left assoc., higher precedence */
%%
list:    /* nothing */
       | list '\n'
       | list expr '\n'    { printf("\t%.8g\n", $2); }
       ;
expr:    NUMBER          { $$ = $1; }
       | expr '+' expr { $$ = $1 + $3; }
       | expr '-' expr { $$ = $1 - $3; }
       | expr '*' expr { $$ = $1 * $3; }
       | expr '/' expr { $$ = $1 / $3; }
       | '(' expr ')'  { $$ = $2; }
       ;
%%
       /* end of grammar */
...
```

There's a lot of new information packed into these few lines. We are not going to explain all of it, and certainly not how the parser works — for that, you will have to read the yacc manual.

Alternate rules are separated by '|'. Any grammar rule can have an associated action, which will be performed when an instance of that rule is recognized in the input. An action is a sequence of C statements enclosed in braces { and }. Within an action, $n (that is, $1, $2, etc.) refers to the value returned by the n-th component of the rule, and $$ is the value to be returned as the value of the whole rule. So, for example, in the rule

```
expr:    NUMBER   { $$ = $1; }
```

$1 is the value returned by recognizing NUMBER; that value is to be returned as the value of the expr. The particular assignment $$=$1 can be omitted — $$ is always set to $1 unless you explicitly set it to something else.

At the next level, when the rule is

```
expr:    expr '+' expr    { $$ = $1 + $3; }
```

the value of the result expr is the sum of the values from the two component expr's. Notice that '+' is $2; every component is numbered.

At the level above this, an expression followed by a newline ('\n') is recognized as a list and its value printed. If the end of the input follows such a construction, the parsing process terminates cleanly. A list can be an empty string; this is how blank input lines are handled.

yacc input is free form; our format is the recommended standard.

In this implementation, the act of recognizing or parsing the input also causes immediate evaluation of the expression. In more complicated situations (including `hoc4` and its successors), the parsing process generates code for later execution.

You may find it helpful to visualize parsing as drawing a *parse tree* like the one in Figure 8.1, and to imagine values being computed and propagated up the tree from the leaves towards the root.

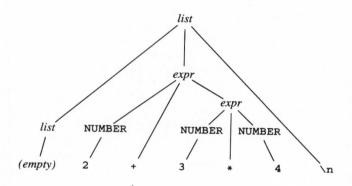

Figure 8.1: Parse Tree for `2 + 3 * 4`

The values of incompletely-recognized rules are actually kept on a stack; this is how the values are passed from one rule to the next. The data type of this stack is normally an `int`, but since we are processing floating point numbers, we have to override the default. The definition

```
#define YYSTYPE double
```

sets the stack type to `double`.

Syntactic classes that will be recognized by the lexical analyzer have to be declared unless they are single character literals like `'+'` and `'-'`. The declaration %token declares one or more such objects. Left or right associativity can be specified if appropriate by using %left or %right instead of %token. (Left associativity means that `a-b-c` will be parsed as `(a-b)-c` instead of `a-(b-c)`.) Precedence is determined by order of appearance: tokens in the same declaration are at the same level of precedence; tokens declared later are of higher precedence. In this way the grammar proper is ambiguous (that is, there are multiple ways to parse some inputs), but the extra information in the declarations resolves the ambiguity.

The rest of the code is the routines in the second half of the file `hoc.y`:

Continuing hoc.y

```
#include <stdio.h>
#include <ctype.h>
char    *progname;      /* for error messages */
int     lineno = 1;

main(argc, argv)        /* hoc1 */
        char *argv[];
{
        progname = argv[0];
        yyparse();
}
```

main calls **yyparse** to parse the input. Looping from one expression to the next is done entirely within the grammar, by the sequence of productions for list. It would have been equally acceptable to put a loop around the call to **yyparse** in main and have the action for list print the value and return immediately.

yyparse in turn calls **yylex** repeatedly for input tokens. Our **yylex** is easy: it skips blanks and tabs, converts strings of digits into a numeric value, counts input lines for error reporting, and returns any other character as itself. Since the grammar expects to see only +, -, *, /, (,), and \n, any other character will cause **yyparse** to report an error. Returning a 0 signals "end of file" to **yyparse**.

Continuing hoc.y

```
yylex()         /* hoc1 */
{
        int c;

        while ((c=getchar()) == ' ' || c == '\t')
                ;
        if (c == EOF)
                return 0;
        if (c == '.' || isdigit(c)) {     /* number */
                ungetc(c, stdin);
                scanf("%lf", &yylval);
                return NUMBER;
        }
        if (c == '\n')
                lineno++;
        return c;
}
```

The variable **yylval** is used for communication between the parser and the lexical analyzer; it is defined by **yyparse**, and has the same type as the **yacc** stack. **yylex** returns the *type* of a token as its function value, and sets **yylval** to the *value* of the token (if there is one). For instance, a floating point number has the type NUMBER and a value like 12.34. For some tokens, especially single characters like '+' and '\n', the grammar does not use the value, only the type. In that case, yylval need not be set.

The yacc declaration %token NUMBER is converted into a #define statement in the yacc output file y.tab.c, so NUMBER can be used as a constant anywhere in the C program. yacc chooses values that won't collide with ASCII characters.

If there is a syntax error, yyparse calls yyerror with a string containing the cryptic message "syntax error." The yacc user is expected to provide a yyerror; ours just passes the string on to another function, warning, which prints somewhat more information. Later versions of hoc will make direct use of warning.

```
yyerror(s)        /* called for yacc syntax error */
        char *s;
{
        warning(s, (char *) 0);
}

warning(s, t)    /* print warning message */
        char *s, *t;
{
        fprintf(stderr, "%s: %s", progname, s);
        if (t)
                fprintf(stderr, " %s", t);
        fprintf(stderr, " near line %d\n", lineno);
}
```

This marks the end of the routines in hoc.y.

Compilation of a yacc program is a two-step process:

```
$ yacc hoc.y              Leaves output in y.tab.c
$ cc y.tab.c -o hoc1      Leaves executable program in hoc1
$ hoc1
2/3
        0.66666667
-3-4
hoc1: syntax error near line 1
$
```

Exercise 8-1. Examine the structure of the y.tab.c file. (It's about 300 lines long for hoc1.) □

Making changes — unary minus

We claimed earlier that using yacc makes it easy to change a language. As an illustration, let's add unary minus to hoc1, so that expressions like

-3-4

are evaluated, not rejected as syntax errors.

Exactly two lines have to be added to hoc.y. A new token UNARYMINUS is added to the end of the precedence section, to make unary minus have highest precedence:

```
%left    '+' '-'
%left    '*' '/'
%left    UNARYMINUS          /* new */
```

The grammar is augmented with one more production for expr:

```
expr:       NUMBER            { $$ = $1; }
        | '-' expr  %prec UNARYMINUS { $$ = -$2; } /* new */
```

The %prec says that a unary minus sign (that is, a minus sign before an expression) has the precedence of UNARYMINUS (high); the action is to change the sign. A minus sign between two expressions takes the default precedence.

Exercise 8-2. Add the operators % (modulus or remainder) and unary + to hoc1. Suggestion: look at frexp(3). □

A digression on make

It's a nuisance to have to type two commands to compile a new version of hoc1. Although it's certainly easy to make a shell file that does the job, there's a better way, one that will generalize nicely later on when there is more than one source file in the program. The program make reads a specification of how the components of a program depend on each other, and how to process them to create an up-to-date version of the program. It checks the times at which the various components were last modified, figures out the minimum amount of recompilation that has to be done to make a consistent new version, then runs the processes. make also understands the intricacies of multi-step processes like yacc, so these tasks can be put into a make specification without spelling out the individual steps.

make is most useful when the program being created is large enough to be spread over several source files, but it's handy even for something as small as hoc1. Here is the make specification for hoc1, which make expects in a file called makefile.

```
$ cat makefile
hoc1:    hoc.o
         cc hoc.o -o hoc1
$
```

This says that hoc1 depends on hoc.o, and that hoc.o is converted into hoc1 by running the C compiler cc and putting the output in hoc1. make already knows how to convert the yacc source file in hoc.y to an object file hoc.o:

```
$ make                          Make the first thing in makefile, hoc1
yacc  hoc.y
cc   -c y.tab.c
rm y.tab.c
mv y.tab.o hoc.o
cc hoc.o -o hoc1
$ make                          Do it again
'hoc1' is up to date.           make realizes it's unnecessary
$
```

8.2 Stage 2: Variables and error recovery

The next step (a small one) is to add "memory" to hoc1, to make hoc2. The memory is 26 variables, named a through z. This isn't very elegant, but it's an easy and useful intermediate step. We'll also add some error handling. If you try hoc1, you'll recognize that its approach to syntax errors is to print a message and die, and its treatment of arithmetic errors like division by zero is reprehensible:

```
$ hoc1
1/0
Floating exception - core dumped
$
```

The changes needed for these new features are modest, about 35 lines of code. The lexical analyzer yylex has to recognize letters as variables; the grammar has to include productions of the form

```
expr:     VAR
        | VAR '=' expr
```

An expression can contain an assignment, which permits multiple assignments like

```
x = y = z = 0
```

The easiest way to store the values of the variables is in a 26-element array; the single-letter variable name can be used to index the array. But if the grammar is to process both variable names and values in the same stack, yacc has to be told that its stack contains a union of a double and an int, not just a double. This is done with a %union declaration near the top. A #define or a typedef is fine for setting the stack to a basic type like double, but the %union mechanism is required for union types because yacc checks for consistency in expressions like $$=$2.

Here is the grammar part of hoc.y for hoc2:

```
$ cat hoc.y
%{
double   mem[26];           /* memory for variables 'a'..'z' */
%}
%union {                    /* stack type */
         double   val;      /* actual value */
         int      index;    /* index into mem[] */
}
%token   <val>    NUMBER
%token   <index>  VAR
%type    <val>    expr
%right   '='
%left    '+' '-'
%left    '*' '/'
%left    UNARYMINUS
%%
list:     /* nothing */
        | list '\n'
        | list expr '\n'          { printf("\t%.8g\n", $2); }
        | list error '\n'         { yyerrok; }
        ;
expr:     NUMBER
        | VAR             { $$ = mem[$1]; }
        | VAR '=' expr    { $$ = mem[$1] = $3; }
        | expr '+' expr { $$ = $1 + $3; }
        | expr '-' expr { $$ = $1 - $3; }
        | expr '*' expr { $$ = $1 * $3; }
        | expr '/' expr {
                if ($3 == 0.0)
                        execerror("division by zero", "");
                $$ = $1 / $3; }
        | '(' expr ')'  { $$ = $2; }
        | '-' expr  %prec UNARYMINUS  { $$ = -$2; }
        ;
%%
        /* end of grammar */
 ...
```

The %union declaration says that stack elements hold either a double (a number, the usual case), or an int, which is an index into the array mem. The %token declarations have been augmented with a type indicator. The %type declaration specifies that expr is the <val> member of the union, i.e., a double. The type information makes it possible for yacc to generate references to the correct members of the union. Notice also that = is right-associative, while the other operators are left-associative.

Error handling comes in several pieces. The obvious one is a test for a zero divisor; if one occurs, an error routine execerror is called.

A second test is to catch the "floating point exception" signal that occurs when a floating point number overflows. The signal is set in `main`.

The final part of error recovery is the addition of a production for `error`. "`error`" is a reserved word in a `yacc` grammar; it provides a way to anticipate and recover from a syntax error. If an error occurs, `yacc` will eventually try to use this production, recognize the error as grammatically "correct," and thus recover. The action `yyerrok` sets a flag in the parser that permits it to get back into a sensible parsing state. Error recovery is difficult in any parser; you should be aware that we have taken only the most elementary steps here, and have skipped rapidly over `yacc`'s capabilities as well.

The actions in the `hoc2` grammar are not much changed. Here is `main`, to which we have added `setjmp` to save a clean state suitable for resuming after an error. `execerror` does the matching `longjmp`. (See Section 7.5 for a description of `setjmp` and `longjmp`.)

```
...
#include <signal.h>
#include <setjmp.h>
jmp_buf begin;

main(argc, argv)          /* hoc2 */
        char *argv[];
{
        int fpecatch();

        progname = argv[0];
        setjmp(begin);
        signal(SIGFPE, fpecatch);
        yyparse();
}

execerror(s, t) /* recover from run-time error */
        char *s, *t;
{
        warning(s, t);
        longjmp(begin, 0);
}

fpecatch()        /* catch floating point exceptions */
{
        execerror("floating point exception", (char *) 0);
}
```

For debugging, we found it convenient to have `execerror` call `abort` (see abort(3)), which causes a core dump that can be perused with `adb` or `sdb`. Once the program is fairly robust, `abort` is replaced by `longjmp`.

The lexical analyzer is a little different in `hoc2`. There is an extra test for a lower-case letter, and since `yylval` is now a union, the proper member has to be set before `yylex` returns. Here are the parts that have changed:

```
    yylex()            /* hoc2 */
    ...
            if (c == '.' || isdigit(c)) {    /* number */
                    ungetc(c, stdin);
                    scanf("%lf", &yylval.val);
                    return NUMBER;
            }
            if (islower(c)) {
                    yylval.index = c - 'a'; /* ASCII only */
                    return VAR;
            }
    ...
```

Again, notice how the token type (e.g., NUMBER) is distinct from its value (e.g., 3.1416).

Let us illustrate variables and error recovery, the new things in hoc2:

```
$ hoc2
x = 355
        355
y = 113
        113
p = x/z                             z is undefined and thus zero
hoc2: division by zero near line 4     Error recovery
x/y
        3.1415929
1e30 * 1e30                         Overflow
hoc2: floating point exception near line 5
...
```

Actually, the PDP-11 requires special arrangements to detect floating point overflow, but on most other machines hoc2 behaves as shown.

Exercise 8-3. Add a facility for remembering the most recent value computed, so that it does not have to be retyped in a sequence of related computations. One solution is to make it one of the variables, for instance 'p' for 'previous.' □

Exercise 8-4. Modify hoc so that a semicolon can be used as an expression terminator equivalent to a newline. □

8.3 Stage 3: Arbitrary variable names; built-in functions

This version, hoc3, adds several major new capabilities, and a corresponding amount of extra code. The main new feature is access to built-in functions:

```
sin     cos     atan     exp     log     log10
sqrt    int     abs
```

We have also added an exponentiation operator '^'; it has the highest precedence, and is right-associative.

Since the lexical analyzer has to cope with built-in names longer than a single character, it isn't much extra effort to permit variable names to be arbitrarily long as well. We will need a more sophisticated symbol table to keep track of these variables, but once we have it, we can pre-load it with names and values for some useful constants:

PI	3.14159265358979323846	π
E	2.71828182845904523536	Base of natural logarithms
GAMMA	0.57721566490153286060	Euler-Mascheroni constant
DEG	57.29577951308232087680	Degrees per radian
PHI	1.61803398874989484820	Golden ratio

The result is a useful calculator:

```
$ hoc3
1.5^2.3
        2.5410306
exp(2.3*log(1.5))
        2.5410306
sin(PI/2)
        1
atan(1)*DEG
        45
...
```

We have also cleaned up the behavior a little. In hoc2, the assignment x=*expr* not only causes the assignment but also prints the value, because all expressions are printed:

```
$ hoc2
x = 2 * 3.14159
        6.28318            Value printed for assignment to variable
...
```

In hoc3, a distinction is made between assignments and expressions; values are printed only for expressions:

```
$ hoc3
x = 2 * 3.14159            Assignment: no value is printed
x                          Expression:
        6.28318              value is printed
...
```

The program that results from all these changes is big enough (about 250 lines) that it is best split into separate files for easier editing and faster compilation. There are now five files instead of one:

hoc.y	Grammar, main, yylex (as before)
hoc.h	Global data structures for inclusion
symbol.c	Symbol table routines: lookup, install
init.c	Built-ins and constants; init
math.c	Interfaces to math routines: Sqrt, Log, etc.

This requires that we learn more about how to organize a multi-file C program, and more about make so it can do some of the work for us.

We'll get back to make shortly. First, let us look at the symbol table code. A symbol has a name, a type (it's either a VAR or a BLTIN), and a value. If the symbol is a VAR, the value is a double; if the symbol is a built-in, the value is a pointer to a function that returns a double. This information is needed in hoc.y, symbol.c, and init.c. We could just make three copies, but it's too easy to make a mistake or forget to update one copy when a change is made. Instead we put the common information into a header file hoc.h that will be included by any file that needs it. (The suffix .h is conventional but not enforced by any program.) We will also add to the makefile the fact that these files depend on hoc.h, so that when it changes, the necessary recompilations are done too.

```
$ cat hoc.h
typedef struct Symbol {  /* symbol table entry */
        char    *name;
        short   type;    /* VAR, BLTIN, UNDEF */
        union {
                double  val;            /* if VAR */
                double  (*ptr)();       /* if BLTIN */
        } u;
        struct Symbol   *next;  /* to link to another */
} Symbol;
Symbol  *install(), *lookup();
$
```

The type UNDEF is a VAR that has not yet been assigned a value.

The symbols are linked together in a list using the next field in Symbol. The list itself is local to symbol.c; the only access to it is through the functions lookup and install. This makes it easy to change to symbol table organization if it becomes necessary. (We did that once.) lookup searches the list for a particular name and returns a pointer to the Symbol with that name if found, and zero otherwise. The symbol table uses linear search, which is entirely adequate for our interactive calculator, since variables are looked up only during parsing, not execution. install puts a variable with its associated type and value at the head of the list. emalloc calls malloc, the standard storage allocator (malloc(3)), and checks the result. These three routines are the contents of symbol.c. The file y.tab.h is generated by running yacc -d; it contains #define statements that yacc has generated for tokens like NUMBER, VAR, BLTIN, etc.

```
$ cat symbol.c
#include "hoc.h"
#include "y.tab.h"

static Symbol *symlist = 0;   /* symbol table: linked list */

Symbol *lookup(s)          /* find s in symbol table */
        char *s;
{
        Symbol *sp;

        for (sp = symlist; sp != (Symbol *) 0; sp = sp->next)
                if (strcmp(sp->name, s) == 0)
                        return sp;
        return 0;          /* 0 ==> not found */
}
Symbol *install(s, t, d)  /* install s in symbol table */
        char *s;
        int t;
        double d;
{
        Symbol *sp;
        char *emalloc();

        sp = (Symbol *) emalloc(sizeof(Symbol));
        sp->name = emalloc(strlen(s)+1); /* +1 for '\0' */
        strcpy(sp->name, s);
        sp->type = t;
        sp->u.val = d;
        sp->next = symlist; /* put at front of list */
        symlist = sp;
        return sp;
}
char *emalloc(n)           /* check return from malloc */
        unsigned n;
{
        char *p, *malloc();

        p = malloc(n);
        if (p == 0)
                execerror("out of memory", (char *) 0);
        return p;
}
$
```

The file init.c contains definitions for the constants (PI, etc.) and function pointers for built-ins; they are installed in the symbol table by the function
init, which is called by main.

```
$ cat init.c
#include "hoc.h"
#include "y.tab.h"
#include <math.h>

extern double    Log(), Log10(), Exp(), Sqrt(), integer();
static struct {              /* Constants */
        char    *name;
        double  cval;
} consts[] = {
        "PI",      3.14159265358979323846,
        "E",       2.71828182845904523536,
        "GAMMA",  0.57721566490153286060,    /* Euler */
        "DEG",    57.29577951308232087680,   /* deg/radian */
        "PHI",     1.61803398874989484820,   /* golden ratio */
        0,         0
};
static struct {              /* Built-ins */
        char    *name;
        double  (*func)();
} builtins[] = {
        "sin",   sin,
        "cos",   cos,
        "atan",  atan,
        "log",   Log,     /* checks argument */
        "log10", Log10,   /* checks argument */
        "exp",   Exp,     /* checks argument */
        "sqrt",  Sqrt,    /* checks argument */
        "int",   integer,
        "abs",   fabs,
        0,       0
};
init()    /* install constants and built-ins in table */
{
        int i;
        Symbol *s;

        for (i = 0; consts[i].name; i++)
                install(consts[i].name, VAR, consts[i].cval);
        for (i = 0; builtins[i].name; i++) {
                s = install(builtins[i].name, BLTIN, 0.0);
                s->u.ptr = builtins[i].func;
        }
}
```

The data is kept in tables rather than being wired into the code because tables
are easier to read and to change. The tables are declared static so that they
are visible only within this file rather than throughout the program. We'll
come back to the math routines like Log and Sqrt shortly.

With the foundation in place, we can move on to the changes in the grammar that make use of it.

```
$ cat hoc.y
%{
#include "hoc.h"
extern  double  Pow();
%}
%union {
        double  val;      /* actual value */
        Symbol  *sym;     /* symbol table pointer */
}
%token  <val>    NUMBER
%token  <sym>    VAR BLTIN UNDEF
%type   <val>    expr asgn
%right  '='
%left   '+' '-'
%left   '*' '/'
%left   UNARYMINUS
%right  '^'      /* exponentiation */
%%
list:     /* nothing */
        | list '\n'
        | list asgn '\n'
        | list expr '\n'          { printf("\t%.8g\n", $2); }
        | list error '\n'         { yyerrok; }
        ;
asgn:     VAR '=' expr { $$=$1->u.val=$3; $1->type = VAR; }
        ;
expr:     NUMBER
        | VAR { if ($1->type == UNDEF)
                        execerror("undefined variable", $1->name);
                $$ = $1->u.val; }
        | asgn
        | BLTIN '(' expr ')'    { $$ = (*($1->u.ptr))($3); }
        | expr '+' expr { $$ = $1 + $3; }
        | expr '-' expr { $$ = $1 - $3; }
        | expr '*' expr { $$ = $1 * $3; }
        | expr '/' expr {
                if ($3 == 0.0)
                        execerror("division by zero", "");
                $$ = $1 / $3; }
        | expr '^' expr { $$ = Pow($1, $3); }
        | '(' expr ')'  { $$ = $2; }
        | '-' expr  %prec UNARYMINUS  { $$ = -$2; }
        ;
%%
        /* end of grammar */
...
```

The grammar now has `asgn`, for assignment, as well as `expr`; an input line that contains just

```
VAR = expr
```

is an assignment, and so no value is printed. Notice, by the way, how easy it was to add exponentiation to the grammar, including its right associativity.

The `yacc` stack has a different `%union`: instead of referring to a variable by its index in a 26-element table, there is a pointer to an object of type `Symbol`. The header file `hoc.h` contains the definition of this type.

The lexical analyzer recognizes variable names, looks them up in the symbol table, and decides whether they are variables (`VAR`) or built-ins (`BLTIN`). The type returned by `yylex` is one of these; both user-defined variables and pre-defined variables like `PI` are `VAR`'s.

One of the properties of a variable is whether or not it has been assigned a value, so the use of an undefined variable can be reported as an error by `yyparse`. The test for whether a variable is defined has to be in the grammar, not in the lexical analyzer. When a `VAR` is recognized lexically, its context isn't yet known; we don't want a complaint that `x` is undefined when the context is perfectly legal one such as the left side of an assignment like `x=1`.

Here is the revised part of `yylex`:

```
yylex()              /* hoc3 */
...
        if (isalpha(c)) {
                Symbol *s;
                char sbuf[100], *p = sbuf;
                do {
                        *p++ = c;
                } while ((c=getchar()) != EOF && isalnum(c));
                ungetc(c, stdin);
                *p = '\0';
                if ((s=lookup(sbuf)) == 0)
                        s = install(sbuf, UNDEF, 0.0);
                yylval.sym = s;
                return s->type == UNDEF ? VAR : s->type;
        }
...
```

`main` has one extra line, which calls the initialization routine `init` to install built-ins and pre-defined names like `PI` in the symbol table.

```
main(argc, argv)           /* hoc3 */
        char *argv[];
{
        int fpecatch();

        progname = argv[0];
        init();
        setjmp(begin);
        signal(SIGFPE, fpecatch);
        yyparse();
}
```

The only remaining file is `math.c`. Some of the standard mathematical functions need an error-checking interface for messages and recovery — for example the standard function `sqrt` silently returns zero if its argument is negative. The code in `math.c` uses the error tests found in Section 2 of the *UNIX Programmer's Manual*; see Chapter 7. This is more reliable and portable than writing our own tests, since presumably the specific limitations of the routines are best reflected in the "official" code. The header file `<math.h>` contains type declarations for the standard mathematical functions. `<errno.h>` contains names for the errors that can be incurred.

```
$ cat math.c
#include <math.h>
#include <errno.h>
extern   int      errno;
double   errcheck();

double Log(x)
        double x;
{
        return errcheck(log(x), "log");
}
double Log10(x)
        double x;
{
        return errcheck(log10(x), "log10");
}
double Exp(x)
        double x;
{
        return errcheck(exp(x), "exp");
}
double Sqrt(x)
        double x;
{
        return errcheck(sqrt(x), "sqrt");
}
```

```
double Pow(x, y)
      double x, y;
{
      return errcheck(pow(x,y), "exponentiation");
}
double integer(x)
      double x;
{
      return (double)(long)x;
}
double errcheck(d, s)    /* check result of library call */
      double d;
      char *s;
{
      if (errno == EDOM) {
            errno = 0;
            execerror(s, "argument out of domain");
      } else if (errno == ERANGE) {
            errno = 0;
            execerror(s, "result out of range");
      }
      return d;
}
$
```

An interesting (and ungrammatical) diagnostic appears when we run yacc on the new grammar:

```
$ yacc hoc.y

conflicts: 1 shift/reduce
$
```

The "shift/reduce" message means that the hoc3 grammar is ambiguous: the single line of input

```
x = 1
```

can be parsed in two ways:

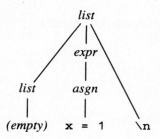
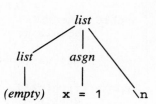

The parser can decide that the *asgn* should be reduced to an *expr* and then to a *list*, as in the parse tree on the left, or it can decide to use the following \n immediately ("shift") and convert the whole thing to a *list* without the intermediate rule, as in the tree on the right. Given the ambiguity, yacc chooses to shift, since this is almost always the right thing to do with real grammars. You should try to understand such messages, to be sure that yacc has made the right decision.† Running yacc with the option -v produces a voluminous file called y.output that hints at the origin of conflicts.

Exercise 8-5. As hoc3 stands, it's legal to say

```
PI = 3
```

Is this a good idea? How would you change hoc3 to prohibit assignment to "constants"? □

Exercise 8-6. Add the built-in function atan2(y,x), which returns the angle whose tangent is y/x. Add the built-in rand( ), which returns a floating point random variable uniformly distributed on the interval (0,1). How do you have to change the grammar to allow for built-ins with different numbers of arguments? □

Exercise 8-7. How would you add a facility to execute commands from within hoc, similar to the ! feature of other UNIX programs? □

Exercise 8-8. Revise the code in math.c to use a table instead of the set of essentially identical functions that we presented. □

Another digression on make

Since the program for hoc3 now lives on five files, not one, the makefile is more complicated:

---

† The yacc message "reduce/reduce conflict" indicates a serious problem, more often the symptom of an outright error in the grammar than an intentional ambiguity.

```
$ cat makefile
YFLAGS = -d                # force creation of y.tab.h
OBJS = hoc.o init.o math.o symbol.o      # abbreviation

hoc3:    $(OBJS)
         cc $(OBJS) -lm -o hoc3

hoc.o:   hoc.h

init.o symbol.o:        hoc.h y.tab.h

pr:
         @pr hoc.y hoc.h init.c math.c symbol.c makefile

clean:
         rm -f $(OBJS) y.tab.[ch]
$
```

The YFLAGS = -d line adds the option -d to the yacc command line generated by make; this tells yacc to produce the y.tab.h file of #define statements. The OBJS=... line defines a shorthand for a construct to be used several times subsequently. The syntax is not the same as for shell variables — the parentheses are mandatory. The flag -lm causes the math library to be searched for the mathematical functions.

hoc3 now depends on four .o files; some of the .o files depend on .h files. Given these dependencies, make can deduce what recompilation is needed after changes are made to any of the files involved. If you want to see what make will do without actually running the processes, try

```
$ make -n
```

On the other hand, if you want to force the file times into a consistent state, the -t ("touch") option will update them without doing any compilation steps.

Notice that we have added not only a set of dependencies for the source files but miscellaneous utility routines as well, all neatly encapsulated in one place. By default, make makes the first thing listed in the makefile, but if you name an item that labels a dependency rule, like symbol.o or pr, that will be made instead. An empty dependency is taken to mean that the item is never "up to date," so that action will always be done when requested. Thus

```
$ make pr | lpr
```

produces the listing you asked for on a line printer. (The leading @ in "@pr" suppresses the echo of the command being executed by make.) And

```
$ make clean
```

removes the yacc output files and the .o files.

This mechanism of empty dependencies in the makefile is often preferable to a shell file as a way to keep all the related computations in a single file. And make is not restricted to program development — it is valuable for packaging any set of operations that have time dependencies.

A *digression on* lex

The program lex creates lexical analyzers in a manner analogous to the way that yacc creates parsers: you write a specification of the lexical rules of your language, using regular expressions and fragments of C to be executed when a matching string is found. lex translates that into a recognizer. lex and yacc cooperate by the same mechanism as the lexical analyzers we have already written. We are not going into any great detail on lex here; the following discussion is mainly to interest you in learning more. See the reference manual for lex in Volume 2B of the *UNIX Programmer's Manual*.

First, here is the lex program, from the file lex.l; it replaces the function yylex that we have used so far.

```
$ cat lex.l
%{
#include "hoc.h"
#include "y.tab.h"
extern int lineno;
%}
%%
[ \t]    { ; }   /* skip blanks and tabs */
[0-9]+\.?|[0-9]*\.[0-9]+ {
          sscanf(yytext, "%lf", &yylval.val); return NUMBER; }
[a-zA-Z][a-zA-Z0-9]* {
          Symbol *s;
          if ((s=lookup(yytext)) == 0)
                  s = install(yytext, UNDEF, 0.0);
          yylval.sym = s;
          return s->type == UNDEF ? VAR : s->type; }
\n        { lineno++; return '\n'; }   /* everything else */
.         { return yytext[0]; }
$
```

Each "rule" is a regular expression like those in egrep or awk, except that lex recognizes C-style escapes like \t and \n. The action is enclosed in braces. The rules are attempted in order, and constructs like * and + match as long a string as possible. If the rule matches the next part of the input, the action is performed. The input string that matched is accessible in a lex string called yytext.

The makefile has to be changed to use lex:

```
$ cat makefile
YFLAGS = -d
OBJS = hoc.o lex.o init.o math.o symbol.o

hoc3:    $(OBJS)
         cc $(OBJS) -lm -ll -o hoc3

hoc.o:   hoc.h

lex.o init.o symbol.o:   hoc.h y.tab.h
...
$
```

Again, make knows how to get from a .1 file to the proper .o; all it needs from us is the dependency information. (We also have to add the lex library -11 to the list searched by cc since the lex-generated recognizer is not self-contained.) The output is spectacular and completely automatic:

```
$ make
yacc -d hoc.y

conflicts: 1 shift/reduce
cc  -c y.tab.c
rm y.tab.c
mv y.tab.o hoc.o
lex  lex.1
cc  -c lex.yy.c
rm lex.yy.c
mv lex.yy.o lex.o
cc  -c init.c
cc  -c math.c
cc  -c symbol.c
cc hoc.o lex.o init.o math.o symbol.o -lm -ll -o hoc3
$
```

If a single file is changed, the single command make is enough to make an up-to-date version:

```
$ touch lex.1              Change modified-time of lex.1
$ make
lex  lex.1
cc  -c lex.yy.c
rm lex.yy.c
mv lex.yy.o lex.o
cc hoc.o lex.o init.o math.o symbol.o -11 -lm -o hoc3
$
```

We debated for quite a while whether to treat lex as a digression, to be illustrated briefly and then dropped, or as the primary tool for lexical analysis once the language got complicated. There are arguments on both sides. The main problem with `lex` (aside from requiring that the user learn yet another language) is that it tends to be slow to run and to produce bigger and slower recognizers than the equivalent C versions. It is also somewhat harder to adapt its input mechanism if one is doing anything unusual, such as error recovery or even input from files. None of these issues is serious in the context of `hoc`. The main limitation is space: it takes more pages to describe the `lex` version, so (regretfully) we will revert to C for subsequent lexical analysis. It is a good exercise to do the `lex` versions, however.

Exercise 8-9. Compare the sizes of the two versions of `hoc3`. Hint: see `size(1)`. □

8.4 Stage 4: Compilation into a machine

We are heading towards `hoc5`, an interpreter for a language with control flow. `hoc4` is an intermediate step, providing the same functions as `hoc3`, but implemented within the interpreter framework of `hoc5`. We actually wrote `hoc4` this way, since it gives us two programs that should behave identically, which is valuable for debugging. As the input is parsed, `hoc4` generates code for a simple computer instead of immediately computing answers. Once the end of a statement is reached, the generated code is executed ("interpreted") to compute the desired result.

The simple computer is a *stack machine*: when an operand is encountered, it is pushed onto a stack (more precisely, code is generated to push it onto a stack); most operators operate on items on the top of the stack. For example, to handle the assignment

```
x = 2 * y
```

the following code is generated:

`constpush`	*Push a constant onto stack*
`2`	*... the constant 2*
`varpush`	*Push symbol table pointer onto stack*
`y`	*... for the variable y*
`eval`	*Evaluate: replace pointer by value*
`mul`	*Multiply top two items; product replaces them*
`varpush`	*Push symbol table pointer onto stack*
`x`	*... for the variable x*
`assign`	*Store value in variable, pop pointer*
`pop`	*Clear top value from stack*
`STOP`	*End of instruction sequence*

When this code is executed, the expression is evaluated and the result is stored in `x`, as indicated by the comments. The final `pop` clears the value off the stack because it is not needed any longer.

Stack machines usually result in simple interpreters, and ours is no exception — it's just an array containing operators and operands. The operators are the machine instructions; each is a function call with its arguments, if any, following the instruction. Other operands may already be on the stack, as they were in the example above.

The symbol table code for hoc4 is identical to that for hoc3; the initialization in init.c and the mathematical functions in math.c are the same as well. The grammar is the same as for hoc3, but the actions are quite different. Basically, each action generates machine instructions and any arguments that go with them. For example, three items are generated for a VAR in an expression: a varpush instruction, the symbol table pointer for the variable, and an eval instruction that will replace the symbol table pointer by its value when executed. The code for '*' is just mul, since the operands for that will already be on the stack.

```
$ cat hoc.y
%{
#include "hoc.h"
#define code2(c1,c2)    code(c1); code(c2)
#define code3(c1,c2,c3) code(c1); code(c2); code(c3)
%}
%union {
        Symbol  *sym;   /* symbol table pointer */
        Inst    *inst;  /* machine instruction */
}
%token  <sym>    NUMBER VAR BLTIN UNDEF
%right  '='
%left   '+' '-'
%left   '*' '/'
%left   UNARYMINUS
%right  '^'      /* exponentiation */
%%
list:      /* nothing */
        | list '\n'
        | list asgn '\n'  { code2(pop, STOP); return 1; }
        | list expr '\n'  { code2(print, STOP); return 1; }
        | list error '\n' { yyerrok; }
        ;
asgn:      VAR '=' expr  { code3(varpush,(Inst)$1,assign); }
        ;
```

```
expr:      NUMBER          { code2(constpush, (Inst)$1); }
        | VAR              { code3(varpush, (Inst)$1, eval); }
        | asgn
        | BLTIN '(' expr ')' { code2(bltin, (Inst)$1->u.ptr); }
        | '(' expr ')'
        | expr '+' expr { code(add); }
        | expr '-' expr { code(sub); }
        | expr '*' expr { code(mul); }
        | expr '/' expr { code(div); }
        | expr '^' expr { code(power); }
        | '-' expr  %prec UNARYMINUS  { code(negate); }
        ;
%%
        /* end of grammar */
...
```

Inst is the data type of a machine instruction (a pointer to a function returning an int), which we will return to shortly. Notice that the arguments to
code are function names, that is, pointers to functions, or other values that
are coerced to function pointers.

We have changed main somewhat. The parser now returns after each
statement or expression; the code that it generated is executed. yyparse
returns zero at end of file.

```
main(argc, argv)          /* hoc4 */
        char *argv[];
{
        int fpecatch();

        progname = argv[0];
        init();
        setjmp(begin);
        signal(SIGFPE, fpecatch);
        for (initcode(); yyparse(); initcode())
                execute(prog);
        return 0;
}
```

The lexical analyzer is only a little different. The main change is that
numbers have to be preserved, not used immediately. The easiest way to do
this is to install them in the symbol table along with the variables. Here is the
changed part of yylex:

```
yylex()          /* hoc4 */
...
         if (c == '.' || isdigit(c)) {    /* number */
                 double d;
                 ungetc(c, stdin);
                 scanf("%lf", &d);
                 yylval.sym = install("", NUMBER, d);
                 return NUMBER;
         }
...
```

Each element on the interpreter stack is either a floating point value or a pointer to a symbol table entry; the stack data type is a union of these. The machine itself is an array of pointers that point either to routines like mul that perform an operation, or to data in the symbol table. The header file hoc.h has to be augmented to include these data structures and function declarations for the interpreter, so they will be known where necessary throughout the program. (By the way, we chose to put all this information in one file instead of two. In a larger program, it might be better to divide the header information into several files so that each is included only where really needed.)

```
$ cat hoc.h
typedef struct Symbol {  /* symbol table entry */
         char     *name;
         short    type;    /* VAR, BLTIN, UNDEF */
         union {
                 double   val;              /* if VAR */
                 double   (*ptr)();         /* if BLTIN */
         } u;
         struct Symbol    *next;  /* to link to another */
} Symbol;
Symbol  *install(), *lookup();

typedef union Datum {    /* interpreter stack type */
         double   val;
         Symbol   *sym;
} Datum;
extern  Datum pop();

typedef int (*Inst)();   /* machine instruction */
#define STOP    (Inst) 0

extern  Inst prog[];
extern  eval(), add(), sub(), mul(), div(), negate(), power();
extern  assign(), bltin(), varpush(), constpush(), print();
$
```

The routines that execute the machine instructions and manipulate the stack are kept in a new file called code.c. Since it is about 150 lines long, we will show it in pieces.

```
$ cat code.c
#include "hoc.h"
#include "y.tab.h"

#define NSTACK   256
static   Datum    stack[NSTACK];   /* the stack */
static   Datum    *stackp;         /* next free spot on stack */

#define NPROG    2000
Inst    prog[NPROG];     /* the machine */
Inst    *progp;          /* next free spot for code generation */
Inst    *pc;             /* program counter during execution */

initcode()      /* initialize for code generation */
{
        stackp = stack;
        progp = prog;
}
...
```

The stack is manipulated by calls to push and pop:

```
push(d)            /* push d onto stack */
        Datum d;
{
        if (stackp >= &stack[NSTACK])
                execerror("stack overflow", (char *) 0);
        *stackp++ = d;
}

Datum pop()        /* pop and return top elem from stack */
{
        if (stackp <= stack)
                execerror("stack underflow", (char *) 0);
        return *--stackp;
}
```

The machine is generated during parsing by calls to the function code, which simply puts an instruction into the next free spot in the array prog. It returns the location of the instruction (which is not used in hoc4).

```
Inst *code(f)    /* install one instruction or operand */
       Inst f;
{
       Inst *oprogp = progp;
       if (progp >= &prog[NPROG])
               execerror("program too big", (char *) 0);
       *progp++ = f;
       return oprogp;
}
```

Execution of the machine is simple; in fact, it's rather neat how small the routine is that "runs" the machine once it's set up:

```
execute(p)       /* run the machine */
       Inst *p;
{
       for (pc = p; *pc != STOP; )
               (*(*pc++))();
}
```

Each cycle executes the function pointed to by the instruction pointed to by the program counter pc, and increments pc so it's ready for the next instruction. An instruction with opcode STOP terminates the loop. Some instructions, such as constpush and varpush, also increment pc to step over any arguments that follow the instruction.

```
constpush()      /* push constant onto stack */
{
       Datum d;
       d.val = ((Symbol *)*pc++)->u.val;
       push(d);
}

varpush()        /* push variable onto stack */
{
       Datum d;
       d.sym = (Symbol *)(*pc++);
       push(d);
}
```

The rest of the machine is easy. For instance, the arithmetic operations are all basically the same, and were created by editing a single prototype. Here is add:

```
add()              /* add top two elems on stack */
{
        Datum d1, d2;
        d2 = pop();
        d1 = pop();
        d1.val += d2.val;
        push(d1);
}
```

The remaining routines are equally simple.

```
eval()             /* evaluate variable on stack */
{
        Datum d;
        d = pop();
        if (d.sym->type == UNDEF)
                execerror("undefined variable", d.sym->name);
        d.val = d.sym->u.val;
        push(d);
}
assign()           /* assign top value to next value */
{
        Datum d1, d2;
        d1 = pop();
        d2 = pop();
        if (d1.sym->type != VAR && d1.sym->type != UNDEF)
                execerror("assignment to non-variable",
                          d1.sym->name);
        d1.sym->u.val = d2.val;
        d1.sym->type = VAR;
        push(d2);
}
print()            /* pop top value from stack, print it */
{
        Datum d;
        d = pop();
        printf("\t%.8g\n", d.val);
}
bltin()            /* evaluate built-in on top of stack */
{
        Datum d;
        d = pop();
        d.val = (*(double (*)())(*pc++))(d.val);
        push(d);
}
```

The hardest part is the cast in bltin, which says that *pc should be cast to "pointer to function returning a double," and that function executed with d.val as argument.

The diagnostics in eval and assign should never occur if everything is working properly; we left them in in case some program error causes the stack to be curdled. The overhead in time and space is small compared to the benefit of detecting the error if we make a careless change in the program. (We did, several times.)

C's ability to manipulate pointers to functions leads to compact and efficient code. An alternative, to make the operators constants and combine the semantic functions into a big `switch` statement in `execute`, is straightforward and is left as an exercise.

A *third digression on* make

As the source code for `hoc` grows, it becomes more and more valuable to keep track mechanically of what has changed and what depends on that. The beauty of `make` is that it automates jobs that we would otherwise do by hand (and get wrong sometimes) or by creating a specialized shell file.

We have made two improvements to the `makefile`. The first is based on the observation that although several files depend on the `yacc`-defined constants in `y.tab.h`, there's no need to recompile them unless the constants change — changes to the C code in `hoc.y` don't affect anything else. In the new `makefile` the `.o` files depend on a new file `x.tab.h` that is updated only when the *contents* of `y.tab.h` change. The second improvement is to make the rule for `pr` (printing the source files) depend on the source files, so that only changed files are printed.

The first of these changes is a great time-saver for larger programs when the grammar is static but the semantics are not (the usual situation). The second change is a great paper-saver.

Here is the new `makefile` for `hoc4`:

```
YFLAGS = -d
OBJS = hoc.o code.o init.o math.o symbol.o

hoc4:   $(OBJS)
        cc $(OBJS) -lm -o hoc4

hoc.o code.o init.o symbol.o:   hoc.h

code.o init.o symbol.o: x.tab.h

x.tab.h: y.tab.h
        -cmp -s x.tab.h y.tab.h || cp y.tab.h x.tab.h

pr:     hoc.y hoc.h code.c init.c math.c symbol.c
        @pr $?
        @touch pr

clean:
        rm -f $(OBJS) [xy].tab.[ch]
```

The '-' before cmp tells make to carry on even if the cmp fails; this permits the process to work even if x.tab.h doesn't exist. (The -s option causes cmp to produce no output but set the exit status.) The symbol $? expands into the list of items from the rule that are not up to date. Regrettably, make's notational conventions are at best loosely related to those of the shell.

To illustrate how these operate, suppose that everything is up to date. Then

```
$ touch hoc.y                               Change date of hoc.y
$ make
yacc -d hoc.y

conflicts: 1 shift/reduce
cc   -c y.tab.c
rm y.tab.c
mv y.tab.o hoc.o
cmp -s x.tab.h y.tab.h ¦¦ cp y.tab.h x.tab.h
cc hoc.o code.o init.o math.o symbol.o -lm -o hoc4
$ make -n pr                                Print changed files
pr hoc.y
touch pr
$
```

Notice that nothing was recompiled except hoc.y, because the y.tab.h file was the same as the previous one.

Exercise 8-10. Make the sizes of stack and prog dynamic, so that hoc4 never runs out of space if memory can be obtained by calling malloc. □

Exercise 8-11. Modify hoc4 to use a switch on the type of operation in execute instead of calling functions. How do the versions compare in lines of source code and execution speed? How are they likely to compare in ease of maintenance and growth? □

8.5 Stage 5: Control flow and relational operators

This version, hoc5, derives the benefit of the effort we put into making an interpreter. It provides if-else and while statements like those in C, statement grouping with { and }, and a print statement. A full set of relational operators is included (>, >=, etc.), as are the AND and OR operators && and ¦¦. (These last two do not guarantee the left-to-right evaluation that is such an asset in C; they evaluate both conditions even if it is not necessary.)

The grammar has been augmented with tokens, non-terminals, and productions for if, while, braces, and the relational operators. This makes it quite a bit longer, but (except possibly for the if and while) not much more complicated:

```
$ cat hoc.y
%{
#include "hoc.h"
#define code2(c1,c2)    code(c1); code(c2)
#define code3(c1,c2,c3) code(c1); code(c2); code(c3)
%}
%union {
        Symbol  *sym;   /* symbol table pointer */
        Inst    *inst;  /* machine instruction */
}
%token  <sym>   NUMBER PRINT VAR BLTIN UNDEF WHILE IF ELSE
%type   <inst>  stmt asgn expr stmtlist cond while if end
%right  '='
%left   OR
%left   AND
%left   GT GE LT LE EQ NE
%left   '+' '-'
%left   '*' '/'
%left   UNARYMINUS NOT
%right  '^'
%%
list:     /* nothing */
        | list '\n'
        | list asgn '\n'  { code2(pop, STOP); return 1; }
        | list stmt '\n'  { code(STOP); return 1; }
        | list expr '\n'  { code2(print, STOP); return 1; }
        | list error '\n' { yyerrok; }
        ;
asgn:     VAR '=' expr  { $$=$3; code3(varpush,(Inst)$1,assign); }
        ;
stmt:     expr           { code(pop); }
        | PRINT expr     { code(prexpr); $$ = $2; }
        | while cond stmt end {
                ($1)[1] = (Inst)$3;     /* body of loop */
                ($1)[2] = (Inst)$4; }   /* end, if cond fails */
        | if cond stmt end {    /* else-less if */
                ($1)[1] = (Inst)$3;     /* thenpart */
                ($1)[3] = (Inst)$4; }   /* end, if cond fails */
        | if cond stmt end ELSE stmt end {  /* if with else */
                ($1)[1] = (Inst)$3;     /* thenpart */
                ($1)[2] = (Inst)$6;     /* elsepart */
                ($1)[3] = (Inst)$7; }   /* end, if cond fails */
        | '{' stmtlist '}'      { $$ = $2; }
        ;
cond:     '(' expr ')'  { code(STOP); $$ = $2; }
        ;
while:    WHILE { $$ = code3(whilecode, STOP, STOP); }
        ;
```

```
if:        IF    { $$=code(ifcode); code3(STOP, STOP, STOP); }
           ;
end:       /* nothing */             { code(STOP); $$ = progp; }
           ;
stmtlist: /* nothing */              { $$ = progp; }
         | stmtlist '\n'
         | stmtlist stmt
           ;
expr:      NUMBER            { $$ = code2(constpush, (Inst)$1); }
         | VAR               { $$ = code3(varpush, (Inst)$1, eval); }
         | asgn
         | BLTIN '(' expr ')'
                   { $$ = $3; code2(bltin,(Inst)$1->u.ptr); }
         | '(' expr ')'   { $$ = $2; }
         | expr '+' expr { code(add); }
         | expr '-' expr { code(sub); }
         | expr '*' expr { code(mul); }
         | expr '/' expr { code(div); }
         | expr '^' expr { code (power); }
         | '-' expr  %prec UNARYMINUS  { $$ = $2; code(negate); }
         | expr GT expr  { code(gt); }
         | expr GE expr  { code(ge); }
         | expr LT expr  { code(lt); }
         | expr LE expr  { code(le); }
         | expr EQ expr  { code(eq); }
         | expr NE expr  { code(ne); }
         | expr AND expr { code(and); }
         | expr OR expr  { code(or); }
         | NOT expr      { $$ = $2; code(not); }
           ;
%%
```

The grammar has five shift/reduce conflicts, all like the one mentioned in hoc3.

Notice that STOP instructions are now generated in several places to terminate a sequence; as before, progp is the location of the next instruction that will be generated. When executed these STOP instructions will terminate the loop in execute. The production for end is in effect a subroutine, called from several places, that generates a STOP and returns the location of the instruction that follows it.

The code generated for while and if needs particular study. When the keyword while is encountered, the operation whilecode is generated, and its position in the machine is returned as the value of the production

```
        while:  WHILE
```

At the same time, however, the two following positions in the machine are also reserved, to be filled in later. The next code generated is the expression that makes up the condition part of the while. The value returned by cond is the beginning of the code for the condition. After the whole `while` statement has been recognized, the two extra positions reserved after the `whilecode` instruction are filled with the locations of the loop body and the statement that follows the loop. (Code for that statement will be generated next.)

```
| while cond stmt end {
        ($1)[1] = (Inst)$3;      /* body of loop */
        ($1)[2] = (Inst)$4; }    /* end, if cond fails */
```

`$1` is the location in the machine at which `whilecode` is stored; therefore, `($1)[1]` and `($1)[2]` are the next two positions.

A picture might make this clearer:

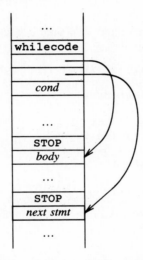

The situation for an `if` is similar, except that three spots are reserved, for the `then` and `else` parts and the statement that follows the `if`. We will return shortly to how this operates.

Lexical analysis is somewhat longer this time, mainly to pick up the additional operators:

```
yylex()              /* hoc5 */
...
        switch (c) {
        case '>':        return follow('=', GE, GT);
        case '<':        return follow('=', LE, LT);
        case '=':        return follow('=', EQ, '=');
        case '!':        return follow('=', NE, NOT);
        case '|':        return follow('|', OR, '|');
        case '&':        return follow('&', AND, '&');
        case '\n':       lineno++; return '\n';
        default:         return c;
        }
}
```

`follow` looks ahead one character, and puts it back on the input with `ungetc` if it was not what was expected.

```
follow(expect, ifyes, ifno)  /* look ahead for >=, etc. */
{
        int c = getchar();

        if (c == expect)
                return ifyes;
        ungetc(c, stdin);
        return ifno;
}
```

There are more function declarations in hoc.h — all of the relationals, for instance — but it's otherwise the same idea as in hoc4. Here are the last few lines:

```
$ cat hoc.h
...
typedef int (*Inst)();  /* machine instruction */
#define STOP     (Inst) 0

extern  Inst prog[], *progp, *code();
extern  eval(), add(), sub(), mul(), div(), negate(), power();
extern  assign(), bltin(), varpush(), constpush(), print();
extern  prexpr();
extern  gt(), lt(), eq(), ge(), le(), ne(), and(), or(), not();
extern  ifcode(), whilecode();
$
```

Most of code.c is the same too, although there are a lot of obvious new routines to handle the relational operators. The function le ("less than or equal to") is a typical example:

```
le()
{
        Datum d1, d2;
        d2 = pop();
        d1 = pop();
        d1.val = (double)(d1.val <= d2.val);
        push(d1);
}
```

The two routines that are not obvious are `whilecode` and `ifcode`. The critical point for understanding them is to realize that `execute` marches along a sequence of instructions until it finds a `STOP`, whereupon it returns. Code generation during parsing has carefully arranged that a `STOP` terminates each sequence of instructions that should be handled by a single call of `execute`. The body of a `while`, and the condition, `then` and `else` parts of an `if` are all handled by recursive calls to `execute` that return to the parent level when they have finished their task. The control of these recursive tasks is done by code in `whilecode` and `ifcode` that corresponds directly to `while` and `if` statements.

```
whilecode()
{
        Datum d;
        Inst *savepc = pc;        /* loop body */

        execute(savepc+2);        /* condition */
        d = pop();
        while (d.val) {
                execute(*((Inst **)(savepc)));  /* body */
                execute(savepc+2);
                d = pop();
        }
        pc = *((Inst **)(savepc+1));  /* next statement */
}
```

Recall from our discussion earlier that the `whilecode` operation is followed by a pointer to the body of the loop, a pointer to the next statement, and then the beginning of the condition part. When `whilecode` is called, `pc` has already been incremented, so it points to the loop body pointer. Thus `pc+1` points to the following statement, and `pc+2` points to the condition.

`ifcode` is very similar; in this case, upon entry `pc` points to the `then` part, `pc+1` to the `else`, `pc+2` to the next statement, and `pc+3` is the condition.

```
ifcode()
{
        Datum d;
        Inst *savepc = pc;        /* then part */

        execute(savepc+3);        /* condition */
        d = pop();
        if (d.val)
                execute(*((Inst **)(savepc)));
        else if (*((Inst **)(savepc+1)))  /* else part? */
                execute(*((Inst **)(savepc+1)));
        pc = *((Inst **)(savepc+2));      /* next stmt */
}
```

The initialization code in init.c is augmented a little as well, with a table of keywords that are stored in the symbol table along with everything else:

```
$ cat init.c
...
static struct {           /* Keywords */
        char    *name;
        int     kval;
} keywords[] = {
        "if",           IF,
        "else",         ELSE,
        "while",        WHILE,
        "print",        PRINT,
        0,              0,
};
...
```

We also need one more loop in init, to install keywords.

```
for (i = 0; keywords[i].name; i++)
        install(keywords[i].name, keywords[i].kval, 0.0);
```

No changes are needed in any of the symbol table management; code.c contains the routine prexpr, which is called when an statement of the form print *expr* is executed.

```
prexpr()          /* print numeric value */
{
        Datum d;
        d = pop();
        printf("%.8g\n", d.val);
}
```

This is not the print function that is called automatically to print the final result of an evaluation; that one pops the stack and adds a tab to the output.

hoc5 is by now quite a serviceable calculator, although for serious programming, more facilities are needed. The following exercises suggest some possibilities.

Exercise 8-12. Modify `hoc5` to print the machine it generates in a readable form for debugging. □

Exercise 8-13. Add the assignment operators of C, such as `+=`, `*=`, etc., and the increment and decrement operators `++` and `--`. Modify `&&` and `¦¦` so they guarantee left-to-right evaluation and early termination, as in C. □

Exercise 8-14. Add a `for` statement like that of C to `hoc5`. Add `break` and `continue`. □

Exercise 8-15. How would you modify the grammar or the lexical analyzer (or both) of `hoc5` to make it more forgiving about the placement of newlines? How would you add semicolon as a synonym for newline? How would you add a comment convention? What syntax would you use? □

Exercise 8-16. Add interrupt handling to `hoc5`, so that a runaway computation can be stopped without losing the state of variables already computed. □

Exercise 8-17. It is a nuisance to have to create a program in a file, run it, then edit the file to make a trivial change. How would you modify `hoc5` to provide an edit command that would cause you to be placed in an editor with a copy of your `hoc` program already read in? Hint: consider a `text` opcode. □

8.6 Stage 6: Functions and procedures; input/output

The final stage in the evolution of `hoc`, at least for this book, is a major increase in functionality: the addition of functions and procedures. We have also added the ability to print character strings as well as numbers, and to read values from the standard input. `hoc6` also accepts filename arguments, including the name "`-`" for the standard input. Together, these changes add 235 lines of code, bringing the total to about 810, but in effect convert `hoc` from a calculator into a programming language. We won't show every line here; Appendix 3 is a listing of the entire program so you can see how the pieces fit together.

In the grammar, function calls are expressions; procedure calls are statements. Both are explained in detail in Appendix 2, which also has some more examples. For instance, the definition and use of a procedure for printing all the Fibonacci numbers less than its argument looks like this:

```
$ cat fib
proc fib() {
        a = 0
        b = 1
        while (b < $1) {
                print b
                c = b
                b = a+b
                a = c
        }
        print "\n"
}
$ hoc6 fib -
fib(1000)
1 1 2 3 5 8 13 21 34 55 89 144 233 377 610 987
...
```

This also illustrates the use of files: the filename "-" is the standard input.
Here is a factorial function:

```
$ cat fac
func fac() {
        if ($1 <= 0) return 1 else return $1 * fac($1-1)
}
$ hoc6 fac -
fac(0)
        1
fac(7)
        5040
fac(10)
        3628800
...
```

Arguments are referenced within a function or procedure as $1, etc., as in the
shell, but it is legal to assign to them as well. Functions and procedures are
recursive, but only the arguments are local variables; all other variables are
global, that is, accessible throughout the program.

hoc distinguishes functions from procedures because doing so gives a level
of checking that is valuable in a stack implementation. It is too easy to forget
a return or add an extra expression and foul up the stack.

There are a fair number of changes to the grammar to convert hoc5 into
hoc6, but they are localized. New tokens and non-terminals are needed, and
the %union declaration has a new member to hold argument counts:

```
$ cat hoc.y
...
%union {
        Symbol  *sym;   /* symbol table pointer */
        Inst    *inst;  /* machine instruction */
        int     narg;   /* number of arguments */
}
%token  <sym>   NUMBER STRING PRINT VAR BLTIN UNDEF WHILE IF ELSE
%token  <sym>   FUNCTION PROCEDURE RETURN FUNC PROC READ
%token  <narg>  ARG
%type   <inst>  expr stmt asgn prlist stmtlist
%type   <inst>  cond while if begin end
%type   <sym>   procname
%type   <narg>  arglist
...
list:     /* nothing */
        | list '\n'
        | list defn '\n'
        | list asgn '\n'  { code2(pop, STOP); return 1; }
        | list stmt '\n'  { code(STOP); return 1; }
        | list expr '\n'  { code2(print, STOP); return 1; }
        | list error '\n' { yyerrok; }
        ;
asgn:     VAR '=' expr { code3(varpush,(Inst)$1,assign); $$=$3; }
        | ARG '=' expr
            { defnonly("$"); code2(argassign,(Inst)$1); $$=$3;}
        ;
stmt:     expr  { code(pop); }
        | RETURN { defnonly("return"); code(procret); }
        | RETURN expr
                { defnonly("return"); $$=$2; code(funcret); }
        | PROCEDURE begin '(' arglist ')'
                { $$ = $2; code3(call, (Inst)$1, (Inst)$4); }
        | PRINT prlist  { $$ = $2; }
...
expr:     NUMBER { $$ = code2(constpush, (Inst)$1); }
        | VAR    { $$ = code3(varpush, (Inst)$1, eval); }
        | ARG    { defnonly("$"); $$ = code2(arg, (Inst)$1); }
        | asgn
        | FUNCTION begin '(' arglist ')'
                { $$ = $2; code3(call,(Inst)$1,(Inst)$4); }
        | READ '(' VAR ')' { $$ = code2(varread, (Inst)$3); }
...
begin:    /* nothing */          { $$ = progp; }
        ;
```

```
prlist:    expr                      { code(prexpr); }
       ¦ STRING                      { $$ = code2(prstr, (Inst)$1); }
       ¦ prlist ',' expr            { code(prexpr); }
       ¦ prlist ',' STRING          { code2(prstr, (Inst)$3); }
       ;
defn:      FUNC procname { $2->type=FUNCTION; indef=1; }
            '(' ')' stmt { code(procret); define($2); indef=0; }
       ¦ PROC procname { $2->type=PROCEDURE; indef=1; }
            '(' ')' stmt { code(procret); define($2); indef=0; }
       ;
procname: VAR
       ¦ FUNCTION
       ¦ PROCEDURE
       ;
arglist:   /* nothing */            { $$ = 0; }
       ¦ expr                       { $$ = 1; }
       ¦ arglist ',' expr          { $$ = $1 + 1; }
       ;
%%
...
```

The productions for `arglist` count the arguments. At first sight it might
seem necessary to collect arguments in some way, but it's not, because each
`expr` in an argument list leaves its value on the stack exactly where it's
wanted. Knowing how many are on the stack is all that's needed.

The rules for `defn` introduce a new `yacc` feature, an embedded action. It
is possible to put an action in the middle of a rule so that it will be executed
during the recognition of the rule. We use that feature here to record the fact
that we are in a function or procedure definition. (The alternative is to create
a new symbol analogous to `begin`, to be recognized at the proper time.) The
function `defnonly` prints a warning message if a construct occurs outside of
the definition of a function or procedure when it shouldn't. There is often a
choice of whether to detect errors syntactically or semantically; we faced one
earlier in handling undefined variables. The `defnonly` function is a good
example of a place where the semantic check is easier than the syntactic one.

```
defnonly(s)      /* warn if illegal definition */
        char *s;
{
        if (!indef)
                execerror(s, "used outside definition");
}
```

The variable `indef` is declared in `hoc.y`, and set by the actions for `defn`.

The lexical analyzer is augmented by tests for arguments — a `$` followed by
a number — and for quoted strings. Backslash sequences like `\n` are interpreted in strings by a function `backslash`.

```
yylex()           /* hoc6 */
...
        if (c == '$') { /* argument? */
                int n = 0;
                while (isdigit(c=getc(fin)))
                        n = 10 * n + c - '0';
                ungetc(c, fin);
                if (n == 0)
                        execerror("strange $...", (char *)0);
                yylval.narg = n;
                return ARG;
        }
        if (c == '"') { /* quoted string */
                char sbuf[100], *p, *emalloc();
                for (p = sbuf; (c=getc(fin)) != '"'; p++) {
                        if (c == '\n' || c == EOF)
                                execerror("missing quote", "");
                        if (p >= sbuf + sizeof(sbuf) - 1) {
                                *p = '\0';
                                execerror("string too long", sbuf);
                        }
                        *p = backslash(c);
                }
                *p = 0;
                yylval.sym = (Symbol *)emalloc(strlen(sbuf)+1);
                strcpy(yylval.sym, sbuf);
                return STRING;
        }
...

backslash(c)      /* get next char with \'s interpreted */
        int c;
{
        char *index();  /* `strchr()' in some systems */
        static char transtab[] = "b\bf\fn\nr\rt\t";
        if (c != '\\')
                return c;
        c = getc(fin);
        if (islower(c) && index(transtab, c))
                return index(transtab, c)[1];
        return c;
}
```

A lexical analyzer is an example of a *finite state machine*, whether written in C
or with a program generator like lex. Our *ad hoc* C version has grown fairly
complicated; for anything beyond this, lex is probably better, both in size of
source code and ease of change.

  Most of the other changes are in code.c, with some additions of function
names to hoc.h. The machine is the same as before, except that it has been

augmented with a second stack to keep track of nested function and procedure calls. (A second stack is easier than piling more things into the existing one.) Here is the beginning of code.c:

```
$ cat code.c
#define NPROG    2000
Inst     prog[NPROG];      /* the machine */
Inst     *progp;           /* next free spot for code generation */
Inst     *pc;              /* program counter during execution */
Inst     *progbase = prog; /* start of current subprogram */
int      returning;        /* 1 if return stmt seen */

typedef struct Frame {  /* proc/func call stack frame */
        Symbol  *sp;       /* symbol table entry */
        Inst    *retpc;    /* where to resume after return */
        Datum   *argn;     /* n-th argument on stack */
        int     nargs;     /* number of arguments */
} Frame;
#define NFRAME   100
Frame    frame[NFRAME];
Frame    *fp;              /* frame pointer */

initcode() {
        progp = progbase;
        stackp = stack;
        fp = frame;
        returning = 0;
}
...
$
```

Since the symbol table now holds pointers to procedures and functions, and to strings for printing, an addition is made to the union type in hoc.h:

```
$ cat hoc.h
typedef struct Symbol { /* symbol table entry */
        char    *name;
        short   type;
        union {
                double  val;            /* VAR */
                double  (*ptr)();       /* BLTIN */
                int     (*defn)();      /* FUNCTION, PROCEDURE */
                char    *str;           /* STRING */
        } u;
        struct Symbol   *next;  /* to link to another */
} Symbol;
...
$
```

During compilation, a function is entered into the symbol table by define, which stores its origin in the table and updates the next free location after the generated code if the compilation is successful.

```
define(sp)          /* put func/proc in symbol table */
        Symbol *sp;
{
        sp->u.defn = (Inst)progbase;    /* start of code */
        progbase = progp;         /* next code starts here */
}
```

When a function or procedure is called during execution, any arguments have already been computed and pushed onto the stack (the first argument is the deepest). The opcode for `call` is followed by the symbol table pointer and the number of arguments. A `Frame` is stacked that contains all the interesting information about the routine — its entry in the symbol table, where to return after the call, where the arguments are on the expression stack, and the number of arguments that it was called with. The frame is created by `call`, which then executes the code of the routine.

```
call()              /* call a function */
{
        Symbol *sp = (Symbol *)pc[0]; /* symbol table entry */
                                      /* for function */
        if (fp++ >= &frame[NFRAME-1])
                execerror(sp->name, "call nested too deeply");
        fp->sp = sp;
        fp->nargs = (int)pc[1];
        fp->retpc = pc + 2;
        fp->argn = stackp - 1;   /* last argument */
        execute(sp->u.defn);
        returning = 0;
}
```

This structure is illustrated in Figure 8.2.

Eventually the called routine will return by executing either a `procret` or a `funcret`:

```
funcret()           /* return from a function */
{
        Datum d;
        if (fp->sp->type == PROCEDURE)
                execerror(fp->sp->name, "(proc) returns value");
        d = pop();       /* preserve function return value */
        ret();
        push(d);
}
```

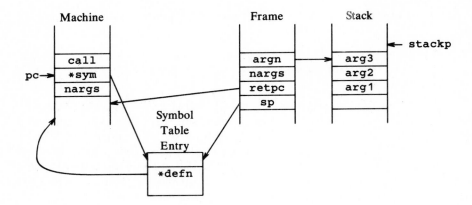

Figure 8.2: Data structures for procedure call

```
procret()           /* return from a procedure */
{
        if (fp->sp->type == FUNCTION)
                execerror(fp->sp->name,
                        "(func) returns no value");
        ret();
}
```

The function `ret` pops the arguments off the stack, restores the frame pointer `fp`, and sets the program counter.

```
ret()               /* common return from func or proc */
{
        int i;
        for (i = 0; i < fp->nargs; i++)
                pop();  /* pop arguments */
        pc = (Inst *)fp->retpc;
        --fp;
        returning = 1;
}
```

Several of the interpreter routines need minor fiddling to handle the situation when a `return` occurs in a nested statement. This is done inelegantly but adequately by a flag called `returning`, which is true when a `return` statement has been seen. `ifcode`, `whilecode` and `execute` terminate early if `returning` is set; `call` resets it to zero.

```
ifcode()
{
        Datum d;
        Inst *savepc = pc;        /* then part */

        execute(savepc+3);        /* condition */
        d = pop();
        if (d.val)
                execute(*((Inst **)(savepc)));
        else if (*((Inst **)(savepc+1))) /* else part? */
                execute(*((Inst **)(savepc+1)));
        if (!returning)
                pc = *((Inst **)(savepc+2)); /* next stmt */
}
whilecode()
{
        Datum d;
        Inst *savepc = pc;

        execute(savepc+2);        /* condition */
        d = pop();
        while (d.val) {
                execute(*((Inst **)(savepc)));  /* body */
                if (returning)
                        break;
                execute(savepc+2);        /* condition */
                d = pop();
        }
        if (!returning)
                pc = *((Inst **)(savepc+1)); /* next stmt */
}
execute(p)
        Inst *p;
{
        for (pc = p; *pc != STOP && !returning; )
                (*(*pc++))();
}
```

Arguments are fetched for use or assignment by getarg, which does the correct arithmetic on the stack:

```
double *getarg()          /* return pointer to argument */
{
        int nargs = (int) *pc++;
        if (nargs > fp->nargs)
            execerror(fp->sp->name, "not enough arguments");
        return &fp->argn[nargs - fp->nargs].val;
}
```

```
arg()    /* push argument onto stack */
{
        Datum d;
        d.val = *getarg();
        push(d);
}

argassign()      /* store top of stack in argument */
{
        Datum d;
        d = pop();
        push(d);              /* leave value on stack */
        *getarg() = d.val;
}
```

Printing of strings and numbers is done by prstr and prexpr.

```
prstr()              /* print string value */
{
        printf("%s", (char *) *pc++);
}

prexpr()             /* print numeric value */
{
        Datum d;
        d = pop();
        printf("%.8g ", d.val);
}
```

Variables are read by a function called varread. It returns 0 if end of file occurs; otherwise it returns 1 and sets the specified variable.

```
        varread()              /* read into variable */
        {
                Datum d;
                extern FILE *fin;
                Symbol *var = (Symbol *) *pc++;
         Again:
                switch (fscanf(fin, "%lf", &var->u.val)) {
                case EOF:
                        if (moreinput())
                                goto Again;
                        d.val = var->u.val = 0.0;
                        break;
                case 0:
                        execerror("non-number read into", var->name);
                        break;
                default:
                        d.val = 1.0;
                        break;
                }
                var->type = VAR;
                push(d);
        }
```

If end of file occurs on the current input file, `varread` calls `moreinput`,
which opens the next argument file if there is one. `moreinput` reveals more
about input processing than is appropriate here; full details are given in Appendix 3.

This brings us to the end of our development of hoc. For comparison purposes, here is the number of non-blank lines in each version:

hoc1	59	
hoc2	94	
hoc3	248	(lex version 229)
hoc4	396	
hoc5	574	
hoc6	809	

Of course the counts were computed by programs:

```
$ sed '/^$/d' `pick *.[chyl]` | wc -l
```

The language is by no means finished, at least in the sense that it's still easy to
think of useful extensions, but we will go no further here. The following exercises suggest some of the enhancements that are likely to be of value.

Exercise 8-18. Modify hoc6 to permit named formal parameters in subroutines as an
alternative to $1, etc. □

Exercise 8-19. As it stands, all variables are global except for parameters. Most of the
mechanism for adding local variables maintained on the stack is already present. One
approach is to have an `auto` declaration that makes space on the stack for variables

listed; variables not so named are assumed to be global. The symbol table will also have to be extended, so that a search is made first for locals, then for globals. How does this interact with named arguments? □

Exercise 8-20. How would you add arrays to hoc? How should they be passed to functions and procedures? How are they returned? □

Exercise 8-21. Generalize string handling, so that variables can hold strings instead of numbers. What operators are needed? The hard part of this is storage management: making sure that strings are stored in such a way that they are freed when they are not needed, so that storage does not leak away. As an interim step, add better facilities for output formatting, for example, access to some form of the C `printf` statement. □

8.7 Performance evaluation

We compared hoc to some of the other UNIX calculator programs, to get a rough idea of how well it works. The table below should be taken with a grain of salt, but it does indicate that our implementation is reasonable. All times are in seconds of user time on a PDP-11/70. There were two tasks. The first is computing Ackermann's function `ack(3,3)`. This is a good test of the function-call mechanism; it requires 2432 calls, some nested quite deeply.

```
func ack() {
        if ($1 == 0) return $2+1
        if ($2 == 0) return ack($1-1, 1)
        return ack($1-1, ack($1, $2-1))
}
ack(3,3)
```

The second test is computing the Fibonacci numbers with values less than 1000 a total of one hundred times; this involves mostly arithmetic with an occasional function call.

```
proc fib() {
        a = 0
        b = 1
        while (b < $1) {
                c = b
                b = a+b
                a = c
        }
}
i = 1
while (i < 100) {
        fib(1000)
        i = i + 1
}
```

The four languages were hoc, bc(1), bas (an ancient BASIC dialect that only runs on the PDP-11), and C (using `double`'s for all variables).

The numbers in Table 8.1 are the sum of the user and system CPU time as

Table 8.1: Seconds of user time (PDP-11/70)		
program	ack(3,3)	100×fib(1000)
hoc	5.5	5.0
bas	1.3	0.7
bc	39.7	14.9
c	<0.1	<0.1

measured by time. It is also possible to instrument a C program to determine how much of that time each function uses. The program must be recompiled with profiling turned on, by adding the option -p to each C compilation and load. If we modify the makefile to read

```
hoc6:    $(OBJS)
         cc $(CFLAGS) $(OBJS) -lm -o hoc6
```

so that the cc command uses the variable CFLAGS, and then say

```
$ make clean; make CFLAGS=-p
```

the resulting program will contain the profiling code. When the program runs, it will leave a file called mon.out of data that is interpreted by the program prof.

To illustrate these notions briefly, we made a test on hoc6 with the Fibonacci program above.

```
$ hoc6 <fibtest                          Run the test
$ prof hoc6 ¦ sed 15q                    Analyze
     name %time  cumsecs  #call  ms/call
     _pop  15.6     0.85  32182     0.03
    _push  14.3     1.63  32182     0.02
   mcount  11.3     2.25
      csv  10.1     2.80
     cret   8.8     3.28
  _assign   8.2     3.73   5050     0.09
    _eval   8.2     4.18   8218     0.05
 _execute   6.0     4.51   3567     0.09
 _varpush   5.9     4.83  13268     0.02
      _lt   2.7     4.98   1783     0.08
 _constpu   2.0     5.09    497     0.22
     _add   1.7     5.18   1683     0.05
  _getarg   1.5     5.26   1683     0.05
 _yyparse   0.6     5.30      3    11.11
$
```

The measurements obtained from profiling are just as subject to chance fluctuations as are those from time, so they should be treated as indicators, not absolute truth. The numbers here do suggest how to make hoc faster, however, *if it needs to be*. About one third of the run time is going into pushing and popping the stack. The overhead is larger if we include the times for the C subroutine linkage functions `csv` and `cret`. (`mcount` is a piece of the profiling code compiled in by `cc -p`.) Replacing the function calls by macros should make a noticeable difference.

To test this expectation, we modified `code.c`, replacing calls to `push` and `pop` with macros for stack manipulation:

```
#define push(d)  *stackp++ = (d)
#define popm()   *--stackp          /* function still needed */
```

(The function `pop` is still needed as an opcode in the machine, so we can't just replace all `pop`'s.) The new version runs about 35 percent faster; the times in Table 8.1 shrink from 5.5 to 3.7 seconds, and from 5.0 to 3.1.

Exercise 8-22. The `push` and `popm` macros do no error checking. Comment on the wisdom of this design. How can you combine the error-checking provided by the function versions with the speed of macros? □

8.8 A look back

There are some important lessons to learn from this chapter. First, the language development tools are a boon. They make it possible to concentrate on the interesting part of the job — language design — because it is so easy to experiment. The use of a grammar also provides an organizing structure for the implementation — routines are linked together by the grammar, and called at the right times as parsing proceeds.

A second, more philosophical point, is the value of thinking of the job at hand more as language development than as "writing a program." Organizing a program as a language processor encourages regularity of syntax (which is the user interface), and structures the implementation. It also helps to ensure that new features will mesh smoothly with existing ones. "Languages" are certainly not limited to conventional programming languages — examples from our own experience include `eqn` and `pic`, and `yacc`, `lex` and `make` themselves.

There are also some lessons about how tools are used. For instance, `make` is invaluable. It essentially eliminates the class of error that arises from forgetting to recompile some routine. It helps to ensure that no excess work is done. And it provides a convenient way to package a group of related and perhaps dependent operations in a single file.

Header files are a good way to manage data declarations that must be visible in more than one file. By centralizing the information, they eliminate errors caused by inconsistent versions, especially when coupled with `make`. It is also important to organize the data and the routines into files in such a way that they are not made visible when they don't have to be.

There are a couple of topics that, for lack of space, we did not stress. One is simply the degree to which we used all the *other* UNIX tools during

development of the hoc family. Each version of the program is in a separate
directory, with identical files linked together; ls and du are used repeatedly to
keep track of what is where. Many other questions are answered by programs.
For example, where is that variable declared? Use grep. What did we
change in this version? Use diff. How do we integrate the changes into that
version? Use idiff. How big is the file? Use wc. Time to make a backup
copy? Use cp. How can we back up only the files changed since the last
backup? Use make. This general style is absolutely typical of day-to-day program development on a UNIX system: a host of small tools, used separately or
combined as necessary, help to mechanize work that would otherwise have to
be done by hand.

History and bibliographic notes

yacc was developed by Steve Johnson. Technically, the class of languages
for which yacc can generate parsers is called LALR(1): left to right parsing,
looking ahead at most one token in the input. The notion of a separate
description to resolve precedence and ambiguity in the grammar is new with
yacc. See "Deterministic parsing of ambiguous grammars," by A. V. Aho, S.
C. Johnson, and J. D. Ullman, *CACM*, August, 1975. There are also some
innovative algorithms and data structures for creating and storing the parsing
tables.

A good description of the basic theory underlying yacc and other parser
generators may be found in *Principles of Compiler Design*, by A. V. Aho and
J. D. Ullman (Addison-Wesley, 1977). yacc itself is described in Volume 2B
of *The UNIX Programmer's Manual*. That section also presents a calculator comparable to hoc2; you might find it instructive to make the comparison.

lex was originally written by Mike Lesk. Again, the theory is described
by Aho and Ullman, and the lex language itself is documented in *The UNIX
Programmer's Manual*.

yacc, and to a lesser degree lex, have been used to implement many
language processors, including the portable C compiler, Pascal, FORTRAN 77,
Ratfor, awk, bc, eqn, and pic.

make was written by Stu Feldman. See "MAKE — a program for maintaining computer programs," *Software—Practice & Experience*, April, 1979.

Writing Efficient Programs by Jon Bentley (Prentice-Hall, 1982) describes
techniques for making programs faster. The emphasis is on first finding the
right algorithm, then refining the code if necessary.

CHAPTER 9: **DOCUMENT PREPARATION**

One of the first applications of the UNIX system was editing and formatting documents; indeed, Bell Labs management was persuaded to buy the first PDP-11 hardware by promises of a document preparation system, not an operating system. (Fortunately, they got more than they bargained for.)

The first formatting program was called `roff`. It was small, fast, and easy to work with, so long as one was producing simple documents on a line printer. The next formatter, `nroff`, by Joe Ossanna, was much more ambitious. Rather than trying to provide every style of document that users might ever want, Ossanna made `nroff` programmable, so that many formatting tasks were handled by programming in the `nroff` language.

When a small typesetter was acquired in 1973, `nroff` was extended to handle the multiple sizes and fonts and the richer character set that the typesetter provided. The new program was called `troff` (which by analogy to "en-roff" is pronounced "tee-roff.") `nroff` and `troff` are basically the same program, and accept the same input language; `nroff` ignores commands like size changes that it can't honor. We will talk mainly about `troff` but most of our comments apply to `nroff` as well, subject to the limitations of output devices.

The great strength of `troff` is the flexibility of the basic language and its programmability — it can be made to do almost any formatting task. But the flexibility comes at a high price — `troff` is often astonishingly hard to use. It is fair to say that almost all of the UNIX document preparation software is designed to cover up some part of naked `troff`.

One example is page layout — the general style of a document, what the titles, headings and paragraphs look like, where the page numbers appear, how big the pages are, and so on. These are not built in; they have to be programmed. Rather than forcing each user to specify all of these details in every document, however, a package of standard formatting commands is provided. A user of the package does not say "the next line is to be centered, in bigger letters, and in a bold font." Instead, the user says "the next line is a title," and the packaged definition of the style of a title is used. Users talk about the logical components of a document — titles, headings, paragraphs, footnotes, etc. — instead of sizes, fonts, and positions.

Unfortunately, what started out as a "standard" package of formatting commands is no longer standard: there are several packages in wide use, plus many local variants. We'll talk about two general-purpose packages here: ms, the original "standard," and mm, a newer version that is standard in System V. We'll also describe the man package for printing manual pages.

We will concentrate on ms because it is standard in the 7th Edition, it exemplifies all such packages, and it is powerful enough to do the job: we used it to typeset this book. But we did have to extend it a bit, for example, by adding a command to handle words in this font in the text.

This experience is typical — the macro packages are adequate for many formatting tasks, but it is sometimes necessary to revert to the underlying troff commands. We will describe only a small part of troff here.

Although troff provides the ability to control output format completely, it's far too hard to use for complicated material like mathematics, tables, and figures. Each of these areas is just as difficult as page layout. The solution to these problems takes a different form, however. Instead of packages of formatting commands, there are special-purpose languages for mathematics, tables and figures that make it easy to describe what is wanted. Each is handled by a separate program that translates its language into troff commands. The programs communicate through pipes.

These preprocessors are good examples of the UNIX approach at work — rather than making troff even bigger and more complicated than it is, separate programs cooperate with it. (Of course, the language development tools described in Chapter 8 have been used to help with the implementations.) We will describe two programs: tbl, which formats tables, and eqn, which formats mathematical expressions.

We will also try to give hints about document preparation and the supporting tools. Our examples throughout the chapter will be a document describing the hoc language of Chapter 8 and a hoc manual page. The document is printed as Appendix 2.

9.1 The ms macro package

The crucial notion in the macro packages is that a document is described in terms of its logical parts — title, section headings, paragraphs — not by details of spacing, fonts and sizes of letters. This saves you from some very hard work, and insulates your document from irrelevant details; in fact, by using a different set of macro definitions with the same logical names, you can make your document appear quite different. For example, a document might go through the stages of technical report, conference paper, journal article and book chapter with the same formatting commands, but formatted with four different macro packages.

Input to troff, whether or not a macro package is involved, is ordinary text interspersed with formatting commands. There are two kinds of

commands. The first consists of a period at the beginning of a line, followed
by one or two letters or digits, and perhaps by parameters, as illustrated here:

```
.PP
.ft  B
This is a little bold font paragraph.
```

`troff` built-in commands all have lower-case names, so by convention commands in macro packages are given upper-case names. In this example, `.PP` is
the `ms` command for a paragraph, and `.ft B` is a `troff` command that causes
a change to the **bold font**. (Fonts have upper case names; the fonts available
may be different on different typesetters.)

The second form of `troff` command is a sequence of characters that
begins with a backslash \, and may appear anywhere in the input; for example,
`\fB` also causes a switch to the bold font. This form of command is pure
`troff`; we'll come back to it shortly.

You can format with nothing more than a `.PP` command before each paragraph, and for most documents, you can get by with about a dozen different
`ms` commands. For example, Appendix 2, which describes `hoc`, has a title, the
authors' names, an abstract, automatically-numbered section headings, and
paragraphs. It uses only 14 distinct commands, several of which come in pairs.
The paper takes this general form in `ms`:

```
.TL
```
Title of document (one or more lines)
```
.AU
```
Author names, one per line
```
.AB
```
Abstract, terminated by `.AE`
```
.AE
.NH
```
Numbered heading (automatic numbering)
```
.PP
```
Paragraph ...
```
.PP
```
Another paragraph ...
```
.SH
```
Sub-heading (not numbered)
```
.PP
...
```

Formatting commands must occur at the beginning of a line. Input between
the commands is free form: the location of newlines in the input is unimpor-
tant, because `troff` moves words from line to line to make lines long enough
(a process called *filling*), and spreads extra space uniformly between words to
align the margins (*justification*). It's a good practice, however, to start each
sentence on a new line; it makes subsequent editing easier.

Here is the beginning of the actual `hoc` document:

```
.TL
Hoc - An Interactive Language For Floating Point Arithmetic
.AU
Brian Kernighan
Rob Pike
.AB
.I Hoc
is a simple programmable interpreter
for floating point expressions.
It has C-style control flow,
function definition and the usual
numerical built-in functions
such as cosine and logarithm.
.AE
.NH
Expressions
.PP
.I Hoc
is an expression language,
much like C:
although there are several control-flow statements,
most statements such as assignments
are expressions whose value is disregarded.
...
```

The `.I` command italicizes its argument, or switches to italic if no argument is given.

If you use a macro package, it's specified as an argument to `troff`:

```
$ troff -ms hoc.ms
```

The characters after the -m determine the macro package.† When formatted with ms, the hoc paper looks like this:

---

† The ms macros are in the file `/usr/lib/tmac/tmac.s`, and the man macros are in `/usr/lib/tmac/tmac.an`.

Hoc - An Interactive Language For Floating Point Arithmetic

Brian Kernighan
Rob Pike

ABSTRACT

Hoc is a simple programmable interpreter for floating point expressions. It has C-style control flow, function definition and the usual numerical built-in functions such as cosine and logarithm.

1. Expressions

Hoc is an expression language, much like C: although there are several control-flow statements, most statements such as assignments are expressions whose value is disregarded.

Displays

Although it is usually convenient that `troff` fills and justifies text, sometimes that isn't desirable — programs, for example, shouldn't have their margins adjusted. Such unformatted material is called display text. The `ms` commands `.DS` (display start) and `.DE` (display end) demarcate text to be printed as it appears, indented but without rearrangement. Here is the next portion of the `hoc` manual, which includes a short display:

```
.PP
.I Hoc
is an expression language,
much like C:
although there are several control-flow statements,
most statements such as assignments
are expressions whose value is disregarded.
For example, the assignment operator
= assigns the value of its right operand
to its left operand, and yields the value,
so multiple assignments work.
The expression grammar is:
```

```
.DS
.I
expr:                   number
         |              variable
         |              ( expr )
         |              expr binop expr
         |              unop expr
         |              function ( arguments )
.R
.DE
Numbers are floating point.
```

which prints as

Hoc is an expression language, much like C: although there are several control-flow statements, most statements such as assignments are expressions whose value is disregarded. For example, the assignment operator = assigns the value of its right operand to its left operand, and yields the value, so multiple assignments work. The expression grammar is:

> *expr:*   *number*
> | *variable*
> | *(expr)*
> | *expr binop expr*
> | *unop expr*
> | *function (arguments)*

Numbers are floating point.

Text inside a display is not normally filled or justified. Furthermore, if there is not enough room on the current page, the displayed material (and everything that follows it) is moved onto the next page. .DS permits several options, including L for left-justified, C, which centers each line individually, and B, which centers the entire display.

The items in the display above are separated by tabs. By default, troff tabs are set every half inch, not every eight spaces as is usual. Even if tab stops were every 8 spaces, though, characters are of varying widths, so tabs processed by troff wouldn't always appear as expected.

Font changes

The ms macros provide three commands to change the font. .R changes the font to roman, the usual font, .I changes to italic, *this font* and .B changes to boldface, **this font**. Unadorned, each command selects the font for the subsequent text:

```
This text is roman, but
.I
this text is italic,
.R
this is roman again, and
.B
this is boldface.
```

appears like this:

> This text is roman, but *this text is italic,* this is roman again, and **this is boldface.**

.I and .B take an optional argument, in which case the font change applies only to the argument. In troff, arguments containing blanks must be quoted, although the only quoting character is the double quote ".

```
This is roman, but
.I this
is italic, and
.B "these words"
are bold.
```

is printed as

> This is roman, but *this* is italic, and **these words** are bold.

Finally, a second argument to .I or .B is printed in roman, appended without spaces to the first argument. This feature is most commonly used to produce punctuation in the right font. Compare the last parenthesis of

```
(parenthetical
.I "italic words)"
```

which prints incorrectly as

> (parenthetical *italic words)*

with

```
(parenthetical
.I "italic words" )
```

which prints correctly as

> (parenthetical *italic words*)

Font distinctions are recognized by nroff, but the results aren't as pretty. Italic characters are underlined, and there are no bold characters, although some versions of nroff simulate bold by overstriking.

Miscellaneous commands

Footnotes are introduced with `.FS` and terminated with `.FE`. You are responsible for any identifying mark like an asterisk or a dagger.† This footnote was created with

```
identifying mark like an asterisk or a dagger.\(dg
.FS
\(dg Like this one.
.FE
This footnote was created with ...
```

Indented paragraphs, perhaps with a number or other mark in the margin, are created with the `.IP` command. To make this:

(1) First little paragraph.
(2) Second paragraph, which we make longer to show that it will be indented on the second line as well as the first.

requires the input

```
.IP (1)
First little paragraph.
.IP (2)
Second paragraph, ...
```

A `.PP` or `.LP` (left-justified paragraph) terminates an `.IP`. The `.IP` argument can be any string; use quotes to protect blanks if necessary. A second argument can be used to specify the amount of indent.

The command pair `.KS` and `.KE` causes text to be kept together; text enclosed between these commands will be forced onto a new page if it won't all fit on the current page. If `.KF` is used instead of `.KS`, the text will *float* past subsequent text to the top of the next page if necessary to keep it on one page. We used `.KF` for all the tables in this book.

You can change most of ms's default values by setting *number registers*, which are `troff` variables used by ms. Perhaps the most common are the registers that control the size of text and the spacing between lines. Normal text size (what you are reading now) is "10 point," where a point is about 1/72 of an inch, a unit inherited from the printing industry. Lines are normally printed at 12-point separation. To change these, for example to 9 and 11 (as in our displays), set the number registers `PS` and `VS` with

```
.nr PS 9
.nr VS 11
```

Other number registers include `LL` for line length, `PI` for paragraph indent, and `PD` for the separation between paragraphs. These take effect at the next `.PP` or `.LP`.

---

† Like this one.

	Table 9.1: Common ms Formatting Commands; see also ms(7)
.AB	start abstract; terminated by .AE
.AU	author's name follows on next line; multiple .AU's permitted
.B	begin bold text, or embolden argument if supplied
.DS *t*	start display (unfilled) text; terminated by .DE
	t = L (left-adjusted), C (centered), B (block-centered)
.EQ *s*	begin equation *s* (eqn input); terminated by .EN
.FS	start footnote; terminated by .FE
.I	begin italic text, or italicize argument if supplied
.IP *s*	indented paragraph, with *s* in margin
.KF	keep text together, float to next page if necessary; end with .KE
.KS	keep text together on page; end with .KE
.LP	new left-justified paragraph
.NH *n*	*n*-th level numbered heading; heading follows, up to .PP or .LP
.PP	new paragraph
.R	return to roman font
.SH	sub-heading; heading follows, up to .PP
.TL	title follows, up to next ms command
.TS	begin table (tbl input); terminated by .TE

The mm *macro package*

We won't go into any detail on the mm macro package here, since it is in spirit and often in detail very similar to ms. It provides more control of parameters than ms does, more capabilities (e.g., automatically numbered lists), and better error messages. Table 9.2 shows the mm commands equivalent to the ms commands in Table 9.1.

Exercise 9-1. Omitting a terminating command like .AE or .DE is usually a disaster. Write a program mscheck to detect errors in ms input (or your favorite package). Suggestion: awk. □

9.2 The troff level

In real life, one sometimes has to go beyond the facilities of ms, mm or other packages to get at some capability of bare troff. Doing so is like programming in assembly language, however, so it should be done cautiously and reluctantly.

Three situations arise: access to special characters, in-line size and font changes, and a few basic formatting functions.

Character names

Access to strange characters — Greek letters like π, graphics like ● and †, and a variety of lines and spaces — is easy, though not very systematic. Each

Table 9.2: Common mm Formatting Commands

.AS	start abstract; terminated by .AE
.AU	author's name follows as first argument
.B	begin bold text, or embolden argument if supplied
.DF	keep text together, float to next page if necessary; end at .DE
.DS	start display text; terminated by .DE
.EQ	begin equation (eqn input); terminated by .EN
.FS	start footnote; terminated by .FE
.I	begin italic text, or italicize argument if supplied
.H n "..."	n-th level numbered heading "..."
.HU "..."	unnumbered heading "..."
.P	paragraph. Use .nr Pt 1 once for indented paragraphs
.R	return to roman font
.TL	title follows, up to next mm command
.TS	begin table (tbl input); terminated by .TE

such character has a name that is either \c where c is a single character, or
\(cd where cd is a pair of characters.

troff prints an ASCII minus sign as a hyphen - rather than a minus −. A
true minus must be typed \- and a dash must be typed \(em, which stands for
"em dash," the character "—".

Table 9.3 lists some of the most common special characters; there are many
more in the troff manual (and the list may be different on your system).

There are times when troff must be told *not* to interpret a character,
especially a backslash or a leading period. The two most common "hands-off"
characters are \e and \&. The sequence \e is guaranteed to print as a
backslash, uninterpreted, and is used to get a backslash in the output. \&, on
the other hand, is nothing at all: it is a zero-width blank. Its main use is to
prevent troff from interpreting periods at the beginning of lines. We used
\e and \& a lot in this chapter. For example, the ms outline at the beginning
of this chapter was typed as

```
\&.TL
.I "Title of document"
\&.AU
.I "Author name"
\&.AB
\&...
...
```

Of course, the section above was typed as

Table 9.3:		Some `troff` special character sequences
-	-	hyphen
`\(hy`	-	hyphen, same as above
`\-`	−	minus sign in current font
`\(mi`	−	minus sign in the mathematics font
`\(em`	—	em dash
`\&`		nothing at all; protects leading period
`\blank`		unpaddable blank
`\¦`		unpaddable half blank
`\e`		literal escape character, usually `\`
`\(bu`		bullet ●
`\(dg`		dagger †
`\(*a`		α. `\(*b`=β, `\(*c`=ξ, `\(*p`=π, etc.
`\f`X		change to font X; X=P is previous
`\f(`XX		change to font XX
`\s`n		change to point size n; n=0 is previous
`\s`$\pm n$		relative point size change

```
\e&.TL
\&.I "Title of document"
\e&.AU
...
```

and you can imagine how that in turn was typed.

Another special character that turns up occasionally is the *unpaddable blank*, a `\` followed by a blank. Normally, `troff` will stretch an ordinary blank to align the margins, but an unpaddable blank is never adjusted: it is like any other character and has a fixed width. It can also be used to pass multiple words as a single argument:

```
.I Title\ of\ document
```

Font and size changes

Most font and format changes can be done with the beginning-of-line macros like `.I`, but sometimes changes must be made in-line. In particular, the newline character is a word separator, so if a font change must be made in the middle of the word, the macros are unusable. This subsection discusses how `troff` overcomes this problem — note that it is `troff` that provides the facility, not the ms macro package.

`troff` uses the backslash character to introduce in-line commands. The two most common commands are `\f` to change font and `\s` to change point size.

The font is specified with `\f` by a character immediately after the f:

```
a \fBfriv\fIolous\fR \fIvar\fBiety\fR of \fIfonts\fP
```

is output as

a **friv**_olous var_**iety** of _fonts_

The font change `\fP` reverts to the previous font — whatever the font was before the last switch. (There's only one previous font, not a stack.)

Some fonts have two-character names. These are specified by the format `\f(XX` where `XX` is the font name. For example, the font on our typesetter in which programs in this book are printed is called `CW` (Courier Constant Width), so `keyword` is written as

```
\f(CWkeyword\fP
```

It's clearly painful to have to type this, so one of our extensions to `ms` is a `.CW` macro so we don't have to type or read backslashes. We use it to typeset in-line words such as `troff`, like this:

```
The
.CW troff
formatter ...
```

Formatting decisions defined by macros are also easy to change later.

A size change is introduced by the sequence `\sn`, where n is one or two digits that specify the new size: `\s8` switches to 8 point type. More commonly, relative changes may be made by prefixing a plus or minus to the size. For example, words can be printed in SMALL CAPS by typing

```
\s-2SMALL CAPS\s0
```

`\s0` causes the size to revert to its previous value. It's the analog of `\fP`, but in the `troff` tradition, it isn't spelled `\sP`. Our extensions to `ms` include a macro `.UC` (upper case) for this job.

Basic `troff` commands

Realistically, even with a good macro package, you have to know a handful of `troff` commands for controlling spacing and filling, setting tab stops, and the like. The command `.br` causes a _break_, that is, the next input that follows the `.br` will appear on a new output line. This could be used, for example, to split a long title at the proper place:

```
.TL
Hoc - An Interactive Language
.br
For Floating Point Arithmetic
...
```

The command `.nf` turns off the normal filling of output lines; each line of input goes directly into one line of output. The command `.fi` turns filling back on. The command `.ce` centers the next line.

The command `.bp` begins a new page. The command `.sp` causes a single blank line to appear in the output. A `.sp` command can be followed by an argument to specify how many blank lines or how much space.

`.sp 3`	*Leave 3 blank lines*
`.sp .5`	*Leave blank half-line*
`.sp 1.5i`	*Leave 1.5 inches*
`.sp 3p`	*Leave 3 points*
`.sp 3.1c`	*Leave 3.1 centimeters*

Extra space at the bottom of a page is discarded, so a large `.sp` is equivalent to a `.bp`.

The `.ta` command sets tab stops (which are initialized to every half inch).

> `.ta` *n n n ...*

sets tab stops at the specified distances from the left margin; as with `.sp`, each number *n* is in inches if followed by 'i'. A tab stop suffixed with R will right-justify the text at the next tab stop; C causes a centered tab.

The command `.ps` *n* sets the point size to *n*; the command `.ft` *X* sets the font to *X*. The rules about incremental sizes and returning to the previous value are the same as for `\s` and `\f`.

Defining macros

Defining macros in full generality would take us much further into the intricacies of `troff` than is appropriate, but we can illustrate some of the basics. For example, here is the definition of `.CW`:

`.de CW`	*Start a definition*
`\&\f(CW\\$1\fP\\$2`	*Font change around first argument*
`..`	*End of definition*

`\$n` produces the value of the *n*-th argument when the macro is invoked; it is empty if no *n*-th argument was provided. The double `\` delays evaluation of `\$n` during macro definition. The `\&` prevents the argument from being interpreted as a `troff` command, in case it begins with a period, as in

> `.CW .sp`

9.3 The `tbl` and `eqn` preprocessors

`troff` is a big and complicated program, both inside and out, so modifying it to take on a new task is not something to be undertaken lightly. Accordingly the development of programs for typesetting mathematics and tables took a different approach — the design of separate languages implemented by separate programs `eqn` and `tbl` that act as "preprocessors" for `troff`. In effect, `troff` is an assembly language for a typesetting machine, and `eqn` and `tbl` compile into it.

eqn came first. It was the first use of yacc for a non-programming
language.† tbl came next, in the same spirit as eqn, though with an unrelated
syntax. tbl doesn't use yacc, since its grammar is simple enough that it's not
worthwhile.

The UNIX pipe facility strongly suggests the division into separate programs.
Besides factoring the job into pieces (which was necessary anyway — troff
by itself was already nearly as large as a program could be on a PDP-11), pipes
also reduce the communication between the pieces and between the programmers involved. This latter point is significant — one doesn't need access to
source code to make a preprocessor. Furthermore, with pipes there are no
giant intermediate files to worry about, unless the components are intentionally
run separately for debugging.

There are problems when separate programs communicate by pipes. Speed
suffers somewhat, since there is a lot of input and output: both eqn and tbl
typically cause an eight-to-one expansion from input to output. More important, information flows only one direction. There is no way, for example, that
eqn can determine the current point size, which leads to some awkwardness in
the language. Finally, error reporting is hard; it is sometimes difficult to relate
a diagnostic from troff back to the eqn or tbl problem that caused it.

Nevertheless, the benefits of separation far outweigh the drawbacks, so
several other preprocessors have been written, based on the same model.

Tables

Let us begin a brief discussion of tbl, since the first thing we want to show
is a table of operators from the hoc document. tbl reads its input files or the
standard input and converts text between the commands .TS (table start) and
.TE (table end) into the troff commands to print the table, aligning columns
and taking care of all the typographical details. The .TS and .TE lines are
also copied through, so a macro package can provide suitable definitions for
them, for example to keep the table on one page and set off from surrounding
text.

Although you will need to look at the tbl manual to produce complicated
tables, one example is enough to show most of the common features. Here is
one from the hoc document:

† It is improbable that eqn would exist if yacc had not been available at the right time.

```
.TS
center, box;
c s
lfCW 1.
\fBTable 1:\fP  Operators, in decreasing order of precedence
.sp .5
^            exponentiation (\s-1FORTRAN\s0 **), right associative
! \-         (unary) logical and arithmetic negation
* /          multiplication, division
+ \-         addition, subtraction
> >=         relational operators: greater, greater or equal,
< <=            less, less or equal,
\&== !=      equal, not equal (all same precedence)
&&           logical AND (both operands always evaluated)
¦ ¦          logical OR (both operands always evaluated)
\&=          assignment, right associative
.TE
```

which produces the following table:

Table 1: Operators, in decreasing order of precedence	
^	exponentiation (FORTRAN **), right associative
! —	(unary) logical and arithmetic negation
* /	multiplication, division
+ —	addition, subtraction
> >=	relational operators: greater, greater or equal,
< <=	less, less or equal,
== !=	equal, not equal (all same precedence)
&&	logical AND (both operands always evaluated)
¦ ¦	logical OR (both operands always evaluated)
=	assignment, right associative

The words before the semicolon (`center, box`) describe global properties of the table: center it horizontally on the page and draw a box around it. Other possibilities include `doublebox`, `allbox` (each item in a box), and `expand` (expand table to page width).

The next lines, up to the period, describe the format of various sections of the table, which in this case are the title line and the body of the table. The first specification is for the first line of the table, the second specification applies to the second line, and the last applies to all remaining lines. In Table 1, there are only two specification lines, so the second specification applies to every table line after the first. The format characters are c for items centered in the column, r and 1 for right or left justification, and n for numeric alignment on the decimal point. s specifies a "spanned" column; in our case 'c s' means center the title over the entire table by spanning the second column as well as the first. A font can be defined for a column; the `tbl` specification `lfCW` prints a left-justified column in the `CW` font.

The text of the table follows the formatting information. Tab characters separate columns, and some `troff` commands such as `.sp` are understood inside tables. (Note a couple of appearances of `\&`: unprotected leading – and = signs in columns tell `tbl` to draw lines across the table at that point.)

`tbl` produces a wider variety of tables than this simple example would suggest: it will fill text in boxes, vertically justify column headings, and so on. The easiest way to use it for complicated tables is to look for a similar example in the manual in Volume 2A of the UNIX *Programmer's Manual* and adapt the commands.

Mathematical expressions

The second `troff` preprocessor is `eqn`, which converts a language describing mathematical expressions into the `troff` commands to print them. It automatically handles font and size changes, and also provides names for standard mathematical characters. `eqn` input usually appears between `.EQ` and `.EN` lines, analogous to `tbl`'s `.TS` and `.TE`. For example,

```
.EQ
x sub i
.EN
```

produces x_i. If the `ms` macro package is used, the equation is printed as a "display," and an optional argument to `.EQ` specifies an equation number. For example, the Cauchy integral formula

$$f(\zeta) \ = \ \frac{1}{2\pi i} \int_C \frac{f(z)}{z-\zeta} dz \tag{9.1}$$

is written as

```
.EQ (9.1)
f( zeta ) ~=~ 1 over {2 pi i} int from C
     f(z) over {z - zeta} dz
.EN
```

The `eqn` language is based on the way that mathematics is spoken aloud. One difference between spoken mathematics and `eqn` input is that braces { } are the parentheses of `eqn` — they override the default precedence rules of the language — but ordinary parentheses have no special significance. Blanks, however, *are* significant. Note that the first `zeta` is surrounded by blanks in the example above: keywords such as `zeta` and `over` are only recognized when surrounded by blanks or braces, neither of which appear in the output. To force blank space into the output, use a tilde character ~, as in `~=~`. To get braces, use `"{"` and `"}"`.

There are several classes of `eqn` keywords. Greek letters are spelled out, in lower or upper case, as in `lambda` and `LAMBDA` (λ and Λ). Other mathematical characters have names, such as sum, int, infinity, grad: $\sum$, $\int$, ∞, ∇. There are positional operators such as sub, sup, from, to, and over:

$$\sum_{i=0}^{\infty} x_i^2 \rightarrow \frac{1}{2\pi}$$

is

```
sum from i=0 to infinity x sub i sup 2 ~->~ 1 over {2 pi}
```

There are operators like sqrt and expandable parentheses, braces, etc. eqn will also create columns and matrices of objects. There are also commands to control sizes, fonts and positions when the defaults are not correct.

It is common to place small mathematical expressions such as $\log_{10}(x)$ in the body of the text, rather than in displays. The eqn keyword delim speci- fies a pair of characters to bracket in-line expressions. The characters used as left and right delimiters are usually the same; often a dollar sign $ is used. But since hoc uses $ for arguments, we use @ in our examples. % is also a suitable delimiter, but avoid the others: so many characters have special pro- perties in the various programs that you can get spectacularly anomalous behavior. (We certainly did as we wrote this chapter.)

So, after saying

```
.EQ
delim @@
.EN
```

in-line expressions such as $\sum_{i=0}^{\infty} x_i$ can be printed:

```
in-line expressions
such as @sum from i=0 to infinity x sub i@ can be printed:
```

In-line expressions are used for mathematics within a table, as this example from the hoc document shows:

```
.TS
center, box;
c s s
lfCW n l.
\fBTable 3:\fP   Built-in Constants
.sp .5
DEG      57.29577951308232087680   @180/ pi@, degrees per radian
E         2.71828182845904523536   @e@, base of natural logarithms
GAMMA     0.57721566490153286060   @gamma@, Euler-Mascheroni constant
PHI       1.61803398874989484820   @( sqrt 5 +1)/2@, the golden ratio
PI        3.14159265358979323846   @pi@, circular transcendental number
.TE
```

This table also shows how tbl lines up the decimal points in numeric (n) columns. The output appears below.

Table 3: Built-in Constants		
DEG	57.29577951308232087680	$180/\pi$, degrees per radian
E	2.71828182845904523536	e, base of natural logarithms
GAMMA	0.57721566490153286060	γ, Euler-Mascheroni constant
PHI	1.61803398874989484820	$(\sqrt{5}+1)/2$, the golden ratio
PI	3.14159265358979323846	π, circular transcendental number

Finally, since eqn italicizes any string of letters that it doesn't recognize, it is a common idiom to italicize ordinary words using eqn. @Word@, for example, prints as *Word*. But beware: eqn recognizes some common words (such as from and to) and treats them specially, and it discards blanks, so this trick has to be used carefully.

Getting output

Once you have your document ready, you have to line up all the preprocessors and troff to get output. The order of commands is tbl, then eqn, then troff. If you are just using troff, type

```
$ troff -ms filenames          (Or -mm)
```

Otherwise, you must specify the argument filenames to the first command in the pipeline and let the others read their standard input, as in

```
$ eqn filenames | troff -ms
```

or

```
$ tbl filenames | eqn | troff -ms
```

It's a nuisance keeping track of which of the preprocessors are really needed to print any particular document. We found it useful to write a program called doctype that deduces the proper sequence of commands:

```
$ doctype ch9.*
cat ch9.1 ch9.2 ch9.3 ch9.4 | pic | tbl | eqn | troff -ms
$ doctype hoc.ms
cat hoc.ms | tbl | eqn | troff -ms
$
```

doctype is implemented with tools discussed at length in Chapter 4; in particular, an awk program looks for the command sequences used by the preprocessors and prints the command line to invoke those needed to format the document. It also looks for the .PP (paragraph) command used by the ms package of formatting requests.

```
$ cat doctype
# doctype:  synthesize proper command line for troff
echo -n "cat $* ¦ "
egrep -h '^\.(EQ¦TS¦\[¦PS¦IS¦PP)' $* ¦
sort -u ¦
awk '
/^\.PP/ { ms++ }
/^\.EQ/ { eqn++ }
/^\.TS/ { tbl++ }
/^\.PS/ { pic++ }
/^\.IS/ { ideal++ }
/^\.\[/ { refer++ }
END {
        if (refer > 0) printf "refer ¦ "
        if (pic > 0)   printf "pic ¦ "
        if (ideal > 0) printf "ideal ¦ "
        if (tbl > 0)   printf "tbl ¦ "
        if (eqn > 0)   printf "eqn ¦ "
        printf "troff "
        if (ms > 0) printf "-ms"
        printf "\n"
} '
$
```

(The −h option to `egrep` causes it to suppress the filename headers on each line; unfortunately this option is not in all versions of the system.) The input is scanned, collecting information about what kinds of components are used. After all the input has been examined, it's processed in the right order to print the output. The details are specific to formatting `troff` documents with the standard preprocessors, but the idea is general: let the machine take care of the details.

`doctype` is an example, like `bundle`, of a program that creates a program. As it is written, however, it requires the user to retype the line to the shell; one of the exercises is to fix that.

When it comes to running the actual `troff` command, you should bear in mind that the behavior of `troff` is system-dependent: at some installations it drives the typesetter directly, while on other systems it produces information on its standard output that must be sent to the typesetter by a separate program.

By the way, the first version of this program didn't use `egrep` or `sort`; `awk` itself scanned all the input. It turned out to be too slow for large documents, so we added `egrep` to do a fast search, and then `sort` −u to toss out duplicates. For typical documents, the overhead of creating two extra processes to winnow the data is less than that of running `awk` on a lot of input. To illustrate, here is a comparison between `doctype` and a version that just runs `awk`, applied to the contents of this chapter (about 52000 characters):

```
$ time awk '... doctype without egrep ...' ch9.*
cat ch9.1 ch9.2 ch9.3 ch9.4 | pic | tbl | eqn | troff -ms

real      31.0
user       8.9
sys        2.8
$ time doctype ch9.*
cat ch9.1 ch9.2 ch9.3 ch9.4 | pic | tbl | eqn | troff -ms

real       7.0
user       1.0
sys        2.3
$
```

The comparison is evidently in favor of the version using three processes. (This was done on a machine with only one user; the ratio of real times would favor the `egrep` version even more on a heavily loaded system.) Notice that we did get a simple working version first, before we started to optimize.

Exercise 9-2. How did we format this chapter? □

Exercise 9-3. If your `eqn` delimiter is a dollar sign, how do you get a dollar sign in the output? Hint: investigate quotes and the pre-defined words of `eqn`. □

Exercise 9-4. Why doesn't

```
$ `doctype filenames`
```

work? Modify `doctype` to run the resulting command, instead of printing it. □

Exercise 9-5. Is the overhead of the extra `cat` in `doctype` important? Rewrite `doctype` to avoid the extra process. Which version is simpler? □

Exercise 9-6. Is it better to use `doctype` or to write a shell file containing the commands to format a specific document? □

Exercise 9-7. Experiment with various combinations of `grep`, `egrep`, `fgrep`, `sed`, `awk` and `sort` to create the fastest possible version of `doctype`. □

9.4 The manual page

The main documentation for a command is usually the manual page — a one-page description in the *UNIX Programmer's Manual*. (See Figure 9.2.) The manual page is stored in a standard directory, usually `/usr/man`, in a sub-directory numbered according to the section of the manual. Our `hoc` manual page, for example, because it describes a user command, is kept in `/usr/man/man1/hoc.1`.

Manual pages are printed with the man(1) command, a shell file that runs `nroff -man`, so `man hoc` prints the `hoc` manual. If the same name appears in more than one section, as does `man` itself (Section 1 describes the command, while Section 7 describes the macros), the section can be specified to `man`:

```
$ man 7 man
```

prints only the description of the macros. The default action is to print all
pages with the specified name, using `nroff`, but `man -t` generates typeset
pages using `troff`.

The author of a manual page creates a file in the proper subdirectory of
`/usr/man`. The man command calls `nroff` or `troff` with a macro package
to print the page, as we can see by searching the man command for formatter
invocations. Our result would be

```
$ grep roff `which man`
        nroff $opt -man $all ;;
        neqn $all | nroff $opt -man ;;
        troff $opt -man $all ;;
        troff -t $opt -man $all | tc ;;
        eqn $all | troff $opt -man ;;
        eqn $all | troff -t $opt -man | tc ;;
$
```

The variety is to deal with options: `nroff` *vs*. `troff`, whether or not to run
`eqn`, etc. The manual macros, invoked by `troff -man`, define `troff` commands that format in the style of the manual. They are basically the same as
the `ms` macros, but there are differences, particularly in setting up the title and
in the font change commands. The macros are documented — briefly — in
man(7), but the basics are easy to remember. The layout of a manual page is:

```
.TH COMMAND section-number
.SH NAME
command \- brief description of function
.SH SYNOPSIS
.B command
options
.SH DESCRIPTION
Detailed explanation of programs and options.
Paragraphs are introduced by .PP.
.PP
This is a new paragraph.
.SH FILES
Files used by the command, e.g., passwd(1) mentions /etc/passwd
.SH "SEE ALSO"
References to related documents, including other manual pages
.SH DIAGNOSTICS
Description of any unusual output (e.g., see cmp(1))
.SH BUGS
Surprising features (not always bugs; see below)
```

If any section is empty, its header is omitted. The `.TH` line and the NAME,
SYNOPSIS and DESCRIPTION sections are mandatory.

The line

```
.TH COMMAND section-number
```

names the command and specifies the section number. The various .SH lines
identify sections of the manual page. The NAME and SYNOPSIS sections are
special; the others contain ordinary prose. The NAME section names the *command* (this time in lower case) and provides a one-line description of it. The
SYNOPSIS section names the options, but doesn't describe them. As in any section, the input is free form, so font changes can be specified with the .B, .I
and .R macros. In the SYNOPSIS section, the name and options are bold, and
the rest of the information is roman. The ed(1) NAME and SYNOPSIS sections, for example, are:

```
.SH NAME
ed \- text editor
.SH SYNOPSIS
.B ed
[
.B \-
] [
.B \-x
] [ name ]
```

These come out as:

NAME

ed − text editor

SYNOPSIS

ed [−] [−x] [name]

Note the use of \- rather than a plain -.

The DESCRIPTION section describes the command and its options. In most
cases, it is a description of the command, not the language the command
defines. The cc(1) manual page doesn't define the C language; it says how to
run the cc command to compile C programs, how to invoke the optimizer,
where the output is left, and so on. The language is specified in the C reference manual, cited in the SEE ALSO section of cc(1). On the other hand, the
categories are not absolute: man(7) is a description of the language of manual
macros.

By convention, in the DESCRIPTION section, command names and the tags
for options (such as "name" in the ed page) are printed in italics. The macros
.I (print first argument in italics) and .IR (print first argument in italic,
second in roman) make this easy. The .IR macro is there because the .I
macro in the man package doesn't share with that in ms the undocumented but
convenient treatment of the second argument.

The FILES section mentions any files implicitly used by the command.
DIAGNOSTICS need only be included if there is unusual output produced by
the command. This may be diagnostic messages, exit statuses or surprising

```
.TH HOC 1
.SH NAME
hoc \- interactive floating point language
.SH SYNOPSIS
.B hoc
[ file ... ]
.SH DESCRIPTION
.I Hoc
interprets a simple language for floating point arithmetic,
at about the level of BASIC, with C-like syntax and
functions and procedures with arguments and recursion.
.PP
The named
.IR file s
are read and interpreted in order.
If no
.I file
is given or if
.I file
is '\-'
.I hoc
interprets the standard input.
.PP
.I Hoc
input consists of
.I expressions
and
.IR statements .
Expressions are evaluated and their results printed.
Statements, typically assignments and function or procedure
definitions, produce no output unless they explicitly call
.IR print .
.SH "SEE ALSO"
.I
Hoc \- An Interactive Language for Floating Point Arithmetic
by Brian Kernighan and Rob Pike.
.br
.IR bas (1),
.IR bc (1)
and
.IR dc (1).
.SH BUGS
Error recovery is imperfect within function and procedure definitions.
.br
The treatment of newlines is not exactly user-friendly.
```

Figure 9.1: /usr/man/man1/hoc.1

variations of the command's normal behavior. The BUGS section is also somewhat misnamed. Defects reported here aren't so much bugs as shortcomings — simple bugs should be fixed before the command is installed. To get a feeling for what goes in the DIAGNOSTICS and BUGS sections, you might browse through the standard manual.

An example should clarify how to write the manual page. The source for hoc(1), `/usr/man/man1/hoc.1`, is shown in Figure 9.1, and Figure 9.2 is the output of

```
$ man -t hoc
```

Exercise 9-8. Write a manual page for doctype. Write a version of the man command that looks in your own man directory for documentation on your personal programs. □

HOC(1)   HOC(1)

NAME
    hoc – interactive floating point language
SYNOPSIS
    hoc [file ...]
DESCRIPTION
    Hoc interprets a simple language for floating point arithmetic, at about the level of BASIC, with C-like syntax and functions and procedures with arguments and recursion.

    The named *file*s are read and interpreted in order. If no *file* is given or if *file* is '−' *hoc* interprets the standard input.

    Hoc input consists of *expressions* and *statements*. Expressions are evaluated and their results printed. Statements, typically assignments and function or procedure definitions, produce no output unless they explicitly call *print*.

SEE ALSO
    Hoc – An Interactive Language for Floating Point Arithmetic by Brian Kernighan and Rob Pike.
    bas(1), *bc*(1) and *dc*(1).

BUGS
    Error recovery is imperfect within function and procedure definitions.
    The treatment of newlines is not exactly user-friendly.

8th Edition   1

Figure 9.2: hoc(1)

9.5 Other document preparation tools

There are several other programs to help with document preparation. The `refer`(1) command looks up references by keywords and installs in your document the in-line citations and a reference section at the end. By defining suitable macros, you can arrange that `refer` print references in the particular style you want. There are existing definitions for a variety of computer science journals. `refer` is part of the 7th Edition, but has not been picked up in some other versions.

`pic`(1) and `ideal`(1) do for pictures what `eqn` does for equations. Pictures are significantly more intricate than equations (at least to typeset), and there is no oral tradition of how to talk about pictures, so both languages take some work to learn and to use. To give the flavor of `pic`, here is a simple picture and its expression in `pic`.

```
.PS
.ps -1
box invis "document"; arrow
box dashed "pic"; arrow
box dashed "tbl"; arrow
box dashed "eqn"; arrow
box "troff"; arrow
box invis "typesetter"
[ box invis "macro" "package"
  spline right then up -> ] with .ne at 2nd last box.s
.ps +1
.PE
```

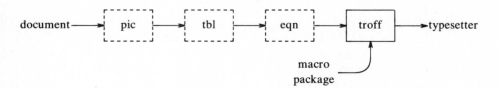

The pictures in this book were all done with `pic`. `pic` and `ideal` are not part of the 7th Edition but are now available.

`refer`, `pic` and `ideal` are all `troff` preprocessors. There are also programs to examine and comment on the prose in your documents. The best known of these is `spell`(1), which reports on possible spelling errors in files; we used it extensively. `style`(1) and `diction`(1) analyze punctuation, grammar and language usage. These in turn developed into the Writer's Workbench, a set of programs to help improve writing style. The Writer's Workbench programs are good at identifying cliches, unnecessary words and sexist phrases.

`spell` is standard. The others may be on your system; you can easily find out by using `man`:

```
$ man style diction wwb
```

or by listing /bin and /usr/bin.

History and bibliographic notes

troff, written by the late Joe Ossanna for the Graphics Systems CAT-4 typesetter, has a long lineage, going back to RUNOFF, which was written by J. E. Saltzer for CTSS at MIT in the early 1960's. These programs share the basic command syntax and ideas, although troff is certainly the most complicated and powerful, and the presence of eqn and the other preprocessors adds significantly to its utility. There are several newer typesetting programs with more civilized input format; TEX, by Don Knuth (*TEX and Metafont: New Directions in Typesetting*, Digital Press, 1979), and Scribe, by Brian Reid ("Scribe: a high-level approach to computer document formatting," 7th Symposium on the Principles of Programming Languages, 1980), are probably the best known. The paper "Document Formatting Systems: Survey, Concepts and Issues" by Richard Furuta, Jeffrey Scofield, and Alan Shaw (*Computing Surveys*, September, 1982) is a good survey of the field.

The original paper on eqn is "A system for typesetting mathematics," (*CACM*, March 1975), by Brian Kernighan and Lorinda Cherry. The ms macro package, tbl and refer are all by Mike Lesk; they are documented only in the *UNIX Programmer's Manual*, Volume 2A.

pic is described in "PIC — a language for typesetting graphics," by Brian Kernighan, *Software—Practice and Experience*, January, 1982. ideal is described in "A high-level language for describing pictures," by Chris Van Wyk, *ACM Transactions on Graphics*, April, 1982.

spell is a command that turned from a shell file, written by Steve Johnson, into a C program, by Doug McIlroy. The 7th Edition spell uses a hashing mechanism for quick lookup, and rules for automatically stripping suffixes and prefixes to keep the dictionary small. See "Development of a spelling list," M. D. McIlroy, *IEEE Transactions on Communications*, January, 1982.

The style and diction programs are described in "Computer aids for writers," by Lorinda Cherry, SIGPLAN Symposium on Text Manipulation, Portland, Oregon (June 1981).

CHAPTER 10: **EPILOG**

The UNIX operating system is well over ten years old, but the number of computers running it is growing faster than ever. For a system designed with no marketing goals or even intentions, it has been singularly successful.

The main reason for its commercial success is probably its portability — the feature that everything but small parts of the compilers and kernel runs unchanged on any computer. Manufacturers that run UNIX software on their machines therefore have comparatively little work to do to get the system running on new hardware, and can benefit from the expanding commercial market for UNIX programs.

But the UNIX system was popular long before it was of commercial significance, and even before it ran on anything but the PDP-11. The 1974 CACM paper by Ritchie and Thompson generated interest in the academic community, and by 1975, 6th Edition systems were becoming common in universities. Through the mid-1970's UNIX knowledge spread by word of mouth: although the system came unsupported and without guarantee, the people who used it were enthusiastic enough to convince others to try it too. Once people tried it, they tended to stick with it; another reason for its current success is that the generation of programmers who used academic UNIX systems now expect to find the UNIX environment where they work.

Why did it become popular in the first place? The central factor is that it was designed and built by a small number (two) of exceptionally talented people, whose sole purpose was to create an environment that would be convenient for program development, and who had the freedom to pursue that ideal. Free of market pressure, the early systems were small enough to be understood by a single person. John Lions taught the 6th Edition kernel in an undergraduate operating systems course at the University of New South Wales in Australia. In notes prepared for the class, he wrote, "... the whole documentation is not unreasonably transportable in a student's briefcase." (This has been fixed in recent versions.)

In that early system were packed a number of inventive applications of computer science, including stream processing (pipes), regular expressions, language theory (yacc, lex, etc.) and more specific instances like the algorithm in `diff`. Binding it all together was a kernel with "features seldom found even in larger operating systems." As an example, consider the I/O structure: a hierarchical file system, rare at the time; devices installed as names in the file system, so they require no special utilities; and perhaps a dozen critical system calls, such as an `open` primitive with exactly two arguments. The software was all written in a high-level language and distributed with the system so it could be studied and modified.

The UNIX system has since become one of the computer market's standard operating systems, and with market dominance has come responsibility and the need for "features" provided by competing systems. As a result, the kernel has grown in size by a factor of 10 in the past decade, although it has certainly not improved by the same amount. This growth has been accompanied by a surfeit of ill-conceived programs that don't build on the existing environment. Creeping featurism encrusts commands with options that obscure the original intention of the programs. Because source code is often not distributed with the system, models of good style are harder come by.

Fortunately, however, even the large versions are still suffused with the ideas that made the early versions so popular. The principles on which UNIX is based — simplicity of structure, the lack of disproportionate means, building on existing programs rather than recreating, programmability of the command interpreter, a tree-structured file system, and so on — are therefore spreading and displacing the ideas in the monolithic systems that preceded it. The UNIX system can't last forever, but systems that hope to supersede it will have to incorporate many of its fundamental ideas.

We said in the preface that there is a UNIX approach or philosophy, a style of how to approach a programming task. Looking back over the book, you should be able to see the elements of that style illustrated in our examples.

First, let the machine do the work. Use programs like `grep` and `wc` and `awk` to mechanize tasks that you might do by hand on other systems.

Second, let other people do the work. Use programs that already exist as building blocks in your programs, with the shell and the programmable filters to glue them together. Write a small program to interface to an existing one that does the real work, as we did with `idiff`. The UNIX environment is rich in tools that can be combined in myriad ways; your job is often just to think of the right combination.

Third, do the job in stages. Build the simplest thing that will be useful, and let your experience with that determine what (if anything) is worth doing next. Don't add features and options until usage patterns tell you which ones are needed.

Fourth, build tools. Write programs that mesh with the existing environment, enhancing it rather than merely adding to it. Built well, such programs themselves become a part of everyone's toolkit.

We also said in the preface that the system was not perfect. After nine chapters describing programs with strange conventions, pointless differences, and arbitrary limitations, you will surely agree. In spite of such blemishes, however, the positive benefits far outweigh the occasional irritating rough edges. The UNIX system is really good at what it was designed to do: providing a comfortable programming environment.

So although UNIX has begun to show some signs of middle age, it's still viable and still gaining in popularity. And that popularity can be traced to the clear thinking of a few people in 1969, who sketched on the blackboard a design for a programming environment they would find comfortable. Although they didn't expect their system to spread to tens of thousands of computers, a generation of programmers is glad that it did.

APPENDIX 1: **EDITOR SUMMARY**

The "standard" UNIX text editor is a program called ed, originally written by Ken Thompson. ed was designed in the early 1970's, for a computing environment on tiny machines (the first UNIX system limited user programs to 8K bytes) with hard-copy terminals running at very low speeds (10-15 characters per second). It was derived from an earlier editor called qed that was popular at the time.

As technology has advanced, ed has remained much the same. You are almost certain to find on your system other editors with appealing features; of these, "visual" or "screen" editing, in which the screen of your terminal reflects your editing changes as you make them, is probably the most common.

So why are we spending time on such a old-fashioned program? The answer is that ed, in spite of its age, does some things really well. It is available on all UNIX systems; you can be sure that it will be around as you move from one system to another. It works well over slow-speed telephone lines and with any kind of terminal. ed is also easy to run from a script; most screen editors assume that they are driving a terminal, and can't conveniently take their input from a file.

ed provides regular expressions for pattern matching. Regular expressions based on those in ed permeate the system: grep and sed use almost identical ones; egrep, awk and lex extend them; the shell uses a different syntax but the same ideas for filename matching. Some screen editors have a "line mode" that reverts to a version of ed so that you can use regular expressions.

Finally, ed runs fast. It's quite possible to invoke ed, make a one-line change to a file, write out the new version, and quit, all before a bigger and fancier screen editor has even started.

Basics

ed edits one file at a time. It works on a copy of the file; to record your changes in the original file, you have to give an explicit command. ed provides commands to manipulate consecutive lines or lines that match a pattern, and to make changes within lines.

Each ed command is a single character, usually a letter. Most commands

319

can be preceded by one or two *line numbers*, which indicate what line or lines are to be affected by the command; a default line number is used otherwise. Line numbers can be specified by absolute position in the file (1, 2, ...), by shorthand like $ for the last line and '.' for the current line, by pattern searches using regular expressions, and by additive combinations of these.

Let us review how to create files with ed, using De Morgan's poem from Chapter 1.

```
$ ed poem
?poem                              Warning: the file poem doesn't exist
a                                  Start adding lines
Great fleas have little fleas
   upon their backs to bite 'em,
And little fleas have lesser fleas,
   and so ad infinitum.
.                                  Type a '.' to stop adding
w poem                             Write lines to file poem
121                                ed reports 121 characters written
q                                  Quit
$
```

The command a adds or appends lines; the appending mode is terminated by a line with a '.' by itself. There is no indication of which mode you are in, so two common mistakes to watch for are typing text without an a command, and typing commands before typing the '.'.

ed will never write your text into a file automatically; you have to tell it to do so with the w command. If you try to quit without writing your changes, however, ed prints a ? as a warning. At that point, another q command will let you exit without writing. Q always quits regardless of changes.

```
$ ed poem
121                                File exists, and has 121 characters
a                                  Add some more lines at the end
And the great fleas themselves, in turn,
   have greater fleas to go on;
While these again have greater still,
   and greater still, and so on.
.                                  Type a '.' to stop adding
q                                  Try to quit
?                                  Warning: you didn't write first
w                                  No filename given; poem is assumed
263
q                                  Now it's OK to quit
$ wc poem                          Check for sure
      8      46     263 poem
$
```

Escape to the shell with !

If you are running ed, you can escape temporarily to run another shell command; there's no need to quit. The ed command to do this is '!':

```
$ ed poem
263
!wc poem                    Run wc without leaving ed
        8       46      263 poem
!                           You have returned from the command
q                           Quit without w is OK: no change was made
$
```

Printing

The lines of the file are numbered 1, 2, ...; you can print the *n*-th line by giving the command *n*p or just the number *n*, and lines *m* through *n* with *m*,*n*p. The "line number" $ is the last line, so you don't have to count lines.

```
1                           Print 1st line; same as 1p
$                           Print last line; same as $p
1,$p                        Print lines 1 through last
```

You can print a file one line at a time just by pressing RETURN; you can back up one line at a time with '-'. Line numbers can be combined with + and -:

```
$-2,$p                      Print last 3 lines
1,2+3p                      Print lines 1 through 5
```

But you can't print past the end or in reverse order; commands like $,$+1p and $,1p are illegal.

The *list* command l prints in a format that makes all characters visible; it's good for finding control characters in files, for distinguishing blanks from tabs, and so on. (See vis in Chapter 6.)

Patterns

Once a file becomes longer than a few lines, it's a bother to have to print it all to find a particular line, so ed provides a way to search for lines that match a particular pattern: /pattern/ finds the next occurrence of *pattern*.

```
$ ed poem
263
/flea/                      Search for next line containing flea
Great fleas have little fleas
/flea/                      Search for next one
And little fleas have lesser fleas,
//                          Search for next using same pattern
And the great fleas themselves, in turn,
??                          Search backwards for same pattern
And little fleas have lesser fleas,
```

ed remembers the pattern you used last, so you can repeat a search with just

//. To search backwards, use *?pattern?* and *??*.

Searches with */.../* and *?...?* "wrap around" at either end of the text:

```
$p                                  Print last line. ('p' is optional)
   and greater still, and so on.
/flea/                              Next flea is near beginning
Great fleas have little fleas
??                                  Wrap around beginning going backwards
   have greater fleas to go on;
```

A pattern search like */flea/* is a line number just as 1 or $ is, and can be used in the same contexts:

```
1,/flea/p                           Print from 1 to next flea
?flea?+1,$p                         Print from previous flea +1 to end
```

Where are we anyway?

ed keeps track of the last line where you did something: printing or adding text or reading a file. The name of this line is '.'; it is pronounced "dot" and is called the *current line*. Each command has a defined effect on dot, usually setting it to the last line affected by the command. You can use dot in the same way that you use $ or a number like 1:

```
$ ed poem
263
.                                   Print current line; same as $ after reading
   and greater still, and so on.
.-1,.p                              Print previous line and this one
While these again have greater still,
   and greater still, and so on.
```

Line number expressions can be abbreviated:

Shorthand:	Same as:		Shorthand:	Same as:
−	.−1		+	.+1
−− *or* −2	.−2		++ *or* +2	.+2
−*n*	.−*n*		+*n*	.+*n*
$−	$−1		.3	.+3

Append, change, delete, insert

The *append* command a adds lines after the specified line; the *delete* command d deletes lines; the *insert* command i inserts lines before the specified line; the *change* command c changes lines, a combination of delete and insert.

```
n a                                 Add text after line n
n i                                 Insert text before line n
m,n d                               Delete lines m through n
m,n c                               Change lines m through n
```

If no line numbers are given, dot is used. The new text for a, c and i commands is terminated by a '.' on a line by itself; dot is left at the last line added. Dot is set to the next line after the last deleted line, except that it doesn't go past line $.

0a	*Add text at beginning (same as* 1i)
dp	*Delete current line, print next (or last, if at* $)
.,$dp	*Delete from here to end, print new last*
1,$d	*Delete everything*
?pat?,.-1d	*Delete from previous 'pat' to just before dot*
$dp	*Delete last line, print new last line*
$c	*Change last line.* ($a *adds after last line*)
1,$c	*Change all lines*

Substitution; undo

It's a pain to have to re-type a whole line to change a few letters in it. The *substitute* command s is the way to replace one string of letters by another:

s/old/new/	*Change first* old *into* new *on current line*
s/old/new/p	*Change first* old *into* new *and print line*
s/old/new/g	*Change each* old *into* new *on current line*
s/old/new/gp	*Change each* old *into* new *and print line*

Only the leftmost occurrence of the pattern in the line is replaced, unless a 'g' follows. The s command doesn't print the changed line unless there is a 'p' at the end. In fact, most ed commands do their job silently, but almost any command can be followed by p to print the result.

If a substitution didn't do what you wanted, the *undo* command u will undo the most recent substitution. Dot must be set to the substituted line.

u	*Undo most recent substitution*
up	*Undo most recent substitution and print*

Just as the p and d commands can be preceded by one or two line numbers to indicate which lines are affected, so can the s command:

/old/s/old/new/	*Find next* old; *change to* new
/old/s//new/	*Find next* old; *change to* new *(pattern is remembered)*
1,$s/old/new/p	*Change first* old *to* new *on each line;* *print last line changed*
1,$s/old/new/gp	*Change each* old *to* new *on each line;* *print last line changed*

Note that 1,$s applies the s command to each line, but it still means only the leftmost match on each line; the trailing 'g' is needed to replace all occurrences in each line. Furthermore, the p prints only the last affected line; to print all changed lines requires a global command, which we'll get to shortly.

The character & is shorthand; if it appears anywhere on the right side of an s command, it is replaced by whatever was matched on the left side:

```
s/big/very &/          Replace big by very big
s/big/& &/             Replace big by big big
s/.*/(&)/              Parenthesize entire line (see .* below)
s/and/\&/              Replace and by & (\ turns off special meaning)
```

Metacharacters and regular expressions

In the same way that characters like * and > and ¦ have special meaning to the shell, certain characters have special meaning to ed when they appear in a search pattern or in the left-hand part of an s command. Such characters are called *metacharacters*, and the patterns that use them are called *regular expressions*. Table 1 lists the characters and their meanings; the examples below should be read in conjunction with the table. The special meaning of any character can be turned off by preceding it with a backslash.

Table 1: Editor Regular Expressions	
c	any non-special character *c* matches itself
c	turn off any special meaning of character *c*
^	matches beginning of line when ^ begins pattern
$	matches end of line when $ ends pattern
.	matches any single character
[...]	matches any one of characters in ...; ranges like a-z are legal
[^...]	matches any single character not in ...; ranges are legal
r*	matches zero or more occurrences of *r*, where *r* is a character, . or [...]
&	on right side of s only, produces what was matched
\\(...\\)	tagged regular expression; the matched string is available as \\1, etc., on both left and right side
No regular expression matches a newline.	

```
Pattern:               Matches:
/^$/                   empty line, i.e., newline only
/./                    non-empty, i.e., at least one character
/^/                    all lines
/thing/                thing anywhere on line
/^thing/               thing at beginning of line
/thing$/               thing at end of line
/^thing$/              line that contains only thing
/thing.$/              thing plus any character at end of line
/thing\.$/             thing. at end of line
/\/thing\//            /thing/ anywhere on line
/[tT]hing/             thing or Thing anywhere on line
/thing[0-9]/           thing followed by one digit
```

```
/thing[^0-9]/            thing followed by a non-digit
/thing[0-9][^0-9]/       thing followed by digit, non-digit
/thing1.*thing2/         thing1 then any string then thing2
/^thing1.*thing2$/       thing1 at beginning and thing2 at end
```

Regular expressions involving * choose the leftmost match and make it as long as possible. Note that x* can match zero characters; xx* matches one or more.

Global commands

The global commands g and v apply one or more other commands to a set of lines selected by a regular expression. The g command is most often used for printing, substituting or deleting a set of lines:

m,n g */re/cmd*	*For all lines between m and n that match re, do cmd*
m,n v */re/cmd*	*For all lines between m and n that don't match re, do cmd*

The g or v commands can be preceded by line numbers to limit the range; the default range is 1, $.

g/.../p	*Print all lines matching regular expression ...*
g/.../d	*Delete all lines matching ...*
g/.../s//repl/p	*Replace 1st ... on each line by 'repl', print changed lines*
g/.../s//repl/gp	*Replace each ... by 'repl', print changed lines*
g/.../s/pat/repl/	*On lines matching ..., replace 1st 'pat' by 'repl'*
g/.../s/pat/repl/p	*On lines matching ..., replace 1st 'pat' by 'repl' and print*
g/.../s/pat/repl/gp	*On lines matching ..., replace all 'pat' by 'repl' and print*
v/.../s/pat/repl/gp	*On lines not matching ..., replace all 'pat' by 'repl', print*
v/^$/p	*Print all non-blank lines*
g/.../cmd1\	*To do multiple commands with a single g,*
cmd2\	*append \ to each cmd*
cmd3	*but the last*

The commands controlled by a g or v command can also use line numbers. Dot is set in turn to each line selected.

g/thing/.,.+1p	*Print each line with* thing *and next*
g/^\.EQ/.1,/^\.EN/-s/alpha/beta/gp	*Change* alpha *to* beta *only between* .EQ *and* .EN, *and print changed lines*

Moving and copying lines

The command m moves a contiguous group of lines; the t command makes a copy of a group of lines somewhere else.

m,n m *d*	*Move lines m through n to after line d*
m,n t *d*	*Copy lines m through n to after line d*

If no source lines are specified, dot is used. The destination line *d* cannot be in the range *m*, *n*−1. Here are some common idioms using m and t:

m+	*Move current line to after next one (interchange)*
m-2	*Move current line to before previous one*
m--	*Same: -- is the same as -2*
m-	*Does nothing*
m$	*Move current line to end (m0 moves to beginning)*
t.	*Duplicate current line (t$ duplicates at end)*
-,.t.	*Duplicate previous and current lines*
1,t	*Duplicate entire set of lines*
g/^/m0	*Reverse order of lines*

Marks and line numbers

The command = prints the line number of line $ (a poor default), .= prints the number of the current line, and so on. Dot is unchanged.

The command k*c marks* the addressed line with the lower case letter *c*; the line can subsequently be addressed as '*c*. The k command does not change dot. Marks are convenient for moving large chunks of text, since they remain permanently attached to lines, as in this sequence:

/.../ka	*Find line ... and mark with* a
/.../kb	*Find line ... and mark with* b
'a,'bp	*Print entire range to be sure*
/.../	*Find target line*
'a,'bm.	*Move selected lines after it*

Joining, splitting and rearranging lines

Lines can be joined with the j command (no blanks are added):

m,nj	*Join lines m through n into one line*

The default range is .,.+1, so

jp	*Join current line to next and print*
-,.jp	*Join previous line to current and print*

Lines can be split with the substitute command by quoting a newline:

s/part1part2/part1\	*Split line into two parts*
part2/	*...*
s/ /\	*Split at each blank;*
/g	*makes one word per line*

Dot is left at the last line created.

To talk about parts of the matched regular expression, not just the whole thing, use *tagged regular expressions*: if the construction \(...\) appears in a regular expression, the part of the whole that it matches is available on both the right hand side and the left as \1. There can be up to nine tagged expressions, referred to as \1, \2, etc.

s/\(...\)\(.*\)/\2\1/   *Move first 3 characters to end*
/\(..*\)\1/   *Find lines that contain a repeated adjacent string*

File handling commands

The *read* and *write* commands r and w can be preceded by line numbers:

n r *file*   *Read file; add it after line n; set dot to last line read*
m,n w *file*   *Write lines m-n to file; dot is unchanged*
m,n W *file*   *Append lines m-n to file; dot is unchanged*

The default range for w and W is the whole file. The default *n* for r is $, an unfortunate choice. Beware.

ed remembers the first file name used, either from the command line or from an r or w command. The *file* command f prints or changes the name of the remembered file:

f   *Print name of remembered file*
f *file*   *Set remembered name to 'file'*

The *edit* command e reinitializes ed with the remembered file or with a new one:

e   *Begin editing remembered file*
e *file*   *Begin editing 'file'*

The e command is protected the same way as q is: if you haven't written your changes, the first e will draw an error message. E reinitializes regardless of changes. On some systems, ed is linked to e so that the same command (e *filename*) can be used inside and outside the editor.

Encryption

Files may be encrypted upon writing and decrypted upon reading by giving the x command; a password will be asked for. The encryption is the same as in crypt(1). The x command has been changed to X (upper case) on some systems, to make it harder to encrypt unintentionally.

Summary of commands

Table 2 is a summary of ed commands, and Table 3 lists the valid line numbers. Each command is preceded by zero, one or two line numbers that indicate how many line numbers can be provided, and the default values if they are not. Most commands can be followed by a p to print the last line affected, or l for list format. Dot is normally set to the last line affected; it is unchanged by f, k, w, x, =, and !.

Exercise. When you think you know ed, try the editor quiz; see quiz(6). □

Table 2: Summary of `ed` Commands

`.a`	add text until a line containing just `.` is typed
`.,.c`	change lines; new text terminated as with `a`
`.,.d`	delete lines
`e` *file*	reinitialize with *file*. `E` resets even if changes not written
`f` *file*	set remembered file to *file*
`1,$g/`*re*`/`*cmds*	do `ed` *cmds* on each line matching regular expression *re*; multiple *cmds* separated by *newline*
`.i`	insert text before line, terminated as with `a`
`.,.+1j`	join lines into one
`.k`*c*	mark line with letter *c*
`.,.l`	list lines, making invisible characters visible
`.,.m` *line*	move lines to after *line*
`.,.p`	print lines
`q`	quit. `Q` quits even if changes not written
`$r` *file*	read *file*
`.,.s/`*re*`/`*new*`/`	substitute *new* for whatever matched *re*
`.,.t` *line*	copy lines after *line*
`.u`	undo last substitution on line (only one)
`1,$v/`*re*`/`*cmds*	do `ed` *cmds* on each line not matching *re*
`1,$w` *file*	write lines to *file*; `W` appends instead of overwriting
`x`	enter encryption mode (or `ed -x` *filename*)
`$=`	print line number
`!`*cmdline*	execute UNIX command *cmdline*
`(.+1)`*newline*	print line

Table 3: Summary of `ed` Line Numbers

n	absolute line number *n*, *n* = 0, 1, 2, ...
`.`	current line
`$`	last line of text
`/`*re*`/`	next line matching *re*; wraps around from `$` to 1
`?`*re*`?`	previous line matching *re*; wraps around from 1 to `$`
`'`*c*	line with mark *c*
N1±*n*	line *N1*±*n* (additive combination)
N1,*N2*	lines *N1* through *N2*
N1;*N2*	set dot to *N1*, then evaluate *N2*
	N1 and *N2* may be specified with any of the above

Hoç - An Interactive Language For Floating Point Arithmetic

Brian Kernighan
Rob Pike

ABSTRACT

Hoc is a simple programmable interpreter for floating point expressions.
It has C-style control flow, function definition and the usual numerical
built-in functions such as cosine and logarithm.

1. Expressions

Hoc is an expression language, much like C: although there are several control-flow
statements, most statements such as assignments are expressions whose value is disregarded. For example, the assignment operator = assigns the value of its right operand
to its left operand, and yields the value, so multiple assignments work. The expression
grammar is:

expr:	*number*
|	*variable*
|	*(expr)*
|	*expr binop expr*
|	*unop expr*
|	*function (arguments)*

Numbers are floating point. The input format is that recognized by *scanf* (3): digits,
decimal point, digits, *e* or *E*, signed exponent. At least one digit or a decimal point
must be present; the other components are optional.

Variable names are formed from a letter followed by a string of letters and
numbers. *binop* refers to binary operators such as addition or logical comparison; *unop*
refers to the two negation operators, '!' (logical negation, 'not') and '−' (arithmetic
negation, sign change). Table 1 lists the operators.

329

Table 1: Operators, in decreasing order of precedence	
^	exponentiation (FORTRAN **), right associative
! —	(unary) logical and arithmetic negation
* /	multiplication, division
+ —	addition, subtraction
> >=	relational operators: greater, greater or equal,
< <=	less, less or equal,
== !=	equal, not equal (all same precedence)
&&	logical AND (both operands always evaluated)
¦¦	logical OR (both operands always evaluated)
=	assignment, right associative

Functions, as described later, may be defined by the user. Function arguments are expressions separated by commas. There are also a number of built-in functions, all of which take a single argument, described in Table 2.

Table 2: Built-in Functions	
abs(x)	$|x|$, absolute value of x
atan(x)	arc tangent of x
cos(x)	$\cos(x)$, cosine of x
exp(x)	e^x, exponential of x
int(x)	integer part of x, truncated towards zero
log(x)	$\log(x)$, logarithm base e of x
log10(x)	$\log_{10}(x)$, logarithm base 10 of x
sin(x)	$\sin(x)$, sine of x
sqrt(x)	$\sqrt{x}$, $x^{\frac{1}{2}}$

Logical expressions have value 1.0 (true) and 0.0 (false). As in C, any non-zero value is taken to be true. As is always the case with floating point numbers, equality comparisons are inherently suspect.

Hoc also has a few built-in constants, shown in Table 3.

Table 3: Built-in Constants		
DEG	57.29577951308232087680	$180/\pi$, degrees per radian
E	2.71828182845904523536	e, base of natural logarithms
GAMMA	0.57721566490153286060	γ, Euler-Mascheroni constant
PHI	1.61803398874989484820	$(\sqrt{5}+1)/2$, the golden ratio
PI	3.14159265358979323846	π, circular transcendental number

2. Statements and Control Flow

Hoc statements have the following grammar:

stmt: *expr*
                        | *variable = expr*
                        | *procedure (arglist)*
                        | *while (expr) stmt*
                        | *if (expr) stmt*
                        | *if (expr) stmt else stmt*
                        | *{ stmtlist }*
                        | *print expr-list*
                        | *return optional-expr*

stmtlist: (nothing)
                        | *stmlist stmt*

An assignment is parsed by default as a statement rather than an expression, so assignments typed interactively do not print their value.

Note that semicolons are not special to *hoc*: statements are terminated by newlines. This causes some peculiar behavior. The following are legal *if* statements:

```
if (x < 0) print(y) else print(z)

if (x < 0) {
        print(y)
} else {
        print(z)
}
```

In the second example, the braces are mandatory: the newline after the *if* would terminate the statement and produce a syntax error were the brace omitted.

The syntax and semantics of *hoc* control flow facilities are basically the same as in C. The *while* and *if* statements are just as in C, except there are no *break* or *continue* statements.

3. Input and Output: *read* and *print*

The input function *read*, like the other built-ins, takes a single argument. Unlike the built-ins, though, the argument is not an expression: it is the name of a variable. The next number (as defined above) is read from the standard input and assigned to the named variable. The return value of *read* is 1 (true) if a value was read, and 0 (false) if *read* encountered end of file or an error.

Output is generated with the *print* statement. The arguments to *print* are a comma-separated list of expressions and strings in double quotes, as in C. Newlines must be supplied; they are never provided automatically by *print*.

Note that *read* is a special built-in function, and therefore takes a single parenthesized argument, while *print* is a statement that takes a comma-separated, unparenthesized list:

```
while (read(x)) {
        print "value is ", x, "\n"
}
```

4. Functions and Procedures

Functions and procedures are distinct in *hoc*, although they are defined by the same mechanism. This distinction is simply for run-time error checking: it is an error for a procedure to return a value, and for a function *not* to return one.

The definition syntax is:

function: func name() stmt

procedure: proc name() stmt

name may be the name of any variable — built-in functions are excluded. The definition, up to the opening brace or statement, must be on one line, as with the *if* statements above.

Unlike C, the body of a function or procedure may be any statement, not necessarily a compound (brace-enclosed) statement. Since semicolons have no meaning in *hoc*, a null procedure body is formed by an empty pair of braces.

Functions and procedures may take arguments, separated by commas, when invoked. Arguments are referred to as in the shell: *$3* refers to the third (1-indexed) argument. They are passed by value and within functions are semantically equivalent to variables. It is an error to refer to an argument numbered greater than the number of arguments passed to the routine. The error checking is done dynamically, however, so a routine may have variable numbers of arguments if initial arguments affect the number of arguments to be referenced (as in C's *printf*).

Functions and procedures may recurse, but the stack has limited depth (about a hundred calls). The following shows a *hoc* definition of Ackermann's function:

```
$ hoc
func ack() {
        if ($1 == 0) return $2+1
        if ($2 == 0) return ack($1-1, 1)
        return ack($1-1, ack($1, $2-1))
}
ack(3, 2)
        29
ack(3, 3)
        61
ack(3, 4)
hoc: stack too deep near line 8
...
```

5. Examples

Stirling's formula:

$$n! \sim \sqrt{2n\pi}(n/e)^n(1+\frac{1}{12n})$$

```
$ hoc
func stirl() {
    return sqrt(2*$1*PI) * ($1/E)^$1*(1 + 1/(12*$1))
}
stirl(10)
        3628684.7
stirl(20)
        2.4328818e+18
```

Factorial function, $n!$:

```
func fac() if ($1 <= 0) return 1 else return $1 * fac($1-1)
```

Ratio of factorial to Stirling approximation:

```
i = 9
while ((i = i+1) <= 20) {
        print i, "  ", fac(i)/stirl(i), "\n"
}
10   1.0000318
11   1.0000265
12   1.0000224
13   1.0000192
14   1.0000166
15   1.0000146
16   1.0000128
17   1.0000114
18   1.0000102
19   1.0000092
20   1.0000083
```

The following is a listing of hoc6 in its entirety.

```
*****   hoc.y  *********************************************************
%{
#include "hoc.h"
#define code2(c1,c2)    code(c1); code(c2)
#define code3(c1,c2,c3) code(c1); code(c2); code(c3)
%}
%union {
        Symbol  *sym;   /* symbol table pointer */
        Inst    *inst;  /* machine instruction */
        int     narg;   /* number of arguments */
}
%token  <sym>   NUMBER STRING PRINT VAR BLTIN UNDEF WHILE IF ELSE
%token  <sym>   FUNCTION PROCEDURE RETURN FUNC PROC READ
%token  <narg>  ARG
%type   <inst>  expr stmt asgn prlist stmtlist
%type   <inst>  cond while if begin end
%type   <sym>   procname
%type   <narg>  arglist
%right  '='
%left   OR
%left   AND
%left   GT GE LT LE EQ NE
%left   '+' '-'
%left   '*' '/'
%left   UNARYMINUS NOT
%right  '^'
%%
list:       /* nothing */
        | list '\n'
        | list defn '\n'
        | list asgn '\n'   { code2(pop, STOP); return 1; }
        | list stmt '\n'   { code(STOP); return 1; }
        | list expr '\n'   { code2(print, STOP); return 1; }
        | list error '\n'  { yyerrok; }
        ;
asgn:       VAR '=' expr { code3(varpush,(Inst)$1,assign); $$=$3; }
        | ARG '=' expr
            { defnonly("$"); code2(argassign,(Inst)$1); $$=$3;}
        ;
```

```
stmt:       expr  { code(pop); }
        |   RETURN { defnonly("return"); code(procret); }
        |   RETURN expr
                { defnonly("return"); $$=$2; code(funcret); }
        |   PROCEDURE begin '(' arglist ')'
                { $$ = $2; code3(call, (Inst)$1, (Inst)$4); }
        |   PRINT prlist  { $$ = $2; }
        |   while cond stmt end {
                    ($1)[1] = (Inst)$3;       /* body of loop */
                    ($1)[2] = (Inst)$4; }     /* end, if cond fails */
        |   if cond stmt end {     /* else-less if */
                    ($1)[1] = (Inst)$3;       /* thenpart */
                    ($1)[3] = (Inst)$4; }     /* end, if cond fails */
        |   if cond stmt end ELSE stmt end {      /* if with else */
                    ($1)[1] = (Inst)$3;       /* thenpart */
                    ($1)[2] = (Inst)$6;       /* elsepart */
                    ($1)[3] = (Inst)$7; }     /* end, if cond fails */
        |   '{' stmtlist '}'          { $$ = $2; }
        ;
cond:       '(' expr ')'  { code(STOP); $$ = $2; }
        ;
while:      WHILE { $$ = code3(whilecode,STOP,STOP); }
        ;
if:         IF    { $$ = code(ifcode); code3(STOP,STOP,STOP); }
        ;
begin:      /* nothing */         { $$ = progp; }
        ;
end:        /* nothing */         { code(STOP); $$ = progp; }
        ;
stmtlist:   /* nothing */         { $$ = progp; }
        |   stmtlist '\n'
        |   stmtlist stmt
        ;
expr:       NUMBER { $$ = code2(constpush, (Inst)$1); }
        |   VAR    { $$ = code3(varpush, (Inst)$1, eval); }
        |   ARG    { defnonly("$"); $$ = code2(arg, (Inst)$1); }
        |   asgn
        |   FUNCTION begin '(' arglist ')'
                { $$ = $2; code3(call,(Inst)$1,(Inst)$4); }
        |   READ '(' VAR ')' { $$ = code2(varread, (Inst)$3); }
        |   BLTIN '(' expr ')' { $$=$3; code2(bltin, (Inst)$1->u.ptr); }
        |   '(' expr ')'  { $$ = $2; }
        |   expr '+' expr { code(add); }
        |   expr '-' expr { code(sub); }
        |   expr '*' expr { code(mul); }
        |   expr '/' expr { code(div); }
        |   expr '^' expr { code (power); }
        |   '-' expr    %prec UNARYMINUS   { $$=$2; code(negate); }
        |   expr GT expr  { code(gt); }
        |   expr GE expr  { code(ge); }
        |   expr LT expr  { code(lt); }
        |   expr LE expr  { code(le); }
        |   expr EQ expr  { code(eq); }
        |   expr NE expr  { code(ne); }
        |   expr AND expr { code(and); }
        |   expr OR expr  { code(or); }
        |   NOT expr      { $$ = $2; code(not); }
        ;
prlist:     expr                  { code(prexpr); }
        |   STRING                { $$ = code2(prstr, (Inst)$1); }
        |   prlist ',' expr       { code(prexpr); }
        |   prlist ',' STRING     { code2(prstr, (Inst)$3); }
        ;
defn:       FUNC procname { $2->type=FUNCTION; indef=1; }
            '(' ')' stmt { code(procret); define($2); indef=0; }
        |   PROC procname { $2->type=PROCEDURE; indef=1; }
            '(' ')' stmt { code(procret); define($2); indef=0; }
        ;
procname:   VAR
        |   FUNCTION
        |   PROCEDURE
        ;
arglist:    /* nothing */         { $$ = 0; }
        |   expr                  { $$ = 1; }
        |   arglist ',' expr      { $$ = $1 + 1; }
        ;
%%
```

```
                /* end of grammar */
#include <stdio.h>
#include <ctype.h>
char     *progname;
int      lineno = 1;
#include <signal.h>
#include <setjmp.h>
jmp_buf begin;
int      indef;
char     *infile;         /* input file name */
FILE     *fin;            /* input file pointer */
char     **gargv;         /* global argument list */
int      gargc;

int c; /* global for use by warning() */
yylex()          /* hoc6 */
{
        while ((c=getc(fin)) == ' ' || c == '\t')
                ;
        if (c == EOF)
                return 0;
        if (c == '.' || isdigit(c)) {    /* number */
                double d;
                ungetc(c, fin);
                fscanf(fin, "%lf", &d);
                yylval.sym = install("", NUMBER, d);
                return NUMBER;
        }
        if (isalpha(c)) {
                Symbol *s;
                char sbuf[100], *p = sbuf;
                do {
                        if (p >= sbuf + sizeof(sbuf) - 1) {
                                *p = '\0';
                                execerror("name too long", sbuf);
                        }
                        *p++ = c;
                } while ((c=getc(fin)) != EOF && isalnum(c));
                ungetc(c, fin);
                *p = '\0';
                if ((s=lookup(sbuf)) == 0)
                        s = install(sbuf, UNDEF, 0.0);
                yylval.sym = s;
                return s->type == UNDEF ? VAR : s->type;
        }
        if (c == '$') { /* argument? */
                int n = 0;
                while (isdigit(c=getc(fin)))
                        n = 10 * n + c - '0';
                ungetc(c, fin);
                if (n == 0)
                        execerror("strange $...", (char *)0);
                yylval.narg = n;
                return ARG;
        }
        if (c == '"') { /* quoted string */
                char sbuf[100], *p, *emalloc();
                for (p = sbuf; (c=getc(fin)) != '"'; p++) {
                        if (c == '\n' || c == EOF)
                                execerror("missing quote", "");
                        if (p >= sbuf + sizeof(sbuf) - 1) {
                                *p = '\0';
                                execerror("string too long", sbuf);
                        }
                        *p = backslash(c);
                }
                *p = 0;
                yylval.sym = (Symbol *)emalloc(strlen(sbuf)+1);
                strcpy(yylval.sym, sbuf);
                return STRING;
        }
        switch (c) {
        case '>':       return follow('=', GE, GT);
        case '<':       return follow('=', LE, LT);
        case '=':       return follow('=', EQ, '=');
        case '!':       return follow('=', NE, NOT);
        case '|':       return follow('|', OR, '|');
        case '&':       return follow('&', AND, '&');
        case '\n':      lineno++; return '\n';
        default:        return c;
        }
```

```
        }
        backslash(c)        /* get next char with \'s interpreted */
                int c;
        {
                char *index();   /* `strchr()' in some systems */
                static char transtab[] = "b\bf\fn\nr\rt\t";
                if (c != '\\')
                        return c;
                c = getc(fin);
                if (islower(c) && index(transtab, c))
                        return index(transtab, c)[1];
                return c;
        }

        follow(expect, ifyes, ifno)       /* look ahead for >=, etc. */
        {
                int c = getc(fin);

                if (c == expect)
                        return ifyes;
                ungetc(c, fin);
                return ifno;
        }

        defnonly(s)        /* warn if illegal definition */
                char *s;
        {
                if (!indef)
                        execerror(s, "used outside definition");
        }

        yyerror(s)        /* report compile-time error */
                char *s;
        {
                warning(s, (char *)0);
        }

        execerror(s, t) /* recover from run-time error */
                char *s, *t;
        {
                warning(s, t);
                fseek(fin, 0L, 2);                      /* flush rest of file */
                longjmp(begin, 0);
        }

        fpecatch()        /* catch floating point exceptions */
        {
                execerror("floating point exception", (char *) 0);
        }

        main(argc, argv)        /* hoc6 */
                char *argv[];
        {
                int i, fpecatch();

                progname = argv[0];
                if (argc == 1) {           /* fake an argument list */
                        static char *stdinonly[] = { "-" };

                        gargv = stdinonly;
                        gargc = 1;
                } else {
                        gargv = argv+1;
                        gargc = argc-1;
                }
                init();
                while (moreinput())
                        run();
                return 0;
        }
```

```
moreinput()
{
        if (gargc-- <= 0)
                return 0;
        if (fin && fin != stdin)
                fclose(fin);
        infile = *gargv++;
        lineno = 1;
        if (strcmp(infile, "-") == 0) {
                fin = stdin;
                infile = 0;
        } else if ((fin=fopen(infile, "r")) == NULL) {
                fprintf(stderr, "%s: can't open %s\n", progname, infile);
                return moreinput();
        }
        return 1;
}
run()    /* execute until EOF */
{
        setjmp(begin);
        signal(SIGFPE, fpecatch);
        for (initcode(); yyparse(); initcode())
                execute(progbase);
}
warning(s, t)    /* print warning message */
        char *s, *t;
{
        fprintf(stderr, "%s: %s", progname, s);
        if (t)
                fprintf(stderr, " %s", t);
        if (infile)
                fprintf(stderr, " in %s", infile);
        fprintf(stderr, " near line %d\n", lineno);
        while (c != '\n' && c != EOF)
                c = getc(fin);    /* flush rest of input line */
        if (c == '\n')
                lineno++;
}

*****    hoc.h    **************************************************************

typedef struct Symbol {  /* symbol table entry */
        char    *name;
        short   type;
        union {
                double  val;            /* VAR */
                double  (*ptr)();       /* BLTIN */
                int     (*defn)();      /* FUNCTION, PROCEDURE */
                char    *str;           /* STRING */
        } u;
        struct Symbol   *next;  /* to link to another */
} Symbol;
Symbol *install(), *lookup();

typedef union Datum {    /* interpreter stack type */
        double  val;
        Symbol  *sym;
} Datum;
```

```
extern   Datum pop();
extern   eval(), add(), sub(), mul(), div(), negate(), power();

typedef int (*Inst)();
#define STOP    (Inst) 0

extern   Inst *progp, *progbase, prog[], *code();
extern   assign(), bltin(), varpush(), constpush(), print(), varread();
extern   prexpr(), prstr();
extern   gt(), lt(), eq(), ge(), le(), ne(), and(), or(), not();
extern   ifcode(), whilecode(), call(), arg(), argassign();
extern   funcret(), procret();


*****    symbol.c  ****************************************************************

#include "hoc.h"
#include "y.tab.h"

static Symbol *symlist = 0;  /* symbol table: linked list */

Symbol *lookup(s)       /* find s in symbol table */
       char *s;
{
       Symbol *sp;

       for (sp = symlist; sp != (Symbol *) 0; sp = sp->next)
              if (strcmp(sp->name, s) == 0)
                      return sp;
       return 0;        /* 0 ==> not found */
}

Symbol *install(s, t, d)  /* install s in symbol table */
       char *s;
       int t;
       double d;
{
       Symbol *sp;
       char *emalloc();

       sp = (Symbol *) emalloc(sizeof(Symbol));
       sp->name = emalloc(strlen(s)+1);  /* +1 for '\0' */
       strcpy(sp->name, s);
       sp->type = t;
       sp->u.val = d;
       sp->next = symlist;  /* put at front of list */
       symlist = sp;
       return sp;
}

char *emalloc(n)        /* check return from malloc */
       unsigned n;
{
       char *p, *malloc();

       p = malloc(n);
       if (p == 0)
              execerror("out of memory", (char *) 0);
       return p;
}


*****    code.c  ****************************************************************

#include "hoc.h"
#include "y.tab.h"
#include <stdio.h>

#define NSTACK  256

static Datum stack[NSTACK];     /* the stack */
static Datum *stackp;           /* next free spot on stack */

#define NPROG  2000
Inst    prog[NPROG];    /* the machine */
Inst    *progp;         /* next free spot for code generation */
Inst    *pc;            /* program counter during execution */
Inst    *progbase = prog;  /* start of current subprogram */
int     returning;      /* 1 if return stmt seen */

typedef struct Frame {  /* proc/func call stack frame */
        Symbol  *sp;     /* symbol table entry */
        Inst    *retpc;  /* where to resume after return */
        Datum   *argn;   /* n-th argument on stack */
        int     nargs;   /* number of arguments */
} Frame;
```

```
#define NFRAME   100
Frame    frame[NFRAME];
Frame    *fp;              /* frame pointer */

initcode() {
        progp = progbase;
        stackp = stack;
        fp = frame;
        returning = 0;
}

push(d)
        Dátum d;
{
        if (stackp >= &stack[NSTACK])
                execerror("stack too deep", (char *)0);
        *stackp++ = d;
}

Datum pop()
{
        if (stackp == stack)
                execerror("stack underflow", (char *)0);
        return *--stackp;
}

constpush()
{
        Datum d;
        d.val = ((Symbol *)*pc++)->u.val;
        push(d);
}

varpush()
{
        Datum d;
        d.sym = (Symbol *)(*pc++);
        push(d);
}

whilecode()
{
        Datum d;
        Inst *savepc = pc;

        execute(savepc+2);       /* condition */
        d = pop();
        while (d.val) {
                execute(*((Inst **)(savepc)));   /* body */
                if (returning)
                        break;
                execute(savepc+2);       /* condition */
                d = pop();
        }
        if (!returning)
                pc = *((Inst **)(savepc+1)); /* next stmt */
}

ifcode()
{
        Datum d;
        Inst *savepc = pc;       /* then part */

        execute(savepc+3);       /* condition */
        d = pop();
        if (d.val)
                execute(*((Inst **)(savepc)));
        else if (*((Inst **)(savepc+1))) /* else part? */
                execute(*((Inst **)(savepc+1)));
        if (!returning)
                pc = *((Inst **)(savepc+2)); /* next stmt */
}

define(sp)      /* put func/proc in symbol table */
        Symbol *sp;
{
        sp->u.defn = (Inst)progbase;    /* start of code */
        progbase = progp;       /* next code starts here */
}
```

```
call()          /* call a function */
{
        Symbol *sp = (Symbol *)pc[0]; /* symbol table entry */
                                      /* for function */
        if (fp++ >= &frame[NFRAME-1])
                execerror(sp->name, "call nested too deeply");
        fp->sp = sp;
        fp->nargs = (int)pc[1];
        fp->retpc = pc + 2;
        fp->argn = stackp - 1;   /* last argument */
        execute(sp->u.defn);
        returning = 0;
}

ret()           /* common return from func or proc */
{
        int i;
        for (i = 0; i < fp->nargs; i++)
                pop();   /* pop arguments */
        pc = (Inst *)fp->retpc;
        --fp;
        returning = 1;
}

funcret()       /* return from a function */
{
        Datum d;
        if (fp->sp->type == PROCEDURE)
                execerror(fp->sp->name, "(proc) returns value");
        d = pop();       /* preserve function return value */
        ret();
        push(d);
}

procret()       /* return from a procedure */
{
        if (fp->sp->type == FUNCTION)
                execerror(fp->sp->name,
                        "(func) returns no value");
        ret();
}

double *getarg()        /* return pointer to argument */
{
        int nargs = (int) *pc++;
        if (nargs > fp->nargs)
                execerror(fp->sp->name, "not enough arguments");
        return &fp->argn[nargs - fp->nargs].val;
}

arg()   /* push argument onto stack */
{
        Datum d;
        d.val = *getarg();
        push(d);
}

argassign()     /* store top of stack in argument */
{
        Datum d;
        d = pop();
        push(d);         /* leave value on stack */
        *getarg() = d.val;
}

bltin()
{
        Datum d;
        d = pop();
        d.val = (*(double (*)())*pc++)(d.val);
        push(d);
}
```

```
eval()              /* evaluate variable on stack */
{
        Datum d;
        d = pop();
        if (d.sym->type != VAR && d.sym->type != UNDEF)
                execerror("attempt to evaluate non-variable", d.sym->name);
        if (d.sym->type == UNDEF)
                execerror("undefined variable", d.sym->name);
        d.val = d.sym->u.val;
        push(d);
}

add()
{
        Datum d1, d2;
        d2 = pop();
        d1 = pop();
        d1.val += d2.val;
        push(d1);
}

sub()
{
        Datum d1, d2;
        d2 = pop();
        d1 = pop();
        d1.val -= d2.val;
        push(d1);
}

mul()
{
        Datum d1, d2;
        d2 = pop();
        d1 = pop();
        d1.val *= d2.val;
        push(d1);
}

div()
{
        Datum d1, d2;
        d2 = pop();
        if (d2.val == 0.0)
                execerror("division by zero", (char *)0);
        d1 = pop();
        d1.val /= d2.val;
        push(d1);
}

negate()
{
        Datum d;
        d = pop();
        d.val = -d.val;
        push(d);
}

gt()
{
        Datum d1, d2;
        d2 = pop();
        d1 = pop();
        d1.val = (double)(d1.val > d2.val);
        push(d1);
}

lt()
{
        Datum d1, d2;
        d2 = pop();
        d1 = pop();
        d1.val = (double)(d1.val < d2.val);
        push(d1);
}
```

```
ge()
{
        Datum d1, d2;
        d2 = pop();
        d1 = pop();
        d1.val = (double)(d1.val >= d2.val);
        push(d1);
}
le()
{
        Datum d1, d2;
        d2 = pop();
        d1 = pop();
        d1.val = (double)(d1.val <= d2.val);
        push(d1);
}
eq()
{
        Datum d1, d2;
        d2 = pop();
        d1 = pop();
        d1.val = (double)(d1.val == d2.val);
        push(d1);
}
ne()
{
        Datum d1, d2;
        d2 = pop();
        d1 = pop();
        d1.val = (double)(d1.val != d2.val);
        push(d1);
}
and()
{
        Datum d1, d2;
        d2 = pop();
        d1 = pop();
        d1.val = (double)(d1.val != 0.0 && d2.val != 0.0);
        push(d1);
}
or()
{
        Datum d1, d2;
        d2 = pop();
        d1 = pop();
        d1.val = (double)(d1.val != 0.0 || d2.val != 0.0);
        push(d1);
}
not()
{
        Datum d;
        d = pop();
        d.val = (double)(d.val == 0.0);
        push(d);
}
power()
{
        Datum d1, d2;
        extern double Pow();
        d2 = pop();
        d1 = pop();
        d1.val = Pow(d1.val, d2.val);
        push(d1);
}
```

```
assign()
{
        Datum d1, d2;
        d1 = pop();
        d2 = pop();
        if (d1.sym->type != VAR && d1.sym->type != UNDEF)
                execerror("assignment to non-variable",
                            d1.sym->name);
        d1.sym->u.val = d2.val;
        d1.sym->type = VAR;
        push(d2);
}
print()  /* pop top value from stack, print it */
{
        Datum d;
        d = pop();
        printf("\t%.8g\n", d.val);
}
prexpr()          /* print numeric value */
{
        Datum d;
        d = pop();
        printf("%.8g ", d.val);
}
prstr()           /* print string value */
{
        printf("%s", (char *) *pc++);
}
varread()         /* read into variable */
{
        Datum d;
        extern FILE *fin;
        Symbol *var = (Symbol *) *pc++;
  Again:
        switch (fscanf(fin, "%lf", &var->u.val)) {
        case EOF:
                if (moreinput())
                        goto Again;
                d.val = var->u.val = 0.0;
                break;
        case 0:
                execerror("non-number read into", var->name);
                break;
        default:
                d.val = 1.0;
                break;
        }
        var->type = VAR;
        push(d);
}
Inst *code(f)    /* install one instruction or operand */
        Inst f;
{
        Inst *oprogp = progp;
        if (progp >= &prog[NPROG])
                execerror("program too big", (char *)0);
        *progp++ = f;
        return oprogp;
}
execute(p)
        Inst *p;
{
        for (pc = p; *pc != STOP && !returning; )
                (*(*pc++))();
}
```

```
*****   init.c   *******************************************************************

#include "hoc.h"
#include "y.tab.h"
#include <math.h>

extern double   Log(), Log10(), Sqrt(), Exp(), integer();

static struct {          /* Keywords */
        char    *name;
        int     kval;
} keywords[] = {
        "proc",         PROC,
        "func",         FUNC,
        "return",       RETURN,
        "if",           IF,
        "else",         ELSE,
        "while",        WHILE,
        "print",        PRINT,
        "read",         READ,
        0,              0,
};

static struct {          /* Constants */
        char *name;
        double cval;
} consts[] = {
        "PI",     3.14159265358979323846,
        "E",      2.71828182845904523536,
        "GAMMA",  0.57721566490153286060,    /* Euler */
        "DEG",    57.29577951308232087680,   /* deg/radian */
        "PHI",    1.61803398874989484820,    /* golden ratio */
        0,        0
};

static struct {          /* Built-ins */
        char *name;
        double  (*func)();
} builtins[] = {
        "sin",  sin,
        "cos",  cos,
        "atan", atan,
        "log",  Log,      /* checks range */
        "log10", Log10,   /* checks range */
        "exp",  Exp,      /* checks range */
        "sqrt", Sqrt,     /* checks range */
        "int",  integer,
        "abs",  fabs,
        0,      0
};

init()  /* install constants and built-ins in table */
{
        int i;
        Symbol *s;
        for (i = 0; keywords[i].name; i++)
                install(keywords[i].name, keywords[i].kval, 0.0);
        for (i = 0; consts[i].name; i++)
                install(consts[i].name, VAR, consts[i].cval);
        for (i = 0; builtins[i].name; i++) {
                s = install(builtins[i].name, BLTIN, 0.0);
                s->u.ptr = builtins[i].func;
        }
}


*****   math.c   *******************************************************************

#include <math.h>
#include <errno.h>
extern  int     errno;
double  errcheck();

double Log(x)
        double x;
{
        return errcheck(log(x), "log");
}
```

```
double Log10(x)
        double x;
{
        return errcheck(log10(x), "log10");
}
double Sqrt(x)
        double x;
{
        return errcheck(sqrt(x), "sqrt");
}
double Exp(x)
        double x;
{
        return errcheck(exp(x), "exp");
}
double Pow(x, y)
        double x, y;
{
        return errcheck(pow(x,y), "exponentiation");
}
double integer(x)
        double x;
{
        return (double)(long)x;
}
double errcheck(d, s)    /* check result of library call */
        double d;
        char *s;
{
        if (errno == EDOM) {
                errno = 0;
                execerror(s, "argument out of domain");
        } else if (errno == ERANGE) {
                errno = 0;
                execerror(s, "result out of range");
        }
        return d;
}

*****   makefile   *************************************************************

YFLAGS = -d
OBJS = hoc.o code.o init.o math.o symbol.o

hoc6:   $(OBJS)
        cc $(CFLAGS) $(OBJS) -lm -o hoc6

hoc.o code.o init.o symbol.o:   hoc.h

code.o init.o symbol.o: x.tab.h

x.tab.h:        y.tab.h
        -cmp -s x.tab.h y.tab.h || cp y.tab.h x.tab.h

pr:     hoc.y hoc.h code.c init.c math.c symbol.c
        @pr $?
        @touch pr

clean:
        rm -f $(OBJS) [xy].tab.[ch]
```

& and signals 150
>> appending output 29
& background process 33, 73, 226
`...` backquotes 86, 139
;; case separator 134
[...], character class 102
. command 89
: command 147
$? command, make 266
- command, make 266
@ command, make 255
; command separator 33, 71
\$ command, troff 301
\& command, troff 298, 304
# comment, awk 117
. current directory 21, 25, 37,
    48, 51, 75
& ed replacement character 323
# erase character 6
\ escape character 6
! escape to shell 9, 35, 92, 184,
    194, 228, 254, 321
^ exponentiation operator 245
< input redirection 29
@ line kill 6
! negation, sed 110
! negation, test 143
^ obsolete ! 36
% operator, awk 117
++ operator, awk 121
+= operator, awk 118
-- operator, awk 121
> output redirection 29
>> output redirection 29
.. parent directory 25, 51, 75
(...) parentheses, shell 72, 73
{...} parentheses, shell 168
* pattern, shell 27
? pattern, shell 28
[...] pattern, shell 28
¦ pipe 31, 72
& precedence 73, 95
; precedence 72
¦ precedence 72
"..." quotes 75, 85
'...' quotes 75, 85
`...` quotes 85
<< redirection 94
$ regular expression 102, 324
(...) regular expression 104
* regular expression 103, 324
+ regular expression 104

. regular expression 103, 324
.* regular expression 109
? regular expression 104
[...] regular expression 102, 324
[^...] regular expression 102,
    324
^ regular expression 102, 324
&& shell AND 143
$# shell argument count 135
"$@" shell arguments 161
$* shell arguments 83, 85, 145,
    155, 161
$@ shell arguments 155
shell comment 7, 77
$? shell exit status 140
¦¦ shell OR 143, 169
* shell pattern 74, 162
$$ shell process-id 146
$ shell variable value 37, 88
${...} variables, shell 148
${...} variables, table of shell
    149
$0 awk input line 116
\0, NUL character 175
$0 shell argument 85
1>&2 redirection 142
2, 3, 4, 5, 6 commands 85
2>&1 redirection 93, 202
2>*filename* redirection 93
411 command 84, 93
4.1BSD x
abort 244
access mode, open 205
ack function 332
Ackermann's function 284, 332
action, embedded 276
adb command 188
add function, hoc4 264
addup command 126
Aho, Al x, 131, 287
alarm signal call 229
ambiguous parse 254
analyzer, lexical 235
AND, && shell 143
appending output, >> 29
ar command 99
arg function 282
argassign function 282
argc 174, 178
argument count, $# shell 135
arguments, blanks in 161
arguments, command 14, 74, 178

arguments, hoc 332
arguments, null 84
arguments, optional 178
arguments, program 174, 220
arguments, shell 82, 160
arguments, troff macro 301
argv 174, 178
arithmetic, awk 118
ASCII character set 42, 106, 107
assign function, hoc4 264
assignment, command-line 90
assignment expression 242, 329
assignment expression, awk 126
assignment, multiple 242, 329
assignment vs. expression 246
associative array, awk 123, 128
associativity 238, 243, 251
at command 35, 129
at command, perpetual 129
atoi 184
awk # comment 117
awk % operator 117
awk ++ operator 121
awk += operator 118
awk -- operator 121
awk arithmetic 118
awk assignment expression 126
awk associative array 123, 128
awk BEGIN pattern 118
awk break statement 121
awk command 114
awk control flow 119
awk END pattern 118
awk exit statement 122
awk -f 114
awk -F 115
awk field, $*n* 115
awk field separators 116
awk fields 115
awk FILENAME variable 121
awk for statement 121, 124
awk FS variable 118, 122
awk functions, table of 123
awk if-else statement 121
awk input line, $0 116
awk I/O redirection 130
awk length function 117
awk, meaning of 131
awk multi-line record 130
awk negated pattern 117
awk next statement 122
awk NF variable 115

awk NR variable 116
awk operators, table of 119
awk pattern range 130
awk patterns 116
awk print statement 114
awk printf statement 116
awk split function 122
awk string concatenation 125
awk strings 119, 125
awk substr function 117
awk variable initialization 118, 119
awk variables, table of 119
awk variables vs. shell variables 115
awk while statement 121
\b backspace convention 43
.B command, ms 294
background process, & 33, 73, 226
backquotes, `...` 86, 139
backquotes, nested 87, 157
backslash 78, 157
backslash, erasing a 6
backslash function 277
backslash into troff, getting 298
backslash, quoting with 6, 29, 75, 324
backspace 6, 172
backspace convention, \b 43
backspace, ctl-h 2, 36
backup, file 60
Backus-Naur Form 234
backwards command 122
bas command 284
BASIC 233
bc command 39, 284
BEGIN pattern, awk 118
Belle chess computer 231
Bentley, Jon x, 287
Berkeley 4.1BSD x
Bianchi, Mike x
Bimmler, Elizabeth x, 34
/bin directory 24, 37, 63, 142
bin directory, personal 81, 90, 134
binary files 47
blank, unpaddable 299
blanks in arguments 161
block device 66
block, disc 14, 50, 66, 203
bltin function, hoc4 264
BNF 234
bootstrap 63, 67
Bourne, Steve 100, 200
.bp command, troff 301
.br command, troff 300
Bradford, Ed x
BREAK 3, 7
break statement, awk 121
break statement, shell 160
buffering 45, 180, 201, 203, 223
BUFSIZ 183, 203
bug, diff 167
bug, ls 14, 60, 163
bug, nohup 151
bug, p 185
bug, pick 188
bug, sed 172
bug, shell 159
bug, sort 47
bug, sqrt 252

bug, system 185, 223
bug, zap 186
built-in functions, hoc3 245
bundle command 98
bundle, reliability of 99
bus error 188
byte 41, 202
.c filename convention 46
\c in echo 78
C program, compiling a 174
C programming language 171
C shell 100
cal command 133, 135
calendar command 9, 127, 129
calendar, design of 128
call function 279
Canaday, Rudd vii
Carfagno, Joe x
carriage return convention, \r 43
Carter, Don x
case conversion 107
case separator, ;; 134
case statement, shell 134
case vs. if 141
cast 211, 264
cat command 15, 203
cat, meaning of 15
cat -u 44
catching interrupts 150, 198
catching signals 153
cc command 174
cc -l 255
cc -o 174
cc -p 285, 286
cd command 25
CFLAGS 285
change, font 299
change, point size 300
changing a password 54
changing directory 25
changing permissions 56
character \0, NUL 175
character class [...] 102
character class, negated 102
character device 66
character names, troff 297
character set, ASCII 42, 106, 107
character set, EBCDIC 42, 107
chdir system call 216
checkmail command 148, 216
checkmail, evolution of 215
Cherry, Lorinda 314
chess computer, Belle 231
child process 34, 222
chmod command 56
chmod -w 56
chmod +x 56, 81
choice of language 170, 171, 181, 258, 277
close system call 206
closure 103, 104
cmp command 20
cmp -s 140, 266
code function, hoc4 263
code generation, hoc4 258
code generation, if 269
code generation, while 268
code.c file, hoc4 262
code.c file, hoc6 278
coercion, type 211, 264
combining programs viii, 30, 32, 170
Comer, Doug 131

comm command 107
command arguments 14, 74, 178
command interpreter 26
command options 13, 14
command separator, ; 33, 71
command-line assignment 90
commands, creating shell 80
commands executable, making 81
commands, ms 291
commands, permuted index to 2, 10
commands, personal 84
commands, table of ed 327
commands, table of file 21
commands, table of sed 112
comment, # shell 7, 77
comment, awk # 117
comparing files 20, 107
compiler-compiler 235
compiling a C program 174
computer-aided instruction 11
concatenation, awk string 125
Condon, Joe 231
conflict, shift/reduce 253, 268
constants, table of hoc 246, 330
constpush function, hoc4 263
continuation, shell line 77
CONTROL 2
control character 2
control flow, awk 119
convention, \b backspace 43
convention, .c filename 46
convention, filename 26
convention, .h 247
convention, .l filename 257
convention, \n newline 43
convention, \r carriage return 43
convention, \t tab 43
convention, .y filename 236
copying a file 17, 61
core dump 188, 225, 242
core dump, ctl-\ 150, 188
correction, spelling 208, 213
counting files 30
counting users 30
counting words 18
cp command 17, 61, 206
crash, system 12, 64
creat permissions 205
creat system call 205
create a program, program to 99, 307
creating a file 202
creating shell commands 80
creation, process 220
CRLF 44, 174
cross-device link 67
crypt command 52, 68
csh command 100
ctl-\ core dump 150, 188
ctl-\ quit signal 225
ctl-c DELETE 3
ctl-d end of file 2, 8, 31, 45
ctl-d to logout 8
ctl-g ring bell 2, 73
ctl-h backspace 2, 36
ctl-i tab 2
ctl-q resuming output 8
ctl-s stopping output 8, 15
ctl-u line kill 6
ctype tests, table of 174
ctype.h header file 173
cu command 39

current directory, . 21, 25, 37, 48, 51, 75
cx command 82
d command, sed 111
data structures, hoc4 262
data structures, hoc6 278
data structures, procedure call 279
date command 4
dates, file 57
dd command 69, 107
.DE command, ms 293
.de command, troff 301
De Marco, Tom x
De Morgan, Augustus 18, 320
dead.letter 8
debugger, adb 188
debugger, sdb 189
debugging 187, 244, 258, 265, 302
default signal handling 225, 227
define function 279
defining troff macros 301
definitions, table of stdio.h 178
defnonly function 276
DELETE 3, 7, 10, 150, 225
DELETE, ctl-c 3
dependency rule, empty 255
descriptor, file 92, 201, 223
design of calendar 128
design of echo 78
design of efopen 182
design of grep family 105
design of idiff 194, 198
design of p 181, 184, 185
design of pick 186
design of set 136
design of spname 209
design of sv 217
design of vis 172, 174, 179, 185
design of zap 198
design, program 110, 134, 147, 154, 165, 170, 222, 265, 286, 302
/dev directory 63, 65
device, block 66
device, character 66
device file 41, 65
device, peripheral 1, 41, 65, 201
/dev/null 69
/dev/tty 68, 160, 183, 223, 224
df command 67
dial-a-joke 84
diction command 313
dictionary, /usr/dict/words 104
diff -b 198
diff bug 167
diff command 20
diff -e 165
diff -h 198
diff -s 140
directories, table of 63
directory 21
directory, . current 21, 25, 37, 48, 51, 75
directory, .. parent 25, 51, 75
directory, /bin 24, 37, 63, 142
directory, changing 25
directory, /dev 63, 65
directory, /etc 63

directory format 51, 59, 209
directory hierarchy 63, 208
directory, home 21, 36
directory, /lib 63
directory, making a 25
directory, moving a 62
directory permissions 55, 56
directory, personal bin 81, 90, 134
directory, removing a 26
directory, root 22, 51
directory structure 48
directory, /tmp 63, 146
directory, /usr 22, 48, 65
directory, /usr/bin 24, 37, 65, 142
directory, /usr/games 25, 90
directory, /usr/include 173
directory, /usr/man 308
directory, /usr/src 48
dir.h header file 209
disc block 14, 50, 66, 203
disc free space 67
discarding output 69
doctype command 307
doctype, evolution of 308
doctype timing 307
double command 120
.DS command, ms 293
du -a 50, 108
du command 50
Duff, Tom x, 100, 231
dump, core 188, 225, 242
dup system call 223
Durham, Ivor 231
\e command, troff 298
EBCDIC character set 42, 107
echo, \c in 78
echo command 27, 77
echo, design of 78
echo -n 78, 160
Echo, UNIX and the 78
ed - 168
ed command 12, 320
ed commands, table of 327
ed editor 11
ed encryption command 327
ed global commands 325
ed line $ 322
ed line . 322
ed line number expressions 322
ed line numbers 320
ed line numbers, table of 327
ed line-moving commands 325
ed mark command 326
ed regular expression examples 325
ed regular expressions, table of 324
ed replacement character, & 323
ed undo command 323
ed.hup 12
editor, screen 11, 319
efficiency 124, 141, 147, 151, 158, 165, 171, 178, 180, 190, 204, 216, 236, 247, 258, 265, 266, 285, 286, 302, 307, 319
efopen, design of 182
efopen function 182
egilops 104
egrep command 69, 103
egrep -f 103

egrep -h 307
emacs screen editor 11
emalloc function 248
embedded action 276
empty dependency rule 255
empty production 237
encryption 52
encryption command, ed 327
encryption, password 53
end of file 44, 202, 203
end of file, ctl-d 2, 8, 31, 45
END pattern, awk 118
EOF 173, 204
eqn examples 304
erase character 7, 29
erase character, # 6
erase character, setting 35
erasing a backslash 6
errcheck function 253
errno 206, 228
errno.h header file 228, 252
error function 207
error handling 218
error message 5, 17, 32, 56, 61, 93, 142, 148, 180, 182, 302
error recovery, hoc2 244, 245
error recovery, hoc3 252
error recovery, hoc6 276
error, standard 32, 92, 177, 202
error status, system call 206
error, write 219
escape character, \ 6
escape to shell, ! 9, 35, 92, 184, 194, 228, 254, 321
/etc directory 63
/etc/group 54
/etc/mount command 66
/etc/passwd password file 53, 103, 115
eval command 156
eval function, hoc4 264
evolution of checkmail 215
evolution of doctype 308
evolution of hoc 233
exception, floating point 242, 243
execerror function, hoc2 244
execlp system call 220
executable, making commands 81
execute function, hoc4 263
execute function, hoc6 281
execvp system call 220
exit command 142
exit function 174
exit statement, awk 122
exit status 140, 142, 144, 174, 222
exit status, $? shell 140
exit status of pipeline 145
exit status of shell file 142
Exp function 252
exponentiation operator, ^ 245
export command 38, 91
expression, assignment 242, 329
expressions, ed line number 322
\f command, troff 291, 299
fac function 274, 333
false command 147, 149
fclose 179
.FE command, ms 296
features 185, 316
Feldman, Stu 287
fflush 183
fgets 183

fgrep command 103
fgrep -f 103
.fi command, troff 300
fib function 274, 284
field command 126
field, $n awk 115
field separator, shell 157, 160, 163, 164
field separators, awk 116
fields, awk 115
fields, sorting on 106
file 11
file access, random 207
file access, simultaneous 203
file backup 60
file command 46
file commands, table of 21
file, copying a 17, 61
file, creating a 202
file dates 57
file descriptor 92, 201, 223
file, device 41, 65
file, moving a 16
file open 176
file, opening a 201
file permissions 52, 54, 205
FILE pointer 177, 202
file, removing a 17
file, renaming a 16
file restore 60
file, shell 81
file structure 41, 47
file system 11, 21, 209
file system hierarchy 24, 63
file system mounting 67
file times 57
file types 46, 47
filename convention 26
filename convention, .c 46
filename convention, .1 257
filename convention, .y 236
filename rules 17
filename search 50
filename shorthand 26
FILENAME variable, awk 121
fileno macro 202
files, comparing 20, 107
files, formatless 47
files, text 47
filling, line 291
filters ix, 101
find command 52
finding a file 50, 52
finite state machine 277
Flandrena, Bob x
fleas 18, 320
floating point exception 242, 243
fold command 125
follow function 270
font change 299
font changes, ms 294
fopen 176
fopen modes 177
for i loop, shell 145
for loop format, shell 95
for statement, awk 121, 124
for syntax, shell 95, 144
fork system call 222
format, directory 51, 59, 209
format independence 290
format, inode 214
format, shell for loop 95
formatless files 47

formatter, nroff 289
formatter, roff 289
formatter, Scribe 314
formatter, TEX 314
formatter, troff 289
FORTRAN 47
FORTRAN 77 39, 287
fortune game 36
fpecatch function, hoc2 244
fprintf 179
fputs 183
free space, disc 67
frexp 241
.FS command, ms 296
FS variable, awk 118, 122
fstat system call 215
.ft command, troff 291, 301
full duplex 2, 4
funcret function 279
function definition, hoc 332
functions, hoc3 built-in 245
functions, table of awk 123
functions, table of hoc 330
functions, table of standard I/O 192
functions, table of string 176
Furuta, Richard 314
game, fortune 36
game, quiz 327
games 11, 25
Gay, David x
get command 168
getarg function 281
getc 177
getchar 172
getchar macro 177
getenv 199
getlogin 216
getname command 109
getopt 179
getting backslash into troff 298
global commands, ed 325
Gosling, James 100
grammar 234
grammar, hoc1 237
grammar, hoc2 243
grammar, hoc3 250
grammar, hoc4 259
grammar, hoc5 267
grammar, hoc6 275
grammar production 235
grep -b 111
grep command 18, 102
grep -e 79
grep examples 102
grep family, design of 105
grep -l 87
grep, meaning of 18
grep -n 102
grep regular expressions 102
grep -v 18, 102, 111
grep -y 85, 102
group-id 52
.h convention 247
hangup signal 150, 225
Hanson, Dave x
Hardin, Ron x
Harris, Marion x
hashing 124, 314
header file 247, 261, 286
header file, ctype.h 173
header file, dir.h 209
header file, errno.h 228

header file, ino.h 219
header file, math.h 252
header file, setjmp.h 227
header file, signal.h 191, 225
header file, stat.h 214
header file, stdio.h 173
header file, types.h 214
here document 94, 98
Hewett, Alan 100
hierarchy, directory 63, 208
hierarchy, file system 24, 63
hierarchy, process 34, 48
hoc arguments 332
hoc constants, table of 246, 330
hoc, evolution of 233
hoc function definition 332
hoc functions, table of 330
hoc input format 331
hoc manual 329
hoc, meaning of 234
hoc operators, table of 330
hoc print statement 331
hoc procedure definition 332
hoc read statement 331
hoc, reliability of 265, 274
hoc sizes, table of 283
hoc stages 233
hoc times, table of 284
hoc1 grammar 237
hoc1 main function 239
hoc1 makefile 241
hoc1 unary minus 240
hoc1 warning function 240
hoc1 yyerror function 240
hoc1 yylex function 239
hoc2 error recovery 244, 245
hoc2 execerror function 244
hoc2 fpecatch function 244
hoc2 grammar 243
hoc2 main function 244
hoc2 yylex function 245
hoc3 built-in functions 245
hoc3 error recovery 252
hoc3 grammar 250
hoc3 hoc.h 247
hoc3 init function 249
hoc3 init.c file 249
hoc3 lex makefile 257
hoc3 lex version 256
hoc3 main function 252
hoc3 makefile 255
hoc3 math.c file 252
hoc3 source files 247
hoc3 yylex function 251
hoc4 add function 264
hoc4 assign function 264
hoc4 bltin function 264
hoc4 code function 263
hoc4 code generation 258
hoc4 code.c file 262
hoc4 constpush function 263
hoc4 data structures 262
hoc4 eval function 264
hoc4 execute function 263
hoc4 grammar 259
hoc4 hoc.h 261
hoc4 main function 260
hoc4 makefile 266
hoc4 pop function 262
hoc4 print function 264
hoc4 push function 262
hoc4 varpush function 263
hoc4 yylex function 261

hoc5 grammar 267
hoc5 hoc.h 270
hoc5 ifcode function 272
hoc5 init.c file 272
hoc5 yylex function 270
hoc6 code.c file 278
hoc6 data structures 278
hoc6 error recovery 276
hoc6 execute function 281
hoc6 grammar 275
hoc6 hoc.h 278
hoc6 ifcode function 281
hoc6 initcode function 278
hoc6 makefile 285
hoc6 yylex function 277
hoc.h, hoc3 247
hoc.h, hoc4 261
hoc.h, hoc5 270
hoc.h, hoc6 278
Holzmann, Gerard x
home directory 21, 36
HOME shell variable 36, 88
Hunt, Wayne 200
.I command, ms 292, 294
ideal command 313
idiff command 193
idiff, design of 194, 198
idiff function 197
idiff main function 195
if code generation 269
if vs. case 141
ifcode function, hoc5 272
ifcode function, hoc6 281
if-else statement, awk 121
if-else statement, shell 140
IFS shell variable 157, 163, 164
ignoring interrupts 228
ignoring signals 151, 153, 226
#include 173
ind command 109, 116
index 218
index to commands, permuted 2, 10
inheritance, open file 223
inheritance, shell variable 89, 91
init function, hoc3 249
init.c file, hoc3 249
init.c file, hoc5 272
initcode function, hoc6 278
initialization, awk variable 118, 119
inode 57
inode format 214
inode table 209
ino.h header file 219
input form, yacc 236
input format, hoc 331
input line, $0 awk 116
input redirection, < 29
input, standard 30, 92, 177, 202
input, troff 290
inserting newline, sed 111
install function 248
instruction, computer-aided 11
integer function 253
interpreter 258
interpreter, command 26
INTERRUPT 3
interrupt signal 150, 225
interrupted system call 228
interrupts, catching 150, 198
interrupts, ignoring 226, 228
i-number 58

i-number, zero 59
I/O library, standard 171
I/O, low-level 201
I/O redirection 29, 30, 47, 74, 80, 92, 180, 183, 202
I/O redirection, awk 130
I/O redirection, shell 159
I/O timing, table of 203
.IP command, ms 296
isascii 173
isprint 173
Johnson, Steve x, 200, 235, 287, 314
Joy, Bill 100
justification, line 291
Katseff, Howard 200
.KE command, ms 296
kernel 1, 7, 23, 32, 43, 53, 55, 99, 201
Kernighan, Brian 39, 131, 171, 314
.KF command, ms 296
kill viii 188
kill -9 152
kill command 34, 225
Knuth, Don 90, 314
.KS command, ms 296
l command, sed 172, 174
.l filename convention 257
Lamb, David 231
language, choice of 170, 171, 181, 258, 277
language development 233, 286
language, special-purpose 286, 290
layout, page 289
lc command 83
le function 271
learn command 11
%left 238
length function, awk 117
Lesk, Mike 200, 287
lex library, -ll 257
lex makefile, hoc3 257
lex regular expressions 256
lex version, hoc3 256
lexical analyzer 235
lexical token 235
/lib directory 63
library, -ll lex 257
library, -lm math 255
limit, open file 206
Linderman, John x
line $, ed 322
line ., ed 322
line continuation, shell 77, 108
line filling 291
line justification 291
line kill 7
line kill, @ 6
line kill character 29
line kill character, setting 35
line kill, ctl-u 6
line number expressions, ed 322
line numbers, ed 320
line numbers, table of ed 327
line printer 16
line spacing 296
line-moving commands, ed 325
link 59, 85, 96
link, cross-device 67
link, making a 59
lint command 190

Lions, John 315
-ll lex library 257
-lm math library 255
ln command 59
Log function 252
Log10 function 252
logout 8, 45
logout, ctl-d to 8
Lomuto, Ann 39
Lomuto, Nico x, 39
longjmp 227, 244
lookup function 248
loop, shell for i 145
loops, shell 94
low-level I/O 201
.LP command, ms 296
lpr command 16
ls bug 14, 60, 163
ls -c 58
ls command 13
ls -d 55
ls -f 51
ls -g 53
ls -i 58
ls -l 13, 14
ls -r 14
ls -t 13, 58
ls -u 58
lseek system call 122, 207
m command 83
macro arguments, troff 301
macro, fileno 202
macro, getchar 177
macro package 289
macro package, man 309
macro package, mm 290, 297
macro package, ms 290
macro, pop 286
macro, push 286
macro, putchar 177
macros, defining troff 301
macros, yacc 255
magic number 46, 191
Mahaney, Steve x
mail command 8
mail, notification of 8, 36, 147, 215
mail, remote 9, 97
mail, sending 8
MAIL shell variable 36, 147
main function, hoc1 239
main function, hoc2 244
main function, hoc3 252
main function, hoc4 260
main function, idiff 195
main function, p 182, 184, 199, 213
main function, pick 187
main function, sv 217
main function, vis 178
main function, zap 191
make $? command 266
make - command 266
make @ command 255
make command 241
make -n 255
make -t 255
makefile, hoc1 241
makefile, hoc3 255
makefile, hoc3 lex 257
makefile, hoc4 266
makefile, hoc6 285
making a directory 25

making a link 59
making commands executable 81
man command 11, 309
man macro package 309
man -t 309
manual, hoc 329
manual organization 10
manual page 308
Maranzano, Joe 200
mark command, ed 326
Martin, Bob x
Mashey, John 39, 100
math library, -1m 255
math.c file, hoc3 252
math.h header file 252
McIlroy, Doug vii, x, 47, 78, 200, 314
McMahon, Lee 131
meaning of awk 131
meaning of cat 15
meaning of grep 18
meaning of hoc 234
meaning of UNIX vii, 1
memory fault 188
mesg command 10, 68
message, error 5, 17, 32, 56, 61, 93, 142, 148, 180, 182, 302
metacharacters 102, 220
metacharacters, shell 74
metacharacters, table of shell 75
mindist function 211
mkdir command 25, 48
mktemp 195
mm commands, table of 297
mm macro package 290, 297
modes, fopen 177
modularity 209, 247, 261, 302
mon.out 285
more command 15
Morris, Bob 70
mounting, file system 67
moving a directory 62
moving a file 16
ms .B command 294
ms commands 291
ms commands, table of 296
ms .DE command 293
ms .DS command 293
ms .FE command 296
ms font changes 294
ms .FS command 296
ms .I command 292, 294
ms .IP command 296
ms .KE command 296
ms .KF command 296
ms .KS command 296
ms .LP command 296
ms macro package 290
ms .PP command 291
ms .R command 294
MULTICS vii, 70
multi-line record, awk 130
multiple assignment 242, 329
mv command 16, 61
$n awk field 115
\n newline convention 43
$n shell argument 82
$n yacc value 237
names, table of troff 298
names, troff character 297
nargs command 158
ncopy function 198
negated character class 102

negated pattern, awk 117
nested backquotes 87, 157
nested quotes 75, 86, 112, 128
netnews command 10
newer command 112
newgrp command 54
newline 13, 43, 202
newline as terminator 44
newline convention, \n 43
newline, sed inserting 111
news command 10, 162, 163, 164
next statement, awk 122
.nf command, troff 300
NF variable, awk 115
nice command 35
nice -n 151
nohup bug 151
nohup command 35, 151
notification of mail 8, 36, 147, 215
NR variable, awk 116
nroff formatter 289
nskip function 198
nu command 80
NUL character \0 175
null arguments 84
NULL pointer 177
null string in PATH 139
number register, troff 296
obsolete ¦, ^ 36
octal numbers in C 205
od -b 42
od -c 42
od command 42
od -d 42, 59
od -x 43
older command 113
on-line dictionary 104
open access mode 205
open, file 176
open file inheritance 223
open file limit 206
open system call 205
opening a file 201
operator, ^ exponentiation 245
operator, awk % 117
operator, awk ++ 121
operator, awk += 118
operator, awk -- 121
operators, relational 266
operators, table of awk 119
operators, table of hoc 330
optional arguments 178, 179, 199
options, command 13, 14
options, parsing 178
OR, ¦¦ shell 143, 169
order of sorting 19, 27, 28
Organick, E. I. 70
organization, manual 10
Ossanna, Joe vii, 289, 314
output, discarding 69
output form, yacc 236
output redirection, > 29
output redirection, >> 29
output, standard 32, 92, 177, 202
overflow 243, 245
overwrite command 153, 155
p bug 185
p command 181, 213
p, design of 181, 184, 185
p main function 182, 184, 199, 213

page layout 289
page, manual 308
parameters, shell 88
param.h header file 206
parent directory, .. 25, 51, 75
parent process 34, 222
parentheses, shell (...) 72, 73
parentheses, shell {...} 168
parse, ambiguous 254
parse function 197
parse tree 238, 254
parser-generator 235
parsing options 178
parsing process, yacc 237
parsing, shell argument 161
Pascal 287
passwd command 54
password 4
password, changing a 54
password encryption 53
password file, /etc/passwd 53, 103, 115
password security 70
PATH, null string in 139
path, search 37, 81, 88, 139, 142, 220
PATH shell variable 37, 81, 88, 138, 139, 142, 220
pathname 23, 25
pathnames, shell patterns in 28
pattern, * shell 74, 162
pattern matching, shell 26, 134, 136, 162
pattern range, awk 130
pattern searching 18
pattern, shell * 27
pattern, shell ? 28
pattern, shell [...] 28
patterns, awk 116
patterns in pathnames, shell 28
patterns, table of shell 136
pclose 190
peripheral device 1, 41, 65, 201
permission, root 55
permission, set-uid 54
permissions, changing 56
permissions, creat 205
permissions, directory 55, 56
permissions, file 52, 54, 205
permissions, /usr/games 56
permuted index to commands 2, 10
perpetual at command 129
personal bin directory 81, 90, 134
personal commands 84
pg command 15
pic command 313
pic example 313
pick bug 188
pick command 87, 156, 160, 186
pick, design of 186
pick function 187
pick main function 187
Pinter, Ron x
pipe, ¦ 31, 72
pipeline 72, 180
pipeline examples 31
pipeline, exit status of 145
point size 296, 300
point size change 300
pointer, FILE 177, 202

pointer, NULL 177
pop function, hoc4 262
pop macro 286
popen 190
portability vii, 190, 209, 218, 234, 252, 315
Pow function 252
.PP command, ms 291
pr command 15
pr -h 95
pr -l 86
pr -m 16
pr -n 16
pr -t 86
%prec 241
precedence 238, 241
precedence, & 73, 95
precedence, ; 72
precedence, | 72
preprocessor 290, 301
prexpr function 272, 282
print function 183
print function, hoc4 264
print statement, awk 114
print statement, hoc 331
printf 173
printf statement, awk 116
procedure call data structures 279
procedure definition, hoc 332
process, & background 33, 73, 226
process creation 220
process hierarchy 34, 48
process status 34
processes 33
process-id 33, 146, 222
process-id, $$ shell 146
procret function 280
production, empty 237
production, grammar 235
prof command 285
.profile 36, 81, 89, 159
.profile example 38
profiling 285
program arguments 174, 220
program design 110, 134, 147, 154, 165, 170, 222, 265, 286, 302
program, stopping a 7, 34
program to create a program 99, 307
programmable formatter 289
programmable shell 99
programming language, C 171
programming, shell 99, 133
programs, combining viii, 30, 32, 170
programs vs. options 185
prompt 4, 26, 72
prompt, secondary 76
protocol, write 9
prpages command 119
prstr function 282
ps -a 34, 191
ps command 34
.ps command, troff 301
PS1 shell variable 36, 82
PS2 shell variable 76
push function, hoc4 262
push macro 286
put command 167
putc 177
putchar 172

putchar macro 177
pwd command 21, 48
q command, sed 110
quit signal 225
quit signal, ctl-\ 225
quiz game 327
quotes 28, 85, 94, 104, 126
quotes, "..." 75, 85
quotes, '...' 75, 85
quotes, `...` 85
quotes, nested 75, 86, 112, 128
quotes, troff 295
quoting with backslash 6, 29, 75, 324
\r carriage return convention 43
.R command, ms 294
random file access 207
range, awk pattern 130
range selection, sed 111
Ratfor 287
read command 159
read statement, hoc 331
read system call 44, 202
readslow command 204, 231
record, awk multi-line 130
recursion 18, 355
redirection, << 94
redirection, < input 29
redirection, > output 29
redirection, >> output 29
redirection, 1>&2 142
redirection, 2>&1 93, 202
redirection, 2>filename 93
redirection, awk I/O 130
redirection, I/O 29, 30, 47, 74, 80, 92, 180, 183, 202
redirection, shell I/O 159
redirections, table of shell 94
refer command 313
regular expression 102, 315, 319
regular expression, $ 102, 324
regular expression, (...) 104
regular expression, * 103, 324
regular expression, + 104
regular expression, . 103, 324
regular expression, .* 109
regular expression, ? 104
regular expression, [...] 102, 324
regular expression, [^...] 102, 324
regular expression, ^ 102, 324
regular expression examples, ed 325
regular expression, tagged 105, 324, 326
regular expressions, grep 102
regular expressions, lex 256
regular expressions, shell vs. editor 138
regular expressions, table of 105
regular expressions, table of ed 324
Reid, Brian 314
relational operators 266
reliability of bundle 99
reliability of hoc 265, 274
reliability of shell programs 133
remote mail 9, 97
removing a directory 26
removing a file 17
renaming a file 16
replace command 155

replacement character, & ed 323
resetting signals 227
restore, file 60
resuming output, ctl-q 8
ret function 280
RETURN 2, 4, 7, 13, 43
rewind 208
%right 238
ring bell, ctl-g 2, 73
Ritchie, Dennis vii, x, 39, 54, 70, 171, 200, 231, 315
rm command 17, 61
rm -f 56, 151
rm -i 187
rmdir command 26
Rochkind, Marc 131, 170
roff formatter 289
root directory 22, 51
root permission 55
root user 52, 55
Rosler, Larry x
RUBOUT 3
rules, filename 17
s command, sed 108
\s command, troff 300
Saltzer, J.E. 314
Saxe, James 231
scanf 173, 329
scapegoat command 219
SCCS 170
Scofield, Jeffrey 314
screen editor 11, 319
screen editor, emacs 11
screen editor, vi 11
Scribe formatter 314
sdb command 189
search, filename 50
search path 37, 81, 88, 139, 142, 220
searching, pattern 18
secondary prompt 76
security, password 70
sed ! negation 110
sed bug 172
sed command 108
sed commands, table of 112
sed d command 111
sed -f 110
sed inserting newline 111
sed l command 172, 174
sed -n 111
sed q command 110
sed range selection 111
sed s command 108
sed stream editor 101
sed w command 112
seek 122
sending mail 8
separator, ; command 33, 71
separator, shell field 157, 160, 163, 164
separators, awk field 116
separators, shell word 86
set command 88, 136, 164
set, design of 136
set -v 136
set -x 136
setjmp 227, 244
setjmp.h header file 227
setting erase character 35
setting line kill character 35
setting tab stops 43
set-uid permission 54

Seventh Edition x, 7, 14, 39, 65, 75, 77, 78, 85, 87, 100, 106, 125, 140, 151, 171, 188, 201, 290, 313, 314
sh -c 221
sh command 80
Shaw, Alan 314
shell ix, 26
shell, ! escape to 9, 35, 92, 184, 194, 228, 254, 321
shell (...) parentheses 72, 73
shell {...} parentheses 168
shell * pattern 27
shell ? pattern 28
shell [...] pattern 28
shell ${...} variables 148
shell ${...} variables, table of 149
shell AND, && 143
shell argument, $0 85
shell argument count, $# 135
shell argument, $n 82
shell argument parsing 161
shell arguments 82, 160
shell arguments, "$@" 161
shell arguments, $* 83, 85, 145, 155, 161
shell arguments, $@ 155
shell break statement 160
shell bug 159
shell case statement 134
shell commands, creating 80
shell comment, # 7, 77
shell exit status, $? 140
shell field separator 157, 160, 163, 164
shell file 81
shell file, exit status of 142
shell for i loop 145
shell for loop format 95
shell for syntax 95, 144
shell if-else statement 140
shell I/O redirection 159
shell line continuation 77, 108
shell loops 94
shell metacharacters 74
shell metacharacters, table of 75
shell OR, || 143, 169
shell parameters 88
shell pattern, * 74, 162
shell pattern matching 26, 134, 136, 162
shell patterns in pathnames 28
shell patterns, table of 136
shell process-id, $$ 146
shell, programmable 99
shell programming 99, 133
shell programs, reliability of 133
shell redirections, table of 94
shell until syntax 145
shell variable inheritance 89, 91
shell variable, TERM 159
shell variable value, $ 37, 88
shell variables 36, 88
shell variables, awk variables vs. 115
shell variables, table of 135
shell vs. editor regular expressions 138
shell while syntax 144
shell word 71, 95, 157
shell word separators 86
shift command 155, 168

shift/reduce conflict 253, 268
shorthand, filename 26
signal call, alarm 229
signal, ctl-\ quit 225
signal handling, default 225, 227
signal, hangup 150, 225
signal, interrupt 150, 225
signal numbers, table of 150
signal, quit 225
signal system call 225
signal, terminate 225
signal.h header file 191, 225
signals 225
signals, & and 150
signals, catching 153
signals, ignoring 151, 153, 226
signals, resetting 227
simultaneous file access 203
Sitar, Ed x
Sixth Edition 100, 208, 315
size change, point 300
size command 258
size, point 296, 300
sizeof 211
sizes, table of hoc 283
sleep 204
sleep command 73
SNOBOL4 131
sort bug 47
sort command 19, 106
sort -d 106
sort -f 106
sort -n 19
sort -n 19, 106
sort -o 106, 152
sort -r 19, 106
sort -u 106, 307
sorting on fields 106
sorting, order of 19, 27, 28
source code control 165, 170
source files, hoc3 247
.sp command, troff 301
spacing, line 296
spdist function 212
special-purpose language 286, 290
spell command 313
spelling correction 208, 213
Spencer, Henry 200
split function, awk 122
spname, design of 209
spname function 210
sqrt bug 252
Sqrt function 252
sscanf 191
stack machine 258
stack trace 188
stack, yacc 238
stages, hoc 233
standard error 32, 92, 177, 202
standard input 30, 92, 177, 202
standard I/O functions, table of 192
standard I/O library 171
standard output 32, 92, 177, 202
startup, system 63, 67
stat system call 215
stat.h header file 214
status, process 34
status return, wait 222
stderr 177, 180
stdin 177
stdio.h 173

stdio.h definitions, table of 178
stdio.h header file 173
stdout 177
Stirling's formula 333
Stone, Harold 200
stopping a program 7, 34
stopping output, ctl-s 8, 15
strchr 218
strcmp 175
stream editor, sed 101
strindex function 192
string concatenation, awk 125
string functions, table of 176
strings, awk 119, 125
strlen 183
strncmp 192
structure, directory 48
structure, file 41, 47
stty command 5, 35, 43
stty -tabs 5, 43
style command 313
su command 52
sub-shell 81, 85, 89, 91, 151, 169
substr function, awk 117
super-user 52, 191
sv command 217
sv, design of 217
sv function 218
sv main function 217
syntax errors, yacc 240
syntax, shell for 95, 144
syntax, shell until 145
syntax, shell while 144
sys_errlist 206
sys_nerr 206
system 184, 220
system bug 185, 223
system call error status 206
system call, interrupted 228
system call, read 44
system call, unlink 195
system crash 12, 64
system dependency 6
system function 224, 229
system startup 63, 67
System V x, 78, 125, 140, 141
Szymanski, Tom 200
\t tab convention 43
.ta command, troff 301
tab convention, \t 43
tab, ctl-i 2
tab stops 5
tab stops, setting 43
table of awk functions 123
table of awk operators 119
table of awk variables 119
table of ctype tests 174
table of directories 63
table of ed commands 327
table of ed line numbers 327
table of ed regular expressions 324
table of file commands 21
table of hoc constants 246, 330
table of hoc functions 330
table of hoc operators 330
table of hoc sizes 283
table of hoc times 284
table of I/O timing 203
table of mm commands 297
table of ms commands 296
table of regular expressions 105

table of `sed` commands 112
table of shell `${...}` variables
    149
table of shell metacharacters 75
table of shell patterns 136
table of shell redirections 94
table of shell variables 135
table of signal numbers 150
table of standard I/O functions
    192
table of `stdio.h` definitions 178
table of string functions 176
table of `troff` names 298
`tabs` command 5
tagged regular expression 105,
    324, 326
`tail` command 19
`tail -f` 204
`tail -n` 20
`tail -r` 122
`tbl` example 303
`tee` command 72
`TERM` shell variable 37, 159
terminal echo 2, 43
terminate signal 225
terminator, newline as 44
`test !` negation 143
`test` command 140
`test -f` 140
`test -r` 140
`test -t` 151
`test -w` 140
`test -x` 140
`test -z` 154
TEX formatter 314
text editor 11
text files 47
Thompson, Ken vii, x, 39, 70,
    204, 219, 231, 315, 319
Tilson, Mike x
`time` command 69, 92
`timeout` command 230
`times` command 152
times, file 57
times, table of `hoc` 284
timing, `doctype` 307
timing, table of I/O 203
`/tmp` directory 63, 146
`%token` 238, 243
token, lexical 235
tools viii, 170, 171, 233, 287
`touch` command 162
`tr` command 107
trace, stack 188
tree, parse 238, 254
`trap` command 150
`troff \$` command 301
`troff \&` command 298, 304
`troff .bp` command 301
`troff .br` command 300
`troff` character names 297
`troff` command 292, 306
`troff .de` command 301
`troff \e` command 298
`troff \f` command 291, 299
`troff .fi` command 300
`troff` formatter 289
`troff .ft` command 291, 301
`troff`, getting backslash into
    298
`troff` input 290
`troff -m` 292
`troff` macro arguments 301

`troff` macros, defining 301
`troff` names, table of 298
`troff .nf` command 300
`troff` number register 296
`troff .ps` command 301
`troff` quotes 295
`troff \s` command 300
`troff .sp` command 301
`troff .ta` command 301
`true` command 147, 149
`tty` command 68
`ttyin` function 184, 185
Tukey, Paul x
`%type` 243
type coercion 211, 264
type-ahead 7
types, file 47
`types.h` 209
`types.h` header file 214
Ullman, Jeff 287
unary minus, `hoc1` 240
undefined variable 251, 276
`undo` command, `ed` 323
`ungetc` 270
`%union` 242, 243, 251, 274
`uniq -c` 107
`uniq` command 106
`uniq -d` 107
`uniq -u` 107
`units` command 39
`/unix` 23, 63
UNIX and the Echo 78
UNIX, meaning of vii, 1
`unlink` system call 195, 206
unpaddable blank 299
`until` syntax, shell 145
USENET 10
user, root 55
user-id 52
`/usr` directory 22, 48, 65
`/usr/bin` directory 24, 37, 65,
    142
`/usr/dict/words` dictionary
    104
`/usr/games` directory 25, 90
`/usr/games` permissions 56
`/usr/include` directory 173
`/usr/man` directory 308
`/usr/pub/ascii` 42
`/usr/src` directory 48
`uucp` command 39
Van Wyk, Chris x, 314
variable initialization, `awk` 118,
    119
variable, undefined 251, 276
variables, shell 36, 88
variables, table of `awk` 119
variables, table of shell 135
`varpush` function, `hoc4` 263
`varread` function 283
`vi` screen editor 11
`vis` command 173, 175, 178
`vis`, design of 172, 174, 179,
    185
`vis` function 179
`vis` main function 178
`vis -s` 174
`w` command, `sed` 112
`wait` command 34
`wait` status return 222
`wait` system call 222
`waitfile` command 222
`warning` function, `hoc1` 240

`watchfor` command 145
`watchwho` command 147
`wc` command 18
`wc -l` 30, 80
Wehr, Larry x
Weinberger, Peter x, 131, 231
Weythman, Jim x
`which` command 141, 143
while code generation 268
`while` statement, `awk` 121
`while` syntax, shell 144
`whilecode` function 271, 281
`who am i` command 5
`who` command 5
word separators, shell 86
word, shell 71, 95, 157
`wordfreq` command 124
words, counting 18
working directory 21
`write` command 9
write error 219
write protocol 9
`write` system call 202
Writer's Workbench 313
`.y` filename convention 236
`yacc` command 240
`yacc -d` 247, 255
`yacc` input form 236
`yacc` macros 255
`yacc` output form 236
`yacc` overview 235
`yacc` parsing process 237
`yacc` stack 238
`yacc` syntax errors 240
`yacc -v` 254
`yacc` value, `$n` 237
`%FLAGS` 255
`y.tab.c` 236
`y.tab.h` 247, 265
`yyerrok` 244
`yyerror` function, `hoc1` 240
`yylex` 236
`yylex` function, `hoc1` 239
`yylex` function, `hoc2` 245
`yylex` function, `hoc3` 251
`yylex` function, `hoc4` 261
`yylex` function, `hoc5` 270
`yylex` function, `hoc6` 277
`yylval` 239, 244
`yyparse` 235, 239
`yytext` 256
`zap` bug 186
`zap` command 157, 158, 191
`zap`, design of 198
`zap` main function 191
zero i-number 59